EMPIRE & COMMONWEALTH

EMPIRE & COMMONWEALTH

STUDIES IN

GOVERNANCE AND SELF-GOVERNMENT

IN CANADA

BY

CHESTER MARTIN

HEAD OF THE DEPARTMENT OF HISTORY
UNIVERSITY OF MANITOBA
CANADA

OXFORD
AT THE CLARENDON PRESS
1929

OXFORD UNIVERSITY PRESS
AMEN HOUSE, E.C. 4
LONDON EDINBURGH GLASGOW
LEIPZIG NEW YORK TORONTO
MELBOURNE CAPETOWN BOMBAY
CALCUTTA MADRAS SHANGHAI
HUMPHREY MILFORD
PUBLISHER TO THE
UNIVERSITY

Printed in Great Britain

PREFACE

IN the play of practical politics there is little scope for that precision which is claimed for jurisprudence or political science. It is possible that studies in politics, however scrupulously historical, may be thought to share the same infirmity. A preface which is the last page of a book to be written and the first to be read may be a convenient place to forecast the nature of these studies without seeming to anticipate the evidence.

The development from the first Empire in America to the modern Commonwealth falls into three clearly marked cycles. The first closed in revolution for all but four or five of the American provinces. Without the concession of 'responsible government' at the middle of the next century, the second Empire, in the opinion of both Elgin and Grey, would have invited the same disaster. Responsible government has since been conceded to a score of British provinces and Dominions, with results that have transformed the second Empire into the Commonwealth.

At each crisis of this trilogy certain decisive factors have been political. For the first, the economic and social background was so complex, on both sides of the Atlantic, that much of it came only subconsciously into the political issues of that day. At the second crisis, however, the lines are more clearly drawn. Responsible government was a political achievement, and it was won by the most distinctive and dynamic agency known to politics after the British model—the agency of dominant political parties. At their best, these parties in Nova Scotia and the old province of Canada conformed to the spirit of Burke's classic definition. They were bodies of men 'united for promoting by their joint endeavours the national interest upon some particular principle in which they are all agreed.' Let it be added that this applies, at the climax of the contest, to Johnston and the Nova Scotia Tories as well as to the followers of Howe, Uniacke, and Huntington. The economic and social background is still as widely varied as the scattered provinces of the second Empire. The evidence here, in each case, must tell its own story. In truth there are few incentives of human conduct that have not contributed, at one time or another, to this historic issue. At the Grand Remonstrance where the contest for 'responsible government' may be said to have begun, the undercurrent was religion. In Prince Edward Island two centuries later it was part of 'the eternal land question'. In the old province of Canada problems of patronage—'the universal thirst for place', as Bagot wrote—played no small part. In the North-West Territories of Canada fifty years later the issue turned largely upon parliamentary technique—the appropriation of federal subsidies by the local Assembly. But while the motives have been infinitely varied the political tendencies have been remarkably constant. The clearing-house for all these issues has been found in the same expedient. It is the genius of British peoples in both hemispheres, exclaimed Robert Baldwin to Lord Durham in 1838, 'to be concerned in the government of themselves'. The next year, two Nova Scotians crossed the Atlantic 'to claim the rights of Englishmen for the people of this country'. 'Your Lordship's declaration', wrote Joseph Howe to Lord John Russell on that occasion, 'tells me, that on this point they will be unsuccessful; but patient perseverance is a political characteristic of the stock from which we spring.' The issue was conceded nearly ten years later, for the first time in the British provinces overseas, but the contest had 'lasted as long as the Trojan war'.

As this contest develops, the theme becomes a study in politics in a narrower sense. Responsible government has sometimes been attributed to the passing of mercantilism and the rise of the economic doctrines of *laissez-faire*, or to the splendid advocacy of Lord Durham's *Report*, Howe's *Letters to Lord John Russell*, and Charles Buller's *Responsible Government for Colonies*. These conclusions, half-true though they may be, are scarcely warranted, in the last analysis, by the evidence. With the passing of mercantilism many devious motives of the old colonial system also passed away, but the doctrine of commercial control from Great Britain, as we shall see, was as imperiously held—and enforced—by Earl Grey, the apostolic free-trader who conceded responsible government, as by William Knox, the mercantilist who had no small share in precipitating the American Revolution. Durham's

Report, too, was not decisive. It heartened the Reformers at the lowest ebb of their fortunes, but its immediate effect was to harden the temper and confirm the doctrine of Lord John Russell; and one of Sydenham's missions both in Nova Scotia and in Canada, as we shall see, was to thwart responsible government by disparaging political parties and binding their formidable powers, like the arms of Samson, by the green withs of specious coalitions. In Nova Scotia the immediate effect of Howe's *Letters to Lord John Russell* was an agreement by Sir Colin Campbell and Lord John Russell himself to bar the man whom both recognized in their dispatches to be the acknowledged leader of the Reformers, from a seat in the Executive Council. In the end responsible government was extorted not by spectacular advocacy but by disciplined political parties, after havoc had been wrought to the old colonial system by every alternative to responsible government in the politics of Nova Scotia and of Canada. There were errors of judgement on both sides, but the political technique of those eventful years will never lose its interest for students of parliamentary government upon the British model.

The process which began with the concession of responsible government is now culminating, it would seem, in the Commonwealth in its final form. Here, too, the honours have gone to the statesman with his empirical methods and pragmatic temper rather than to the jurist or the doctrinaire. Inconsistencies and anomalies still abound, but they no longer daunt the exponents of politics. *Solvitur ambulando.*[1] Precision is not after all the pearl of great price. This may not be an unmixed blessing. Lord Morley once confessed himself 'amazed and a trifle horrified' in contrasting the 'loose free-and-easy way in which politicians form their judgements with the strict standards of proof, evidence, fact, observed by every conscientious critic or historian'.[2] The compromises and accommodations of politics are apt to be very irksome to the jurist. Many a great lawyer has confessed ruefully that politics have played havoc with his law. Too arid a legal temper, on the other hand, has been known to play havoc with politics. The statesmen of the Commonwealth now respond more

[1] See *Great Britain and the Dominions*, Harris Foundation Lectures, 1927. University of Chicago Press, p. 210.

[2] *Recollections*, p. 190.

confidently to the sure instincts of historical imagination; and the future historian will understand little indeed of their problems who does not add to the precision of the jurist the sovereign faculty of historical insight.

A note may be added with regard to the evidence. Bibliographies of these studies would almost amount to a bibliography of Canadian, to say nothing of early American, history. It has been necessary to forgo so pretentious a plan, but no apology is made for relying upon ample references and apt quotations in the attempt to purvey not merely conclusions but convincing evidence to the reader. In dealing with controversial topics like the *Quebec Act*, or the relations between Howe and Falkland in Nova Scotia, or the 'Metcalfe crisis' in the old province of Canada, opinions without proof would be valueless. To proffer them in the present transitional state of Canadian history would be a poor compliment either to the importance of the subject-matter or to the reader's discernment.

An additional reason for ample documentation is to be found in the fact that the sources are as yet so largely unpublished or inaccessible. This is particularly true of Nova Scotia, not only for the period of the first Empire but for the whole critical period from the War of 1812 to responsible government. Much of the early official correspondence relating to reform in Upper and Lower Canada is to be found in the *British Parliamentary Papers* or in the provincial *Journals*; but as the contest approached its climax, less and less was entrusted to official papers that were liable to be called up, like Samuel's ghost, in the form of parliamentary returns, by those who fancied themselves 'greater witches than their neighbours'. By the time of Lord Sydenham's administration blue-books are abridged or suspended altogether, and the 'confidential' dispatch tends to disappear from the official correspondence. The truth was that official intercourse, far from being interrupted or curtailed, was simply following a safer channel. The thin routine of the *G. Series* was being supplemented by the intimacies of private and confidential intercourse like the *Bagot Papers* and the *Grey-Elgin Correspondence*. In truth, Elgin and Grey more than once resort to the harmless guile of advising each other in private what to put into their official dispatches.

But even these, the most brilliant collections of private papers, perhaps, in Canadian history, can no longer be regarded as the thesaurus of evidence for responsible government. Bagot and Elgin may have dealt incomparably with the situation, but they did not create it. The springs of responsible government were in Nova Scotia and in Canada. In the *Howe Papers*, the *Baldwin Papers*, the *La Fontaine Papers*, and similar collections, is to be found the spontaneous and confidential intercourse of the Reformers themselves; and nothing demonstrates more clearly than the confidential letters of Sydenham and Metcalfe and Sir Colin Campbell how completely sometimes the official mind was at fault in gauging the forces that were already at work. From the *La Fontaine Papers* (to cite a single instance) it is clear that the alliance between the Baldwin Reformers of Upper Canada and the French *bloc* under La Fontaine in June, 1841—one of the historic alliances of Canadian politics which Sydenham scathingly denounced at that time as the work of men 'not known for 24 hours' to each other—had been patiently and secretly built up for more than two years. The relations between Hincks, Baldwin, and La Fontaine in Canada, between La Fontaine, Girouard, Viger and Morin, between Howe, Huntington, and Uniacke in Nova Scotia, and above all between Howe and Charles Buller in the final concession of responsible government, are to be traced only in papers of this nature. An attempt has been made in these studies to give them the place to which they are entitled.

My obligations are so numerous that it will be possible to acknowledge by name only the deepest of them here. Dr. Doughty, Dr. Adam Shortt, and Mr. William Smith of the Public Archives at Ottawa will be gratefully remembered not only for a hundred kind offices in making the vast resources of the Archives accessible, but for placing so generously at the disposal of every serious investigator the store of their own ripe wisdom and experience. I have been under obligation to the Provincial Librarian of Nova Scotia for the use of valuable papers and Letter-Books, and to Mr. Smith again for copies supplied to me for further reference. To the use of the *Grey-Elgin Correspondence* which I owe to Dr. Doughty I must add the use of the excellent copies in the Shortt Collection which Professor Morton was good enough to lend me from the University of Saskatchewan. Acknowledgement is due to the Royal Society of Canada, to the *Canadian Historical Review*, and to the Association of Canadian Clubs, for the use, in several of these studies, of details already published under their auspices. For innumerable details of documentation and indexing I have been happily indebted to my wife. Grateful thanks also which I hoped to be able to express for the kindly interest of the late Professor Egerton and of the late Professor Davis can now be inscribed only to their memory. With that eager band of scholars whose periodical gatherings at Ottawa have long made of the Public Archives there a veritable clearing-house for Canadian history, there have been stimulating discussions without number. Under the enthusiastic scholarship of these and other experienced investigators it is altogether a heartening thing to see the cause of Canadian history coming at last into its own.

C. M.

UNIVERSITY OF MANITOBA,
August, 1928.

CONTENTS

INTRODUCTORY

I

THE six studies in this series, though self-contained essays in Canadian history, will be found to follow a very clearly marked theme. The first three relate to the first Empire and the disaster which overtook it at the American Revolution; the last three to the truly British solution of 'the American question' in the practice of responsible government. The slow but steady growth in the scope of responsible government has culminated in the Commonwealth as we know it to-day. Taken together these stages mark the transition from governance to full self-government; and it is a curious coincidence that the recurring cycles in the process have come at almost exactly equal intervals of seventy-five years—from the beginning of the American Revolution which destroyed the first Empire to the achievement of responsible government in Nova Scotia and in Canada which saved the second, and from the full concession of responsible government to the culmination of that process in the report of the Committee on Inter-Imperial Relations at the Imperial Conference of 1926.

The pursuit of such a theme is not without its dangers. Much of the unity and inevitableness of history is lost when the attempt is made to break it up, like a ray of white light, into its component prismatic colours. For a variety of reasons, however, a comprehensive history for Canada may long remain a counsel of perfection. Canadian history is highly complex, and in truth it is only by focusing broken lights and by fusing all the cardinal colours that it is ever likely to be reconstructed in its entirety. Much of it has been the by-product of larger issues. Many issues that were Canadian in their origin have been distorted almost beyond recognition by external influences. Many, too, have complicated each other by appearing at the same time, thus forcing an attempt at simultaneous solution under conditions which invited disaster for them all.

Of the three or four major problems in Canadian political history—the fundamental issues of colonial government inherited from the first Empire, the problem of race after 1763, the project of combining scattered British provinces into a transcontinental Dominion—not one, it would be safe to say, was singled out for settlement upon its merits. The first of these it will be the aim of these studies to trace in some detail. The second, though contemplated by the Board of Trade upon principles of toleration and of magnanimity unexampled at that time, came almost immediately within the orbit of the American Revolution, and was launched by that cataclysm upon a meteoric course through Canadian history which it has followed ever since. Successful as the Canadian solution of the problem of race may now seem to the South African or to the Irishman, a closer view of its earlier history is less inspiring. Never perhaps since the great *Report* of 1769 has the chance occurred to solve it upon so lofty a plane of mutual confidence, of toleration, and of compromise.

The Canadian Confederation too arose from a welter of conflicting forces. Beyond a doubt it was the stronger for them in the end. Federal powers by comparison with provincial or state powers are stronger in Canada than in the United States or in Australia or in Brazil—a fact which would seem to warrant the inference that this ratio stands in direct proportion to the pressure under which such powers are usually extorted. In so far as the Canadian Confederation was the 'child of deadlock', the result of 'impending anarchy', the escape from 'perpetual ministerial crises' in the old province of Canada after the Union, the turmoil of that day may now be regarded with a measure of resignation not conspicuous sixty-five years ago. Thus even Confederation is scarcely a clear theme in Canadian history. It had its rise in a dozen tributaries with sources as remote as race and religion, constitutional defects of the Union, economic pressure, relations with the United States, territorial expansion, and the stirrings of a national spirit.

The theme here attempted—the transition from governance to self-government in British America—is still more complex, for it is complicated by all the others. It was the first to appear and it has been the last to approach finality; for though the general principles of responsible government were established nearly eighty years ago, it has required more than two generations to reach the stage epitomized in the report of the Imperial Conference of 1926. Not even this complexity, however, can conceal its importance. The principles of responsible government, vindicated here seventy-five years ago, have since been applied to British dominions in every quarter of the world. In Elgin's deliberate opinion they saved the second Empire from the fate of the first. In the process, they transformed the whole nature of its unity, and the present Commonwealth became inevitable. In that sense the cause of the reformers of that day, as Howe and Baldwin instinctively believed, concerned vastly more than the petty local interests of Nova Scotia or of Canada. Howe wrote prophetically of the security and peace of millions in every clime. In truth responsible government was the watershed between the old Empire and the Commonwealth, and it is from the rugged outline of that 'great divide' that the long approach from the first Empire and the prospect for the future Commonwealth are alike most clearly discernible.

II

The approach from the first Empire is not illuminated by the traditions of constitutional history in Canada. The conventional approach to the second Empire is the Battle of the Plains of Abraham. The *Quebec Act*, following closely upon the conquest of New France, was so complete a reversal of the old colonial system of the first Empire that the return to that system at the *Constitutional Act* seemed almost a new creation. The loyalist migrations further buried the origins of British colonial government beneath a new stratum of conventional, not to say parochial, prepossessions. A curtain was drawn across Canadian history at the American Revolution, and even the *Quebec Act*, detached from its real setting in British policy at the most critical period of the Revolution, was long regarded as though it were purely local in its origin with no bearing upon the larger issue.

Traditions of Virginia, New Hampshire, and other 'royal' provinces of the first Empire—prototypes of Nova Scotia which was taken in turn as the model for Quebec in 1763—faded into memories of an incomprehensible tragedy. The phenomenal growth of the Canadas, particularly after the Union, and the fact that the name of that province was eventually given to the whole Dominion, further confirmed these prepossessions. New France thus became the background, and the problem of race became the staple of Canadian history. In so far as Confederation was the solution of that problem by providing 'home rule' for Quebec, this also confirmed the conventional approach. The loyalist traditions of Upper Canada, the problem of race in Lower Canada, the process of Confederation—these have bulked so large in the growth of the Dominion that it requires almost a *tour de force* to trace self-government in Canada to its real origin not in the 'paternal despotism' of

New France but in the traditions of the old colonial system, defective though it was, in New England. These traditions were already to be found in the wake of the New England migrations into Nova Scotia nearly a generation before the American Revolution, and they continued there uninterruptedly until they were vindicated in responsible government. 'We seek for nothing more than British subjects are entitled to', wrote Howe in the fourth of his *Letters to Lord John Russell*, 'but we will be contented with nothing less.'

The preliminary outline of *The Old Colonial System* (Chapter I) is an attempt to supply in very brief compass this indispensable approach to the study of self-government in Canada. After the volumes of Osgood and the brilliant studies of a host of British and American scholars, one would be bold indeed to aspire to any original contribution in such a field. So many interpretations of the first Empire and its dissolution, however, have survived the most exacting scholarship on both sides of the Atlantic that a less pretentious claim may perhaps be allowed. That part of the first Empire which remained British may be entitled, without false modesty, to a point of view which is somewhat distinctively Canadian.

Despite the admirable poise and detachment of recent scholarship in the United States, there is an assumption of inevitableness in the complete breakdown of mutual confidence, resulting in violent separation and traditions on both sides which can never, in all probability, be harmonized. On the other hand Professor Egerton, while inclined to concede the inevitableness of revolution, lodges a justifiable claim to consideration for a 'British, and not an American, attitude of mind'.[1] Viewing in retrospect as an accomplished fact a solution of the 'American question' in the achievement of responsible government, a Canadian may perhaps be permitted a third and less desperate thesis in reflecting upon the tendencies at work in the first Empire. Many of these appear strangely familiar. Unlike the United States, the provinces which remained British found little but tragedy in the Revolution. Unlike Great Britain they found the first fifty years of the second Empire poignantly reminiscent of the first. But better counsels prevailed. The achievements of the Commonwealth thus predispose the Canadian to seek the elements of promise as well as the elements of disruption in the old colonial system. The voices cry-

[1] 'Without prejudices derived from the traditional struggles of English Whigs and Tories.' *The American Revolution*, Oxford, 1923, Preface.

ing in the wilderness at that time—the counsels of Burke, the 'piercing and terrible note' of Chatham—are but echoes in the traditions of the American republic. In Canadian history they remain the law and the prophets, and the prophets of our own Commonwealth have more than once replenished the sacred fire from the same altar.

III

Nova Scotia after 1713 and particularly after the New England migrations and the granting of an Assembly in 1758 was an integral part of the 'American Empire'. After wavering for many years between the rival types of 'chartered', 'royal', and 'proprietary' provinces in America, the Board of Trade finally fixed upon 'royal' prototypes in Virginia and New Hampshire. Thus the Nova Scotia Assembly—now the oldest in British America and the only Assembly to precede and survive the Revolution—has a tradition which is unique in the development of self-government in the second Empire. Shirley's 'Great Plan', moreover, for New England expansion northward—so successfully carried out by Halifax and the Board of Trade in Nova Scotia—was projected by the Board and by Halifax himself for the new province of Quebec at the close of the Seven Years' War. In all this, as we shall see, there was no departure from the accepted forms of colonial government which obtained elsewhere in the fourteen or fifteen chief provinces at that time in America. Nova Scotia thus remained without intermission a factor in 'the American question', and the secret Addresses of the Nova Scotia Assembly within a few weeks of Lexington are not without interest in the larger struggle. The brief study of *Nova Scotia and the Old Empire* is an attempt to reconstruct this natural bridge, in one sense the only unbroken bridge, between the first Empire and the second.

For Quebec the 'Great Plan' of Shirley and of Halifax never matured. At the approach of the Revolution, for reasons which we shall try to trace, the project was reversed by the *Quebec Act*, with a violence which almost obliterated the original design of the Board of Trade and its context in an undivided Empire. This reversal of the old colonial system for Quebec long remained one of the most controversial themes in Canadian history. '*New Subjects*' *in Quebec* (Chapter III) is a study of the *Quebec Act* in its effect upon the policy originally contemplated for Quebec by the Board of Trade from 1763 to the great *Report* of 1769. There are many aspects of that Act which have been omitted in this survey. To Canadians of French origin these features are among the most important in their history since the conquest—the 'charter of the special privileges which the French-Canadians have enjoyed ever since'—and the presence to-day of a French civilization upon the banks of the St. Lawrence attests the greatest achievement of the French race upon this continent. But for the process here under review the *Quebec Act* not only reversed the normal tendencies towards self-government in America in 1774 but introduced into Quebec an exotic tradition of racial separatism which eventually embittered the whole issue of responsible government both there and elsewhere. The part of La Fontaine and Morin and Girouard and the solid French *bloc* after the Union went far to restore their race to its rightful place in the working of those representative institutions which the Board of Trade had solemnly avowed in 1769 'can alone ensure their affection, and fix their attachment to the British Government'. But it was then too late, for racial dualism was soon irremediable. In the end it brought disaster to the Union, though it forced the happier solution of 'home rule' within a broader federation of the British provinces.

In that sense the century in the Canadas from Carleton's first project of the *Quebec Act* to Confederation is surely unique in colonial history. Far from being the staple of colonial development from governance to self-government, it is marked at every stage by violent reactions. The original policy of Halifax and the Board of Trade, as we shall see, provided in Quebec as in other 'royal' provinces in America, for an Assembly and the spontaneous growth of an organic constitution. The growth of the primitive Assemblies of Nova Scotia from 1758, of Prince Edward Island from 1773, and of New Brunswick from 1785, to the achievement of 'responsible government' in the middle of the next century was effected by the 'conventions' of the constitution unbroken by a single Act of imperial legislation. Into that system the Board of Trade in 1765 and in 1769 sought to admit the 'eighty thousand brave and loyal Subjects' in Quebec, by removing the disabilities of Roman Catholics at that time, and by a sustained effort 'to extend to his Majesty's new Subjects those Privileges, which exist in the principles of a British Constitution'. It required the highest legislative authority of the Empire—an Act of the Imperial Parliament—to reverse that policy in the *Quebec Act* of 1774. That reversal forced the *Constitutional Act* of 1791 which marked a partial return to 'the principles of a British Constitution'. This in turn after two rebellions forced the *Act of Re-union* in 1841, and when the *Act of Re-union* broke down, the *British North America Act* became necessary. Thus there are three successive attempts, all by Act of Parliament, to deal with the situation created by the *Quebec Act*. The implications of that measure are thus very far-reaching in Canadian history, and no apology is offered for travelling so far out of the record in tracing its bearing upon the problem of self-government.

IV

The loss of the first Empire was followed by an attempt to apply the lessons of that still incomprehensible disaster to the second.

The hiatus which lies between the first three studies in this series and the last three, would form a theme for a volume in itself, for the history of the second 'American Empire' from the loss of the thirteen colonies to the contest for responsible government has yet to be written. Much of it has long been known in considerable detail. The story of Upper and of Lower Canada forms the conventional 'history of Canada' for fifty years, but there would seem to be room for a series of provincial histories for the other provinces and for that vast area comprising more than a quarter of the continent which lay for fifty years under the control of the Hudson's Bay Company. A synthesis of all these might then supply for the study of the second Empire in America what Osgood has so admirably compiled for the first.

In the essay which bears the somewhat pretentious title of *Nova Scotia and the Second Empire* (Chapter IV) something has been included by way of introduction to the more detailed study of responsible government in that province. The background for *Responsible Government in Canada* (Chapter V) is already a familiar story. The former of these was the first formal concession of that great reform, but the second, following almost immediately upon it, was a much more critical experiment with even more decisive results for the Empire. With responsible government the menace which threatened the second Empire with the fate of the first passed away, and with the passing of the second Empire came the sure foundations of the Commonwealth.

The concluding study on *The Commonwealth and its Corollaries* was published in substance by the Royal Society of Canada in

1923.[1] Though it may serve to carry forward the theme towards the denouement which has since been formally recognized by the Imperial Conference of 1926, the field of Canadian history with which it deals, it is scarcely necessary to add, has yet to be explored in systematic detail. For obvious reasons it is even less known and less accessible for historical investigation than the course of the second Empire with its wealth of state papers, pamphlet literature, and invaluable collections of private correspondence. Yet the crowning glory of British statesmanship is perhaps to be found in the patient empirical methods, the 'day to day opportunism', by which the scope of responsible government has been slowly but steadily enlarged until it has come to embrace for the British Dominions all the attributes of potential nationhood. Not without heart-burnings and at times very plain dealing have the anomalies of the old Empire been discarded for the recognized 'conventions' of the Commonwealth. In that process all the Dominions have had their part, and the exclusively Canadian point of view advanced in these essays would be indefensible in a more general survey. But despite the conflicts of opinion and of policy, concord has been in the ascendant; and it may well be said that the manner and spirit of this development, together with its attendant consequences, have been without a parallel in the history of government.

In 1783, the younger Pitt, contemplating the ruins of the first Empire, spoke with poignant recollections of that 'memorable era of *England's* glory'.[2] Whatever poignancy attaches to the Imperial Conference of 1926 is of a different sort—the poignancy of 'parental recollection' upon seeing the vigorous young nations of the family coming of age, as Elgin had predicted in 1850, passing from direct parental authority and arraying themselves for direct participation in those international issues which are now abroad in the world. In the historic words of the report on Inter-Imperial Relations, the self-governing Dominions are now '*autonomous Communities within the British Empire, equal in status, in no way subordinate one to another in any aspect of their domestic or external affairs, though united by a common allegiance to the Crown, and freely associated as members of the British Commonwealth of Nations*'.

The nature of the 'unity' which emerges from this conception of

[1] *Responsible Government and its Corollaries in the Canadian Constitution, Transactions,* Third Series, 1923, vol. xvii, pp. 41–56.

[2] Quoted in Professor Coupland's *Quebec Act,* Oxford, 1925, p. 1.

the British Commonwealth is altogether profounder than the mechanics of governmental control. 'The very idea of subordination of parts', exclaimed Burke in the most dynamic of his speeches, 'excludes this idea of simple and undivided unity.'

> 'Do not entertain so weak an imagination, as that your registers and your bonds, your affidavits and your sufferances, your cockets and your clearances, are what form the great securities of your commerce. Do not dream that your letters of office, and your instructions, and your suspending clauses, are the things that hold together the great contexture of this mysterious whole. These things do not make your government. Dead instruments, passive tools as they are, it is the spirit of the English communion that gives all their life and efficacy to them.'

'Wild and chimerical' as that conception appeared in 1775 to those 'mechanical politicians . . . . who think that nothing exists but what is gross and material', it finds a better vindication in the happier omens of our own day. The Commonwealth, says Lord Balfour, is 'held together far more effectually by broad loyalties and common feelings of interest and devotion to the great world ideals of peace and freedom than by anything else. That is the bond . . . . and if it is not enough nothing else will be'.[1] What this may mean for the nations of the Commonwealth itself, and what the same conception might mean if projected into international relations, it would be rash to speculate, but Burke's vain appeal a century and a half ago ought now to merit a more prophetic response. 'We ought to auspicate all our public proceedings in America, with the old warning of the Church, *Sursum corda!* We ought to elevate our minds to the greatness of that trust.'

[1] House of Lords, Dec. 8, 1926.

I
THE OLD COLONIAL SYSTEM

THE functions of government exercised by the British Dominions now amount in practice to self-government and potential equality with Great Britain in the British Commonwealth. If traced back to the middle of the eighteenth century, these functions would be found in a bewildering variety of institutions, many of them from the beginning so directly under imperial control that colonists had scarcely contemplated the possibility of any other.

A Canadian protective tariff at the present time would be announced by a Canadian Minister of Finance at Ottawa. It would be collected by officials appointed by the Minister of Customs. It would be enforced by Canadian courts under the administration of the Canadian Department of Justice. The revenues thus accruing would find their way automatically into the consolidated fund of the Dominion. In 1765 not one of these functions was controlled by colonial legislation or administered by colonial officials acting in the interests of the colonies. In this field, therefore, governance was the rule, confirmed, as Burke pointed out upon the eve of the American Revolution, 'even more by usage than by law'. On the other hand there had scarcely been a time when British settlers in America had failed to feel and to exercise certain instinctive aptitudes which colonial patriots could call 'the inalienable rights of British subjects'. An Assembly of freeholders came to be regarded as indispensable in a British province. By the middle of the eighteenth century the law officers of the Crown and the Lords of Trade had laid down the principle that no government 'can be properly carried on without such an Assembly'.[1] In a resolution which Dickinson in his *Farmers' Letters* called 'the American Declaration of Rights', the Stamp Act Congress at New York, October 19, 1765, declared that 'His Majesty's liege subjects in the Colonies are intitled to all the inherent rights and liberties of his natural-born subjects within the Kingdom of Great

[1] William Murray and Sir Richard Lloyd, Apr. 29, 1755; Lords of Trade to Gov. of N.S., May 7, 1755. *Pub. Arch. Can., Nova Scotia, A. Series*, vol. lvii.

Britain'.[1] In 1758 the humblest Assembly in North America at its first session could arraign a citizen of Halifax at the bar of the House to answer for aspersions upon the dignity of the Assembly.

Between these two poles—governance through the mercantile system on the one hand, and self-government through the local Assembly on the other—lay vast areas of government over which the control was almost constantly shifting. The adjustments that took place were normally as peaceful and almost as imperceptible as the slow changes of nature. At times they were the result of deliberation. Occasionally there was an angry contest which enlarged rather than closed the issue, and left a scar behind. But though no serious attempt was made to fix the boundaries, certain very marked tendencies were discernible. The abounding commerce of North America was everywhere obvious; but without questioning the general principles of mercantilism, close observers had already begun to suspect that much of this prosperity arose not only through the mercantile system but in spite of it. On the other hand a series of ineffectual attempts to circumscribe the scope and progress of self-government had revived in the new world many of the issues of the revolt against the Stuarts and the Revolution Settlement in the old. Without drawing upon the century and a half of experience and more than a score of experiments in self-government since the American Revolution, it is not difficult to trace in the American colonies of the eighteenth century certain tendencies that are now so familiar as to be commonplaces of British government in every quarter of the world. So prevalent had these become by the middle of the century, despite the widest diversities of environment in America, that they seemed a part, as Burke said, of 'the natural operation of things which left to themselves generally fall into their proper order'.

THE MERCANTILE SYSTEM

I

Neither in its origin nor perhaps in practice did the mercantile system of the eighteenth century deserve the obloquy which overtook it in the wake of the American Revolution. By comparison with Spanish greed for gold and silver during the fifteenth and sixteenth centuries, the ideals of British mercantilism were plausible and enlightened. Nearly half the years of the eighteenth cen-

[1] See however Knox, *Controversy between Great Britain and her Colonies Reviewed*, London, 1769, p. 26, and Appendix, p. cii, &c.

tury before 1765 were years of war when national aggrandizement was naturally associated with conquest. Trade was to be sought not through the prosperity of potential enemies but in the expansion of a self-sufficing Empire. The mercantile system was thus the product of its age and can scarcely be appraised apart from the conditions which called it into being.

Many features of the system, moreover, subserved the best interests of the nation. One of its cardinal principles was that British commerce must be carried on in British ships, commanded by British masters, and manned by predominantly British crews. The great *Navigation Act* of 1651 was directed against the Dutch carrying-trade, and beyond a doubt was instrumental in establishing that maritime supremacy which, until the brief but disastrous intermission at the most critical period of the American Revolution, was never broken. In an age of sailing-ships when a sailor's skill was the result of a lifelong aptitude for the sea, and when naval stores were largely interchangeable between the navy and the mercantile marine, the one was almost the counterpart of the other. The oft-quoted dictum of Adam Smith may be taken to justify this phase at least of the mercantile system: 'defence is more important than opulence'. In fact defence, in this instance, produced opulence. The avowed object of the *Navigation Act* of the seventeenth century was an accomplished fact by the middle of the eighteenth: 'the increase of shipping and the encouragement of the navigation of this nation'. Policy in this respect was merely a reinforcement of natural tendencies. The growth of colonial shipping in particular filled the traveller in America with astonishment. Long after the American Revolution this feature of the system was held to be justified by results. 'I would ask the most interested colonist', wrote one of the best-informed of British officials, 'to shew upon what *other principle* he founds his expectation of security in his possessions and protection in his trade.' [1]

Other features of the system, however, were highly artificial, and invited the fate of all systems which depend for success upon the defiance of nature. Colonial governors were under the most positive instructions to prohibit manufactures which might compete with the mother country: 'it is Our express Will and Pleasure', read the *Instructions* to Governor Murray in Quebec, 'that you do not, upon any Pretence whatever, upon pain of Our highest Displeasure, give your Assent to any Law or Laws for setting up any Manufac-

[1] William Knox in *Extra Official State Papers*, 1789, ii. 54.

tures and carrying on any Trades, which are hurtful and prejudicial to this Kingdom.'[1]

For the 'tropical' as distinct from the 'continental' plantations perhaps the worst feature of this was the stark avowal of colonial subordination to British interests. Between sugar-islands in the West Indies and industrial Britain competition was negligible. For primitive 'continental' colonies too the regulations frequently conformed to natural conditions, and the British Government sometimes relied upon constructive enterprise rather than prohibitions. Thus Bridger, Surveyor of Woods, strove to convince the frontiersman that tar or potash was more profitable than homespun: he could 'earn enough at it to buy two coats in the same time he spent in the actual manufacture of one'. But few communities in the north temperate zone could develop far without aspiring to primitive industries of their own. The manufacture of beaver hats flourished in New York and Pennsylvania, while 'the country people or planters are entered so far into making their own woolens that not one in forty but wears his own carding, spinning, &c.'.[2] The prohibition of American manufactures, though continued on paper, seems to have been ignored in practice. Had such measures as the *Hat Act* and the *Iron Act* been vigorously enforced, or, indeed, had there been in the nature of things any possibility of enforcing them, this feature of the mercantile system might have ended in disaster. The fact that so little was done to enforce them is perhaps the best proof that the theory was thoroughly untenable, and that no legislation in defiance of nature could crib and confine the illimitable resources of the new world.

II

Two other features of the mercantile system were closely related, and it is difficult to appraise them. The general purpose of scores of Acts was to give the mother country a virtual monopoly both of colonial exports, chiefly raw materials, for her own and foreign markets, and of colonial markets for her own and foreign exports. To both of these categories, however, there were many exceptions, and the element of monopoly was not devised exclusively in the interests of the mother country.

[1] 'And that You do use your utmost Endeavours to discourage, discountenance and restrain any Attempts which may be made to set up such Manufactures, or establish any such Trades.' Shortt and Doughty, *Documents relating to the Constitutional History of Canada, 1759–1791*, i. 200.

[2] Dickerson, *American Colonial Government, 1696–1765*, p. 307.

The colonial products which were to be exported to Great Britain or to foreign countries through British warehouses were those only which were 'enumerated' from time to time by the various Acts of trade; and two observations are in order with regard to them. In the first place many of the most valuable products of the colonies were not 'enumerated'; thus the fisheries which the New England colonies developed with phenomenal skill and resourcefulness were unfettered by restrictions of trade except that a clipper which carried the season's catch of cod-fish to the European market was supposed to return either in ballast or with foreign goods by way of a British port. Similarly European salt, an indispensable commodity for the fisheries, was supposed to reach the fishing-grounds only by the same circuitous route. The resourceful New England skipper was scarcely to be bound by regulations like these. In the second place there were many bounties even upon 'enumerated' colonial products, and many heavy duties upon the competitive foreign products in the British market. Thus Virginian tobacco had the advantage of a tax upon Spanish tobacco in Great Britain, while the cultivation of tobacco was prohibited in any form in Great Britain and Ireland—a regulation which in Beer's opinion 'entailed far greater sacrifice than did British restrictions on Colonial manufacturing'.[1] But while there were constant protests from British and Irish farmers against the colonial monopoly of the British market, the Virginian planters had a right to protest that more than three-quarters of their tobacco found its way to foreign markets. For this lucrative trade Great Britain was the staple, and, despite the rebate of the British duty to the colonial exporter, the British merchant reaped the middleman's profits.

With regard to one class of colonial exports—masts and naval stores—'defence' rather than 'opulence' was still the order of the day, and the long controversies over bounties and preferences and reservations of pine timber for the navy ought not perhaps to be separated from that division of the system. Had the bounties on hemp, pitch, tar, masts, and other naval stores in the colonies, even when reinforced by the duties on Baltic timber, availed to meet the needs of the navy and of ship-builders in Great Britain, the friction might have been negligible. But measures deemed necessary in the interests of naval security were frequently administered in a way which left an ugly impression of coercion rather than encourage-

[1] *British Colonial Policy, 1754–1765*, p. 196.

ment. Comfortable fortunes were made in colonial ship-yards upon masts and spars for the British market, but the Surveyor of Woods was constantly embroiled with the pioneer settler, and the 'enumeration' of lumber cut off the colonial exporter from direct contact with the European market, perhaps the most lucrative field in the whole range of colonial enterprise.

There were those like Martin Bladen who claimed boldly that colonies ought thus to subserve 'the advantage of the mother state' as the price of colonial 'privileges and protection': 'if this use cannot be made of them it will be much better for the state to be without them.'[1] At the close of the American Revolution it was still roundly asserted by an Under-Secretary of State as 'the principle I meant to found the regulations upon . . . that *it was better to have no colonies at all, than not to have them subservient to the maritime strength and commercial interests of Great Britain*'.[2] But the benefits of control over colonial products were believed to be reciprocal. 'It became hard to say', writes Professor Egerton, 'what was the final result, on a balancing of accounts.'[3] Almost the last defence of the mercantile system in the nineteenth century was the protest from Canada, Nova Scotia, and New Brunswick against the repeal of British duties on Baltic timber. Perhaps the chief defects of this branch of the system would have appeared under any regulations which interfered with the natural course of trade. Those who profited prospered in silence or agitated for still greater profits. Those who were hit could be relied upon to make themselves heard. Perhaps the most dangerous feature was that in the midst of grave controversies so artificial a system lent itself, as we shall see, to manipulation for ulterior purposes.

III

The remaining features of the system were also highly artificial, and still more fatally invited exploitation. The attempt to monopolize the colonial market and to make Great Britain the staple even for foreign exports invited systematic evasion by every rank

[1] *Colonial Records of North Carolina*, ii. 626–7, quoted by Professor Egerton in *The American Revolution*, p. 5.

[2] 'This principle I make no secret of, for I have ever avowed it, even in America, and as an American planter, when I was deeply interested in the prosperity and security of that country, and its continuing to be a member of the British Empire.' William Knox, *Extra Official State Papers*, ii. 54.

These papers were addressed to the 'Members of the Two Houses of Parliament Associated for the Preservation of the Constitution and Promoting the Prosperity of the British Empire'.

[3] *American Revolution*, p. 59.

of society in North America from the skipper of the New England schooner to the relatives of the judge upon the bench. Unlike the ban upon manufacturing in the colonies, the regulation of colonial imports was supposed in theory to be thoroughly practicable. The laws of trade were British, and they were administered by an organization which was imperial in every detail. The commissioners of customs were British officials over whose appointment and conduct even the Board of Trade exercised no control. Until 1767 these commissioners were resident in Great Britain, and commissioners then came to America not to conciliate American opinion but to enforce the regulations at close quarters. The Vice-Admiralty Courts for the enforcement of trade and maritime regulations sat without juries, and were presided over by British judges who, like the customs officials, were supposed to be independent of local influence as they were of local control. Behind the whole moved the pervasive power of the Royal Navy, which on occasion could exert a direct and invincible domination. On paper the system seemed remarkably complete and responsive to central control.

In practice the system, like Charon's boat beneath the weight of Aeneas, leaked at every joint. Smuggling went on until the atmosphere reeked with it. The customs officials were venal until it was said that 'a very small office in the customs in America has raised a man a fortune sooner than a Government'.[1] Many of the officials lived in Great Britain and sent deputies whose fortunes were observed to bear an inverse ratio to their salaries. It was stated that 'without bribery and corruption they must starve';[2] but every vacancy in the customs was thronged with candidates for starvation. Even in time of war fortunes were made by trading with the enemy and particularly by the indirect trade with the French through the Spanish island of Monte Cristi. The evidence cited by Beer leaves an impression of utter lawlessness wherever evasion was possible. Chatham, with righteous indignation, condemned 'this dangerous and ignominious trade', and attributed to it the protraction of 'this long and expensive War'. Fifteen years later, on the eve of the American Revolution, Chatham could still speak of 'little paltry peddling fellows, vendors of twopenny wares, and

[1] James Otis, *Rights of the British Colonies Asserted and Proved*, Boston, 1764, p. 58; quoted by Beer, *British Colonial Policy, 1754–1765*, p. 210.
Otis had been prosecuting-attorney in Vice-Admiralty Court until 1761.

[2] *Ibid.* Hutchinson to Richard Jackson, Sept. 17, 1763.

falsehoods, who, under the idea of trade, *sell* everything in their power—Honour, Trust, and Conscience'.[1]

If families like the Livingstons and De Peysters of New York could dabble in this filthy lucre in time of war, the tendencies in time of peace must have been irresistible. The prevalence of smuggling could scarcely have escaped the most casual observer. The *Molasses Act* of 1733 imposing duties upon foreign molasses, sugar, and rum in the American colonies yielded less than £5,700 during the twenty-one years preceding the outbreak of the Seven Years' War—an average of £259 a year;[2] yet the molasses annually brought into Rhode Island alone amounted to 14,000 hogsheads of which scarcely 2,500 came from the British sugar-islands. Of the 1,500,000 lb. of tea consumed annually in the North American colonies, scarcely one-tenth was imported directly from Great Britain. The irregularities involved in these practices included everything from mere evasion to fraudulent declarations and downright perjury. At a time when the total export trade of Great Britain to the North American colonies amounted to less than £2,000,000 a writer in London estimated the smuggling at £700,000 a year.[3] In a secret Address to the House of Commons in 1775 the Nova Scotia Assembly deplored 'that corruption of manners and that contempt of the crime of perjury which is now become so open and flagrant'.[4]

Natural *versus* Official Tendencies

I

The net results of the mercantile system at the close of the Seven Years' War would be hard to estimate, but it seems obvious that a system which lent itself to this monstrous perversion could scarcely have commanded the moral respect without which law is worse than useless. Professor Egerton has finely said that 'perhaps in the long run the worst result of the system was the lowering of the public conscience, which is the inevitable outcome of continuous successful evasion of the law'.[5] It is but a step from the evasion of

[1] *Speech of the Rt. Hon. the Earl of Chatham in the House of Lords*, Jan. 20, 1775, p. 91.

[2] Dickerson, *American Colonial Government, 1696–1765*, p. 118; Beer, *op. cit.*, p. 240.

[3] Beer, *op. cit.*, p. 246.

[4] *Nova Scotia, A. Series*, 94. 11. (Transcripts of *C.O. 217* in the Public Record Office.) *Pub. Arch. Can.*

[5] *Origin and Growth of the English Colonies*, p. 119.

a bad law to contempt for all law. To this polluted source have been traced certain evil tendencies which tainted American public life far into the nineteenth century. A system which induced venality and evasion on such a scale must have had a taint of original sin in its own nature. The most flagrant instances of fraud and perjury, indefensible under any circumstances, were winked at in high places or deplored as inevitable corollaries of the system. The Governor of Massachusetts wrote that 'if conniving at foreign sugar and molasses, and Portugal wines and fruit, is to be reckoned Corruption, there was never, I believe, an uncorrupt Custom House Officer in America until within twelve months'.[1] Yet the *Molasses Act* and other intolerable regulations remained upon the statute-books until Grenville found them there and a fatal train of circumstances led to an attempt for the first time to enforce them.

The normal and what may be called the natural tendencies of the system, therefore, may be inferred from the evasions that went on under it. For economic as well as for bodily health the subversion of nature is a costly process; and though not yet reduced to a body of economic doctrine many saving principles were acted upon in detail with determined conviction. The Boston skipper, part-owner of his ship and 'working on shares' with his crew, was accustomed to spend the season on 'the banks' and to take his catch of dried and salted cod to Portugal in the autumn. He was not likely to come back in ballast if he could fill the hold with 'Portugal wines and fruit', or better still, with salt for the next season's fishing. The New York merchant who bought so lavishly of British goods was frequently able to buy British goods only because he had first prospered, sometimes in devious ways, by buying and selling foreign and particularly West Indian goods. The British manufacturer was not deeply concerned how the customer who bought British woollens in Philadelphia got the *dollars* to pay for them, or how Spanish or Dutch bullion came to gravitate so mysteriously to Britain by way of the North American colonies. It was scarcely by chance that the dollar passed into the currency of the United States.

This abounding commerce, moreover, was as potent in the colonial Assembly as it was in the British House of Commons. For the governor of a colony the merchant was frequently a thorn in the flesh: he was 'not so nearly concerned in its Welfare', Governor Lawrence protested, as the 'landed people' whose enormous hold-

[1] Beer, *op. cit.*, p. 239.

ings of unimproved wilderness cluttered colonial development for fifty years.[1] But it could scarcely be gainsaid that the prosperity of the pre-revolutionary Empire was largely commercial. In resourcefulness, in enterprise, in that practical contact with affairs as distinct from theories which distinguished the mercantile from the official mind; above all, in that species of expediency which Sir Charles Lucas calls 'day to day opportunism', the merchant adventurer deserved better of his critics than he sometimes received. Chatham, with all his contempt for the 'little paltry peddling fellows' who sold honour, trust, and conscience, had a tribute for the men who solved with unprecedented skill the problems of the commissariat. Burke, with his fierce denunciation of 'the rotten contract-hunting part of the mercantile interest' snuffing 'the cadaverous *haut goût* of lucrative war', reserves one of his highest tributes to the American colonies for their commercial enterprise: 'Nothing in the history of mankind is like their progress. For my part, I never cast an eye on their flourishing commerce and their cultivated and commodious life too, but they seem to me rather ancient nations grown to perfection through a long series of fortunate events, and a train of successful industry, accumulating wealth in many centuries, than the colonies of yesterday.'[2]

Much of the systematic evasion of the laws of trade, therefore, may perhaps be interpreted as the trend of practical commerce towards a sounder economic policy. Beer has traced much of the prosperity of the North American colonies not to the flaunted virtues but to the ineffectiveness of the system. The trade which the Englishman balanced under exports and imports was, in fact, triangular or multilateral. Thus while the export trade to the 'tropical' West Indies—the ideal type of colony from the mercantilist's point of view—increased by £326,000 during the period from 1747 to 1767, that of the 'continental' colonies increased by £1,232,000, virtually trebling in twenty years and nearly doubling the West Indian trade in total volume. The truth seems to have been that the 'continental' colonies got their first impulse to wealth by domestic and foreign trade, legitimate or otherwise. With these acquired riches they could then afford to buy British manufactures and especially woollens in rapidly increasing volume.

[1] Governor Lawrence to the Lords of Trade, Dec. 8, 1755, *Nova Scotia, A. Series*, 58. 166. In Prince Edward Island the grants of 1769 were not finally disposed of until the close of the nineteenth century.

[2] Burke to Rockingham, Aug. 23, 1775; *Speech on American Taxation*, 1774.

In 1764 Governor Colden of New York claimed it was 'evident to a demonstration that the more Trade the Colonies in North America have with Foreign Colonies, the more they consume of the British Manufactures'.[1] The opinion of William Knox was equally positive, and few could have been better informed. Knox was the confidant in turn of Grenville, of Hillsborough, of Germain, and of North himself. He had spent six years in the North American colonies before their independence, and he stated in 1789 that there had been 'a free though illicit trade with all the world there'. Elsewhere in the *Extra Official State Papers* Knox states his conviction that 'had America continued a part of the British empire for half a century longer, under the same mode of Government as subsisted in the several provinces before the war, the navigation, manufactures, and a great part of the people of Great Britain and Ireland, would probably have transported themselves thither'.[2]

II

It is clear, therefore, that to the colonist at least the practice was less objectionable than the theory, so long as normal tendencies were permitted to develop without exploitation for ulterior purposes; and indeed the hostility to the system traditionally associated with the American Revolution is found to be almost altogether apocryphal. Daniel Dulany, who was among the first to protest against the right of the Commons of Great Britain by 'giving and granting' the stamp tax 'to be thus munificent at the Expense of the Commons of America', conceded that 'the Authority of the Mother Country to regulate the Trade of the Colonies' was 'unquestionable. . . . A Right to regulate their Trade without their Consent is admitted'.[3] Gervase Parker Bushe, who in 1769 dared to suggest that 'if the cause of the Americans be just, their firmness is virtue', allowed that 'they must be subject to British navigation laws, and trade-regulations', and that 'the sea, the common benefit of mankind, may be denied them'.[4] Robinson Matthews in 1774, after exhausting satire and argument against arbitrary taxation for revenue in America, asserted that 'our colonies are content that we

[1] Quoted by Beer, *op. cit.*, p. 292. *N.Y. Col. Documents*, vii. 612.

[2] *Extra Official State Papers*, ii. 23, 12.

[3] *Considerations on the Propriety of Imposing Taxes in the British Colonies*, London (reprinted), 1766, p. 49.

[4] *The Case of Great Britain and America, Addressed to the King and Both Houses of Parliament*, London, 1769, pp. 19, 29.

should at our pleasure regulate their trade provided that what we do is bona fide, really, truly and sincerely for that purpose': this fact 'has been corroborated by their perpetual and constant consent and acquiescence'.[1]

John Adams, whose fierce invective in 1774 questioned the whole sovereign authority of Parliament, adds the proviso 'excepting to regulate their trade'. 'There is no need of any other Power than that of regulating Trade; and this the Colonies ever have been, and will be, ready and willing to concede to her.'[2] James Otis, who was referred to in 1769 as 'the first leader in the American disputes', had conceded in 1764 that 'the Act of Navigation is a good Act, so are all that exclude foreign manufactures from the plantations, and every honest man will subscribe to them'.[3] Burke, who was agent for New York, admitted in his *Speech on American Taxation* that commercial restraint was

> 'as vigorous servitude as men can be subject to. But America bore it from the fundamental Act of Navigation till 1764. Why? Because men do bear the inevitable constitution of their original nature with all its infirmities. The Act of Navigation attended the colonies from their infancy, grew with their growth, and strengthened with their strength. They were confirmed in obedience to it even more by usage than by law.'

The fourth article in the Declaration of the first Continental Congress, 1774, avowed this acquiescence in the clearest language: 'from the necessity of the case, and a regard to the mutual interest of both countries, we cheerfully consent to the operation of such Acts of the British Parliament, as are bona fide restrained to the regulation of our external commerce, for the purpose of securing

[1] 'Who are . . . to determine whether any money is wanted for such purposes; they who pay it or they who take it? They who take it. Who are to determine the quantity wanted? They who take it. Who are to determine how often it is wanted? They who take it. . . . Suppose the Americans should be of opinion or declare that the money so raised is not for their advantage but the contrary; is that a bar to raising? No. . . . Suppose them to signify, that the money alledged to be used in their military defence is employed in paying troops to enslave them, or which they had rather be without. . . . Wherein then does this differ from will and pleasure in the most absolute sense?' *Considerations on the Measures carrying on with Respect to the British Colonies in North America*, London, 1774, pp. 7, 8, 10.

[2] *History of the Dispute with America from its Origin in 1754. Written in the Year 1774.* London, 1774, pp. 23, 33.

[3] *A Vindication of the British Colonies, By James Otis, Esq. of Boston*, reprinted 1769, Advertisement. *Rights of the British Colonists Asserted and Proved*, Boston, New-England (1764). Reprinted, London, 1766.

the commercial advantages of the whole empire to the mother country, and the commercial benefits of its respective members.'[1] What with British capital, British naval defence, and free intercourse within the Empire, the commercial advantages of the old colonial system may well have exceeded the commercial hazards of political independence. Beer, 'the best qualified of men to speak on the subject of the Mercantile System', has the remarkable statement that in this respect 'the system tended in the direction of greater imperial cohesion, and ran counter to the strongly marked tendency towards political disintegration'.[2]

III

It would be idle, perhaps, to speculate upon the result had other events permitted a peaceful evolution. The glories of the Seven Years' War brought disaster in their train—a staggering debt, disillusionment and impatience at home, the demand for adequate taxation of the colonies, and a temptation to exploit this specious imperial system as a short cut to solvency. Is it conceivable that if divested of more fundamental issues the transition from monopoly to reciprocity under Huskisson and to free trade under Peel might have taken place in the thirteen colonies as quietly as in those which eventually remained British?

Whatever be the answer to that question there was one attribute of the system—to the official mind perhaps its most attractive feature—which like the heel of Achilles invited a mortal arrow. While the mercantile interests, with feet firmly planted upon the bed-rock of economic facts, could be relied upon sooner or later to recognize stubborn realities, the official method was not always so empirical; and official as distinct from natural tendencies were never perhaps more sorely tried than at the close of the Seven Years' War. Whatever the varying fortunes of the conflict with the provincial Assemblies, here was one phase of the colonial system which was admittedly under imperial control. The laws of trade, the commissioners of customs in London, the customs officials at the American ports, the Vice-Admiralty Courts, admiralty law without juries and without recourse to local legislation, the Royal Navy with traditions which were the pride and glory of

[1] S. E. Morison, *Sources and Documents illustrating the American Revolution*, Clarendon Press, 1923, p. 120.

[2] Egerton, *The American Revolution*, p. 50. *British Colonial Policy, 1754–1765*, p. 210. See the excellent summary in Schlesinger, *The Colonial Merchants and the American Revolution*, New York, 1918, pp. 591–3.

every Briton—all these were imperial. For the official type of mind with its hard virtues and its impatience of anomalies this glittering array of organization must have exercised a fascination which it was scarcely in human nature to resist.

By all the orthodox canons of officialdom the Right Honourable George Grenville must have been one of the most virtuous and admirable of men. William Knox, who defended the policy, and, after Grenville's death, 'the memory of that great and excellent man', claims to have been admitted to a closer intimacy with him than 'that great Minister's nearest relations'.[1] Neither to his friends nor to himself, wrote Knox in 1789, 'would he warp the public interest or service in the smallest degree; rigid in his opinions of public justice and integrity, and firm to inflexibility in the construction of his mind, he reprobated every suggestion of the political expediency of overlooking frauds or evasions in the payment or collection of the revenue, or of waste and extravagance in its expenditure'.[2]

> 'With a masculine understanding and a stout and resolute heart (says Burke in the memorable lines on *American Taxation*), he had an application undissipated and unwearied. . . . But it may be truly said that men too much conversant in office are rarely minds of remarkable enlargement. . . . Mr. Grenville thought better of the wisdom and power of human legislation than in truth it deserves. He conceived, and many conceived along with him, that the flourishing trade of this country was greatly owing to law and institution, and not quite so much to liberty; for but too many are apt to believe regulation to be commerce and taxes to be revenue.'

The laws against illicit trade were already upon the statute-books. Why not enforce them? In 1764 it was determined to enforce the *Molasses Act* at 3*d*. per gallon. The *Sugar Act* of the same year under the guise of commercial regulation avowed the ominous principle that it was 'just and necessary that a revenue be raised in

[1] *Extra Official State Papers*, ii. 31–2.

[2] *Id.*, p. 34. Cf. Grenville to Knox, Aug. 28, 1768: 'I may appeal to you as a private man, and as a Member of Parliament, to my public declarations, that my opinions upon this subject have ever been uniformly the same.' *Id.*, Appendix, No. IV, p. 19. Cf. also Grenville's diary for July 10, 1765, at the time of his resignation: 'he besought His Majesty, as he valued his own safety, not to suffer any one to advise him to separate or draw the line between his British and American dominions . . . that if any man ventured to defeat the regulations laid down for the Colonies, by a slackness in the execution, he should look upon him as a criminal and the betrayer of his country.' *Grenville Correspondence*, 1853, iii. 215–16.

your Majesty's said dominions in America for defraying the expenses of defending, protecting, and securing the same'. It was now resolved to establish a Vice-Admiralty Court for the whole of British America and to enforce confiscations for illicit trade. As First Lord of the Admiralty Grenville had already urged vigorous action against clandestine foreign trade. Closer observers were aware that from these hidden springs flowed much of the prosperity which enriched British trade with the colonies and 'filled all its proper channels to the brim'. 'Any of these innumerable regulations, perhaps', says Burke, 'would not have alarmed alone; some might be thought reasonable; the multitude struck them with terror.' When the thin disguise of commercial regulation was dropped and a revenue boldly sought by the ill-fated *Stamp Act* in 1765, it was to the Vice-Admiralty Courts that Grenville turned with his 'stout and resolute heart' to secure its enforcement. It was natural that opposition should vent itself against the immediate instruments of this insensate policy; and this may account for much of the apocryphal hostility to the mercantile system. But there was a deeper issue than this. Apart altogether from the instruments used to enforce the policy, what was the motive for the policy itself? Was it justifiable in 1765? What was its ultimate purpose? These were questions which could not be answered from the standpoint of eighteenth-century mercantilism, for they concerned those 'inalienable rights of British subjects' which were to be sought and perhaps understood only at the other pole of the old colonial system—the stubborn faith which British peoples in every quarter of the world have always retained in the efficacy of self-government.

Colonial Government

I

The Seven Years' War closed with seventeen or eighteen British provinces in North America, stretching from the Gulf of Mexico to the Arctic Ocean. There were those who rejoiced with Benjamin Franklin that 'the foundations of the future grandeur and stability of the British empire' were now laid, and that these were 'broad and strong enough to support the greatest political structure that human wisdom ever yet erected'.[1] On the other hand there were officials like Governor Murray in Quebec, or William Knox, Under-

[1] *Works*, ed. Bigelow, i. 399.

Secretary for the Southern Department, who contemplated 'this American Empire' from another point of view, for 'empire' in the sense of organized dominion was nowhere in evidence. The mercantile system, it is true, was imperial in every detail, and the laws of trade and navigation were placed in the hands of every governor without differentiation. But at the sea-coast this conception of 'empire' virtually came to an end, and the forms of local government in the British provinces were truly bewildering in their variety. When Knox went to America in 1756, 'it was with no small degree of astonishment' that he 'perceived a total want of plan or system in the British Government'. 'Something more than the powers of paper and parchment', he afterwards observed in those invaluable revelations, the *Extra Official State Papers*, would have been necessary 'to render them useful, and retain them in subordination to Great Britain'.[1]

No 'colonial system' could have been more varied than the conditions under which these provinces and 'plantations' had been founded, or the courses which they had run in their spontaneous and sturdy development. The new England colonies of Massachusetts, Rhode Island, and Connecticut had been havens for Puritan refugees during the royalist ascendancy under the Stuarts; Virginia proved a haven for royalist refugees under the Commonwealth. Pennsylvania was a refuge for Quakers, German Mennonites, and Tunkers; Maryland at first for Roman Catholics. In New York the Dutch of New Amsterdam and the English of the Restoration had coalesced into a province whose commercial future was already assured. In Nova Scotia French and British had lived together until 'the expulsion' scattered the Acadian exiles along the Atlantic seaboard from New Hampshire to Georgia. The basic population of Florida was Spanish; of Quebec and Grenada, French; of Rupert's Land, native Indian. The Carolinas marked the colonizing enterprise of the Stuarts after the Restoration; Georgia that of the Georges after the Revolution Settlement.

The forms of government were scarcely less varied. Even the 'royal' provinces were far from uniform; but the 'proprietary' and 'chartered' provinces exhibited in their local institutions almost every combination of relationship between governor, council, and Assembly it was possible to find in North America. The Hudson's Bay Charter of 1670—still in existence as the act of incorporation of the Hudson's Bay Company—conferred upon British stock-

[1] *Extra Official State Papers*, 1789, ii. 11, 20.

holders an iron-bound monopoly of trade and proprietary rights. It was not until the nineteenth century that a resident 'governor' was appointed in Rupert's Land and a 'Council of Assiniboia' was convened to discharge the most primitive functions of government. The charter of Pennsylvania on the other hand provided for an elective Assembly and a governor nominated by the proprietors, but no functions of legislation were accorded to the council. A popular 'single chamber' legislature and an executive controlled by the proprietary interests were thus brought into direct juxtaposition, with disastrous results to the peace and good name of the province.[1] More devastating still was the chronic feud between the Assembly and the proprietors of Maryland. For a brief period after 1691 the proprietary governor was replaced by a royal appointee, leaving, however, the other proprietary rights under the charter practically intact. After the restoration of the proprietary régime in 1715 the old feud was renewed under the old auspices, and was made memorable by the appearance of Daniel Dulany as the champion of *The Right of the Inhabitants of Maryland*. 'The proprietorships', says Osgood, 'were the weakest and on the whole the least satisfactory of the three forms of colonial government'.[2] They were also the least responsive. The sordid conflict between proprietor and pioneer, between private and public interests, could scarcely be expected to breed public spirit or devotion to a national cause. It is significant that among all the British provinces during the Seven Years' War, Pennsylvania and Maryland distinguished themselves by their stolid and perhaps disingenuous apathy.[3]

Another series of diversities was to be found in the 'chartered' provinces of Massachusetts, Rhode Island, and Connecticut. All three had narrowly escaped the aggressive royalist policy of James II. All three charters had been attacked by writs of *Quo Warranto*. That of Massachusetts in fact had been formally annulled in Chancery.[4] There was a return of chartered rights with the Revolution of 1689, though the royal governor installed in Massachusetts by James II remained a permanent institution of the province. The *Massachusetts Province Charter* of 1691 under William and Mary left both the Council and the House of Representatives elective: the latter by popular franchise, the former by

[1] For the effect of this conflict upon Indian relations and the apathy of Pennsylvania during the Seven Years' War see Osgood, *American Colonies in the 18th Century*, iv. 297, 298, 351, &c.

[2] *Id.*, iv. 25.

[3] 'They availed themselves of these disputes to shirk their simple duty.' Beer, *op. cit.*, p. 69.

[4] Greene, *The Provincial Governor*, p. 16.

the Council itself and the House of Representatives in joint session as the 'General Court' of the province. Of the royal governor also Stanhope observes in 1715 that he 'draws all his subsistance from the people and has nothing but his Commission from the King'.[1]

In Rhode Island even the governor was elective; and though there was a British statute providing that all governors must receive the approval of the Crown, the local government of the province was practically republican.[2] The right of disallowance of provincial Acts and the appointment of judges 'during pleasure'—which usually meant the pleasure of the local Assembly—were almost equally negligible as guarantees of 'subordination'. The nebulous rights of British parliamentary supremacy were seldom invoked except in the field of trade and navigation, and nowhere were the regulations more systematically evaded. 'It would be too much', wrote Governor Bernard of New Jersey to Lord Halifax, 'to require an elective governor to be in earnest in discovering & prosecuting frauds of trade.' Stephen Hopkins, the Governor of Rhode Island, stated in public in 1764 that 'the Parliament of Great Britain had no more right to make laws for them than they had for the Mohawks'. Connecticut also enjoyed an elective government protected by royal charter. 'These two Republics then', wrote Bernard, 'are the Allies of Great Britain & not the Subjects.'[3]

II

The 'royal' provinces of Virginia and Georgia, North and South Carolina, New York, New Jersey, New Hampshire, and Nova Scotia had much more in common. By the middle of the eighteenth century the Commissions under which the royal governors were supposed to administer their governments had become stereotyped, and the Instructions which accompanied the Commissions had begun to reflect a settled policy. Despite many inconsistencies and anomalies there was more hope and perhaps more actual harmony here than appeared upon the surface. Many of the differences which impressed observers like Knox or Abercromby were due not to different tendencies but to wide differences of environment and to the rapid progress of the more highly favoured provinces through the primitive stages of settlement to self-support and self-govern-

[1] Stanhope, Secretary of State to Council of Trade, May 15, 1715, *Nova Scotia, A. Series*, vi. 198.

[2] 7 and 8 Wm. III, c. 22. Greene, *The Provincial Governor*, p. 22.

[3] Bernard to Halifax, Dec. 14, 1764, quoted by Beer, *op. cit.*, pp. 240, 310.

ment. The rate of development naturally varied. The stages in the process reached by the several 'royal' provinces at any one time were correspondingly varied. But the general direction was unmistakable, and the tendencies were remarkably constant.

With few exceptions—New Hampshire and Nova Scotia before the Seven Years' War, and Quebec, East and West Florida, and Grenada at its close—all the 'royal' provinces had originated like the 'proprietary plantations' in royal grants to companies or proprietors whose obligations implied, as Greene points out, the old feudal 'association of rights in the soil with rights of government'.[1] Thus Virginia was granted by James I to the Virginia Company until a writ of *Quo Warranto* was served against the company in 1624 and the charter annulled. The direct royal government then established continued, with a brief intermission under the Commonwealth, until the American Revolution. The Commission and Instructions throughout came from the Crown but the mutual relations between governor, council, and House of Burgesses adjusted themselves as in England by the operation of unwritten custom and 'convention'. Thus as early as 1641 Sir William Berkeley is instructed to 'summon the Burgesses . . . which together with the Governor and Councill shall have Power to make Acts and Laws for the Government of that Plantation correspondent, as near as may be, to the Laws of England'.[2] That organic growth which after the Revolution Settlement in England settled into the ordered evolution of the British constitution was thus veritably transplanted to American soil. Despite the most determined attempts to restrict and discipline that growth, the process of erosion and adjustment by which governor, council, and Assembly sought to settle their working conditions with each other continued, on one side of the Atlantic as on the other, almost without intermission. Indeed, in the only province with a representative Assembly that remained British at the American Revolution—in Nova Scotia—it may be said that the process has never ceased.[3] Largely by virtue of priority Virginia became the model

[1] 'The King parts with a portion of his prerogative, and exempts this particular piece of territory from the ordinary jurisdiction, very much as his predecessors had done when they created the palatinates of Lancaster and Durham.' Greene, *The Provincial Governor*, p. 9.

[2] See the Commissions and Instructions in Greene, *op. cit.*, Appendix A, pp. 207–64.

[3] The same could be claimed for Prince Edward Island from 1773, for New Brunswick from 1784 and in a measure for Upper and Lower Canada from 1791; though in the last instance, since an Assembly had been abrogated altogether

of 'royal' governments for other provinces. Not a few of the usages there established found their way into general practice, until superseded in turn by precedents established elsewhere.

The Carolinas had been granted, like Virginia, to proprietors in 1663, but under conditions still more reminiscent of feudalism. New York was granted to the Duke of York in 1664, and a part of the grant transferred to other proprietors to form the province of New Jersey. When the Duke of York succeeded to the Crown as James II the transition from proprietary to royal government took place automatically. In New Jersey a conflict between the proprietary governors and the royal customs officials, a feud amongst the proprietors themselves, and a very general popular demand for law and order, paved the way for the surrender of the charter and the establishment of royal government in 1702. The Carolinas, North and South, were the next to pass through a similar ordeal of anarchy and turmoil. Danger from the Spaniards, a struggle with the Tuscarora Indians, and the constant menace of the 'Carolina pirates' who infested the waters of the Bahama Islands, all reinforced the popular discontent. Here as in the Jerseys the proprietary system came to an end by surrender of the charter in 1729 and the appointment of a governor by commission from the Crown. The transition, however, was not complete. In the Carolinas as in Prince Edward Island and Rupert's Land in Canadian history, certain proprietary rights in the land survived the old régime—a costly legacy to be redeemed by an innocent posterity.

In Georgia a royal government was contemplated from the first in the original grant to the Georgia trustees in 1732. By the terms of the charter the government of the province was to revert to the Crown at the end of twenty-one years. The disfavour into which proprietary government had fallen was warranted by the facts in Georgia. When William Knox went there with Governor Ellis in 1756, two years after the transfer to the Crown, he reported 'not a trader in the country who imported goods from England, except the merchant whose first cargo went in the ship with us, and we were six months before we saw another topsail'. Within six years the annual exports amounted to £38,000. 'Such (adds Knox) are the effects of a good and of a bad Constitution.' [1]

It is noteworthy, therefore, that of all the 'royal' provinces in

by statute in the *Quebec Act* it required another statute—the *Constitutional Act* of 1791—to begin the process which began elsewhere by the mere prerogative of the Crown.

[1] *Extra Official State Papers*, ii. 20.

North America upon the eve of the Seven Years' War, two only, New Hampshire and Nova Scotia, had not evolved from the semi-feudal status of 'proprietary plantations'. The former had come into existence under royal commission in 1680. In Nova Scotia, which had become finally British after the Treaty of Utrecht in 1713, the final decision to continue the 'royal' government after the model of Virginia was reached only after years of discussion during which the advantages of both the other forms of government were exhaustively canvassed. Stanhope, the Secretary of State in 1715, had favoured annexation to Massachusetts with the double design of conciliating the New Englanders and of strengthening the hands of the Governor there by increasing his resources in the contest with the House of Representatives.[1] As late as 1748 Governor Shirley of Massachusetts advocated a charter based upon that of his own province as 'a great advantage . . . for attracting New England Settlers to live there'.[2] The Lords of Trade in 1737 had recommended Coram's plan for a proprietary government like that of Georgia, to revert from the trustees 'entirely to the Crown' twenty-one years from the date of the charter. In the end the royal Commissions to Governor Vetch (January 20, 1715) and to Governor Philipps (August 17, 1717) were amplified to conform to those in the royal provinces 'immediately under His Majesty's protection', and an Assembly was duly convened in 1758.

III

The 'royal' as distinct from the 'chartered' and the 'proprietary' provinces thus promised to become the dominant type in North America. There were quarters, it is true, where these tendencies were viewed askance. In the chartered provinces of Massachusetts, Rhode Island, and Connecticut, and in the proprietary provinces of Maryland and Pennsylvania, the whole policy of the Crown was interpreted as a studied encroachment upon chartered rights; and indeed it could scarcely bear a construction entirely disinterested. For those provinces, however, which eventually became 'royal', the transition, as Greene has pointed out, was due not to the 'natural hostility of a tyrannical government to the local liberties of the colonies', but upon the whole to the desire of Crown and colonists alike for stable government.[3] In that sense it was parallel

1 Stanhope to Council of Trade, May 15, 1715, *Nova Scotia, A. Series*, vi. 198–200.

2 Shirley to the Duke of Bedford, *Nova Scotia, A. Series*, xxxiii. 177–180.

3 *Op. cit.*, p. 19.

to that process which delivered England from the anarchy and selfishness of feudalism by the 'popular despotism' of the New Monarchy. The rule of the Tudors at least began the phenomenal 'Expansion of England'. It was equally necessary for the ordered development of parliamentary government against the Stuarts.

In the 'royal' provinces, indeed, popular institutions suffered no eclipse in the process; for once representative institutions began to function, no 'paper chains' (in Burke's phrase) could restrain their slow but relentless growth. The Crown could and did instruct the governor of Nova Scotia to follow certain usages which were favourable to the Crown in Virginia and Georgia and New Hampshire; and in due time the governor of Quebec was instructed to follow similar usages which favoured the Crown in Nova Scotia. But there were limitations to this prerogative. James Abercromby, the agent for Virginia and North Carolina, observed in 1752 that 'Assemblys in America Do not look upon Instructions alone as binding on Representatives of the People'. Thus the governor's Instructions were 'very positive (continues Abercromby) not to allow the sole Right of Money Bills to the Assembly, but such Instructions have never been able to Establish a Right in the Council'.[1] In truth the New York Assembly secured and exercised 'the power of the purse' as effectively as any House of Commons under the Georges, and the primitive Assembly of Nova Scotia at its first session began to follow suit. Above all, British precedents themselves were invoked in the contest until 'every great principle which they teach, every phrase of freedom to be gleaned from them', as Joseph Howe was wont to boast in Nova Scotia, became 'familiar as household words'.[2]

Thus while the 'chartered' provinces came to look to the barriers of the written bond to protect them from the encroachments of the Crown, the 'royal' provinces were forced to rely upon those empirical adjustments which had already prevailed in Great Britain. It would be rash to say that in this respect the royal province was looking discerningly forward while the chartered province was inclined to look backward; or that the one grasped the full meaning of the Revolution Settlement while the other was still perhaps in thrall to the *Instrument of Government*. Neither perhaps was in a position to forecast the organic growth of 'the law and custom of the constitution'. It required, to be sure, the eye of faith to see in

[1] *Shelburne Manuscripts*, xlvii. 131. *Pub. Arch. Can.*

[2] *Letters to Lord John Russell*, Egerton and Grant, *Canadian Constitutional Development*, p. 248.

the embryonic powers of the provincial Assembly the 'responsible government' of the British Dominions. The preference of the chartered province for written guarantees was natural from the conditions under which they themselves had flourished; when dislodged from so inadequate a defence they had no recourse but to 'natural rights' and independence. The 'royal' governments on the other hand were miniature monarchies with Assemblies as tenacious of their 'birthright' as Britain itself, and capable of the same organic evolution. Had the Crown in Britain maintained its supremacy for another generation or two it is conceivable that the ultimate ascendancy of parliaments might have been established *pari passu* on both sides of the Atlantic. Professor Egerton has raised the interesting speculation 'what would have been the consequences had an able king boldly adopted this doctrine and recognized them as a new realm for which a third crown might have to be provided'.[1] It is significant that the provinces which remained British and eventually evolved 'responsible government' were all 'royal' provinces and won their case by an appeal to British parliamentary analogies without the necessity of invoking 'natural rights' or written 'guarantees'. It will perhaps suffice therefore to outline that particular form of government in order to gauge at the outset a few of these far-reaching tendencies.

(*a*) *The 'Royal' Governor and Council*

I

The governor in the 'royal' province was appointed directly in the name of the Crown without regard to intermediary proprietors as in Pennsylvania or to popular electors as in Rhode Island. In his own person, therefore, he represented his sovereign as actively as a 'burgess' in Virginia represented his constituency. In truth the 'royal prerogative' which was entrusted to his keeping was supposed to be wider in its range than that which the sovereign exercised at home. The defence of it was his first preoccupation. Among the gravest objections urged by Governor Lawrence against the newly-elected Assembly in Nova Scotia in 1758 was the fear that they might 'dispute the Royal Prerogative'.[2]

The Commission which the governor received from the Crown, though no longer issued like that of Charles I to Governor

[1] *American Revolution*, p. 10.

[2] Lawrence to Lords of Trade, Sept. 26, 1758, *Nova Scotia, A. Series*, 61.

Berkeley of Virginia in 1641 'per ipsum Regem',[1] ran in the king's name. By the middle of the eighteenth century it had become stereotyped, and variations to meet local contingencies were provided as a rule only in the Instructions which accompanied the Commission, or in Additional Instructions which were added from time to time. The distinction between the Commission which was a letter patent under the great seal and Instructions under the privy seal was quickly grasped, as Abercromby noted in 1752, by the colonial Assembly. Since by the former the governor was authorized to make laws only 'by and with the advice and Consent of our said Council and Assembly', the organic 'constitution' thus created quickly developed unwritten 'conventions', as we have seen, analogous to those which attended parliamentary government in Great Britain. The governor might seek to confirm his prerogative, or he might be instructed to add to it; but his success, like that of the king himself in Britain, depended upon forces vastly more complicated than the arbitrary will of the Crown.

Thus while the Charter, a 'written' bond, would appear at first sight more effectively to safeguard local rights and to prescribe the limitations of royal interference,[2] there is a sense in which the 'royal' province was much more congenial to the growth of parliamentary control by traditional British methods. The influence of Massachusetts which was undoubtedly dominant in the never-ending contest with the 'royal prerogative' may have been due in no small measure to the fact that there was a 'royal' governor in that province in direct juxtaposition to the most popular 'chartered' legislature, with the exception of the single chamber of Pennsylvania, to be found in North America. But the 'royal' province in the end was in a still stronger position than its 'chartered' ally. The Assembly of Nova Scotia originated, like the House of Commons itself, by summons of the Crown, and in the end the colonial governor shared the fate of the Crown and the royal prerogative in Great Britain.[3] The whole achievement of 'responsible government' is a commentary upon this fact.

[1] For Berkeley's Commission see Greene, *op. cit.*, Appendix A, p. 218.

[2] Cf. Osgood, *American Colonies in the 18th Century*, i. 34: 'In a certain sense the governors' commissions ranked with colonial charters, but commissions did not imply a contract and could be recalled or modified at any time without judicial action. This made them much less permanent and reliable, when viewed from the standpoint of the colonists and considered as embodying the element of a constitution for the individual colony.'

[3] In Upper and Lower Canada after 1791 Assemblies were established by Act of Parliament because an Act of Parliament—the *Quebec Act*—had previously

The 'royal' governor in the eighteenth century, however, was but a pale reflection of monarchy in Great Britain. The Crown under George III had so far won back the prestige lost under the Stuarts that it aspired, upon the whole with success, to dominate the rest of Parliament. The hereditary principle, life-long training, exemplary industry, the prerogatives which controlled the creation of peers, the whole range of honours and of patronage which the Crown could use when it chose with almost overwhelming effect, enabled George III very effectively to follow his mother's injunction, 'George, be King!' 'The power of the crown', wrote Knox in 1768, 'was, indeed, never more visibly extensive over the great men of the nation'.[1]

But the king's representative in the colonies could rely upon few of these advantages. His tenure of office was 'during pleasure' and was often precarious. With the exception of the period of the Board of Trade's ascendancy under Halifax, the colonial patronage was usually a perquisite of the Southern Department. The unblushing jobbery of the period of the Restoration was not in evidence, but each new constellation in the political firmament had its satellites. A governor had frequently to fear not only the friendly rivalry of those of his own circle whose prospects of employment at home were less than first rate, but the more deadly rivalry of hostile factions in both countries. Threats of recall by a hostile ministry were frequently flaunted before the governor's face by the officials of his own administration. Where backstairs influence prevailed, he was known to lament, like the humble policeman in *The Pirates of Penzance*, that his lot was 'not a happy one'.

There were administrations like Legge's in Nova Scotia or Belcher's in New Jersey where this resource was upon the whole salutary. A hopeless misfit in the colonies could thus be ushered gently into oblivion through the back door. But with rapacious place-hunters besetting every dispenser of political patronage in Great Britain, the best of governors frequently found their pathway, as one of them expressed it, 'very slippery'. The agent who was sent home to procure the recall of Governor Burnet of Massachusetts came back with a governor's Commission for

abrogated an Assembly altogether. But though the 'constitutions' under the *Constitutional Act*, the *Union Act* of 1841, and the *B.N.A. Act* of 1867, were statutory, the relations between the Assembly and the Executive were still left indeterminate, and were, of course, eventually settled by the same method as in the other provinces.

[1] *The Present State of the Nation*, Dublin, 1768, p. 64.

himself.[1] Governor Murray of Quebec was a protégé of James Oswald, the Earl of Bute, and 'the King's friends'.[2] His administration was embittered by a vindictive feud with General Burton and the Shelburne interests. Burton's chief supporter in Montreal openly predicted the governor's recall—'not only tells them so', wrote Murray, 'but he lays considerable Wagers in public that it Shall be so.' 'Every post brings news that I am to be Superseded the next.' When Murray's recall seemed at last inevitable, he wrote bitterly that he was to be 'made a Sacrifice of, to Convince the Mob, that the present Administration, have no Connection with Lord Bute'.[3] Carleton, Murray's successor in Quebec, immediately associated himself with the rival faction, and described two of Murray's friends in the Council—one of them his relative—as a 'Surgeon's Mate' and 'a strolling Player'.[4] Carleton himself was to drink the same bitter cup to the dregs under the administration of Lord George Germain.

Within the colony itself the governor's footing was equally 'slippery'. Though James Otis declared that 'a very small office in the customs in America had raised a man a fortune sooner than a Government',[5] many a 'Government' was still obviously lucrative, and many a governor, by methods legitimate or otherwise, must have retired with a fortune.[6] It is suggestive that the office was sometimes held by an absentee and discharged by a deputy, while gifts from the Assembly and grants of land within the governor's own province were strictly prohibited. But as a rule the governor found himself as cramped in the regular emoluments as in the tenure of his office. In a few provinces like Virginia, Georgia, and Nova Scotia, his salary was assured either by a fixed civil list or

[1] Greene, *op. cit.*, pp. 48, 50.

[2] Murray to Eglintoun, Oct. 27, 1764, *Murray Papers*, i. 170; Cramahé to Murray, Feb. 9, 1765, *id.*, iii. 262; Murray to Sir James Cockburn, Jan. 26, 1764, *id.*, i. 60; Murray to Ross, Dec. 4, 1765, *id.*, i. 289, &c. *Pub. Arch. Can.*

[3] Murray to Burton, Oct. 17, 1765; to Ross, Dec. 4, 1765. *Murray Papers*, i. 289, 265.

[4] Carleton to Shelburne, Oct. 25, 1766, *Shortt and Doughty*, i. 277.

[5] *Rights of the British Colonies Asserted and Proved*, Boston, 1764, p. 58.

[6] Professor Egerton cites the attempt to purchase the governorship of New York from Lord de la Warr for £1,000, and Greene cites the sale of that of Massachusetts and New Hampshire for the same sum. *American Revolution*, p. 38; *Provincial Governor*, p. 47.

Governor Murray in Quebec sold captured stores of brandy for £2,400, and considered himself entitled to the proceeds because he 'had been the first Military Man, who had ever accounted for such things'. *Murray Papers*, i. 85; iii. 255, &c. *Pub. Arch. Can.*

directly by the British Treasury. No effort was spared to make the office equally independent in the other provinces, but in the end the governor was forced to rely upon the Assembly for his salary, frequently in the form of annual grants accompanied by much huckstering and unseemly compromise.

With these poor trappings of majesty to rely upon in the colonies, the governor was expected to wield almost the prerogatives of the Crown under the Tudors. The right of veto had lapsed in Great Britain since the time of Queen Anne; the governor by his Commission was to 'enjoy a Negative Voice' over all provincial legislation.[1] The *Bill of Rights* and the *Mutiny Act* had disposed of a standing army under royal control in time of peace; the governor was given 'full power & Authority to Levy, Arm, Muster Command, and Employ all persons whatsoever'[2]—powers which the Assembly had little difficulty in reducing to a hollow mockery. In Great Britain the *Mutiny Act* and the *Septennial Act* with the 'power of the purse' had long since ensured both the continuity of parliament and the periodical election of the House of Commons; the governor's Commission authorized him to summon, adjourn, prorogue, and dissolve the Assembly at will, and his Instructions authorized him to fix the franchise and the electoral districts.[3] A *Triennial Bill* was vetoed in New Jersey in 1739, and a similar bill from New York disallowed in 1737 as against the royal prerogative of 'calling and continuing the Assembly at such times and for as long as it was thought necessary for the public service'. In 1767 governors were expressly forbidden to assent to any Act fixing the duration of the Assembly.

In Great Britain a century of controversy with regard to the position of the judges had been brought to a close by the *Act of Settlement* in 1702, in keeping with the settled convictions of the whole nation. Instead of being in effect a part of the executive—'lions under the throne' as Bacon had advocated—their independence was assured by appointment during good behaviour. In the colonies every judicial officer from chief justice to justice of the peace held office during pleasure; and if the judges were not always responsive to control it was because the pleasure of

[1] *Shortt and Doughty*, i. 176.

[2] . . . 'To march, Embark, or Transport, from one place to another for the resisting and withstanding of all enemies, pirates & Rebels both at land and sea: and to Transport such Forces to any of our Plantations in America. . . .' *Shortt and Doughty*, i. 177.

[3] Cf. Instructions to Belcher, s. 13, in Greene, *op. cit.*, p. 237.

the Assembly was frequently more important than the pleasure of the Crown.

II

The Council of the 'royal' province was regarded as a bulwark of the royal prerogative, and the natural ally of the governor. The primary function of the Council was 'to assist . . . in the Administration of Government', but it normally exercised through the same personnel, usually of twelve members, legislative functions as a second chamber and certain judicial functions as a court of appeal. In the provinces originally organized as 'royal' governments the governor was directly authorized to 'nominate and establish a Council'. For the regular members the governor's nomination continued as a rule to prevail. Certain *ex officio* members, the Lieutenant-Governor, the Surveyor-General of Customs, and the Chief Justice, were more directly appointed from Great Britain. In all three capacities the Council was thus as completely irresponsible as the governor himself to the House of Assembly, while it was supposed to be attached by every bond of self-interest and subordination to the governor's own office.[1]

In practice, however, an appointment to the Council during pleasure usually meant an appointment for life, and a coterie of life appointees seldom failed to reverse the official order of ascendancy. Governors might come and governors might go, but the self-interest of resident councillors remained a permanent if not always a stabilizing factor in colonial life. Thus, instead of the governor dominating the Executive Council as George III dominated the Cabinet, the Council when it was not itself overawed by the Assembly frequently dominated the governor. Their 'advice and Consent' was necessary in summoning the Assembly, in all legislation, in creating courts of judicature, in establishing cities and fortifications, fairs, harbours, and markets, in issuing warrants for the expenditure of 'all publick monies', in the granting of public lands, and in a variety of other functions.[2] Using their privileged position to establish a monopoly over the advice upon which the governor was supposed to act, they usually contrived to bend policy to their own interests, leaving the governor responsible to the home government and before the province for the consequences.[3]

But members of the Council were not always so fortunate. In

[1] Murray's Instructions, *Shortt and Doughty*, i. 182–205. [2] *Ibid.*

[3] For a classic outline of this process see Howe's *Letters to Lord John Russell* in *Egerton and Grant*, pp. 209–12.

primitive provinces like Nova Scotia or Quebec the governor could sometimes ride rough-shod over them. Even in the older provinces governors like Shirley and Spotswood, Morris and Sharpe and Pownall, no doubt wielded occasionally a truly vice-regal influence. But more insidious influences normally prevailed in the other direction, and indeed the most pervasive influence at work came from another quarter. Popular opinion when thoroughly aroused was sometimes irresistible, and the Council in their own interests did not venture to run counter to it. When the Council was elective as in Massachusetts it merely reinforced the House of Representatives. In Rhode Island where the governorship itself was elective, the royal prerogative was little more than a shadow. The governor himself frequently bent before the storm, masking the surrender behind the advice of his Council. Governor Denny of Pennsylvania signed an Act taxing proprietary lands in that province on condition that the Assembly should indemnify him for the bond he was compelled to forfeit to the proprietors for violating his instructions.[1] Knox, writing in 1789, avowed that Rhode Island and Connecticut 'were not a whit more under the control of the King's civil authority before the revolt, than they now are as Independent States'.[2]

While the mutual relationship between governor and Council thus varied with the personnel and the state of popular opinion, that between the Council and the Assembly was almost invariably hostile; and this chronic conflict almost invariably resulted in the ascendancy of the Assembly. The most precise instructions were powerless to reverse this tendency. The governor was directed to resist the pretensions of the Assembly to 'Privileges no ways belonging to them', and particularly to 'the sole framing of Money Bills, refusing to let the Council alter or amend the same; all which Practices are very detrimental to Our Prerogative'. It was the pleasure of the Crown 'that the Council have the like power of framing Money Bills as the Assembly'.[3] We have already noted Abercromby's observation that 'such Instructions have never been able to Establish a Right in the Council'. The 'convention' established by practice did not accord with the pleasure of the Crown. Knox found this

> 'middle estate . . . by way of apology for an aristocratic power . . . too inconsiderable to give the Crown or its Governor any effectual

[1] Dickerson, *op. cit.*, p. 171. [2] *Extra Official State Papers*, ii. 14.
[3] Murray's Instructions, *Shortt and Doughty*, i. 187.

support against the Assembly . . . and as almost all the public appointments, and all the jobs are made by the Assembly, the poor Counsellors have nothing to console themselves with, for the loss of popularity, by being considered as dependants of the Governor, but the barren and temporary title of Honourable. Hence it is that the men of the greatest property and weight in the province prefer being members of the Assemblies to seats in the Council.' [1]

In the British provinces after the Revolution Knox's favourite design of strengthening the Councils, of fortifying an endowed church, and of circumscribing the powers of Assemblies, was pursued with greater success. The conflict was thus confined to the province, and took the form of a contest between rival local interests, aspiring, the one by virtue of royal appointment, the other by virtue of popular representation, to control the executive. Before the Revolution the conflict was more deadly because it could not be localized. The governor and the Assembly—and through them the home government and the province—were brought directly into collision. These were the nominal, if not always the real, protagonists of governance on the one side and of self-government on the other. The duel between them is fought out in practically every province of 'the American empire'—sometimes with rancour and bitterness, sometimes with mutual forbearance which gave promise of better things.

(*b*) *The Assembly*

I

If the governor was but a pale reflection of monarchy, the Assembly was a very vital counterpart of the House of Commons. Nothing in Britain before the *Reform Bill* of 1832, or perhaps long after it, compared with the colonial Assembly in its immediate responsiveness to popular opinion. The franchise was broader, the indirect resources at the disposal of the Crown for controlling or corrupting the electorate were incomparably fewer, and there was nothing but 'an apology for an aristocratic power' or an established church to redress the balance.

Professor Egerton has traced among the fundamental causes 'almost inevitably leading the way to separation', this fatal divergence between parliamentary institutions in Britain and in America. Despite a common origin and in the end a common destiny in

[1] *Extra Official State Papers*, ii. 21.

virtually democratic government, the crisis came upon them in the eighteenth century at vastly 'different stages of development'.[1] The first revolt against the Stuarts was still a vital and creative tradition in America. Thus the governor of New Jersey reported in 1743 that the members of his Assembly were 'generally so fond of the example of the parliament of 1641 & that of their neighbours in Pensilvania & New England, that until some measures are taken in England to reduce them to propper limits I suspect they will not mend much'.[2] In England these traditions had so far been tempered, first by the Restoration, and even after the Revolution Settlement by the reascendancy of the monarchy, that few dared openly to avow them. While British parliamentary government in relation to the total population of Britain was in effect an oligarchy which tended to 'narrow' until power rested in the hands of a close landed aristocracy, it was obvious to every observer that the other branch of the family was passing rapidly to another polity. 'However long the forms and appearance of a Royal Government might be kept up', wrote William Knox, 'a real and pure democracy must soon be the true description of their Constitutions.'[3]

This variation in development was still further accentuated by the reaction in Britain after the Seven Years' War. Never surely was there a more ominous conjunction of Mars and Saturn in the horoscope of the nation. The obliteration of party distinctions during a victorious but ruinously wasteful war now enabled a 'patriot king' to play the 'despot among the ruins of parliamentary parties'.[4] By the king's policy of 'dependent administrations' even the aristocratic oligarchy had been brought to submit to a sedulous and vigilant monarchy. In *The Present State of the Nation*, 1768, it is stated that 'the power of the crown was, indeed, never more visibly extensive over the great men of the nation; but then (Knox was constrained to add) the great men have lost their influence over the lower order of the people; even parliament has lost much of its reverence with the subjects of the realm. . . . Government relaxed in every sinew, and a corrupt selfish spirit pervading the whole!'[5] The accuracy of this dismal picture was commended by Grenville himself, to whom it was dedicated, and whose confidence Knox was still proud to possess.[6]

1 *American Revolution*, pp. 21, 22.
2 Quoted in Greene, *op. cit.*, p. 178.
3 *Extra Official State Papers*, ii. 22.
4 Hertz, *The Old Colonial System*, p. 36.
5 *The Present State of the Nation*, Dublin, 1768, pp. 64–5.
6 'I have read over the Papers (*The State of the Nation*) . . . with the greatest

The glories of victory were thus swallowed up in the disillusionments of peace. Even Chatham moved in a 'dim twilight of popularity'. 'I do not suppose', wrote Burke in 1772, 'that there was ever anything like this stupor in any period of our history.'[1] The House of Commons was 'mortgaged to the court'. The public seemed so 'utterly careless and supine' that exertion was taken to indicate rather 'a restlessness of spirit than a manly zeal'.

> 'I am satisfied (continued Burke) that within a few years there has been a great change in the national character. We seem no longer that eager, inquisitive, jealous, fiery people which we have been formerly. . . . The people look back, without pleasure or indignation; and forward, without hope or fear. . . .
>
> If things are left to themselves, it is my clear opinion that a nation may slide down fair and softly from the highest point of grandeur and prosperity to the lowest state of imbecility and meanness, without any one's marking a particular period in this declension. . . . I am certain that if pains, great and immediate pains, are not taken to prevent it, such must be the fate of this country.'[2]

II

While this torpor benumbed the nation at home, the political aptitudes of Britons in America were not unlike those of their ancestors from the accession of James I to the Revolution Settlement in Great Britain. Differences of environment, though less marked than those now everywhere recognized within the British Commonwealth, already reflected grave differences of outlook and temper. The economic 'frontier' had already appeared in American life. But we are here concerned with the political 'frontier' of British policy in the old colonial system, and in this the colonial Assembly was running true to form. Parliamentary government was perhaps more instinctive in America than in England, and in more than one province, 'royal' as well as 'chartered' or 'proprietary', it was asserted with a spirit

pleasure. They are written with so much temper and force, with so much knowledge and precision, that I am persuaded they will do you great honour, if ever you shall think fit to avow yourself as the author of them. The general opinions laid down in them, correspond so much with my declared opinions, and are so favourable to the public measures I have pursued, that to express my approbation of them to you, who are so *perfectly acquainted with them both*, must be unnecessary.' Rt. Hon. George Grenville to Knox, Oct. 9, 1768, *Extra Official State Papers*, ii. Appendix, p. 23.

[1] Burke to Wm. Dowdeswell, Oct. 27, 1772.

[2] Burke to Rockingham, Aug. 23, 1775.

nearer perhaps than that of the House of Commons itself to the traditions of the Revolution Settlement.

If being British, therefore, consisted of doing what Britons themselves had done under similar circumstances, the North American colonies of the eighteenth century were unmistakably British. The controversy between governance and self-government took many forms, but there was scarcely a phase of it where precedent or analogy was not to be found in British history. Legalists might maintain that the colonial Assembly was merely an elaborate town council under a sovereign Parliament; or that two millions and a half of Britons in America like 50,000 Britons in Manchester before the *Reform Bill* were 'virtually represented' in the House of Commons. Tories like Knox could still scout the pretensions of the colonists to 'all the liberties, rights, and privileges of his majesty's subjects in Great Britain'; or 'the absurdity of their idea of a *polypus* government, where a head sprouts out of every joint'.[1] But those who had courage to face realities—to sweep aside 'the monstrous idea of Virtual Representation' and even Chatham's fine-spun distinction between general legislation and taxation—confronted not a theory but a fact. The colonists in America were disconcertingly like their ancestors at home. America 'had the image of the British constitution. She had the substance'. In methods of growth, in procedure, and above all in power, the Assembly did not belie its lineage. With two millions and a half of Britons in America and every prospect of four millions within that generation, 'metaphysical distinctions' would not long suffice. Nobody, Burke exclaimed, will be argued into slavery; and even the advocates of coercion conceded that boasted claims 'if not speedily and effectively enforced, will soon (be) found as ridiculous, as the Cham of Tartary's gracious permission to the potentates of the earth to sit down to their dinners'.[2]

Thus the issues that were petty current politics in Britain were charged with history in America. The *Triennial Bill* which New York and New Jersey passed in vain in 1737 and 1739 were strangely reminiscent of the *Triennial Act* by which the Long Parliament sought to remedy 'the discontinuance of Parliaments' after the eleven years of Charles I's arbitrary government. The

[1] *The Controversy between Great Britain and her Colonies Reviewed*, William Knox, London, 1769, pp. 10, 96.

[2] *A Letter to the Rt. Hon. Wills Earl of Hillsborough on the Connection between Great Britain and her American Colonies*, London, 1768, p. 14.

struggle for the independence of the judges was merely a repetition of the earlier struggle to free the bench from 'the rod over them'. Parliament had vindicated this independence for England. Were Englishmen in America to be content with 'lions under the throne'? The supremacy of the Commons over money bills was nowhere contested in Great Britain. The royal instructions to accord to Councils in America 'the like Power of framing Money Bills as the Assembly' could bear but one interpretation. If the claims of James I arbitrarily to tax currants going into London imperilled parliamentary control of taxation, what was to be said of the arbitrary taxation of tea going into Boston? Could the resistance to it be dismissed, as William Knox dismissed it, as 'an instance of infatuation unparalelled in the history of mankind'? [1] The rooted suspicions of a standing army had been a national obsession from the *Petition of Right* to the *Bill of Rights*. A standing army of 10,000 men in America in time of peace could scarcely fail to prompt Daniel Dulany's ironical inquiry if these men were intended 'to defend the Colonists against Themselves'.[2]

'The feelings of the colonies', Burke said truly, 'were formerly the feelings of Great Britain. Theirs were formerly the feelings of Mr. Hampden when called upon for the payment of twenty shillings. Would twenty shillings have ruined Mr. Hampden's fortune? No! but the payment of half twenty shillings, on the principle it was demanded, would have made him a slave.'[3] Could an Englishman in America pay stamp-money for a standing army without reflecting upon ship-money in England? There was much to be said about 'duty' and patriotism and fair play to the British tax-payer, but there was more than rhetoric in Chatham's solemn warning against 'dragooning the Bostonians into what is called their duty'.

> 'Full well I knew that the offspring of such ancestors would resist upon the same principles, and on the same occasions. . . . If then we applaud our ancestors for obtaining such liberties for us, at a time when all the rights of Englishmen were trampled upon, and despotism had trodden down the laws—surely we cannot in reason, deny that portion of liberty . . . to our own brethren—brethren by the same common parent, and who are unquestionably heirs of the same glorious inheritance.'[4]

[1] *Extra Official State Papers*, ii. 9.

[2] *Considerations on the Propriety of Imposing Taxes in the British Colonies, for the Purpose of Raising a Revenue by Act of Parliament*, London (reprinted), 1766, p. 59.

[3] *Speech on American Taxation.*

[4] *Speech of the Rt. Hon. the Earl of Chatham in the House of Lords, Friday, the 20th of January, 1775*, Dublin (n.d.), pp. 91, 93.

In that sense the gravest danger lay not in the recognition of political differences but in the failure to recognize fundamental resemblances. In truth the differences merely accentuated the resemblances, for while the powers of governance in the hands of the governor and the British Government were technically as formidable as those of the Tudors, the agencies for self-government were as dynamic as those which destroyed the Stuarts. The bottles were older, the wine was newer, and the disaster was devastating beyond calculation. Thus, while Britain itself was passing through an eclipse of parliamentary government at home, 'a scheme of government new in many things' began to cast its shadow across the Atlantic. The American colonists, trained in the rugged school of colonial politics to the exercise of initiative and self-reliance, found themselves involved for the first time in a controversy which went to the roots of parliamentary government. In the memorable words of Burke, 'they were, it is true, as yet novices; as yet unaccustomed to direct attacks upon any of the rights of parliament'.[1] As the issues clarified it is impossible to ignore the stirrings of a new spirit. With faith in their star and without false modesty they began to look beyond 'metaphysical distinctions' and to contemplate realities; for as the greatest of them was slowly driven to suspect, the 'systematic assertion of an arbitrary power' not only ran counter to 'an innate spirit of freedom' but was 'subversive of the laws and constitution of Great Britain itself, in the establishment of which some of the best blood in the kingdom has been spilt'.[2]

NATURAL *VERSUS* OFFICIAL TENDENCIES

I

From the humble beginnings of self-government in the Virginian House of Burgesses in 1619 to the first Continental Congress in 1774 nothing was more remarkable than the spontaneous growth of the Assemblies planted by the Crown in that fertile and fallow soil. As in Britain itself the secret of this was the power of the purse.

The sums voted by provincial Assemblies for civil government were almost incredibly small. If British liberties, as Hallam remarks, have been as a rule 'purchased by money',[3] never surely

1 *Speech on American Taxation.*

2 Washington to Bryan Fairfax, Aug. 24, 1774; Washington to Capt. Robert Mackenzie, Oct. 9, 1774. *Writings*, ed. Jared Sparks, ii. 397, 400.

3 *Middle Ages*, iii. 162.

was there thriftier bargaining than in the process by which the colonial Assemblies acquired power in North America. 'The Taxes which the People pay in this Country', wrote General Loudoun in 1757, 'are really so trifling, that they do not deserve the Name.'[1] The civil establishment of New Jersey was less than £1,500; that of Rhode Island scarcely £3,500; of Connecticut £4,000; of Virginia £8,000; of New York less than £5,000. That of Massachusetts in time of peace was given by Governor Pownall as 'sterling 12,937£. 10s.'. These petty sums, however, were scrutinized as jealously as the House of Commons had ever scrutinized a maletote; and they sufficed in the end to thwart the most ingenious devices of the Crown to reverse the normal functions of taxation. In a few of the provinces the Crown had the advantage of permanent civil lists; but the independence thus secured to the service was seldom repaid in the form of sound administration. The negligence of absentees and the venal abuses too often chargeable against resident officials were not calculated to commend the experiment to others. In provinces without fixed civil lists a corrupt régime like that of the egregious Governor Cornbury in New York was usually sufficient to create a demand for direct supervision as well as vigilance on the part of the Assembly. By the middle of the eighteenth century there was not an Assembly in North America where the subtle relationship between taxation and control was not thoroughly understood.

The royal province of New York may be taken to illustrate these tendencies. As early as 1704 the Assembly had refused to permit the amendment of a money bill by the Council, in defiance of the most explicit instructions to the contrary. Not satisfied with the control of supply the Assembly took steps to control expenditure. Although the governor's instructions forbade him to 'suffer any publick money whatsoever to be issued or disposed of otherwise than by warrant under your hand', the House enforced its claim first to scrutinize the public accounts, then to appoint its own treasurer, to supervise expenditure through its own commissioners, and finally to restrict the payment of public funds to their warrants and 'no other order mandate or warrants whatsoever'.[2] By 1739 the fiscal supremacy of the Assembly was assured. 'Salaries of officers were ordered paid by name and amount', usually in the form of annual grants. The governor still issued warrants for

[1] Beer, *op. cit.*, p. 292.

[2] Dickerson, *op. cit.*, pp. 159–61. Osgood, *op. cit.*, ii. 84.

officials directly appointed by the Crown, but the names appeared also in the appropriation bills, and the governor's unfettered control appears to have been restricted to a contingent fund of £100 per year. All this was termed by the Board of Trade 'a violation of the constitution of the government of that province . . . derogatory to her Majesty's royal prerogative'.[1]

The practice in New York was emulated by less assertive provinces and inspired in some respects by others still more aggressive. Thus North Carolina where there was supposed to be a permanent civil list not only appointed its own treasurer but controlled expenditure through its own commissioners whose supervision extended to almost every sphere of administration from the building of bridges to the making of treaties with the Indians. In New Jersey the Assembly not only overrode the Council on money bills but refused in 1761 to vote the salary of any judge who should accept a commission from the Crown 'during pleasure'. It was not until Governor Hardy had issued commissions accordingly 'during good behaviour' and had been dismissed 'as a necessary example to deter others' that the Assembly could be induced to waive the point.[2] In the chartered provinces the power of the purse was still more ruthlessly exercised. On one occasion Governor Shute of Massachusetts found it necessary to forego his salary, and Governor Belcher implied that the House of Representatives there was virtually governor of the province since 'they that have the controul of the money will certainly have the power'.[3]

II

By regarding the forms of colonial government as static rather than kinetic, it is possible to represent this development as a 'subversion of the whole constitution' of the colonies. Perhaps it would be nearer the truth to say that tendencies so spontaneous, had they been magnanimously recognized, would have been less subversive than the attempt to thwart and to circumscribe them; for success in that design might have subverted a nobler tradition. 'At some time or other', said Burke, 'it will come home to England.' Lord Morley has the dictum that 'the ruin of the American cause would have been also the ruin of the constitutional cause in England'.[4] Tendencies so clearly discernible in England during the seventeenth century could scarcely have reappeared in nine-

[1] Dickerson, *op. cit.*, pp. 163–5.
[2] *Id.*, p. 153.
[3] *Id.*, pp. 168–9.
[4] Morley's *Burke*, 1888, p. 87.

teen separate British colonies during the eighteenth and in more than a score during the nineteenth without a touch of organic nature in their kinship.

To the student of Canadian history especially there is something strangely familiar in these chronic symptoms of the first Empire. It is true that there were elements of hope in the nineteenth century that were almost altogether wanting in the eighteenth. There was free trade with a Whig ascendancy, instead of eighteenth-century mercantilism and a 'patriot king'. There was an Earl Grey at the Colonial Office with Charles Buller in the background instead of a Grenville or a Hillsborough in office served by the mordant toryism of William Knox. But the problem was essentially the same, and the infirmities of human nature responded to the same narrow impulses. Reformers under Governor Bernard and Sir Francis Head alike are 'rebels' and 'republicans'. Let it be added also that Assemblies are alike factious and short-sighted. Can it be said that Papineau in Lower Canada was nearer 'the great *arcanum*' than Franklin in Pennsylvania? In truth the American colonies were working out their own salvation in their own way. The plaint of the 'poor Commons' under James I was at last redressed. It was the prerogative of the Crown which was now 'at an everlasting stand'.[1]

The control hitherto exercised indirectly by the Crown was in truth effective enough only to be thoroughly vexatious. The powers of veto and of disallowance—Dickerson has recorded nearly four hundred instances from 1696 to 1765[2]—were not in themselves objects of general attack. Still less was the practice of 'suspending' the operation of colonial laws pending the approval of the Crown. There were ready means of circumventing all these. In certain parts of the field, it is true, the Crown stubbornly held its own. It refused to countenance anything in the nature of an Act to secure the frequency or continuity of the Assemblies. It fixed the electoral districts, and as a rule adjourned, prorogued, and dissolved at pleasure, though it could not prevent a dissolved Assembly arising like Antaeus stronger than ever. Perhaps the most determined measure of indirect control was the appointment of the judges 'during pleasure'. After the experience of Governor Hardy in New Jersey and of Governor Clinton in New York, colonial governors were forbidden 'upon pain of being removed from your govern-

[1] Apology of the Commons, June 20, 1604, Prothero, *Statutes and Constitutional Documents, 1559–1625*, p. 289.

[2] Dickerson, *op. cit.*, p. 227.

ment' to grant commissions other than 'during pleasure only'.[1] But these instances of successful control were exceptional. As a rule the home government, in the scathing words of Professor Egerton, 'combined the opposite faults of excessive meddlesomeness and of excessive weakness', and indeed scarcely deserved 'the praise it has sometimes received for leaving the colonies alone'.[2] With the outbreak of the Seven Years' War, as in those wars of the Edwards which had established the early powers of the House of Commons, the ascendancy of the Assemblies could scarcely be withstood.

> Every shekel that he doth receive
> Doth cost a limb of his prerogative.

With every will to confirm 'the dependence which the colonies ought to have upon the government of the mother country', and to make the governor and the executive officers of the colony, like the judges before them, 'independent of the factious will and caprice of an assembly', it would be necessary, as Governor Dobbs of North Carolina suggested, to await 'a glorious peace', when 'His Majesty will have no great demands upon this province'.[3] Meanwhile the exigencies of war wrought havoc with these lilliputian calculations, and the measures that were finally devised to deal with them belong to another category.

III

In 1754, on the eve of the Seven Years' War, an intercolonial congress, convened by Lieut.-Governor De Lancey of New York under the directions of the Board of Trade, met at Albany for the purpose of devising some unity of action with regard to the French wars and the Indians. Resolving unanimously that united action was 'absolutely necessary', the delegates under the influence of Benjamin Franklin approved of a *Plan of Union* to be established by Act of Parliament. In Franklin's plan the central command was to be vested in a President General to be appointed by the Crown. A Grand Council, to be elected by the colonial Assemblies

[1] *Id.*, p. 204. Governor Clinton had granted a commission to Chief Justice De Lancey 'during good behaviour', and the grant was pronounced by the law officers of the Crown 'good in point of law'. Both Clinton's and Hardy's commissions had to be revoked by inducing the judges to resign and to accept commissions 'during pleasure'. *Id.*, pp. 200, 205.

[2] Egerton, *American Revolution*, p. 41.

[3] Board of Trade, Nov. 11, 1761, quoted in Dickerson, *op. cit.*, p. 204; *id.*, p. 179.

for three years, was to be charged with the task of raising and voting the funds necessary for their security and defence. The spontaneity of this plan is illustrated by the fact, according to Stephen Hopkins of Rhode Island, that the delegates 'forbid their Secretary to give any Copy, except to the Colonies'. De Lancey sent the plan to the Board of Trade but the whole scheme miscarried. The colonial Assemblies failed to ratify it 'with the same unanimity with which their representatives had adopted the plan'. As late as 1789 Franklin maintained that had the Albany plan been put into operation the separation from the mother country might have been postponed for a century.[1]

More intent than Franklin himself upon the cause of inter-colonial union for self-defence was another colonist who after his appointment as governor of his adopted province naturally approached the problem from another angle. Shirley, 'the ablest colonial governor of his time',[2] was not present at the Albany Congress, though he had not only commended it to other governors in America, but had been instrumental in sending from Massachusetts the only commissioners to the Congress with a mandate to conclude 'articles of Union and Confederation . . . for the General Defence of his Majesty's Subjects and Interests in North America as well in time of Peace as of War'.[3] Shirley objected, however, to Franklin's *Plan of Union* that it followed too closely 'the old charter form of government', and was therefore unsuited for an 'Imperium over all the Colonies'. 'I am labouring this point, totis viribus', he wrote to Governor Morris of Pennsylvania. 'Lose no time for promoting the Plan of an Union of the Colonies for their mutual Defence to be concerted at home, and establish'd by Act of Parliament, as soon as possible.' [4]

From the record of Shirley's private intercourse with Franklin it is clear that the governor contemplated a Grand Council, appointed like the provincial Councils by the Crown, and an Act of Parliament to assess the quota for each province, leaving it 'to their Choice to raise the Sum assessed upon them according to their own discretion'.[5] Shirley's days of influence in America were numbered—he was recalled in 1756—and his labours for colonial

[1] Beer, *op. cit.*, pp. 18–23, 313, &c.; Osgood, *op. cit.*, iv. 316–21.

[2] Beer, *op. cit.*, p. 49. For a brilliant analysis of Shirley's methods and success see Osgood, *Massachusetts under Shirley*, *op. cit.*, Part III, ch. iv.

[3] *Correspondence of William Shirley*, ed. Lincoln, ii. 61.

[4] Shirley to Sir Thomas Robinson, Dec. 14, 1754, *id.*, ii. 116; *id.*, ii. 96.

[5] *Id.*, ii. 103; Beer, *op. cit.*, p. 49.

defence passed into the hands of others; but the project of this greatest and most popular imperialist of his day has a melancholy interest far beyond the range of its immediate influence. It drew from Franklin a memorandum of prophetic insight that might almost have been written after Franklin himself as plenipotentiary for thirteen independent colonies had affixed his signature to the Treaty of Versailles:

> 'In Matters of General Concern to the People, and especially where Burthens are to be laid upon them, it is of Use to consider as well what they will be apt to think and say, as what they *ought* to think....
>
> First, they will say, and perhaps with Justice, that the Body of the People in the Colonies are as loyal ... as any Subjects in the King's Dominions; ... That the People in the Colonies ... are likely to be better judges of the Quantity of Forces necessary to be raised and maintain'd ... than the Parliament of England at so great a Distance. ... That it is suppos'd an undoubted Right of Englishmen not to be taxed but by their own Consent given thro' their Representatives.... That to propose taxing them by Parliament, and refusing them the Liberty of chusing a Representative Council to meet in the Colonies, and consider and judge of the Necessity of any General Tax and the Quantum, shews a Suspicion of their Loyalty to the Crown, or Regard for their Country, or of their Common Sense and Understanding which they have not deserv'd.... That a Power in Governors to march the Inhabitants from one End of the British and French Colonies to the other ... would put them on a Footing with the Subjects of France in Canada.... That if the Colonies in a Body may be well governed by Governors and Councils, appointed by the Crown, without Representatives, particular Colonies may as well or better be so governed; a Tax may be laid on them all by Act of Parliament; for Support of Government, and their Assemblies dismiss'd, as a useless Part of their Constitution....
>
> Then, the Administration ... not having any Representative Body of the People to approve and unite in its Measures, and conciliate the Minds of the People to them, will probably become suspected and odious. Animosities and dangerous Feuds will arise between the Governors and the Governed, and every Thing go into Confusion.'[1]

Meanwhile a third project was being matured at the Board of Trade under the directions of the ablest administrator who had ever presided over that much-maligned body. Five days before the opening of the Albany Congress the same problem had been referred to the Board by the king himself, and the dominant influence of Lord Halifax is found in the most promising plan ever

[1] Franklin to Shirley, Dec. 4, 1754, *Shirley Correspondence*, ii. 103-7.

devised for the defence of the first Empire. The appointment of a Commander-in-Chief over all forces in America was to be made by the Crown, but the obligations of the several provinces were to be reviewed by commissioners selected by the provinces themselves, seven to constitute a quorum, with powers to determine the force required, the cost, and the quota to be contributed by each. The plan was to be drafted in its final form by the provincial commissioners themselves, submitted by them to the provincial legislatures for approval or amendment, and finally ratified by the Crown.[1]

The restriction of the project to defence and Indian relations, and its adaptability, as Halifax emphasized, to colonial conditions and government, were features of remarkable promise; but by the time the plan had run the gauntlet of official criticism it was apparent that something more than defence was in the minds of British officialdom. 'The provinces', objected Charles Townshend, 'have been for many years engaged in a skillful design of drawing to themselves the ancient and established prerogatives wisely preserved in the crown as the only means of continuing the superintendency of the mother country.' The Crown would be 'sacrificing our only security for their dependence upon us' if the granting of supply were to be left to the colonies. Townshend commended the principle of a permanent revenue in America by Act of Parliament. 'Thus spoke reinvigorated officialdom', adds Osgood, 'and it was quite time that the policy to which it referred was tried if the imperial system . . . was ever to be put in operation'.[2]

IV

But there were yet to be thirteen years of grace before Townshend's scheme of taxing the colonies as 'security for their dependence' was so light-heartedly launched in the port duties of 1767. Meanwhile the storm for which Franklin and Shirley and Halifax had been desperately preparing was already upon them. The Seven Years' War had begun, and what Shirley had called 'the natural tendency of their government' in America was reinforced by conditions almost altogether unforeseen to make such a policy as Townshend's forever impossible.

Chatham's practice of subsidizing the provincial Assemblies in proportion to their exertions in the war produced, in the aggregate, results that were unprecedented in colonial history. No

[1] Osgood, *op. cit.*, iv. 323 ff.

[2] *Id.*, pp. 326–7.

British appeal had ever inspired a nobler response than the circular letter of December, 1757, drew from Massachusetts, New York, and Connecticut. The traditions of Shirley's governorship in Massachusetts had shown what could be done in the most popular of colonial governments through the agency of faith and goodwill without compromising the just prerogatives of the Crown. The traditions of the Chatham régime during the Seven Years' War showed what could be done by a British minister who, instead of exploiting the checks upon popular institutions, dared to appeal boldly to their virtues in order to command their confidence and thus to liberate their incomparable energies. Not without knowledge and not without reason was Chatham's passionate appeal in 1775 directed to some measure of 'mutual confidence'—'something to trust to'—before the first drop of blood should make reconciliation impossible.

But the magic of Chatham's influence in itself revealed how sudden was the emergency and how rare his magnanimity. To William Knox 'the new mode of application to the Assemblies introduced by Mr. Pitt' was only an incitement to colonial 'ideas of their own future greatness'—a fatal policy 'which having opened to them a direct intercourse with the throne, led them to assume all the importance of Parliaments'.[1] The war with its inequalities of sacrifice, moreover, had left behind a legacy of odious comparisons. Beer has estimated that seven-tenths of all the colonial troops raised during the war were contributed by Massachusetts, New York, and Connecticut, with less than one-third of the population. On the other hand, the proprietary Assemblies and several of the others availed themselves of local disputes with their governors or Councils 'to shirk their simple duty'. The system was declared to be 'inherently vicious'. The fact that the British Government might go farther and fare much worse—and conversely that the voluntary response of self-governing British Dominions would one day dwarf the entire armaments of the Seven Years' War—was of course beyond the ken of eighteenth-century statesmanship. Much, therefore, from the standpoint of fair play was to be said for a more ambitious scheme devised to rest more equitably upon the resources of 'the American empire' as a whole.[2] Had the issue been confined scrupulously to the problem of colonial defence, had no

[1] *Extra Official State Papers*, ii. 23.

[2] For contemporary thought in favour of parliamentary taxation for America see Egerton, *American Revolution*, pp. 70–7.

ulterior purposes lurked beneath the project of securing a revenue in America, had suspicion, that most malignant of political infirmities, not been aroused among those whose goodwill would have been cheap at any price, had the menace of foreign war and French power to the north continued to operate, it is conceivable, as Franklin himself admitted in 1764, that 'a revenue arising out of the American trade' might have passed unchallenged.[1]

But with the advent of peace there was a new heaven and a new if not a better earth. Neither the urgency of the problem nor the outlook and temper of the colonies themselves could ever again be the same. Knox afterwards maintained that the colonies already contemplated 'an American empire, in which the British isles and possessions should be absorbed'.[2] Franklin himself after the reduction of Canada wrote that the 'foundations of the future grandeur and stability of the British empire lie in America'. Yet the very provinces which had flung themselves most ardently into the war without counting the cost now found themselves in common with the other colonies 'proceeded against as delinquents, or, at best, as people under suspicion of delinquency; and in such manner, as they imagined, their recent services in the war did not at all merit'. In addition to the general indictment attuned to 'duty' and 'a fair share of the burden', they had reason to reflect with some bitterness upon the contemptuous criticism which colonial conditions and in particular the colonial militia had almost invariably received at the hands of British officers.[3] To this source the greatest of the Chief Justices of the United States has attributed much of the irremediable bitterness of the Revolutionary War. French power was broken, national danger was past, and the chronic conflict between governance and self-government could be fought out, like Sir Lucius O'Trigger's duel, 'in peace and quietness'. Such were the auspices under which a design that might have been defensible in 1754 became one of the most devastating and mischievous projects in British history.

V

The determination to maintain by parliamentary taxation a standing army of 10,000 men in America at the close of the most victorious of colonial wars, was not unattended by other designs

[1] Egerton, *American Revolution*, p. 73. [2] *Extra Official State Papers*, ii. 23.

[3] Not merely officers of the type of Braddock and Loudoun but men like Generals Amherst, Murray, and Wolfe. See Egerton, *American Revolution*, p. 19; Beer, *op. cit.*, 173 ff.

which went far to justify colonial suspicions and to make them in the end ineradicable. We have seen that the temptation to reverse the normal functions of taxation and to make British officials 'independent of the factious will and caprice of an assembly' was not new. Stanhope, in proposing to annex Nova Scotia to Massachusetts in 1715, observed that it would make the governor 'more independent, and much better able to serve the Crown than he is at present, while he draws all his subsistence from the people'.[1] The whole struggle over fixed salaries and a permanent civil list had turned upon the policy of liberating the officials of government from 'the power of the purse' in the hands of the Assembly. In the very act of surrender, when permission to accept annual grants was made general in 1735, the Board advised, for the governor at least, a fixed salary payable out of permanent royal revenues 'by which the governor will become entirely independent of the people'.[2] Martin Bladen's project of a Stamp Tax in 1726—the prototype of Grenville's ill-starred measure—was devised with the same object in view. Governor Shirley himself wrote in 1755 that 'Independency' was impossible in America, 'whilst His Majesty hath 7000 Troops kept up within them, & in the Great Lakes upon the back of six of them, with the Indians at command . . . provided the Governors and principal Civil Officers are Independent of the Assemblies for their Subsistence'.[3]

And thus it came to pass that perhaps the first clear-cut issue of 'independence' imported into 'the American question' was the design of making the imperial system independent of the local Assemblies. With a standing army of twenty battalions in America in view, the *Sugar Bill* was introduced in 1764. For the first time it was stated that 'it is just and necessary that a revenue be raised' in America, and that it should 'be from time to time disposed of by Parliament towards defraying the necessary expenses of defending, protecting, and securing the British colonies in America'. Burke has recorded in words too well known to require repetition 'the symptoms of a great change' at this time—'a scheme of government new in many things' defended in parliament by the brilliant talents of Charles Townshend who 'did dazzle them by playing before their eyes the image of a revenue to be raised in America'. The implications of the *Sugar Act* were scarcely seen

[1] *Nova Scotia, A. Series*, vi. 198.
[2] The case of Governor Belcher in Massachusetts. Dickerson, *op. cit.*, p. 188.
[3] Beer, *op. cit.*, p. 266.

at the time in America, though with the tightening of the mercantile system, the extension of Vice-Admiralty Courts and the *Mutiny Act*, and the other regulations of the Grenville régime it was obvious that the whole glittering machinery of imperial organization was being put into motion. With the *Stamp Act* of the following year Grenville advanced to direct parliamentary taxation, to be enforced in Vice-Admiralty Courts in which British officials administered British laws without even the formalities of a jury.

The resistance which culminated in the Stamp Act Congress of October, 1765, and led to the repeal of the Act was the measure of the awakening in America to the meaning of 'the new colony system'. James Otis wrote that it did more in a few months to stir opinion in the colonies than all that had gone before. When the measure was repealed by the Rockingham administration Burke maintained that the calm after so violent a storm was 'without parallel in history'. But Grenville solemnly assured the king that 'if any man ventured to defeat the regulations laid down for the Colonies, by a slackness in the execution, he would look upon him as a criminal and the betrayer of his country'.[1] The *Declaration Act* itself which accompanied the repeal, stated that Parliament 'had, hath, and of right ought to have, full power and authority to make laws . . . in all cases whatsoever'. When Townshend, therefore, again advanced to the attack by the duties of 1767, the least suspicious of colonists could scarcely ignore their import. In order to observe the American distinction between internal and external taxation the duties were laid at the American ports, but the object was unmistakable—'a more certain and adequate provision for defraying the charge of the administration of justice and the support of civil government'. Accompanying the *Revenue Act* of 1767 came resident commissioners of customs for America and the suspension of the New York Assembly until it should comply with the *Quartering Act* by supplying certain provisions to the standing army in New York. 'How is this mode', asked John Dickinson in the first of his *Farmer's Letters*, 'more tolerable than the Stamp Act?'[2] Indeed the design is bluntly stated by William Knox himself. The system of port duties, he wrote in 1789, was 'expressly appropriated to defray the expence of *their* Civil government'; and it was so far from proceeding 'by *sap*, as the stamp duties would

[1] *Grenville Correspondence*, iii. 216.

[2] Morison, Documents on *The American Revolution*, p. 36.

have done, that it was attacking them by storm in open day; every man therefore saw into the design'.[1]

When the duties on glass, lead, colours, and paper were removed, the duty on tea remained: what was the colonist to make of Hillsborough's 'Canonical book of ministerial scripture', as Burke called it—'the general epistle to the Americans'—the circular letter in which the minister in the name of the Crown renounced 'any further taxes upon America, for the purpose of Raising a Revenue'? In the letters of Washington it is possible to follow the perplexities which British policy thus forced upon a resolute mind until suspicion became at last a settled conviction. As late as 1774 Washington, in the most solemn language, wrote from the first Continental Congress at Philadelphia that 'it is not the wish or interest of that government (Massachusetts), or any other upon this continent, separately or collectively, to set up for independence'.[2] But though long 'unsuspicious of design', Washington was now 'convinced beyond the smallest doubt, that these measures are the result of deliberation', and that there had been 'a regular systematic plan formed to enforce them'. 'Government is pursuing a regular plan at the expense of law and justice to overthrow our constitutional rights and liberties.'[3] It is surely one of the ironies of history that much of the systematic tyranny at this stage was a desperate attempt of a blundering ministry to save its own precious dignity.

[1] 'For every man was able to satisfy himself, that if the civil expences of the Colony were defrayed by duties imposed by Parliament, and all the officers paid out of it and appointed by the Crown, their Sun of independence would be much longer a rising than they wished or hoped for.' *Extra Official State Papers*, ii. 27.

Knox's whole theory, written of course 'after the event', was the characteristic Tory doctrine that the colonists had independence in view from the first; though in reality when Knox claims to have observed 'a general disposition to independence of this country' it is clear that it is the same type of 'independence' which he finds 'in the first plantation in every one of them', and that it arose through 'a total want of plan or system'. (*Extra Official State Papers*, ii. 11.) What Knox seems to have had in mind was not sovereign political independence and separation from Great Britain but *the dependence of officials upon the local Assemblies*: a vastly different thing which has been regarded throughout this essay as a very natural and indeed inevitable process.

[2] 'This I advance with a degree of confidence and boldness, which may claim your belief, having better opportunities of knowing the real sentiments of the people you are among, from the leaders of them, in opposition to the measures of the administration, than you have.' Washington to Capt. Robert Mackenzie, Philadelphia, Oct. 9, 1774. *Washington's Writings*, ed. Sparks, ii. 401. In Washington's Diary for Sept. 28, is the entry: 'spent the afternoon with the Boston gentlemen.' *Ibid.*

[3] Washington to Bryan Fairfax, *id.*, ii. 398; *id.*, ii. 392.

Thus events moved on to a crisis which Burke in 1774, and posterity after him, could not contemplate without despair:

> 'If intemperately, unwisely, fatally, you sophisticate and poison the very source of government, by urging subtle deductions, and consequences odious to those you govern, from the unlimited and illimitable nature of supreme sovereignty, you will teach them by these means to call that sovereignty itself in question.... If that sovereignty and their freedom cannot be reconciled, which will they take? They will cast your sovereignty in your face. Nobody will be argued into slavery.
>
> ... Your scheme yields no revenue ... and such is the state of America, that after wading up to your eyes in blood, you could only end just where you begun; that is, to tax where no revenue is to be found, to—my voice fails me; my inclination indeed carries me no further—all is confusion beyond it.'

The Loss of an Empire

I

The consequences which followed the breakdown of mutual confidence lie beyond the scope of this essay, but the reflections which occur to a Canadian a century and a half after the catastrophe are apt to differ from those which have been traditional either in Great Britain or in the United States. Both countries, perhaps, have come to regard the American Revolution with a measure of fatalism: the one with resolute acquiescence in the inevitable, the other in a more exultant spirit of unquestioning vindication. Viewing in Canada the results of the conflict at closer range, and contemplating also as an accomplished fact what may be regarded as a truly British solution to the old 'American question' in the achievement of 'responsible government', it is not so easy to aspire to either form of equanimity. In such a context the inevitableness of revolution is less obvious; perhaps because it seems belied by the inevitableness of the evolution which saved the second Empire and was already so far advanced in the first when the springs of mutual confidence were recklessly poisoned.

In truth the similarity of organic growth between the first Empire and the second is borne in upon one at every point. Not only are the local problems the same but with the exception of Nova Scotia the process of colonial government begins again almost *de novo*; and if the second Empire, like the first, came to the brink of disaster it was not because it had not a fair chance. Nor was it because there was 'a total want of plan or system' as Knox had urged in extenuation of the earlier catastrophe.[1] Knox himself, who had no small share in starting that second Empire on its way, could scarcely have desired material more to his liking. Quebec, which alone among the provinces of the first Empire seems to have commanded his unqualified approval,[2] had no Assembly whatever until 'the zealots for universal liberty', as Knox wrote upon the eve of the *Constitutional Act*, 'come with their fine spun theories, for promoting the happiness of the French Canadians, by converting them into English Republicans'.[3] The Nova Scotia Assembly, it is true, continued the New England traditions, but neither there nor in Upper Canada and New Brunswick and Prince Edward Island was a basis of mutual confidence in the British connexion ever wanting. With the loyalist migrations a fair trial for another régime of the old colonial system was doubly assured.

All the approved specifics for making the officials of government 'independent of the factious will and caprice of an assembly' are tried again. The same catchwords of 'due subordination' and 'the rights and liberties of British subjects' appear on either side. The same bitter struggle ensues, a struggle wholly indigenous to Canadian soil but complicated by false analogies drawn from the results of the earlier conflict. Within fifty years the same malignant disease had run its course. Fortunately there was no recourse to surgery, though the poisoning of mutual confidence threatened the same dissolution. Governor Bernard never vilified his political opponents in Massachusetts more heartily than Sir Francis Head berated the 'republicans' of Upper Canada. Before the struggle was over, men as staunchly British as Robert Baldwin and Joseph Howe had become very nearly as desperate as Washington in 1774. Baldwin solemnly warned Lord Durham in 1838 that without responsible government 'England will continue to retain these Colonies by means of her troops alone'.[4] Howe advised Charles Buller as late as 1846 that if men like those who 'drove the old Colonies to separation' had their way, the problem would be

[1] *Extra Official State Papers*, ii. 11.

[2] 'It might be expected that in those which are denominated Royal Governments, something more than the powers of paper and parchment would have been employed to render them useful, and retain them in subordination to Great Britain. But there is really no material difference between any of them, (except Quebec) and the others.' *Id.*, ii. 20.

[3] *Id.*, ii. 6.

[4] Baldwin to Durham, Aug. 23, 1838, *Calendar of the Durham Papers*, ed. William Smith, *Pub. Arch. Can.*, 1923, p. 326.

'discussed in a different spirit, ten years hence, by the Enemies of England, not by her friends'.[1] Happily the 'friends' on both sides of the Atlantic prevailed; and though the old colonial system remained much the same, it was the happier lot of the second Empire to deal with men who were vastly different.

II

From the vantage ground of responsible government, therefore, one is impressed not merely with the difficulties but with the elements of promise in the first Empire. It was the fact that the colonies were already so far upon the way to self-government which made them doubly jealous of it; and in the end they 'made their stand', to repeat the oft-quoted words of Moses Coit Tyler, 'not against tyranny inflicted, but only against tyranny anticipated'. Thus Beer has recorded the opinion that revolution 'might not have followed had the British government, after 1763, been willing to relax still further the political ties, and to allow the colonies in bulk to assume the virtually complete powers of self-government that Rhode Island and Connecticut enjoyed'.[2] Is it true that this was impossible?

Whatever answer to that question came from the one side of the Atlantic, the tendencies already outlined seem conclusive for the other. The achievement of political power by the Assembly was not a subversive but a natural process; and it was as nearly inevitable as any process in government. Who could have been ignorant in 1765 that this was one of the cardinal facts of British history? In America the same truth was written in the journals of every Assembly. It continued in a score of British provinces after the Revolution until the control of local administration was finally achieved. British Dominions have survived to encounter the same tendencies in the government of their own subordinate territories. 'It is the genius of the English race in both hemispheres', exclaimed Baldwin, 'to be concerned in the Government of themselves'.[3]

How near were the American provinces to self-government? No British province in 1836 wielded the power over local administration that the average colony exercised in 1763. Their method, it is true, was not ours; nor was this power unaccompanied by fric-

[1] Howe to Buller, Oct. 28, 1846, *Howe Papers*, vi. 80. *Pub. Arch. Can.*
[2] *Op. cit.*, p. 313.
[3] *Calendar of the Durham Papers, Pub. Arch. Can.*, 1923, p. 328.

tion and anomalies. Even before Grenville with his 'stout and resolute heart' took the helm, it is impossible, as Professor Egerton has shown so convincingly, to say that all was well in the best of all possible worlds. The ceaseless friction must have irritated unspeakably a mind like Lord Halifax's, attuned to system and tangible results. But there had been considerable friction in Great Britain in disposing of the Stuarts. Perhaps there was more hopeless friction and less compromise in Lower Canada in 1838 than in any province of the old Empire. Nor did it cease with responsible government. It ceased to fill the ears of the Colonial Secretary merely because it was left to work itself out, as all representative government on the British analogy must work itself out, in the provinces themselves. Good government is not synonymous with self-government, but as Campbell-Bannerman so wisely said, it can never be a satisfactory substitute.

If nothing but force, then, could have stopped this process, was the temper of Britain such in 1770 that the use of force was inevitable? Had Grenville and Townshend been vouchsafed a vision of the results of their desperate experiment in constructive imperialism, would they still, as a Whig pamphleteer in America expressed it, have 'hardened their hearts like unto Pharaoh'? Could the wells, poisoned by false dignity on the one side, and suspicion —much of it ill-founded—on the other, have yet been purified and sweetened by a touch of statesmanship, a flash of historical imagination?

The answer to these questions, to be sure, was not to be found in America. The outlook in Britain has been painted by those who speak with authority; and it must have been black indeed. When Burke and Knox can agree, there must be little room for disagreement. Perhaps the most desperate outlook was the temper of the British public. What had the colonist to hope if no virtue was to be found here? During the momentous elections of 1768 when Knox professed to see 'a spirit rising in this country', Franklin found the 'whole venal nation is now at market, will be sold for about two millions, and might be bought . . . by the very devil himself'. But this did not prevent Knox from interpreting the election *ex cathedra* to the colonies in America:

'Do not flatter yourself, that she is yet so despicable as to be terrified by your threats, or so ignorant of your affairs, as to imagine you can carry them into execution. There is a spirit rising in this country, which will make you to know its strength and your own weakness, that will convince you of its authority and of your dependence. . . . If you do not avail yourselves of the information I have given you, perhaps the people of England may be led by it to conceive more justly of their *Rights*, and of your *Intentions*, than they have hitherto done; and may compel you to submit, if they unhappily find no argument, but force can induce you to obey. It is time indeed for my countrymen to bestir themselves, and to vindicate the honour of the state.'[1]

Such desperate wickedness as this flourishing in high places was enough, as James Otis had said, to 'make the wisest mad and the weakest strong'.[2] But the people of England remained apathetic. As late as 1774 Burke wrote that the public was 'perfectly careless and supine'. 'Any remarkable highway robbery at Hounslow Heath would make more conversation than all the disturbances of America.'[3] They might be stirred to escape 1*s*. of land tax in the £ by taxing America; and they still talked, with an air of joint sovereignty, as Franklin found, of '*our subjects in the colonies*'. But in the end the ministry had to resort to Catherine the Great of Russia and Hessian troops to implement the programme of William Knox. In truth, this apathy, however hopeless, indicated no rooted determination to subjugate the colonies; and indeed the *Stamp Act* passed the House itself almost unnoted, except for the inflexible determination of George Grenville. We have seen that Townshend's measure in 1767, despite Burke's description of that fine-spun scheme of 'exquisite policy', was much more than a device on the part of the darling of the House to win its applause. The applause of the House nevertheless was won, and won easily; and it was as easily lost. The sequel went far to justify the language of Burke:

'What woeful variety of schemes have been adopted; what enforcing, and what repealing; what bullying, and what submitting; what doing, and undoing; what straining and what relaxing; what assemblies dissolved for not obeying, and called again without obedience; what troops sent out to quell resistance, and on meeting with resistance, recalled; what shiftings, and changes, and jumblings of all kinds of men at home, which left no possibility of order, consistency, vigour, or even so much as a decent unity of colour in any one public measure.'[4]

[1] *The Controversy between Great Britain and her Colonies Reviewed*, London, 1769, pp. 204–5.

[2] *Rights of the British Colonies Asserted and Proved.*

[3] Burke to Rockingham, Feb. 2 and Dec. 5, 1774. *Letters*, ed. Laski, pp. 179, 189.

[4] *Speech on American Taxation.*

This is not the manner of inexorable tyranny; and thus one is led to attach more and more importance to that ill-fated project of imperialization which 'ran counter to the tendency towards autonomy'.[1] Had Grenville and Townshend held their hand the problem assuredly would not *ipso facto* have been solved. But at least its solution would not have been made for ever impossible. Nor would the problem have been solved had Burke's tentative plan of conciliation been immediately adopted. But the first step would have been taken and, as it happens, that particular process usually requires but one step at a time.

III

Was it then, to quote the ruthless verdict of Professor Egerton, 'because the men of the eighteenth century were puffed up with a stupid pride and ignorance which forbade their realizing the possibilities of the future, however remote, that the first English Empire . . . came to an unhonoured and irreparable end'? Was revolution inevitable because British ministers were, like George Grenville, 'altogether lacking in that quality which is the touchstone of great statesmanship, the quality of historical imagination'?[2]

It is a hard saying and it is not easy to subscribe to it without qualification. None but an archangel, assuredly, could have foreseen the British Commonwealth of to-day. None but Franklin seems to have approached such a vision. But lack of imagination is an infirmity which may reveal itself in two very different ways. Both have much to answer for, but it will be conceded that they are not of equal malignancy.

Sins of omission are as a rule venial and remediable. With few exceptions statesmen of the eighteenth century were denied prophetic insight into the potentialities of colonial conditions and character. Until the very eve of the Revolution Britain was more intent upon winning an American empire than upon understanding it. The absence of system was not unnatural, and there were many compensations. Colonial growth was organic. Its diversity was at once the inspiration and the result of natural aptitudes. Like Topsy the average colony 'just growed'. There was no 'empire' in a literal sense, but there was never wanting a certain practical empiricism, a 'day to day opportunism' which Sir Charles Lucas has called 'the highest genius of the race'.[3]

[1] Beer, *op. cit.*, p. 287.
[2] *American Revolution*, pp. 200, 70.
[3] *Greater Rome and Greater Britain.*

But there is a lack of imagination which belongs to another category: that of Clarendon who thought the absolutism of Charles I could have been 'covered under a bushel' at the time of the Grand Remonstrance; or that of a Wentworth to whose masterful spirit Charles I's fatal policy was 'well laid but miserably lost in the execution'. No policy of 'thorough' ever had a slighter chance of success than Grenville's in America. Resistance came not because the colonists were Americans but because they were British. Could any autocrat have hoped for success in America who had not begun by belying the instincts of Britons in Great Britain? The lack of imagination here is the failure to understand the spirit of a free people, a people who believed themselves substantially free and discovered that they were not. The political virtues which may accompany such statesmanship may be as exemplary as those which Burke conceded to Grenville: fearless self-confidence, a genius for responsibility, an imperviousness to criticism, and the loftiest motives in the world for 'saving the Empire'. But in the last analysis is there any refinement of constructive statesmanship which can take the place of simple confidence among men—confidence, like peace, to be 'sought in its natural course and in its ordinary haunts'?

Thus while Chatham pleaded for 'mutual confidence'—'something to trust to'—and Burke implored the nation to restore at any cost '*the former unsuspecting confidence of the colonies in the Mother Country*', the government, always ready to do too late what might have saved the day had it been done in time, passed from one paltry subterfuge to another, in retreat upon what was deemed to be its last line of defence, the defence of its own dignity. Meanwhile suspicion spread like the plague, the deadliest of all political maladies because it throve not upon facts but upon itself. In that sense the period from the *Sugar Bill* to the Declaration of Independence is the Black Death of colonial history. In such an atmosphere even Paine's *Common Sense* seemed a breath of fresh air. 'The fate of Charles the First', he cried, 'hath only made kings more subtle—not more just'.[1] The time came when Knox himself, in his *Project of a permanent Union and Settlement with the Colonies*, conceded that 'state chicane or lawyers craft will not do with the

[1] *Common Sense*, Philadelphia, February, 1776, reprinted London, 1776, 2nd edition, p. 6.

In America alone over 120,000 copies of this pamphlet were sold within three months. Egerton, *American Revolution*, p. 195.

Colonies, they have lost all confidence in the integrity of Parliament, and until confidence is restored, treaty is impossible. Parliament must therefore endeavour to beget confidence by putting it out of its own power to deceive.'[1]

And thus 'reinvigorated officialdom' in person proclaimed its own bankruptcy.

[1] *Extra Official State Papers*, ii., Appendix xi.

II

NOVA SCOTIA AND THE OLD EMPIRE

I

WITH the final cession of Acadie to the British Crown by the Treaty of Utrecht in 1713, Nova Scotia became an integral part of 'the American empire'. By the same treaty the British claims to the Hudson's Bay territories, pursuant to the Charter of 1670, were also finally confirmed. This monopolistic proprietary 'plantation' of Charles II, however, bore little resemblance to the thriving proprietary provinces of Maryland and Pennsylvania. The oldest continuously British territory on the continent of North America slumbered peacefully through the American Revolution in the swaddling charter of the Hudson's Bay Company.

It was at first proposed to annex Nova Scotia to Massachusetts. Every argument of conquest and of provincial rights seemed to warrant that expectation. More than three-quarters of Colonel Nicholson's force against Port Royal in 1710 had been colonial militiamen; and Massachusetts had contributed half as many again as all the other colonies together. Of the garrison which remained under Colonel Samuel Vetch of Boston until the signing of the peace, more than half were colonial volunteers.[1] Annexation to Massachusetts, in fact, had already been implied in the charter of William and Mary to that province. Stanhope himself, the Secretary of State, conceded that 'it would be a violation of the very words of that Charter to erect a new Government there'. Rivalry in trade and the fisheries, moreover, would render the two provinces 'very ill friends; tho' very near neighbours'; whereas the Governor of Massachusetts if entrusted with the government of Nova Scotia would be 'more independent, and much better able to serve the Crown that he is at present, while he draws all his subsistance from the people and has nothing but his Commission from the King'.[2]

The sequel for Canadian history had the boundaries of Massachusetts been extended to the Gulf of St. Lawrence would defy calculation; but the British Government decided otherwise. A separate 'royal' province was established upon the model of Vir-

[1] Osgood, *American Colonies in the 18th Century*, i. 436 ff.

[2] Stanhope, to Council of Trade, May 15, 1715, *Nova Scotia, A. Series*, 6. 199. (Transcripts of *C.O. 217*, Public Record Office) *Pub. Arch. Can.*

ginia. The first Commission and Instructions to Colonel Philipps were not 'so extensive as those for His Majesty's other Governors in America', since both the fisheries and the fur trade were seasonal, and the settled white population remained almost exclusively French. The instructions with regard to the laws of trade and navigation were 'in the usual form', though the prominence of timber and naval stores—the boundless reserves of which were placed under the direct supervision of the continental Surveyor-General of Woods—pointed to 'defence' rather than 'opulence' as a dominant motive in organizing the new province. The choice of Virginia as the prototype was designed, moreover, to strengthen the hands of the Crown in the contest with the 'proprietary' and 'chartered' provinces. The Instructions to the Governor of Virginia were supplied to Governor Philipps for use in 'cases that may happen . . . till His Majesty's further pleasure shall be known'.[1]

The early government of the new province was necessarily primitive. The permanent white population, almost exclusively Acadian French, was estimated by Nicholson at 2,500, of whom 1,290 were in the vicinity of Annapolis and Minas Basin. Ten years later Philipps reported the trade and fisheries to be 'intirely hitherto in favour of Boston'—an excellent illustration of the prevailing tendencies in eighteenth-century mercantilism. Cured fish from Nova Scotia already found its way 'to all the markets of Portugal, the Mediterranean and West Indies'. Furs to the value of £10,000 were traded for 'West India Commodityes, and Provissions of New England and some European goods', at a profit of four or five hundred per cent., 'without paying the least duty or impost towards the support of this Government'. There was 'a very good coal mine, which the people of Boston fetch at their pleasure'. Meanwhile Philipps had difficulty in assembling twelve councillors for the nominal administration of the province. 'This has been hitherto', he wrote from Annapolis, 'no more than a Mock Government—Its authority haveing never yet extended beyond cannon reach of this Fort'.[2]

[1] Council of Trade to Lords Justices, June 19, 1719. *Id.*, 10. 128.

[2] Philipps to Lords of Trade, Aug. 6, Sept. 26 and 27, 1720. *Id.*, 1. 186 ff.; 12. 91 ff., &c. The Council included Capt. Doucett, Major Armstrong, afterwards Lieut.-Governor, Paul Mascarene 'Chief Engineer and a Person of great prudence and Capacity', the Chaplain of the Garrison, a surveyor, the Collector of Customs, two merchants, a surgeon, and the son of an eminent merchant of Boston. *Id.*, 11. 108.

The ultimate form of government, however, was never in question, though the contest between the 'chartered' and 'royal' types was by no means over. By 1725 the settlements at Canso, the head-quarters of the New England fishing fleets, had so far altered the political conditions of the province that Lieut.-Governor Armstrong sought directions from the Duke of Newcastle 'for constituting an Assembly . . . the People so much desiring it'.[1] To Alured Popple, Secretary of the Board of Trade, Armstrong added that an Assembly was particularly necessary for the New England settlers, 'otherways the best man on Earth cannot manage and govern them'. To Newcastle himself, two years later, Armstrong reported the activities of 'some Boston antimonarchical traders'.[2] In 1727, however, the Board of Trade drew up a formal report upon the civil government of the province. The governor was 'to declare in His Majesty's Name by Proclamation or otherwise, that such persons as shall settle in Nova Scotia shall be entitled to all the like Privileges, Liberties and advantages which are at present enjoy'd by the rest of His Majesty's Subjects in His other American Colonies and particularly to that of an Assembly, as soon as their circumstances will admit of it'.[3] These pledges, as we shall see, were duly redeemed in Nova Scotia. The Board itself was the first to see that no British settlement on a large scale was possible without a prospect of enjoying 'a Civil Government there' such as Britons in America everywhere took for granted; and conversely British institutions could be expected to function only when 'there are English enough to compose an Assembly'.[4]

II

Twenty years passed before systematic British settlement was begun, and more than thirty before an Assembly brought the province into conformity with the usual type of 'royal' government in America. The schemes of settlement and of government projected during this period must have exhausted the range of colonial precedent. Governor Richard Philipps returned to Nova Scotia in 1729 with new Commission and Instructions, directed, it would seem, to a new policy. In truth the wealth of the fisheries alone must have commanded the attention of the Board. As early as

[1] 'Which will not only add to the authority of the Government but in a little time very much lessen the Public Charge.' Sept. 5, 1725. *A. Series*, 16. 128.

[2] *Id.*, 16. 162–3; 17. 102 ff.

[3] Lords of Trade to the Privy Council, June 7, 1727. *Id.*, 18. 122 ff.

[4] Lords of Trade to Armstrong, Sept. 18, 1735. *Id.*, 33. 160.

1722 these had been reported to be 'the best in His Majesty's dominions'. Philipps found at Canso no fewer than 250 vessels with some 2,000 men engaged in the fisheries. The industry, he wrote to Newcastle, contributed from £30,000 to £40,000 per year to the revenues of Great Britain—more than any other province in America except Virginia.[1] The new seal of the province bore the appropriate motto 'Terrae Marisque Opes'.

But projects of settlement—at least six are on record during this period—yielded very meagre results. It was decided in 1729 to extend the boundaries of the province westward to the Kennebec River, upon the basis of 'the ancient limits' as surrendered by the French in 1713. The district between the Kennebec and the St. Croix was to be named 'Georgia'; and David Dunbar, whose stormy career as Surveyor of Woods and Lieut.-Governor of New Hampshire brought him into constant conflict with Governor Belcher of Massachusetts, was authorized by Order in Council to settle it with Protestant settlers from Ireland and German settlers from the Palatinate.[2] But in 1732 the law officers of the Crown upheld the claims of Massachusetts to the whole area in dispute, and even the name of Dunbar's settlement was appropriated for the new province in South Carolina.[3] The wealthiest of the 'Palatinates' were induced—by 'the intrigues of Boston', Philipps complained—to settle in the south. And thus the two provinces, as Stanhope had predicted, became 'very ill friends; tho' very near neighbours'.

A few years later a still more pretentious scheme found favour with the Board of Trade. In 1736 Thomas Coram, an influential merchant of London, proposed a government for Nova Scotia upon the model of the new province of Georgia, but with provision for self-government at the earliest stages of adequate settlement. Trustees were to be incorporated for twenty-one years. The councillors, instead of being appointed by the trustees or the governor, were to be elected annually by the Assembly, though the deputy-governor was to have an 'absolute negative upon each of them'. At the end of twenty-one years the trustees were to surrender their charter, and the government of the province was to 'return entirely to the Crown . . . as in New York or any other plantation immediately under His Majesty's protection'. The

1 Oct. 2, 1729, Sept. 2, 1730; *America and West Indies*, 29. 165; 30. 11, &c.
2 *Board of Trade, Nova Scotia*, 33. 158, 227, &c.
3 Osgood, *op. cit.*, iii. 329–330.

Board commended the project and agreed that the settlement of Nova Scotia was 'of very great consequence to His Majesty's interests in America, and to the interests of this kingdom'; but Coram's scheme came to nothing, and it seems clear, from a memorandum of 1741, that the Board still retained its decided preference for a 'royal' government 'in the same manner and form as His Majesty's other Plantations in America'.[1]

In truth the growing insecurity of British interests between a French and Indian population within the province and the direct menace of French power from Louisbourg must have jeopardized settlement under any auspices. 'No more striking proof exists of the neglect of colonial interests', says Osgood, 'than is afforded by the history of Nova Scotia for nearly forty years after the Treaty of Utrecht'.[2] Project after project—for French protestants, for Irish settlers in the Chignecto peninsula, for Protestant settlers from Germany—came to grief. Philipps himself left the province to deputies after 1731, and Armstrong died by his own hand in 1739. Mascarene, who returned from Boston to take over the administration in the following year, reported that there were scarcely half a dozen British families left exclusive of the garrisons at Annapolis and Canso. Depredations upon the New England fishing fleets and finally open war with France brought the fortunes of the province to the lowest ebb. Canso itself was taken in 1744 by a French force from Louisbourg. Gallant old Mascarene beat off attack after attack upon Annapolis, but it was clear that the cause of British settlement and of stable government alike in Nova Scotia was not to be made good without an appeal to the fortunes of war.

SHIRLEY'S 'GREAT PLAN'

I

The lean years of military occupation closed with a project of more than passing interest, for it was the work of the greatest colonial governor of his time, and it was one of the most cherished projects of his career. Indirectly, at least, it proved to be the turning-point in the history of Nova Scotia.

William Shirley, Governor of Massachusetts, was too magnanimous to share the narrow provincial jealousies which had embittered the relations between the two provinces. It was Shirley's conviction that 'Nova Scotia was the key to British interests and

[1] *A. Series*, 33. 160; 25. 105.

[2] *Op. cit.*, iii. 512.

dominion in America'; that it was 'the key of all the Eastern Colonies upon the Northern Continent'. It had 'more safe and commodious harbours . . . than the same extent of Sea coast in any part of the world'. Its loss would be fatal to the whole area of 'the King's woods whence the Royal Navy is almost wholly supply'd with masts yards and bowsprits', and fatal to the 'Cod fishery' from New England to the Gulf of St. Lawrence. In the end its loss would jeopardize the naval control of the North Atlantic. These convictions Shirley affirmed in season and out of season—to his own General Court in Massachusetts, to the Duke of Bedford, to Newcastle, to the Admiralty, to Sir Thomas Robinson, to Benning Wentworth of New Hampshire and other governors of the nothern provinces, and finally, in his own defence, to the Crown itself.[1] To Shirley the meagre garrison of British settlers in Nova Scotia came to look as their champion and protector. In war he was their defender. With the advent of peace his name must be associated with that of Halifax in the final establishment of Nova Scotia as a British province.

More than once during the war Shirley had saved Annapolis by dispatching timely supplies and reinforcements from Boston. His old friend Mascarene 'did Nothing of Moment', Shirley afterwards remarked, 'without either my Directions, Approbation, or Advice, transmitting even his Correspondence with his Majesty's Ministers thro' my hands'.[2] In that field, says Osgood, he was 'the most alert and the best informed man in New England'. Pledging the General Court of Massachusetts to secrecy, he launched the project for the capture of Louisbourg, and became 'the moving spirit' of that most successful colonial enterprise of the war. More than three-quarters of Pepperrell's force—4,300 in all—were men of that province. From Louisbourg itself (October 29, 1745) Shirley wrote to Newcastle of the future government and settlement of the province; two years later he claimed Newcastle's promise 'that his Majesty design'd to bestow on me the Government of Nova Scotia, to hold with that of the Massachusetts Bay'. Shirley was among the first to urge the fortification of Chebucto, afterwards Halifax, and a settlement there to be drawn from the hardy stock of New England. And finally it was 'in Obedience to his Majesty's Commands' (October 3, 1747) through Newcastle

[1] Osgood, *op. cit.*, iii. 574; *Correspondence of William Shirley*, ed. Lincoln, ii. 148 ff.; i. 346 ff., 470 ff., 499 ff.; ii. 592 ff., &c.

[2] Shirley to Newcastle, Mar. 28, 1750. *Id.*, i. 499.

himself that Shirley drew up his 'Plan of a Civil Government for the Province of Nova Scotia, to be laid before his Majesty for his Royal Consideration'.[1]

The immediate sequel might well have daunted a temper less serene and tenacious than Shirley's, for he was not to become Governor of Nova Scotia, and his *Plan of a Civil Government*, based upon the Charter of his own province, was finally passed over in favour of an orthodox 'royal' government. Deeper than either disappointment must have been his chagrin when Louisbourg, the prize won by New England blood and treasure, was returned to France in exchange for Madras at the Treaty of Aix-la-Chapelle in 1748. Fortunately, in the end, the cause which Shirley had at heart for Nova Scotia was upon the whole not seriously impaired by these accumulated calamities, for his chief project was nothing less than the systematic settlement of the province to ensure a decided British ascendancy. He had preferred the 'chartered' government of Massachusetts because 'a near conformity of the Civil Government of Nova Scotia to that of this Province, may be a great advantage to the former for attracting New England Settlers to live there'.[2] In two exhaustive letters to Bedford, Secretary of State, accompanied by plans and memoranda of sites and estimates, Shirley proposed to settle 6,000 families in Nova Scotia within ten years. Of these 2,000 were to be drawn from the northern colonies at a cost of £48,900, 2,000 from Europe at a cost of £78,900, and 2,000 disbanded troops at the close of the war. Thus was a British ascendancy to be established, the fishery to be secured and developed, and the cost of the whole to be defrayed in a few years by the increase of trade.[3] Such indeed proved to be the ingredients of British settlement in Nova Scotia upon the eve of the American Revolution.

II

The first systematic British settlement in Nova Scotia took place under the able administration of Lord Halifax at the Board of Trade, and the new capital of the province bore his name. More than 1,400 British settlers, originally intended for the Annapolis district, reached Halifax in 1749, followed by a smaller party which founded Dartmouth on the other side of the harbour in 1750. A

[1] Shirley to Newcastle, Mar. 28, 1750, *Shirley Correspondence*, i. 500, 470.
[2] Shirley to Bedford, Feb. 27, 1748, *id.*, i. 470; *Nova Scotia, A Series*, 33. 177 ff.
[3] *America and West Indies*, 63. 102 ff., 108 ff., &c.

second type, chiefly German protestants, began to arrive in 1751, and finally, in 1753, peopled the southern districts of Lunenburg County. Their struggle from destitution to prosperity is a remarkable chapter of stolid thrift, though it complicated rather than simplified the immediate problems of civil government. Neither of these migrations, in fact, proved to be a dominant factor in the political development of the province. Halifax grew rapidly by the arrival of 'useful men from New England', but Cornwallis, who had come out as governor with the expedition of 1749, was not favourably impressed with the original personnel. The discharged soldier was seldom a resourceful pioneer, and there were but too many of 'the King's bad bargains'.

The Halifax settlement, however, was intended to be but 'part of a great plan'. Shirley, who was now in England, reported that 'when the Supply for the Maintenance of Nova Scotia came on in the House of Commons . . . it was not only unanimously voted, but with the most visible Satisfaction on the Countenance of every Member that was ever known there upon any such occasion, most explicit strong declarations were made by the Minister in favour of its Support and of the Importance of it to the Nation'.[1] The Board of Trade, like Shirley himself, had now come to rely upon the New England settler to 'add strength' and cohesion to less resourceful elements of colonization.[2] Even Colonel Lawrence, who could scarcely be charged with a taste for civil as distinct from military traditions of government, was known to express a downright preference for the pioneer settler ready-made in the rugged school of New England.

This was the personnel of settlement in the province when the whole basic problem with which Shirley and every administrator in Nova Scotia had been struggling for fifteen years was transformed by the expulsion of the Acadians in 1755. Neither the idyll which tradition has woven about the Acadians in Nova Scotia nor the tragedy of their exile was primarily a matter of government, though it is on record that Lieut.-Governor Armstrong had proposed an Assembly in 1732 with the French Acadians represented in order to 'secure obedience to their own Acts'.[3] The problem of

[1] Shirley to Josiah Willard, Apr. 27, 1753, *Shirley Correspondence*, ii. 10. Shirley was one of the commissioners for the adjustment of the boundaries between Nova Scotia and New France. See Osgood, *op. cit.*, iii. 574, &c.

[2] Lords of Trade to Cornwallis, Oct. 16, 1749, *Board of Trade, Nova Scotia*, 34. 163 ff.; Lords of Trade to Bedford, Mar. 9, 1750, *id.*, 206 ff.

[3] Armstrong to Newcastle, Nov. 15, 1732, *America and West Indies*, 30. 29.

'the neutral French', however, had complicated the security of British interests in Nova Scotia at every point; and to Shirley, as we have seen, that security was the key not only to 'the King's Woods' and the fishery but to the safety of New England and the control of the North Atlantic. Thus the two specifics unceasingly advocated to this end by Shirley and his school were nothing less than basic strategy in the impending struggle for a continent. One was to take Louisbourg and to hold Nova Scotia in force as the key to the whole Atlantic seaboard. The other, as we have seen, was to fill the rich lands on the frontiers with 6,000 British settlers under a form of government capable of 'attracting New England Settlers to live there'.

Had both—or perhaps either—of these projects been carried out in time, it is conceivable that the attitude of the Acadians might never have invited disaster. The correspondence of old Mascarene with his courtly French manners and humane concern for 'the perilous situation' of the Acadians bears witness that even during the perils of open war they were not incapable of responding to generosity.[1] But the return of Louisbourg to France in 1748, the weakness of the British occupation in Nova Scotia, the sparsity of British settlement, the desperately unscrupulous intrigues of the French agents, the vicissitudes of colonial warfare already overshadowed by signs of a final struggle for colonial power in America, left all the elements of tragedy at large in the land. Shirley himself, in default of vigorous action by the British Government or an unequivocal oath of allegiance by the Acadians, was prepared to deal summarily with the intrigues from Louisbourg and Quebec, and to transport the most troublesome of the French population from the frontiers to less exposed locations at Annapolis.[2] But by 1755—the year of Braddock's defeat—the beginnings of the Seven Years' War were already smouldering from Beausejour to Fort Duquesne. Lieut.-Governor Lawrence[3] and his Council decided to cut the Gordian knot, and the Acadian exiles were scattered

[1] Mascarene to Shirley, July 28, 1744, *British Museum*, add. 19071, 516; to Lords of Trade, May 12, 1747, *America and West Indies*, vol. 595; to Secretary of State, June 15, 1748, *id.*, 31. 4, &c.

[2] Shirley to Bedford, Mar. 3, 1748. *America and West Indies*, 63, 108 ff.

[3] Governor Philipps had visited the province only twice during his long governorship from 1719 to 1749. Cornwallis who succeeded Philipps was followed by Hopson, Apr. 4, 1752. Lawrence was appointed Lieut.-Governor Aug. 6, 1754, and upon Hopson's resignation the following year was appointed 'Captain General and Governor-in-Chief', Dec. 18, 1755. *Board of Trade, Nova Scotia*, 13. H. 85; 15. H. 248; 16. I. 1.

along the Atlantic seaboard from Georgia to New Hampshire. Not until three years later, after disasters had ravaged the frontiers from Oswego to Ticonderoga, did the struggle between France and Britain enter upon its last phase in the final capture of Louisbourg in 1758.

By that time Shirley himself, the most consistent advocate of British power in Nova Scotia, was no longer directly associated with British policy. His work in America was over; but in his lodgings on Conduit Street in London whence this 'ablest colonial governor of the time' was constrained to beg of Newcastle a petty governorship in the Bahama Islands 'after so many Years in faithfull Services to the Crown',[1] Shirley must have reflected with some bitterness upon the vicissitudes of fortune in the final achievement of the 'Great Plan' for Nova Scotia.

III

'Cruel and unnecessary'[2] as the expulsion of the Acadians may finally have proved to be in the military struggle for Nova Scotia, the indirect results upon the development of the province were very far-reaching. In 1755, upon the eve of the expulsion, Chief Justice Belcher estimated the number of Acadians at 8,000,[3] and the British at scarcely more than 3,000. As it happened, the removal of the Acadians not only simplified the problem of government for those who remained but resulted indirectly in quickening the tendencies which Shirley had encouraged from the beginning. The settlement of New Englanders in the wake of the Acadian exile, and in increasing numbers after the fall of Louisbourg, introduced a basic element into the population which profoundly modified the prospects of representative government and left a mark upon Nova Scotian history for many generations to come.

The forerunners of this migration had long since found their way to Nova Scotia under the normal incentives of private enterprise. They were already familiar with the fur trade and the almost inexhaustible resources of timber and naval supplies. They had already exploited the fisheries and the trade, not always strictly legitimate, with the French inhabitants and even with the French authorities at Louisbourg. But the New Englanders who now

[1] *Shirley Correspondence*, ii. 599.

[2] Osgood, *op. cit.*, iv. 361.

[3] Of these 1,000 were at Annapolis, 1,500 at Minas, 1,500 at Piziquid (Windsor), and 4,000 at Chignecto. *America and West Indies*, 597. 101.

settled the rich lands on the St. John River, at the head of the Bay of Fundy, in the Annapolis Valley, and on the south shore, came to live upon the soil and to establish what Chatham afterwards called 'a permanent—natural right in the place'. Such 'ever speak the voice of the people', and perhaps there were no more enterprising and resourceful pioneers upon the Atlantic seaboard.

During the early years of the Seven Years' War the atrocities of border warfare not only halted this migration but forced the abandonment of Lawrencetown and other pioneer settlements. With the final reduction of Louisbourg in 1758 the tide set in with silent but steady flow. Lawrence, it is clear, had fallen under the spell of Shirley's doctrine, with more than Shirley's optimism. In the autumn of 1757 he wrote that 20,000 families could be settled in the districts from Annapolis to Chignecto alone. Two proclamations were issued, one almost immediately after the fall of Louisbourg (October 12, 1758) and another in the following February.[1] Two months later agents from associations of settlers in Rhode Island and Connecticut were already upon the ground with surveyors and every resource of skill and enterprise. The response from Massachusetts, New York, and Pennsylvania was equally prompt. The settlements of Horton, Cornwallis, Falmouth, and Newport in the Annapolis Valley, of Oromocto on the St. John River, of Sackville and Cumberland at the head of the Bay of Fundy, were drawn from this tried material. 'Their mark', writes Dr. MacMechan, 'is on every settlement they made to this day; and the beautiful valley of Annapolis, one long, watered garden between its sheltering hills, testifies to their character and justifies the policy that planted them there.'[2]

Many were already accounted 'rich'.[3] Thus while Lawrence bluntly complained that 'every soldier that has come into this province since the establishment of Halifax has either quitted it or become a dram-seller', the New Englanders prospered from the outset by their own thrift and sobriety and enterprise. The party which settled at Liverpool on the 'south shore' of the province brought not only horses and cattle and sheep with them but thirteen fishing schooners of their own. The crews sailed at once for

[1] *Board of Trade, Nova Scotia*, 16, I. 46, 87, 90.

[2] *Canada and its Provinces*, xiii. 110.

[3] Belcher to Lords of Trade, Dec. 12, 1760. *Board of Trade, Nova Scotia*, 18. L. 17.

the Banks leaving the rest of the party to erect three saw-mills on the river and to build from native pine and oak their houses for the winter. Seven years later a census of the province showed more than 25,000 head of live-stock, an output of more than 1,250,000 feet of sawn 'lumber', a catch of over 50,000 quintals of cod and 10,500 barrels of salmon and other fish, a fleet of nearly 500 schooners, fishing-boats, and larger ships, and a crop of 67,000 bushels of grain. More than half the population was classified as 'Americans'. To most of them the traditions of colonial self-government were already familiar. Without relinquishing their intercourse with the provinces from which they had come they developed in the land of their adoption a spirited and sturdy self-reliance which survived in many curious ways until 'the American question' was solved upon British soil by the practice of responsible government.

The First Assembly

I

The issues in colonial government which accompanied and followed the achievement of Shirley's 'Great Plan' at the hands of Lawrence, his disciple in Nova Scotia, and of Halifax, were more than usually notable; for the next decade and a half sealed the fate of the first Empire, and the Nova Scotia Assembly of 1758 was the only one in America which did not eventually side with the Revolution. Though representing a predominantly New England population, it supplied, as we shall see, a commentary—not without poignant contrasts—upon the policy of Carleton and 'the King's friends' in the adjoining province of Quebec in discarding the scheme of settlement and of government prescribed for both provinces by Halifax and the Board of Trade.

Governor Cornwallis's Commission and Instructions contained directions for calling a General Assembly 'according to the usage of the rest of our Colonies and plantations in America'. No attempt was made by Cornwallis to carry these instructions into effect, and it must be admitted that the first settlers at Halifax showed little desire and less aptitude for self-government. The New Englanders were less complacent. There was already a skilfully directed claim on foot for an Assembly when Jonathan Belcher, Jr., arrived as Chief Justice of the province in 1754. Belcher who was a son of a former governor of Massachusetts—now Governor of New Jersey—immediately raised the issue in the council. Writing to John

Pownall, the indefatigable Secretary of the Board of Trade under Halifax, he quoted the historic phrase in the governor's Commission authorizing governor and council to legislate for the province only '*by and with the consent of the General Assembly of the Province*', and submitted the vital question 'whether the Provincial Laws are binding as they have not been assented to by an Assembly'.[1]

It has been customary to charge the Board of Trade during these critical years preceding the Revolution with every delinquency from mere negligence to narrow and selfish meddlesomeness. After Hillsborough, long a member of the Board, had supplanted its functions as first Secretary of State for the Colonies in 1768, it was sent like the scapegoat into the wilderness; with none to defend it, all sorts of apocryphal and vicarious sins could safely be laid upon its head by the high-priests of royal power in England. The evidence from Nova Scotia and Quebec during this period does not warrant that tradition. The dominant influence of Lord Halifax and the unassuming ability of John Pownall, the permanent Secretary of the Board, are traceable in many ways throughout the critical period of early New England settlement and the calling of the first Assembly in Nova Scotia. It is noteworthy too that Halifax was in the Southern Department and John Pownall back at the Board of Trade when the instruments for the government of Quebec—almost identical in policy with those for Nova Scotia—were drafted after 1763. In neither province, as we shall see, was the policy of the Board wanting in consistency or discernment, and more than one project of coercion in the early stages of the Revolution met here a resolute opposition.

The action of the Board in 1755 was prompt and decisive. Chief Justice Belcher's letter was dated January 16, 1766. By April 29 the issue had been referred by the Board to the Attorney- and Solicitor-General, William Murray and Sir Richard Lloyd, and a report obtained that 'the Governor & Council alone are not Authorized . . . to make Laws'. Scarcely more than a week later instructions were on their way to Lawrence in Halifax that

> 'tho' the calling an Assembly may, in the present Circumstances of the Colony, be difficult, and attended with some Inconveniences, yet as the Attorney and Solicitor General are of opinion that the Governor and Council have no power to enact Laws, We cannot see how the Government can be properly carried on without an Assembly.

[1] Jan. 16, 1755, *A. Series*, 57. 58.

. . . It is of the greatest consequence to the peace & Welfare of the Province, that the opinion of His Majesty's Attorney and Solicitor General should not be made publick, until an Assembly can be convened, and an Indemnification passed for such Acts as have been done under Laws enacted without any proper Authority.'[1]

II

To Lawrence's brusque military temper this pother about an Assembly was 'altogether a point of Law', and the governor's resourcefulness in putting off the evil day must have brought a smile to the more indulgent members of the Board. It would be necessary 'to provide for the expence of a House for the Assembly to sit in, and for a Clerk and such Salary'd Officers as may be thought necessary for their Attendance'.[2] Since their lordships were 'pressing on the affair', the governor begged 'an Additional Instruction thereon'. An Assembly would 'serve only to create heats, Animosities and disunion among the People'. There were a few 'malevolent and ill-designing Men' in the province, but the 'well disposed part' were 'not in the least uneasy', and if any had joined in the petition for an Assembly they had been 'led into it thro' inadvertancy and the Specious pretences of the Persons I have been just now describing'.[3]

For two years the governor had his way. The Board's policy was urged from London with conviction tempered by a measure of indulgence, but in Nova Scotia the governor's will was not to be challenged with impunity. One hundred and eighty-six merchants of Halifax, having 'time after time, applyed to the Governor and Council' for the rights 'enjoyed in all other His Majesty's Colonys in America' as promised by 'His Majesty's Proclamation . . . at the beginning of the Settlement', raised a subscription to engage an agent in Great Britain for the purpose of urging 'the earnest and almost unanimous desire of the people'. Anonymous letters with less restraint found their way to the Board, seeking protection from the 'Fury & Resentment of the Governors, & all the placemen' against those who had petitioned for an Assembly, and imploring the Board to 'recall the present Governor, and send out another divested of Military Lawless Principles'. Monckton,

[1] *Board of Trade, Nova Scotia,* 15. H. 293; Lords of Trade to Lawrence, May 7, 1755, *id.*, 36. 118. Murray was afterwards Lord Chief Justice.

[2] Lawrence to the Lords of Trade, Dec. 8, 1755, *id.*, 68. 166.

[3] Lawrence to the Lords of Trade, Nov. 3, 1756, *id.*, 60. 156.

the Lieut.-Governor, was 'a thorough paced, Military, Arbitrary, and Inconstitutional Man'.

Grand juries with conspicuous moderation cited the practical inconveniences to trade and industry. For Englishmen to be deprived of proper legislation was 'not known in Any other Place in his Majesty's Dominions. . . . We should not have troubled your Lordships could We have Obtain'd any Relief here'. The memorial is certified by Chief Justice Belcher. And finally a memorial by four members of the council itself must have convinced the Board that peremptory measures were necessary. Despite the urgent advice of the council, the governor 'was pleased to declare that he would not issue the Writ, but should leave the Matter to the discretion of the Lieut. Governor as Commander in Chief in his Absence'. The council, therefore, 'did move the Lieut. Governor at the Council Board, that the Writ might issue'; but 'to our great surprise we were inform'd by the Lieut. Governor that it was his Excellency's Opinion and his own that it was not a proper time to Call an Assembly'. The appeal to the Board of Trade was their last resort since no minutes of their protest were entered 'tho' desired, in the Council Books. . . . We have hitherto silently submitted to the weight of His Excellency's Power and Influence'.[1]

The patience of the Board, however, had been exhausted, and instructions which admitted of no evasion were already upon the way. The fact that the same problem arose in the province of Quebec at the most critical stage of the American Revolution—not only the same problem but the same policy urged by the same Board—may warrant a careful examination of the principles underlying this clear precedent in Nova Scotia. The inconveniences pointed out by Governor Lawrence were conceded:

> 'Yet We cannot but be of opinion (continued the Board) that the Want of a proper Authority in the Governor and Council to enact such Laws as must be absolutely necessary in the Administration of Civil Government, is an Inconvenience and Evil still greater than all these. . . . We can by no means think, that that or any other Reason can justify the Continuation of the Exercise of an illegal Authority. . . . What you say with regard to the Council of Virginia passing Laws in the first infancy of that Colony is very true; but then . . . it was a power of very short duration, and in later times, since the Constitution of this Country has been restored to its true Principles, has never been thought adviseable to be executed.'[2]

[1] *Board of Trade, Nova Scotia*, 61. 1 ff., 158 ff., 109 ff., &c.

[2] *Id.*, 59. 22 ff.

There was no escape from these instructions. The governor issued the writs, and on October 2, 1758, met the first Assembly in what is now British North America—the only British Assembly upon the continent that preceded and survived the American Revolution.[1]

III

Nova Scotia now took its place as the youngest, if not perhaps the humblest, among the normal provinces of the first Empire. Three years before, an Assembly had finally been convened in Georgia with a population of less than 4,000 whites. This also, it is clear, was part of the deliberate policy of the Board. Perhaps the primitive house about which Lawrence had been so concerned 'for the Assembly to sit in' at Halifax was as comely in its architecture as that described to the Board of Trade by Governor Reynolds in Savannah where the chimney and one end of the building once 'fell with a crash and the magistrates came near being buried in the ruins'.[2] At all events when Governor Ellis, William Knox's old friend, was transferred from Georgia to Nova Scotia after the death of Lawrence in 1760, the new charge was regarded as a promotion.

But 'dependency' in Nova Scotia was accentuated not only by policy but by nature and by self-interest. With little immediate prospect of paying its own way, the Assembly had little incentive either to use or to abuse the power of the purse by which the other powers of provincial Assemblies in America had so diligently been extorted. In Nova Scotia as in Georgia the deficits in the cost of civil government were met by the House of Commons, and the power of the purse in effect lay with the British Government. Much of the early prosperity of the province, moreover, was the result of lavish military and naval expenditures during the Seven Years' War. Fish and naval stores were the staple exports. The situation of the province at the threshold of New France gave it an importance out of all proportion to its population and revenues. A measure of accommodation could scarcely fail to result from these mutual interests. Governor Lawrence greeted his first Assembly amidst the rejoicings that attended the final capture of Louisbourg. The first session closed in the midst of Wolfe's

[1] The writs, &c., were based upon the precedents of New Hampshire and Georgia. Twelve out of the twenty members of the first Assembly were elected from the province at large. *Board of Trade, Nova Scotia*, 36. 273; *A. Series*, 61. 1; *Journals*, Oct. 2, 1758.

[2] Osgood, *op cit.*, iv. 246.

campaign against Quebec. The House was duly impressed with 'the Happiness and prosperity . . . from His Majesty's Royal Favour to this Infant Colony'.

Without local traditions and without the central dignity which comes only with administrative responsibility, newly constituted popular assemblies have seldom been noted for studied moderation. From many of these normal tendencies the first Assembly in Nova Scotia was saved by the temper and experience of the men who composed it. Many of them were native New Englanders with more than the average knowledge of the issues of the day. Despite the bitterness of 'the seven years' war for an Assembly', the mutual misgivings between the governor and the House quickly vanished.[1] Before the first session was over Lawrence found himself playing the benevolent mediator between council and Assembly, and begging them 'to Record nothing . . . to tarnish the Credit of your proceedings'.[2]

With a spirit and a knowledge of precedent which the Board of Trade, in reviewing the *Journals*, shrewdly traced to an origin in New England, the House lost no time in asserting privileges both legitimate and otherwise. A resolution for a return of fees and perquisites by all officers of civil government in the province was generally complied with; but John Collier, a member of the council and judge of probate, was also a judge of the Vice-Admiralty Court, and in that capacity quite properly declined to obey the order of the House. The Assembly voted his conduct 'an high Contempt of the Authority of this House', and the excessive fees of the Vice-Admiralty Court 'oppressive to the People and without Colour of Law'. The council tactfully retorted 'that the Resolution, had it been any other than that of the Assembly, would have been a rude and groundless aspersion'.[3] A Bill was passed for the regulation of future elections, 'to which His Excellency Answered that such Power certainly lay with him and Him alone'.[4] The legal adviser of the Board noted from the *Journals* that a Bill had been 'brought in, Read three times, Ingrossed and Ordered to be

[1] Cf. Lawrence to Lords of Trade, Sept. 26, 1758: 'I hope I shall not find in any of them a disposition . . . to dispute the Royal Prerogative, though I observe that too many of the Members chosen are such as have not been the most remarkable for promoting Unity, or Obedience to his Majesty's Governm^{t}. here.' *Board of Trade, Nova Scotia*, 16. I. 75.

[2] Governor's *Messages*, *Journals*, Nov. 3, 1758, Aug. 1, 1759.

[3] *Minutes of Council*, Mar. 29, 1759. Collier, in fact, had signed the protest of the council in favour of an Assembly. *A. Series*, 61. 109.

[4] *Journals*, Feb. 17, 1759.

sent up for Concurrence, all in one Day'. There had also been 'Encroachment upon the Right of the Governor', and it was imperative that 'some stop may be put to their continuing to Intermeddle therein'.[1]

But these were the views of critics; upon safer grounds the Assembly was spirited enough to hold its own. Perhaps the most discerning measure of the session was a motion for the appointment of a provincial treasurer after the model of New York. The 'Hinshelwood incident' too became historic. One of the members of the House was cursed roundly in the streets of Halifax for the meddlesomeness of the Assembly in criticizing Hinshelwood's office. The offender was summoned to the bar of the House where he humbly apologized both orally and in writing, and was placed in custody until the following day. In 1759 the first Assembly was dissolved. They had 'unanimously resolved . . . that they would all serve without Reward'. The writs for the new House were delayed until the new 'Freeholders of King's County' could reach their farms—the vanguard, as we have seen, during the summer of 1759, of a steady and almost spontaneous migration which changed the whole outlook of the province. Thenceforth, until the coming of the Loyalists, the control of the Assembly and of the province at large passed steadily into their hands.

IV

For the decade and a half preceding the outbreak of the American Revolution the *Journals* of the Assembly contain little evidence of an unaccommodating temper except in the periodical contests with the council in which the House usually looked, not in vain, for support from the Board of Trade. The governor and council, fortified by their control over British parliamentary grants and local administration, regulated the franchise, the electoral districts, and 'all Rules for the Electing of Members'.[2] The dissolution of the House was long determined by resolution of the council,[3] and more than one attempt was made to regulate the quorum and the standing rules of the House in the interests of the administration.

The response of the House to these encroachments was always

[1] Sir Matthew Lamb to Lords of Trade, Mar. 5, 1760. For the influence of legal counsel upon constitutional development in the colonies see Dickerson, *American Government, 1696–1765*, 264 ff.

[2] *Minutes of Council*, July 5, 1775.

[3] Cf. *Minutes of Council*, Apr. 2, 1770: 'Resolved that the General Assembly (elected May, 1765) be Disolved.'

spirited and frequently reached a high level of political sagacity. The 'quorum controversy' may be taken to illustrate tactics on the part of the Assembly which became traditional in Nova Scotia, and remained an unwritten law of political strategy until responsible government itself was finally achieved. The difficulty of securing a quorum in regular attendance in the Assembly was the subject of a report from a committee of the council. The report went to Dartmouth, Secretary of State for the Colonies, who returned it to the governor with instructions to lay it before the Assembly. The resolution of the Assembly in reply was written within a few weeks of Lexington. They had not 'words to express the high sense we have of the goodness and Justice of Our Gracious King & His Ministers on this occasion, who by referring Your Excellency to the Legislature of this Province on this most interesting & constitutional measure, have shown their strict regard to the rights of the People in this Province'. The proposal of the council to fix the quorum at nine instead of twelve, and to allot four additional members to the town and county of Halifax, was 'subversive of real Representation & in its consequences must render a Governor of this province absolute', since it would 'command a Quorum at all times on the spot'.

> 'With a dependant Council & a Majority of such a Quorum of Assembly, what might not an Ambitious Governor effect.
>
> Dictatorial powers may be necessary to quell insurrections or to rule a disaffected People; but where no such principles exist, the exertion of such Powers will create them. . . .
>
> These great and good purposes will be best promoted by preserving the freedom of Elections & rendering the applications of the House of Assembly to the King & Parliament for the Redress of Grievances, easy.'

In preserving the 'Privileges of the People' His Excellency would 'best defend the prerogatives of Our Common Sovereign'.[1]

In such an atmosphere the stand of the thirteen colonies—'not against tyranny inflicted but only against tyranny anticipated'—awakened little response. The Kings County farmer had brothers or cousins among the 'patriots' of Massachusetts or Rhode Island, and his rugged opposition to the whole official policy of coercion is everywhere in evidence; but extreme measures were generally deplored. Lord William Campbell, the governor, reported in 1770 that he could not discover in the Nova Scotia Assembly 'any of

[1] *Minutes of Council*, June 29, 1775.

that Licentious principle, with which the Neighbouring Colonies are so highly infected'.[1] The apathy of the province invited caustic criticism from New England where the Nova Scotian Assembly's professed 'sense of the Greatest Loyalty and Gratitude' was interpreted after Hobbes's definition as a lively sense of favours to come.

In truth every interest predisposed the province to the constitutionalist point of view. After lavish expenditures upon the military and naval establishments as well as the civil government of the province, the prospect of parliamentary taxation for imperial purposes was not alarming, while the direct benefits to be anticipated from the new imperial policy in America were out of all proportion to the revenues or population of the province. There was a suggestion that Nova Scotia might become the 'Head Quarters of the British Land and Sea Forces in America'.[2] The imperial project of making executive officers of government and the military forces of the Crown in America independent of the local Assemblies was not only an accomplished fact but a commonplace in Nova Scotia. The province had long been familiar with the supremacy of Parliament 'which they have never thought a Burden';[3] hitherto the result had not been tyranny. In the contest with the council and eventually with the governor himself, the Assembly was to find its staunchest allies in the Board of Trade and the Secretary of State. In the Address on the 'quorum controversy' the House recorded its conviction that both Crown and Parliament of Great Britain 'have nothing more at Heart than that His Majesty's American Subjects should enjoy constitutional freedom'.[4]

While this may have been the general faith of the Assembly, there were extremists on both sides. In both council and Assembly there were those whose attachment to the British cause was marked by a degree of subserviency which betrayed the presence of less creditable motives. On the other hand there were a few who were as 'licentious' as the bands that were tarring and feathering Vice-Admiralty officials in Massachusetts. As the Revolution took form in the other colonies these extremists asserted themselves in Nova Scotia; the one type, as was to be expected, openly and at times

[1] To Hillsborough, June 13, 1770, *Colonial Correspondence, Nova Scotia*, 5. 36.

[2] *Address of the Assembly*, June 23, 1775, *A. Series*, 94. 11 ff.

[3] Mauger to Pownall, Oct. 16, 1775. *Id.*, 93. 213.

[4] Quoted in *Minutes of Council*, June 29, 1775.

arrogantly; the other cautiously and in secret. Nothing contributed more to separate the two, to confirm the one in abject subserviency and to drive the other to desperation, than the arrival of Francis Legge as governor of the province in October, 1773.

THE 'ALARMING CRISIS'

I

Governor Legge must have belonged to that school of British officers to whose arrogance and narrow prejudices much of the irremediable bitterness of the Revolutionary War was directly attributable. He was a relative of the Earl of Dartmouth who had succeeded Hillsborough as Secretary for America in 1772. Both Dartmouth and his protégé bore a name long favourably known in America.[1] Even Legge's enemies—and before he left Nova Scotia there were few indeed who did not belong to that number—could not deny him courage in danger and honesty in administration. After Lexington he sent off four regiments of troops to Gage's assistance, and at one period the dockyards and stores at Halifax, valued at half a million pounds, were guarded by exactly three dozen ragged regulars. But in Legge's forthright character arrogance itself was ingenuous almost beyond belief; and such was the vindictiveness of his temper, the truculence which marked his personal relations with all but the narrow circle of favourites who enjoyed his confidence, the almost unbelievable fury with which he pursued his personal animosities—against Lieut.-Governor Francklin, against the aged Chief Justice, against the Attorney-General, the Secretary of the Province, the chief members of the council, the Speaker of the Assembly—that his name in Nova Scotia is still held in popular execration.

Legge came to Nova Scotia at the most critical period in the American Revolution. His views of that struggle seem to have been unrelieved by a single ray of discernment. In May, 1774, he assured the Secretary of the Board of Trade that the disorders in America would yield to nothing but 'coercive measures', and that the 'single example made of the Town of Boston will be a means to convince the Americans, that it is their Interest as well as duty to be amenable to the Laws of Great Britain'. He wrote to Admiral

[1] But cf. Dartmouth to Legge, May 4, 1774: 'The Governorship of Nova Scotia will probably be vacant for you very soon, if not, another will, to one or other of wch. you will be appointed.' *Dartmouth Papers*, I. 2. 853. *Pub. Arch. Can.*

Graves in July that 'the Americans have nothing in view more than publishing some impertinent resolves which they will never be able to carry into execution'. 'I am clear in my opinion', he stated to Dartmouth, 'that His Majesty's Governors should be invested with greater authority' in order to 'Suppress in embrio opposition to government, and to preserve a due Subordination'.[1] Members of his own council wrote of 'this Ignorant Tyrant our Governor'. The British Government, deluged with petitions against him, was at last moved to express His Majesty's 'Displeasure that . . . the public peace should be disturbed and His Majesty's Service obstructed by Ill humour, Anger and Resentments in Matters of the most trivial moment respecting merely the Domestick Oeconomy of the Province'.[2] When Legge was at last recalled there is a tradition that he was seen upon the decks of the frigate shaking his fist at the shores of Halifax.

Governor Legge's administration was one long feud with what he called 'the inveterate party' in Nova Scotia. There can be no doubt that 'the Mauger influence' was a dominant factor in the commercial life of the province. Joshua Mauger, once a resident of Halifax, later the agent of the Nova Scotia Assembly, was at this time member for Poole in the British House of Commons. A long intimacy with John Pownall, the Secretary of the Board of Trade, and an assured access to Dartmouth himself are obvious from the *Dartmouth Papers*. More than one member of the council owed their appointment to 'the Mauger influence'; the appropriations of the little Assembly too seem to indicate a measure of those petty accommodations with which eighteenth-century mercantilism must have been riddled. The correspondence of Mauger's agent at Halifax—a member of the council—throws a curious light upon this 'seamy side' of colonial government in which fishing-fleets and smuggling, West Indian molasses, rum and local distilleries, army contracts and backstairs influence, must have played no small part. It is clear, however, that the 'Mauger interests' were by no means associated with much of that indigenous opinion in Nova Scotia during the Revolution which had its remoter origin in New England. Mauger's agent himself deplores the signs of this 'Levelling Principle' in the Assembly, and charges the most conspicuous of their leaders with that 'Levelling Spirit that has Ruin'd America'.[3]

[1] Legge to Pownall, May 29, 1774, *A. Series*, 90. 162; 90. 196; 94. 113.
[2] Suffolk to Legge, Oct. 16, 1775. *Id.*, 94. 207.
[3] Butler to Mauger, May 6, 1775. *Dartmouth Papers*, I. 2. 1119.

But these subtle distinctions were lost upon Governor Legge, who seems to have been initiated into the feud by the opposing faction. By January, 1775, Legge had entered the fray with an invincible conviction that 'these Menopolizers' had been responsible for filling 'Every Coffee House in London . . . with Falsehood and unjust aspersions against every Governor his Majesty has thought fit to appoint'. Michael Francklin of Windsor, the Lieut.-Governor, was in 'total dependance on this Party'. They had 'so compleatly acquired the Influence and Command of the Inhabitants of this Town that there is at present scarce a Merchant, Shop Keeper, Tradesman, Retailer of Spirituous Liquors, and all other Labourers and low Macanicks but intirely have their dependance on this Party'.[1] In an official dispatch to Dartmouth four members of the council are roundly charged with guilty collusion in fiscal irregularities which the governor hoped to detect. Against one of them, Jonathan Binney, whose name had headed the subscription list for an agent to press for an Assembly in 1757 and who had been elected to the first House the following year, the governor pursued a relentless vendetta which did not cease even with his recall. Despite the recorded advice of the council, the governor directed an action against Binney in the Courts, and according to a petition of five members of the council headed by the Chief Justice himself, caused him 'to be unjustly sued and imprisoned'. A special Exchequer Court was constituted for nine months 'for the more effective investigation' of such cases. The governor appeared in person 'at Trials instituted by his Order . . . overawing and influencing the Jury and Officers of Justice'.[2] Binney was confined in the Halifax jail with his wife and children for nearly two months and a half, and finally sought redress, not in vain, in London.

Not to be outdone, the governor gave Burrow, the Inspector-General of Customs, leave of absence and sent him home to defend his interests. The egregious correspondence between Legge and Burrow is an almost incredible record of petty vindictiveness. When Burrow finally advised the governor that he was to be summoned home[3] it was still with the hope of 'effectually crushing

[1] Legge to Dartmouth, *A. Series*, 93. 83.

[2] Jan. 1, 1776. *Id.*, 95. 14. Cf. charges against Legge, *id.*, 95. 139: 'even sent to his own house for Wine and other refreshment to be brought him to the Court House, that he may not be absent on said Trial.'

[3] 'In which I most cordially joined; on the proviso, Francklin was dismissed.' Burrow to Legge, Feb. 28, 1776. *Id.* 95. 148.

Dartmouth, who supported his kinsman unreservedly until the investigation

these Vipers, & nest of Cormorants'. Dartmouth, however, had left the American Department, and Germain's measures were prompt and decisive. Legge was not to return to Nova Scotia. A British Order in Council directed the governor to assent to a Bill passed by the Assembly 'for the relief of Jonathan Binney'. For Francklin, whose magnanimous and exemplary conduct throughout this ordeal shines like a beacon, a 'kind and friendly letter' from Pownall, the Joint Secretary of the American Department, at last brought 'Balm for the Wound' he had received after sixteen years of public service.[1]

Legge's relations with almost every interest in the province were poisoned by the same narrow and suspicious temper. William Smith of Halifax, Justice of the Peace, Judge of the inferior Court of Common Pleas, and member of the Assembly, invited a few merchants of the town to meet him 'on business of consequence', the business of consequence being the disposal of a shipment of tea from New England which did not belong to the East India Company. Smith, when summoned before the governor and council, admitted that 'were it the property of the East India Company the People wou'd be prejudiced against it', and that he 'would have had nothing to do with it'. After the 'Boston tea party'—Dartmouth himself had sent directions for disposing of the Company's tea in Nova Scotia—this savoured of sedition. Smith's commission was cancelled and he was 'removed from those & all other his Employments under Government'. Fillis, another member of the Assembly, suffered the same fate for his 'sentiments in opposition to the importation of Tea'. Both were charged with complicity in the burning of hay intended for Gage's cavalry in Boston. The Assembly in defending them as 'dutiful and loyal subjects' was 'unanimously of Opinion that the said Reports are base infamous and false'. This action the governor interpreted as a combination with his enemies, and attributed it to the fact that 'the Majority of our Assembly are Persons born in New England'.[2]

II

The confusion which finally overwhelmed Legge's administration in Nova Scotia arose from his active measures against the thirteen colonies. In Nova Scotia under Legge, as in Quebec

in London, finally withdrew his protection. *Dartmouth Papers*, I. 2. 1255, 1305, &c.

[1] *A. Series*, 95. 320.

[2] *Minutes of Council*, Sept. 16, 1774; *Journals*, M. 397. 11, p. 26; Legge to Dartmouth, July 31, 1775, *A. Series*, 94. 48.

under Carleton, there is discernible a deliberate reversal of the 'Great Plan' of Shirley and of Halifax for the northern provinces.

Legge lost no opportunity of girding at the New Englanders. The Acadians had been driven out and their fertile lands appropriated by wealthy settlers who had 'never . . . contributed towards the charges and expenses of Government from their Real and Personal Estates, one Shilling'.[1] The atrocities of Indian warfare and the insoluble problems of the 'neutral French' during the Seven Years' War were now forgotten. In June, 1775, Gage in Boston instructed Legge to raise the newly arrived 'Hylanders' of the Pictou district and to 'secure the Indians to our Side . . . I may possibly have occasion for them, in these parts; . . . I wish you would likewise try the temper of the Accadians, remaining in your Province. Its possible that some of them may be tempted to rise for the King'.[2] Legge responded with a proposal to raise a regiment 'to be compos'd of Germans, Neutrals and Irish'. The New Englanders, he added, were 'too much of the same Sentiment with the people of the Country from whence they come'.[3] Here was a strange reversal of the policy of Lawrence. The governor hoped for a third of his regiment from the Acadians, and more than a hundred men actually responded. Martial law was declared in December, 1775. When two measures were finally forced through the Assembly for the levying of every fifth man in the province by ballot and an assessment in specie for the defence of the province, the result was 'an universal uproar'[4] which the governor characteristically attributed to treasonable motives.

Petitions poured in against both measures. In Truro specie was so scarce that it was 'impossible . . . to raise money if it were to save our lives'. The inhabitants of Yarmouth were 'true Friends and Loyal Subjects to George our King', but they were 'almost all . . . born in New England'. 'We have Fathers, Brothers and Sisters in that Country', they added, 'divided between natural affection to our nearest relations, and good Faith and Friendship to our King and Country.' From Cumberland County nearly 250 petitioners protested that 'it must be the greatest piece of Cruelty and Imposition, for them to be subjected to march . . . in arms against their Friends and Relatives'.[5]

[1] Legge to Dartmouth, Nov. 15, 1774. *A. Series*, 91. 110.

[2] 'Gain their Priest (if there is one with them) and you will succeed.' Gage to Legge, June 7, 1775. *Id.*, 94. 133.

[3] *Id.*, 94. 59, 151.

[4] *Id.*, 94. 289; 95. 61, 108.

[5] *Id.*, 95. 34; 94. 300, 328.

From the Annapolis Valley there were fewer petitions, but the egregious Captain Stanton, sent by the governor to 'discover their Principles—Views—Sentiments—Wishes—Hopes—and Fears' sent in a report which confirmed Legge's worst prepossessions. 'Their Principles are Republican—Their Views, to Subvert the English Constitution in this Province—Their Sentiments, taken generally, are, that there is too much power vested in the Governor. . . . Their Wishes are, that the Rebels . . . may invade this Province. . . . Their Hopes are, to profit by the confusion. . . . Their Fears are, least by mistake they should join the weaker Party.' 'As nineteen out of twenty are natives of New England,' Stanton concluded, 'to put a Confidence in such Fellows would be acting like the man who cherished a snake in his bosom, till heated with the warmth of his blood, it bit him to death.' In commending Stanton's report to Dartmouth, the governor found in these 'most accurate and pertinent observations' evidence alike of Stanton's 'capacity and good conduct', and of the 'base principles which actuate the greater part of the People of this Province'.[1]

Perhaps the best commentary upon this desperate conclusion is to be found in the sequel. Germain replied almost savagely that the promotion proposed by Legge for Captain Stanton was 'entirely disapproved by the King, and he is ordered to return immediately to join his Regiment'.[2] Legge himself was to return at once to England. Francklin, after many ineffectual protests against the governor's 'coercive measures', was at last authorized to adopt other methods. Among the New Englanders of Kings County he enrolled 'more than nine-tenths of all the able men in those Townships' as a volunteer militia under oath for the defence of the province against a projected American invasion.[3]

Petitions for the governor's recall came from almost every free agency in the province. Five members of the council, 'in the most publick manner', formed an association pledged to maintain the British connexion with their lives and fortunes; but in a petition to the Crown they solemnly asserted in the name of 'duty to Your Majesty and Love to Our Country' that 'unless this Gentleman be speedily removed this valuable Province may be lost'.[4] One member of the council, not without a personal interest in the matter, wrote to Mauger that the governor could not remain

[1] *A. Series*, 94. 272, 343.
[2] Feb. 24, 1776, *id.*, 95. 118.
[3] Francklin to Pownall, May 4, 1776, *id.*, 95. 320. For the oath of the volunteers, *id.*, 95. 199.
[4] *Id.*, 95. 14.

'without ruin to the Province'. 'If he is not moved we shall be all in Flame.' A general petition bearing among others the names of the Rector of St. Paul's, the Speaker of the Assembly, a Deputy Judge of Vice-Admiralty, and a Judge of the Court of Common Pleas, affirmed that 'this Your Majesty's valuable Province may be irrecoverably lost, unless Governor Legge be speedily removed'.[1] Francklin too urged his years of public service in Nova Scotia as a warrant for defending the good name of the province. The governor had made

> 'representations highly injurious to the Characters, and reputations of the Officers of Government, and that few or none of the Inhabitants of the Province in General, not even the very Officers of this Government, but what are disaffected, and are inclinable to give countenance and assistance to the Rebells. . . . I do avow and assert that such representations are totally untrue, and without foundation, which can be made appear by a thousand instances'.[2]

III

The weightiest protest, however, came from another quarter, and in the end Dartmouth himself was daunted by it. In the Assembly the deadly animosities which embittered the governor's personal relations were less in evidence. Here, a few weeks after Lexington, an attempt was made to lift the conflict above the level of personal vindictiveness, and to reaffirm in the form of some practicable policy a hope that traditional British methods of reform might yet avail 'in this dreadful and alarming crisis'. In some quarters—perhaps in the minds of the secret drafting committee of the House as they toiled through the long June days of 1775—this hope was scarcely more than an instinctive and desperate faith. But the attempt to formulate that faith constructively is remarkable for its magnanimity and for its courage; for among these humble legislators in the only British Assembly (except that of Prince Edward Island, convened in 1773) destined to survive that 'alarming crisis', there were those who dared to hope that the 'proceedings in this Assembly may possibly have some influence with other Assemblies in America'.

The immediate object of the Address of June 24, 1775, was to urge 'such Regulations, as we conceive most likely to preserve the Inhabitants of this province, in duty and allegiance'. For reasons that are easily surmised the Address is not to be found in the

[1] *A. Series*, 95. 18.
[2] *Id.*, 95. 26.

Journals of the House. Even the record of the drafting committee was 'concealed from me', wrote the governor, 'until it came out in their Printed votes'. After ten days of dour deliberation the Address was finally drawn up in triplicate, one copy going to the King in Council, one to the Speaker of the House of Commons, and one to the Lord Chancellor for the House of Lords.[1] Legge reported that 'on the best information, it . . . contains some projection for the alteration of Government upon the American System of Popularity, which if attended to, may produce the same convulsions in this as in the other Provinces'.[2] The leading spirit was 'a Member Mr. Day, who . . . had resided at Philadelphia where the Legislative Power consists only of Governor and Representatives, the most popular Government in America. . . . The Majority of our Assembly are Persons born in New England'. Their secrecy was 'double dealing'. It was clear to the governor that he required greater authority in order to 'Suppress in embrio opposition to government, and to preserve a due Subordination'.[3]

The temper of the Address itself is a remarkable commentary upon that of the governor. The Assembly was 'animated with the firmest attachment to the Mother Country, Zealous to support her power and consequence, over all the British Dominions, and dreading a Separation from her Government, and protection, as the greatest political evil which can befall us or our posterity'. There was an acknowledgement, unanimously given, of the legislative supremacy of the British Parliament and of an 'indispensable Duty to pay a due proportion of the Expence of this great Empire'. The discharge of this duty without resorting to British parliamentary taxation was undoubtedly the chief constructive feature of the Address, and the method proposed is best summarized perhaps in Day's original motion:

> 'that the Legislature of this Province may be permitted to grant to His Majesty a certain duty of Impost on all Commodities imported into the said Province, not being the Growth of His Majesty's *European* or *American* Dominions (Salt only excepted) and that the Same may be accepted in Lieu of all Taxes, payable in this Province

[1] The Address to the House of Commons is in *A. Series*, 94. 11 ff.

[2] Legge to Dartmouth, June 27, 1775, *id.*, 93. 303.

[3] *Id.*, 94. 48, 113: 'There can be no ill consequences arise from such Powers, because . . . every Honest Man, that has the interests of his King and Country at heart, and his own Reputation, will always take care that no just complaint shall be formed against him.'

It is impossible in this to doubt Legge's honesty and ingenuousness.

by virtue of any Acts of Parliament.' 'So conscious (adds the Address) are we of your Justice and Humanity that we request to know what proportion would be pleasing or agreeable to you.'

In support of their plan they urged that it would never be necessary to alter it, that it would increase automatically with the affluence of the province, that it would not be affected by the increase of gold and silver in the world, and that its effectiveness could be ensured by stringent regulations against illicit trade and fraudulent dealings. It would dispense with a multitude of officials and 'prevent that corruption of manners and that contempt of the crime of perjury which is now become so open and flagrant'. Finally 'appoint good and sufficient Salarys, to the Officers of the Customs and absolutely forbid them to take any Fee'.

The Assembly sought other reforms of less immediate urgency; assemblies to be elected triennially and by ballot; revenue officers to be ineligible for both council and Assembly; judges of the Supreme Court to 'have their Commission during good behaviour in the same manner as in England'; the boundaries of the counties to be fixed by the Legislature; sheriffs to preside over elections instead of a Provost-Marshal—'if we are not relieved in this particular, we can have no pretensions even to the name of Freemen'.

> 'Finally, we most humbly request, that the Assembly of this province may be called together annually, and that no Governor may be allowed to dissolve, or Prorogue them, when he shall be informed that they are preparing a petition to our Gracious King and Parliament of Great Britain.'
>
> 'May the Spirit of Concord, Justice, and publick Virtue, direct the Councils of the British Senate, and may the Father of mercies preserve constitutional Freedom, to the British Race, in every part of the Globe.' [1]

'A Loyal and Devoted People'

I

Had Governor Legge been sustained by the British Government there can be little doubt that the overtures of Congress might have met a different response from Nova Scotia. The charges were referred to the Board of Trade. Their decision was based upon 'the

[1] *A. Series*, 94. 11 ff. A very interesting sidelight upon the 'Mauger interests' is found in the petition of the Assembly that no native of the province should be appointed Governor, Lieut.-Governor or Judge of the Supreme Court. 'The Ambitions of affluent Individuals . . . have led to faction and partys. . . . The present disputes in America, may have been promoted by this cause.'

unanimous voice of the Province of Nova Scotia, by their representatives in General Assembly', and Dartmouth himself added emphatically that 'the advice . . . will not be disapproved by the Crown'.[1] Early in 1776 Burrow had reported to Legge that Germain's administration was likely to prove a reversal of the Dartmouth régime. Carleton was to be recalled from Quebec. 'General Gage does not go out again.' Admiral Graves was to be tried at his own request by court martial, and '22,000 foreign Troops are taken into pay'.[2] In Nova Scotia Legge's recall was interpreted as the vindication of a 'loyal and devoted people'; and thus it came to pass that conflict with the governor led not to conflict but to increasing concord with the Board of Trade and the American Department. The 'unsuspecting confidence', conspicuous seventy years later in the transition from governance to self-government in Nova Scotia, is thus to be found at the earlier crisis in its history; and it may be added that it was never again altogether wanting.

For a few months after Legge's departure from Nova Scotia the state of the northern part of the province was still precarious. In Cumberland County on the mainland, and on the St. John, sympathy with the cause of the thirteen colonies was undoubtedly active. At one time it was reported that Arnold's expedition against Quebec by way of the Kennebec River was intended for Nova Scotia. Charles Dixon, a well-informed but friendly critic at Sackville, deplored the two obnoxious Acts which had caused the 'universal uproar' in the province. 'The Country will be in Rebellion', he wrote in January, 1776. 'Such a plan has been already adopted, till the persons who were most active, were oblig'd, to publickly discourage it', pending the use of 'all Lawfull means' to repeal the two Acts.[3] There can be no doubt that two members of the Assembly, Jonathan Eddy and John Allan, sought from the first to commit the province to revolution. But after Carleton's brilliant defence of Quebec, Nova Scotia was never seriously in danger.[4] Of the 600 men promised by Eddy and Allan in case of

[1] *Dartmouth Papers*, I. 2. 1308, 1305.

[2] Burrow to Legge, Mar. 8, 1776, *A. Series*, 95. 179.

[3] 'For God's Sake use your Interest & Wisdom in this Matter, and the Lord give you and those concern'd a discerning Spirit, to discern what may be for our present and future Peace.' Charles Dixon to John Butler, Jan. 14, 1776. *Id.*, 95. 108.

[4] Lieut.-Governor Arbuthnot (who succeeded to the administration after Legge's departure) to Germain, July 8, 1776, *Colonial Correspondence, Nova Scotia*, 10. 262.

an invasion, fewer than 200 appeared in arms for the futile attack upon Fort Cumberland in November, 1776, and more than 100 laid down their arms upon the promise of amnesty. Among the number was 'a talented young Irishman of huge stature', twenty-two years of age, whose name in characteristic script had already been writ large, very literally, in one of the earliest petitions against Governor Legge's administration. It was yet to be writ large, in another sense, in the history of the province; for R. J. Uniacke lived to be Speaker of the Assembly, and afterwards Attorney-General and Executive Councillor until the very eve of responsible government. His was one of the first projects on record for the confederation of the British provinces after the Revolution; and his son was to be the first premier of a British province under responsible government.

> 'No man', wrote the Hon. R. J. Uniacke in 1826, 'has had a better opportunity of forming an opinion on this subject than I have had. In the year 1774 I travelled through a large part of those Colonies. I saw their first Congress assemble at Philadelphia the same year, and I continued in America from the very commencement of the revolution to its conclusion. . . .
>
> Had the administration of His late Majesty met the wishes of the North American Colonies fifty years ago with the same liberality and enlightened wisdom that influences His present Majesty's Government, there cannot be a doubt that the separation of that Country from the British Crown would not have taken place.' [1]

The uprising in the north was not reflected in the Assembly. By resolution of the House the members for the 'rebellious' township of Onslow were unseated, and the Assembly elected in 1770 continued to sit throughout the Revolutionary War. The old controversy was closed by an Address of thanks on behalf of council and Assembly for the removal of Legge from the government of the province.[2] Thereafter Lieut.-Governor Arbuthnot—Francklin was now Superintendent of Indian Affairs—had little but harmony to report of the Nova Scotia Legislature. In truth issues of reform and self-government were no longer imperative. The Speaker of the Assembly was assured by John Pownall himself that the secret Address of 1775 had been received 'very graciously', and that 'the fullest consideration will be given to the several Propositions con-

[1] *A. Series*, 167. 344 ff.

[2] *Id.*, 10. 253. Instructions for the dissolution of the Assembly, May 9, 1781, were lost in transit, *Colonial Office, Nova Scotia*, i. 333; *America and West Indies*, 597. 223.

tained therein'.[1] But the years that followed belong to the military history of the Revolution. The immediate solution of 'the American question' was to be found in the field and not in the forum; and in the wake of war came the loyalists who trebled the population of the province, and submerged every other consideration in the desperate struggle for existence.

II

The effects of the War of Independence upon Nova Scotia were curiously paradoxical. On the one hand the issues of the Revolution left the province British—in many respects more stolidly British than they found it. The political temper of the province, its faith in constitutional methods of reform, its instinctive adherence to British precedent, passed into a tradition. On the other hand, the promise of the pre-revolutionary Assembly under the spirited and resourceful leadership of Day and Denson and Tonge and Morris, was quickly overshadowed by the urgent problems of the war and the still more imperative problems of peace. Even the moderate programme of 1775 was lost to sight. For the first generation of loyalists the gloom of exile seldom lifted from the horizon. Traces of the old spirit are still to be found, but not again in the ascendant until settled conditions of life began at last to emerge from the vicissitudes of the loyalist migrations.

Many conditions combined to effect the security of the province during the war and to fix its British character at the close. The geographical advantages of the province for naval defence were obvious. Sea power, as Washington saw, was to have 'the casting vote' in the Revolutionary War; but though British sea power could be broken by the allies long enough to force the surrender of Cornwallis at Yorktown, it could not be destroyed or seriously shaken in its control of the North Atlantic. Half of Nova Scotia was a peninsula; and the coming and going of British troops between Halifax and 'the continent', as the other provinces were usually termed, went on almost uninterruptedly. During the early years of the war 'O'Brien's gang' and swarms of other privateers played havoc with sea-coast settlements, frequently visiting the penalties of 'non-intercourse' upon friends and foes alike. In time the balance was effectively reversed by a few frigates in the Bay of Fundy, and by British posts at Castine on the Penobscot and at Fort Howe at the mouth of the St. John. Thus the brief

[1] *A. Series*, 94. 180.

siege of Fort Cumberland in November, 1776, was finally raised by a body of marines who marched north from Windsor. Even had Jonathan Eddy and John Allan succeeded at Cumberland as Ethan Allen and Benedict Arnold succeeded at Ticonderoga and Crown Point, the conquest would have been jeopardized at a dozen points on the Atlantic seaboard. None saw this more clearly than Washington himself, and it was one of his reasons in 1775 for refusing to sanction an invasion of the province.

A second source of security, however, belongs to another category; and without it Nova Scotia might conceivably have shared the fate of Georgia after Yorktown, or of the hinterlands of the Province of Quebec south of the Great Lakes. In 1775 Washington wrote that to attack Nova Scotia was 'a measure of conquest rather than defence'; and under the conditions which subsequently formed the basis of the Franco-Spanish-American alliance, Washington's decision in 1775 became doubly conclusive after 1778. For reasons to be noted in another context, the only basis of alliance which could meet Spanish jealousy of the American provinces on the Mississippi and American jealousy of French power on the St. Lawrence was Vergennes' formula of independence but no conquest.[1] For Quebec, as we shall see, Montgomery's invasion had preceded the French alliance, and indeed had been projected as a measure not of conquest but of defence. In any event, justification for a renewed attack might perhaps have been found in the fact that the hinterlands north of the Ohio for which the British provinces had fought in the Seven Years' War had been swept within the boundaries of the new province by the *Quebec Act* of 1774. In the absence of an Assembly, moreover, there was no proof forthcoming that claims of popular support in Quebec for the revolutionary cause were unfounded. Vergennes' formula thus applied only partially to Quebec; and the Quebec hinterlands south of the Great Lakes went to the United States at the treaty of 1783.

For Nova Scotia, on the other hand, Vergennes' formula was less ambiguous; for had the Assembly declared in favour of Congress, or had an Assembly been denied to Nova Scotia as it was denied to Quebec after 1769, an invasion of the province or its acquisition by diplomacy at the treaty of 1783 might have been interpreted as the liberation of an oppressed people seeking independence rather than as the conquest of a province which

[1] See Sparks, *Writings of George Washington*, i. 312 ff.

had declared in the most solemn manner for the British connexion. In that sense the attitude of the Nova Scotia Assembly may perhaps rank with the important decisions of the war. After Legge's recall, at least, the concord within the province was such that nothing short of conquest could have changed its allegiance.

A third source if not of security during the war at least of devotion to the British connexion after the peace is to be found in the deluge of loyalist immigration from the older colonies. From the evacuation of Boston in March, 1776, to that of New York in 1783, some 35,000 loyalists found their way to Nova Scotia; with results scarcely less distinctive than those which attended the earlier migrations from New England. For many of the refugees Nova Scotia, as their oppressors derisively predicted, was to mean 'Nova Scarcity' and destitution. Like the tattered boots in which the Rev. Jacob Bailey landed at Halifax, their shattered fortunes bore all the 'marks of sedition and independence'; and not all of them could command Bailey's grim and steadfast humour. The tragic experiences of the Revolution were stamped indelibly into the temper of the loyalist settlements. For better or for worse the results were traceable on every hand. The fortitude of the thousands who grappled with adversity and passed on their indomitable spirit to posterity is perhaps as brave a tradition of character and of unconscious heroism as Canadian history has to record. On the other hand, where destitution proved too strong an adversary, there were tendencies at work to destroy initiative and to hasten the easy descent from self-reliance to government aid, paternalism, and dependency.

III

For the northern part of the province 'the coming of the loyalists' marked a new era. More than 10,000 settled on the St. John River, and 'the City of the Loyalists', as the city at the mouth of the river came to be called, 'was born in a day'. Upon the upper reaches of the St. John many of the loyalist regiments of the Revolutionary War were to be ranged in blocks of twelve miles on either side of the river—the Maryland Loyalists, the Royal Guides, the Queen's Rangers, the Pennsylvania Loyalists, de Lancey's, Loyal American, 1st, 2nd, and 3rd New Jersey Volunteers, King's American Dragoons, New York Volunteers, King's Regiment of Foot, Arnold's American Legion. Some 2,000 settled on Passamaquoddy Bay, and nearly 1,000 in the Cumberland district.[1] The pre-revolutionary settlements from New England upon the mainland were thus completely engulfed in a population which had every incentive, as William Knox wrote, to be 'loyal and abhorrers of Republicanism'.[2] Within a year of their arrival there were complaints of the distances and delays of administration from Halifax. Thinly veiled allusions to the 'treasonable practices' among the old settlers and the 'prevalence of republican ideas' in the Assembly were followed by a demand for the organization of a new province north of the Bay of Fundy.

The uncanny speed with which the British Government seemed to comply with this request was not altogether the result of local preferences. Before the New Brunswick loyalists had reached their destination, Knox had submitted to Lord North a memorandum for the *New Establishments for the American Loyalists*. He proposed to

> 'erect the country from the river St. Croix, to the Gulph of St. Lawrence, and from the Line across the Isthmus to the Line of Canada, into a new province, placing the seat of Government on the river St. John. . . . They will gladly receive a Constitution calculated to cherish monarchical principles, and to repress republican ideas, and of a tendency to bind them to Great Britain; and it will be the fault of Administration if such a Constitution be not established, as will render their union with this country happy and permanent.'[3]

New Brunswick thus became, *par excellence*, the province of the loyalists, with traditions born of an uncompromising and unavailing struggle. In such an atmosphere not only the sympathies of the original New England settlers but all innovations which savoured of 'republicanism' or 'democracy' were instinctively suspect. The first governor, Colonel Thomas Carleton, younger brother of Sir Guy Carleton, hoped complacently that with 'better habits' than in the older province of Nova Scotia, the New Brunswick loyalists could be relied upon to counteract 'the American spirit of innovation'.[4] Contests between the pre-loyalist 'Whigs'—the Hazens, the Davidsons, the Simondses and the Dicksons—and the loyalists are to be found from the first gathering of the New Brunswick Assembly in 1786; but the cause of reform which

[1] Raymond, in *Canada and its Provinces*, xiii, pp. 145, 149, 151.

[2] Knox, *New Establishments for the American Loyalists*, submitted to Lord North in 1783. *Extra Official State Papers*, ii, Appendix xiv, p. 53.

[3] *Id.*, ii. 52, 54.

[4] Raymond, *op. cit.*, xiii. 158, 162, &c.

triumphed two generations later in New Brunswick owed less to traditions which survived the period of the Revolution than to political problems that were indigenous to the new province. Never, surely, did the old colonial system receive a fairer trial than under the loyalist régime in New Brunswick. No experiment could have been devised in which time and place and personnel were more auspiciously blended to correct, as Knox himself prescribed, 'those vices which . . . sprung up from the constitution of those which have revolted, and occasioned their separation from us'.[1] New Brunswick thus began with every predisposition against the tendencies which were held to have destroyed the first Empire. How inevitable were these tendencies Knox little knew; for despite this tried material, the second Empire, organized at leisure to secure 'the *permanency* of their connection'[2] with Great Britain, went step by step the way of the first until it invited the same disaster.

The original province was further dismembered by the establishment of a separate government in Cape Breton under a lieut.-governor and council without an Assembly. Prince Edward Island narrowly escaped the same fate, for the Secretary of State, Thomas Townshend, now Baron Sydney, once assured Governor Parr that both Cape Breton and 'the Island of St. John (Prince Edward Island), after reducing the Civil Establishment of it to a parallel with Cape Breton, shall both . . . be subordinate to you'.[3] Thus the old province of 1713 was broken into four unequal and dissimilar fragments. Cape Breton was reunited to Nova Scotia in 1820 after a generation of petty government during which the most valuable resources of the island passed to the control of vested interests; but New Brunswick, Prince Edward Island, and Nova Scotia were left to find their way by separate routes to the achievement of responsible government and finally into the Canadian Confederation.

How far this disintegration—against which recurring movements for 'Maritime Union' have struggled in vain—was the result of deliberate policy it is difficult to determine. All the woes of the Revolution, it seemed, had sprung from popular Assemblies,

[1] *Extra Official State Papers*, ii, Appendix xiv, p. 49.

[2] *Id.*, p. 47.

[3] *Colonial Correspondence, Nova Scotia*, 15. 198. The Secretaryship for the Colonies and the Board of Trade were both abolished in 1782 by 22 Geo. III, c. 82. The administration of the colonies was taken over again by the Southern Department, now termed the Home Department. *Shortt and Doughty*, ii. 739 n.

and particularly from the fact that the disunion among them which every observer from Franklin to Shirley had at one time deemed an insuperable barrier to colonial co-operation had been overcome by the sovereign expedient of a Continental Congress. The only settled provinces to remain British, on the other hand, had been Nova Scotia and Prince Edward Island where popular Assemblies were still in their primitive stages, and Quebec where there was no Assembly whatever. Did the path of safety lie through the concentration of executive authority and the disintegration of popular institutions? When Knox was called upon by Lord North to assist in 'framing regulations for our remaining Colonies', he laid it down as his first principle that 'the *permanency* of their connexion with this country should . . . be the ground of every measure respecting our Colonies'. It was part of Knox's original project to erect another province, under the name of New Ireland, east of the Penobsçot River, and yet another separate government on the St. Croix.[1] It seems to have been 'the policy of the British Government (Durham afterwards observed) to govern its Colonies by means of division, and to break them down as much as possible into petty isolated communities, incapable of combination, and possessing no sufficient strength for individual resistance to the Empire'.[2]

A distinctive interest, however, attaches to the older province of Nova Scotia. Here alone pre-revolutionary popular traditions survive in some measure without the devastating effects of transplanting to another soil. 'The American question' as it appeared to the Nova Scotia Assembly at the outbreak of the Revolution is never solved, and despite the intervening period of reaction, is never regarded as solved, until the final achievement of responsible government. Among the 20,000 loyalists at Shelburne, at Annapolis, at Halifax, and elsewhere in the peninsula in 1784,[3] many of the aptitudes which appeared in New Brunswick are clearly discernible. Many of the loyalists had 'had enough of Assemblies'. The only traditions of self-government that survived among them from the thirteen colonies had been torn up by the roots, and it required the growth of another season in a new soil before the political harvest of the second Empire could reach the maturity of

[1] The former went to the United States by the Treaty of Paris, 1783. *Extra Official State Papers*, ii. 60 n.; Appendix, xiv, p. 53.

[2] *Report*, ed. Lucas, ii. 66–7.

[3] *Colonial Correspondence, Nova Scotia*, 16. 18.

the first. The fact that the season was inclement beyond all expectation delayed the growth but could not repair the tendencies which developed two generations later into responsible government.

Yet the second Empire began, as we shall see, with many of the hardest lessons learnt, and above all with goodwill once more in the ascendant. There is a tradition that R. J. Uniacke, whose long career as assemblyman, Speaker of the Assembly, and Attorney-General, filled the remarkable span of forty-six years from 1784 to 1830, was once twitted with his association with the 'Cumberland rebels' of 1776. He retorted with much truth that the change was to be found not in his own views but in the temper of British colonial policy. The forms of the Old Colonial System, it is true, survived almost intact; in many respects confirmed rather than discredited by disaster. But in Nova Scotia there survived also the spirit which had robbed the system of many of its terrors—the goodwill which Chatham and Burke had invoked in vain for the older colonies—'*the former unsuspecting confidence of the colonies in the Mother Country*'. Nowhere were traditional British methods of reform more carefully dissociated from violence and revolution than in Nova Scotia; though not without restraint and searchings of spirit were they finally vindicated. At the passing of the second Empire both the dominant traditions in Nova Scotia were fittingly represented. Joseph Howe, the son of a Massachusetts loyalist, became the prophet of the new Commonwealth, and James Boyle Uniacke, son of the old 'Cumberland rebel', became the first premier under responsible government in the British dominions overseas.

III

'NEW SUBJECTS' IN QUEBEC

I

To outward appearances the contest with France for domination in America closed in a blaze of glory. The prospect of an 'American empire' at the close of the Seven Years' War was one which no other generation of the British race has ever contemplated. In extent of territory it stretched from the Arctic Ocean to the Gulf of Mexico. It contained some two millions and a half of the most resourceful and enterprising settlers in modern history—a population which had doubled in twenty years, with every prospect of increasing for another generation in the same ratio. So vast were the hinterlands and so illimitable the resources that William Knox after the Revolution predicted a series of people-wanderings like those of the Scythians and Tartars for 4,000 years before the 'Transallegany mountain people' should be able to found a settled state.[1] This was the heritage which British statesmen were privileged for a little more than ten years to hold and if possible to safeguard.

The conquest of New France has been regarded as an epoch in the first Empire. It liberated the southern colonies from the menace of French power to the north which had always overshadowed their expansion and government. Henceforth a British army and even the British navy would have a different meaning for colonists in America. With the close of the Seven Years' War also came a transformation in British mercantile policy. During the decade and a half before the war British exports to the West Indies had increased only 10 per cent. to the annual value of £877,571 while those to the 'continental' colonies had increased by 186 per cent. to the annual value of £1,832,948. It was clear that markets could be as important as raw materials, and that British settlers in America by buying British woollens could be of more value than all the tropical products of the Indies. The ascendancy which British manufacturers and their natural allies the landed interests thus gained over the purely commercial interests of the nation culminated, according to Beer, in the decision to retain Quebec at

[1] *Extra Official State Papers*, ii. 50.

the Treaty of Paris. It is not flattering to modern Canadian sensibilities to reflect that the whole of New France was weighed in the balance against the little French sugar island of Guadaloupe; but the new province was to be a field where 'perpetual Settlement and Cultivation ought to be encouraged'.[1] The further purposes of the British Government are traceable in a great variety of official documents, and it must be stated at the outset that there is no consciousness of the vexed problem of race as the Revolution was soon to leave it, dominating, like a mountain range, the length and breadth of Canadian history.

Quebec was to become part of the 'American empire'. The 60,000 inhabitants of the new province were to 'become subjects of the King' and fellow-subjects with more than forty times that number of British subjects already in America. Among the questions referred to the Board of Trade by the Secretary for the Southern Department was the query 'what Privileges are reserved to His Majesty's New Subjects by the Terms of their Capitulations' and 'how far it is expedient to retain, or depart from the Forms of Government which His Most Christian Majesty had established in those Colonies'.[2] 'The free exercise of their religion' was guaranteed to the Canadians in the capitulation of Montreal, but it was made clear that 'the obligation of paying the tithes . . . will depend on the King's pleasure', while at the Treaty of Paris privileges in religion were granted only 'as far as the laws of Great Britain permit'. The French plenipotentiaries 'proposed to insert the Words *comme ci-devant*, in order that the Romish Religion should continue to be exercised in the same manner as under their Government', but they were 'plainly told that it would be deceiving them to admit those Words'. The demand at the capitulation of Montreal that 'the French and Canadians shall continue to be governed according to the custom of Paris, and the Laws and Usages established for this country' was refused with the significant reply that 'They become subjects of the King'.[3]

Thus while the present prescriptive rights of Canadians of French origin are not less sacred in the Dominion than treaty rights or fundamental law of other nations they are not to be found in the policy contemplated for Quebec in 1763. Despite

[1] Beer, *op. cit.*, p. 139; Grant, *Canada versus Guadaloupe, Amer. Hist. Rev.*, July, 1912; Lords of Trade to Egremont, June 8, 1763, *Shortt and Doughty*, i. 140.
[2] Egremont to Lords of Trade, May 5, 1763, *id.*, i. 128.
[3] *Id.*, i. 30; *id.*, i. 115; Egremont to Murray, Aug. 13, 1763, *id.*, i. 169; *id.*, i. 34.

three rapid changes of ministry the measures for the government of the new province were drafted by the Board of Trade after 'most serious Consideration'. The Board itself still bore the stamp of Halifax's brilliant reorganization of that much-maligned body, and Halifax himself was now in control at the Southern Department. John Pownall, the indefatigable Secretary of the Board, whose influence had sometimes been all-powerful during the Halifax régime, was now, after a brief leave of absence with Halifax in Ireland, back again at his old office. Hillsborough, another of Halifax's staff in Ireland, was at the head of the Board. It was under Halifax's own instructions of September 19, 1763, that the Board undertook to 'declare the Constitution of the new Governments, as established for the present, & intended in future'.[1] 'The form', writes Dr. Alvord, 'was undoubtedly due to the influence of Pownall', and the final policy was 'due to Lord Halifax'.[2] For Quebec as for Nova Scotia it is reasonable to suppose that Shirley's 'Great Plan' was again in the ascendant. In the early reports and correspondence of the Board, in the resulting Order in Council, in the Proclamation of October 7, 1763, issued by Halifax himself—the constitution of Quebec until the *Quebec Act*—in the Commission to Governor Murray, in the elaborate Instructions which followed, in the Commission to Carleton as governor in 1768, in the *Report* of the Board of Trade in 1765, and above all in the incisive *Report* of 1769, next to the *Quebec Act* itself perhaps the most important document of the period in Canadian history, one searches in vain for any official departure from the recognized forms and functions of British colonial government in North America.

II

During the debates on the *Quebec Act* the attempt was made to attribute the policy of 1763 to haste and inadvertence. Evidence to the contrary is to be found in a score of documents of every degree of historical conclusiveness.

Prevailing conceptions in the mercantile system were of course taken for granted. The Board advised the 'secure settling' of the country either by European emigration 'or from the Overflowing of Your Majesty's ancient Colonies'. Among all the conquests of

[1] *Shortt and Doughty*, i. 127–63. The Proclamation of Oct. 7, 1763, the Commission to Murray, Nov. 21, 1763, and the Instructions of Dec. 7, 1763, were all drafted in detail by the Board of Trade. *Id.*, i. 154.

[2] *The Mississippi Valley in British Politics*, Cleveland, 1917, pp. 201 n., 199.

the Seven Years' War Canada was placed first among the 'Places where Planting, and perpetual Settlement and Cultivation ought to be encouraged and consequently where regular Forms of Government must immediately be established'. In the formal Instructions to Murray no fewer than sixteen sections relate to the 'advantageous and effectual Settlement' of the new province. The governor was instructed, no doubt with Lawrence's experience in Nova Scotia in mind, to invite British settlement by 'Proclamation in all the Colonies in North America'.[1]

Nowhere was the incorporation of Quebec into the old colonial system more clearly foreshadowed than in the proposed form of government. Variations in law and legal practice were of course taken for granted. Hillsborough afterwards stated that 'it never entered into Our Idea to overturn the Laws and Customs of Canada, with regard to Property', though justice was to be administered 'according to the Laws of England'.[2] With regard to franchise and legal rights the law officers of the Crown decided from the outset that Roman Catholics were 'not subject, in those Colonies, to the Incapacities, disabilities, and Penalties, to which Roman Catholics in this Kingdom are subject by the Laws thereof'.[3] In truth neither law nor religion was vitally related to the issues that were already overshadowing the whole problem of colonial government in America. Boundaries and Indian policy were more significant. But the form of government itself was fundamental. From the decision in Nova Scotia in 1756 to the great *Report* of 1769 there is no deviation here in the deliberate policy of the Board. In the end, as we shall see, their insistency was such that the whole problem of government for Quebec was summarily removed from their hands and dealt with as 'a matter of State Politics' at the most critical stage of the American Revolution.

Traditions of arbitrary governance in Quebec were not unknown either to the Board or to the American colonies. In 1754 Benjamin Franklin objected to Shirley's scheme of a Commander-in-Chief and Council for America because such a system 'would put them on a Footing with the Subjects of France in Canada. . . . If the

[1] *Report on Acquisitions in America*, June 8, 1763, *Shortt and Doughty*, i. 132–47. The report is signed by eight members of the Board, including Shelburne, Soame Jenyns, John Yorke, Orwell, and Bamber Gascoyne. *Instructions*, ss. 44–59, *id.*, i. 194–9. *Id.*, i. 199. [2] *Id.*, i. 297.

[3] *Report of Atty. and Sol. Gen.* re *Status of Roman Catholic Subjects*, June 10, 1765, *Shortt and Doughty*, i. 236.

Colonies in a Body may be well governed by Governors and Councils, appointed by the Crown, without Representatives, particular Colonies may as well or better be so governed'.[1] It is true that Murray during the military occupation of Quebec had opposed an Assembly,[2] but this was not the first record of a military governor's distaste for the 'heats, Animosities and disunion' usually associated with representative institutions. More than one indulgent member of the Board must have recalled the instructions to Governor Lawrence in Nova Scotia in 1758. Thus the Board of Trade, after nearly five months' deliberation and two preliminary reports, placed in the hands of Lord Halifax, who had himself presided over the Board in 1758, the instruments which formed the constitution of Quebec until the *Quebec Act*. And since it would 'give Confidence and Encouragement (they added), to such Persons as are inclined to become Settlers in the new Colonies, That an immediate and public Declaration should be made of the intended permanent Constitution and that the power of calling Assemblies should be inserted in the first Commissions, We have therefore drawn the Proclamation agreeable to this Opinion, and have prepared the Commissions accordingly'.[3]

III

In Proclamation, Commission, and Instructions accordingly the 'intended permanent Constitution' is outlined in ascending degrees of incisiveness. The first of these, in the interests of 'speedy settling', established the normal type of 'royal' province:

> 'We have, in the Letters Patent under our Great Seal of Great Britain, by which the said Governments are constituted, given express Power and Direction to our Governors of our Said Colonies respectively, that so soon as the state and circumstances of the said Colonies will admit thereof, they shall, with the Advice and Consent of the Members of our Council, summon and call General Assemblies . . . in such Manner and Form as is used and directed in those Colonies and Provinces in America which are under our immediate Government.'[4]

Murray's Commission, drafted by the Board in complete accord with the Proclamation, contained the same provisions for a representative Assembly which had forced the summoning of the Nova Scotia Assembly in 1758.[5] At the time of the *Quebec Act* the

[1] *Shirley Correspondence*, ii. 105.
[2] *Pub. Arch. Can., Q. Series*, i. 23.
[3] Oct. 4, 1763, *Shortt and Doughty*, i. 156.
[4] *Id.*, i. 165.
[5] *Id.*, i. 175.

Advocate-General, James Marriott, suggested that these provisions were applied to Quebec, 'inadvertently, and in the hurry of office'.[1] It is impossible to suppose that the Board of Trade which drafted them, or Lord Halifax who carried them into execution, could have been ignorant of the principles which both had been at such pains to enforce against Governor Lawrence's scruples in Nova Scotia. It had then been agreed that 'the Governor & Council alone are not Authorized . . . to make Laws', and that neither the governor's objections nor 'any other Reason can justify the Continuation of the Exercise of an illegal Authority'. The truth was, as Lord Mansfield stated in the case of *Campbell* v. *Hall* in 1774, that by the Proclamation and Commission 'the King had immediately and irrevocably granted' an Assembly 'in like manner as in the other provinces under the King'.[2]

And finally the Instructions were perhaps the most insistent of all. Here alone the Board had provided for the necessary interval pending the summoning of an Assembly. The governor and council were expressly forbidden to pass any ordinance 'that shall any ways tend to affect the Life, Limb or Liberty of the Subject, or to the imposing any Duties or Taxes'; and since by his Commission the governor was to 'summon and call a General Assembly' he was to 'give all possible attention to the carrying this important Object into Execution'. No fewer than twelve paragraphs of the Instructions relate to 'tacking', to 'the sole framing of Money Bills', and to other tendencies of Assemblies in the 'royal' provinces. It came to pass that more than one ordinance of Murray and his council had to be disallowed 'from a consideration of the Want of a due authority to enact them'. As late as 1769 the Board was ready to stake its own existence upon the summoning of an Assembly 'for the establishment of which it is humbly conceived the Faith of the Crown stands fully pledged'.[3]

It is a remarkable fact that for eleven years no attempt was made to call an Assembly in Quebec. At the end of that period the constitution of 1763 was altogether abrogated. It required nothing short of the highest legislative authority of the Empire, an Act of Parliament, to effect this. For the first time 'since the Constitution of this Country has been restored to its true Principles',[4] the *Quebec Act* formally dispensed with an Assembly and vested legislative authority in a governor and council. So complete a reversal

[1] *Id.*, i. 449. [2] See above, pp. 68, 70. *Shortt and Doughty*, i. 531.
[3] *Id.*, i. 185 ff.; 381. [4] *Nova Scotia, A. Series*, 59. 22.

of policy would have been remarkable even had it been the result of gradual and spontaneous conviction. But the reversal was effected within a much shorter period—between the *Report* of the Board of Trade in 1769 and the *Quebec Act*. It thus synchronized with the most critical period of the American Revolution, and it is safe to say that neither the purposes nor the results of the measure are to be found altogether within the orbit of purely Canadian history.

'The New Subjects' and the Old

I

The problems of civil government in Quebec were not unlike those of Governor Lawrence in Nova Scotia, which had been commended for Murray's guidance, or those of Governor Melville in the conquered French islands of Grenada which like Quebec had been created a 'royal' province by the same Proclamation. In neither the older province nor the new, however, were the immediate difficulties so formidable.

In Nova Scotia the problem of 10,000 implacable Acadians had been complicated by the German Protestants of Lunenburg and by the proximity of Louisbourg; but the Seven Years' War had closed with Cape Breton in British possession, with the Acadians in exile, and with an influx of New England immigration which completely transformed the political outlook of the province. The primitive stages of self-government thus passed with every promise of progress and harmony. Grenada was perhaps a closer parallel. As in Quebec the basic population was French. In both cases the Crown, by the same Proclamation, 'had immediately and irrevocably' granted an Assembly 'in like manner as in the other provinces under the King'. In the opinion of Yorke, then Attorney-General, the oath required of Roman Catholics there was 'matter of political judgment . . . the statute does not apply to them'. 'An assembly was at once established . . . all the French freeholders were allowed to vote and, catholics though they were, to sit and hold office'.[1]

The technical difficulties in Quebec, therefore, were not formidable. The policy of the Board had already been vindicated, as we have seen, by the law officers of the Crown: 'His Majesty's Roman Catholick Subjects . . . are not subject, in those Colonies,

[1] *Shortt and Doughty*, i. 267 n. Higham, *The General Assembly of the Leeward Islands*, *Eng. Hist. Rev.*, July, 1926, p. 367.

to the Incapacities, disabilities, and Penalties, to which Roman Catholicks in this Kingdom are subject by the Laws thereof'. The Board of Trade, now under Dartmouth himself—sponsor of the *Quebec Act* nine years later—prescribed an Assembly for Quebec, with a franchise to include 'all the Inhabitants . . . seeing that we know of no Law by which Roman Catholicks, as such, are disqualified from being Electors'.[1]

Other difficulties, however, were less tractable. The preponderance of the French in numbers was overwhelming—even the British petitioners for an Assembly at the time of the *Quebec Act* conceded that they numbered 75,000 while the British or 'ancient subjects' numbered but 3,000, exclusive of traders in the 'up-country' and the fishing population on the Gulf.[2] At the beginning of civil government their numbers were estimated by Murray at a few hundreds, and from their relations with the governor it is easy to surmise why the instructions for the encouragement of further immigration by 'Proclamation in all the Colonies in North America' remained unavailing.[3]

It would seem from Murray's caustic references to the merchants in his letters to some of his patrons, and from his defence after his recall, that the chief causes of disagreement were religious. 'He could not be prevailed upon to persecute his Majesty's Roman catholic subjects in Canada'. The British traders were 'Licentious Fanaticks' who sought nothing less than 'the expulsion of the Canadians'. They were a set of 'cruel, Ignorant, rapacious Fanatics', made up of 'Quakers—Puritants, Anabaptists, Presbeterians, Atheists, Infidels, and even the Jews', all bent upon preventing 'any Consideration being paid to the Poor Canadians'.[4]

But it is impossible to account for the relations between Murray and the merchants upon the basis merely of toleration on the one side and intolerance on the other. Murray's broadmindedness in

[1] Norton and de Grey, Lincoln's Inn, June 10, 1765, *Shortt and Doughty*, i. 236. Sept. 2, 1765, *id.*, i. 248.

[2] *Petition to the Commons*, Nov. 12, 1774, *id.*, i. 593. The Petition of Dec. 31, 1773, however, claimed that several of the British 'possess the largest and best cultivated Seigniorys in the Province' and that their 'personal Estates by far exceed those of the new Subjects.' *Id.*, i. 500. Four-fifths of the total trade of the province was also said to be in their hands. *Id.*, i. 592.

[3] A Proclamation, Mar. 1, 1765, was published in the *Quebec Gazette* on Mar. 7, 1765, but with no reference, as in Lawrence's Proclamations, to the form of government. *Report*, *Pub. Arch.*, 1918, Appendix C, 3 ff.

[4] Murray to Eglinton, Oct. 27, 1764, *Pub. Arch. Can.*, *Murray Papers*, i. 170; Murray's *Memorandum* in reply to the charges against him, *id.*, iii. 211 ff.; Murray to Lords of Trade, Oct. 29, 1764, *Shortt and Doughty*, i. 231.

matters of race and religion reflects imperishable credit upon his own name and upon his office. But the British traders themselves sought the franchise for the French-Canadians—for the first time on record—'without burdening them with such Oaths as in their present mode of thinking they cannot conscientiously take';[1] while they accused Murray himself of fomenting racial and religious discord. 'Instead of promoting Harmony and an Union between His Majesty's British and Canadian Born Subjects, to which both parties were inclined, the whole Tenor of his Policy and Conduct has been to kindle Animositys, and to raise jealousies among them, and to keep them Disunited'.[2] It must be conceded that there is enough evidence to give some colour to this charge.[3]

II

In truth less praiseworthy differences are not far to seek, and to these Murray's recall was undoubtedly due. The governor's patrons were Lord Bute, James Oswald, Lord Eglinton, and 'the King's friends'; and his term of office was filled with a desperate attempt to keep his footing in the slippery by-ways of political patronage. With the passing of Bute's ascendancy Murray found himself everywhere in conflict with the opposite faction: with General Gage who after commanding at Montreal was made Commander-in-Chief in America, and with General Burton who succeeded to the command at Montreal. The full implications of the new imperial

[1] *Shortt and Doughty*, i. 234. This petition was drawn up more than a year before the Board of Trade formally recommended the same measure, and before the opinion of the law officers of the Crown could have been known in Quebec.

[2] Murray's *Memorandum* in reply to the charges against him, Article 11, *Murray Papers*, iii. 238.

[3] Cf. Murray to Halifax, June 26, 1764: 'Several from New England now established here are most inveterate Fanaticks, a little address however may make even them of advantage, a proper conviction of their insults will gain and strengthen the confidence of the Canadians to Government which confidence being the Main Spring must be perpetually kept in order and cannot fail of perfecting the Business I charge myself with which is no less then (*sic*) the reformation of the greatest part of the inhabitants of this Colony. I shall not at present enter into a detail of my project.'

Murray's 'project' was based largely upon the co-operation of the notorious renegade Jesuit, Roubaud. *Murray Papers*, i. 139.

Even Murray's ordinance admitting French jurors and barristers to the Court of Common Pleas was overruled by additional royal instructions not because it extended privileges to the Roman Catholics, but because it tended to 'restrain Our Canadian Subjects in those Privileges they are entitled to enjoy in common with our Natural born Subjects' in every court in the province. *Shortt and Doughty*, i. 247, n. 2. Cf. *Report of the Board of Trade*, Sept. 2, 1765: 'This Distinction and Exclusion seem to us to be as inconsistent with true Policy, as it is unwarrantable upon the Principles of Law and Equity.' *Id.*, i. 241.

policy in America scarcely appeared above the northern horizon; but finding himself as civil governor 'degraded from *the Profession of Arms*', Murray spent the best energies of a fiery and impulsive temper in a vain attempt to retain his military command.[1]

Murray's relations with Burton thus developed into a deadly feud in which the most incongruous allies were sought on both sides: by Murray in Thomas Walker (of 'Walker's ear' fame) and a few of the Montreal merchants against Burton, and by Burton still more successfully in the Quebec merchants against Murray.[2] The governor wrote to Montreal that 'the poor Mercantile Devils at your place have been hardly dealt by'. Burton returned the compliment by inspecting the garrison at Quebec with studied affronts to the civil governor, and a 'huge entertainment for the Malcontents'. Wagers were laid in public upon the governor's recall. Murray ruefully assured his patrons that he was struggling manfully against his 'natural vivacity' of spirits, while his enemies were being encouraged from home 'with a View to make an Explosion of my Temper'.[3] But the friction between Murray and the merchants was older than the feud with Burton. It was part of a chronic conflict which was to be found in Halifax and Boston and Philadelphia as well as in Quebec; and it was this undercurrent which eventually dragged the governor down and led, by methods that are not pleasant to reflect upon, to his recall.

On both sides the quarrel was instinctive, and it had begun long before Murray found himself 'degraded from *the Profession of Arms*' by promotion to civil government. The 'new subjects' had found in Murray's military régime 'all the justice that we could have expected from the most enlightened jurists'. The 'ancient subjects' were not so easily satisfied. They submitted, 'hoping Time

[1] Murray to Halifax, Oct. 15, 1764, *Shortt and Doughty*, i. 211. 'Mr. Gage and Mr. Burton have long been ploting to ruin me, this mine they have Sprung is the most extraordinary thing which ever happened . . . to turn me out of the Army. . . . If . . . You find that His Majesty has come to a Resolution to allow no Civil Governor to have any Military Command, for God sake get me as handsomely out of this Civil Embrassement as possible. The Government of the Province will be a good thing for some dependent of the Ministers, and I am ready to resign it for an Old Regiment.' Murray to Oswald, Oct. 16, 1764, *Murray Papers*, i. 164.

[2] 'Walker and Knipe have been here. . . . I have had much Conversation, and if any Confidence may be put in them we may hope to find the People at Montreal very tractable: to contribute to it I have made Walker and Knipe Justices of the Peace, the first is certainly a sensible Man.' *Murray Papers*, i. 203.

[3] Murray to Oswald, Nov. 11, 1765, *id.*, i. 276; *id.*, i. 265, 289, &c. Cf. *Memorials of Rt. Hon. James Oswald*, Edinburgh, 1825, p. 347.

with a Civil Establishment would remedy this Evil'. Murray afterwards acknowledged he had 'often severely repremanded some of the traders'; and the traders in due time charged Murray with 'a Rage and Rudeness of Language and Demeanour'.[1] With civil government after the peace, it was not long before there was 'the greatest Enmity raging between the Troops and the Inhabitants'. In Montreal Thomas Walker, who had made himself particularly obnoxious to the troops, was assaulted in his own house by masked men[2] who flogged him in the presence of his family and cut off one of his ears. When the trials were transferred to Quebec and failed to produce a conviction, the utterly false inference was drawn that the governor had taken the offenders under his protection. Walker's ear, like Jenkyns's and Prynne's before him, proved more potent than the head to which it belonged. The incident was soon known from Quebec to Georgia. Daniel Dulany, afterwards a loyalist at the Revolution, asked if the new standing army in America was 'to be employed in the national Service of Cropping the Ears, and Slitting the Nostrils of the civil magistrates, as marks of Distinction'.[3]

Murray's scorn for 'contemptible subtlers' was repaid by a stubborn and inveterate hostility, and neither side emerged from the conflict with dignity. A month after the establishment of civil courts by the ordinance of September 17, 1764, the grand jury of Quebec made the egregious presentment which Murray never ceased to cite against his enemies, and which the Board of Trade justly stigmatized as 'indecent, unprecedented and unconstitutional'.[4] The demands ranged from the 'due observance of the Sabbath' and the inspection of public accounts 'at least twice a year' by the grand jury, to the exclusion of Roman Catholics from juries and 'Gentlemen of the Army' from 'exercising any Judicial Authority'. The last were added in a postscript from which the names of the seven French members of the grand jury were

[1] *Shortt and Doughty*, i. 227. *Murray Papers*, iii. 211, in reply to Article 8; *Shortt and Doughty*, i. 233.

[2] See *The Mystery of Walker's Ear*, by Professor Burt, in *Can. Hist. Rev.*, Sept. 1922, pp. 233–55.

[3] Walker, in fact, had been Murray's protégé. The case was taken to Quebec, as Murray stated, by 'Mr. Walker's own Obstinency (in demanding a Protestant jury) and the Intrigues practised upon him by Cunningham the Attorney'. *Murray Papers*, iii. 211. Dulany's footnote: 'See the Narrative of the Outrages committed by the Soldiery on Mr. Justice Walker in Canada.' *Considerations on the Propriety of imposing Taxes in the British Colonies*, London (reprinted), 1766, p. 59.

[4] *Shortt and Doughty*, i. 246.

significantly omitted. The French jurors thereupon disclaimed responsibility, and a petition to the King was promoted with the governor's approval, attributing the action of the British jurors to 'the base anxiety for their own interests'. The petitioners had no doubt of 'the Beneficence of the Government . . . if Messrs. the English jurors were as submissive to the wise decisions of the Governor and his Council, as we are'.[1]

III

Murray would scarcely have been flesh and blood had he not seized this opportunity of discrediting his 'factious and licentious' critics. But when the inevitable petition for Murray's recall was drawn up by the Quebec traders and their patrons in London, it was found to be a much more formidable document than the crude findings of the grand jury. In addition to complaints of 'Rage and Rudeness of Language and Demeanour', they charged the governor with 'flagrant Partialities, by fomenting Parties and taking measures to keep your Majesty's old and new Subjects divided'. They prayed for an Assembly 'exclusive of Military Officers', and a 'Governor over us, acquainted with other maxims of Government than Military only'.[2] In the background, beyond a doubt, uglier rumours of irregular duties and captured French brandies were insidiously circulated in London by Fowler Walker, the self-accredited agent of the province. In vain Murray sent Panet, one of his French-Canadian protégés, and his 'Bosom friend Cramahé' upon a confidential mission to Bute and Hillsborough and Knox to counteract 'the Intrigues of Brigadiers, Judges, Laweyers & Fanatics' against him.[3]

Murray was recalled in 1766, but the charges were never tried. He left behind him in Canada a reputation which does him credit,

[1] See, however, the explanation of the Protestant jurors in *Shortt and Doughty*, i. 215. *Id.*, i. 229.

[2] *Id.*, i. 232 ff.

[3] Murray to his brother, the Master of Elibank, Oct. 27, 1764; to Lord Adam Gordon, Oct. 3, 1765; to Ross, his agent, Dec. 4, 1765; Cramahé to Murray, Jan. 12 and Feb. 9, 1765, &c. *Murray Papers*, i, pp. 172, 247, 289; iii. 255, 262, &c.

Murray had disposed of the brandies for £2,400, but the proceeds were regarded as his own perquisites. Cf. Murray to Hon. George Murray, Feb. 23, 1764: 'I am determined to do no wrong thing. . . . If the king gives me the money for which the Stores not Military were sold for, I shall be rich. . . . I was given to understand, that as I had been the first Military Man, who had ever accounted for such things I certainly would not be refused the Demand.' *Murray Papers*, i. 85; iii. 255, &c.

if not as a statesman at least as a man. It is difficult either to credit or to debit Murray with a policy in Quebec, since policy implies a degree of consistency and discernment which was seldom conspicuous in Murray's conduct. He scorned the trader much as Falstaff recognized the true prince—by instinct; and his instinct carried him perhaps insensibly into a bias on 'the American question' which was scarcely less obstructive to sound policy than that of Gage in Boston or Legge in Nova Scotia. His position was 'very slippery' and he took friends where he could find them. Thus in 1762 after nearly three years of military governorship in Quebec he reported that the seigneurs were 'extremely vain and have an utter contempt for the trading part of the Colony, tho' they make no scruple to engage in it, pretty deeply too, whenever a convenient opportunity served; They were great Tyrants to their Vassals who seldom met with redress let their grievances be ever so just'. Six months later he wrote to Amherst that 'they may become very usefull to us if properly managed'.[1] In 1762, the *habitants*, though strong and healthy, virtuous in their morals and temperate in their living, were 'extremely ignorant . . . few can read or write, and all receive implicitly for truth, the many arrant falsehoods and atrocious lies industriously handed among them'. Two years later Murray predicted that if indulged with a few privileges denied to Roman Catholics at home they could 'become the most faithful and most useful set of Men in this American Empire'.[2]

The Quebec Act: its Origin

I

The measure by which the official British policy for Quebec from 1763 to 1769 was formally reversed passed the British Parliament in an interval of political twilight fitfully illuminated by flashes of the coming storm. If ministerial speeches and semi-official polemics in 1774 were the only source of information with regard to the origin and purposes of the *Quebec Act*, it would be hard to find a measure more severely local in its scope or more benevolently disinterested in its aim. In addition to this there have been far-reaching results from the Act which have wielded in Canadian traditions all the force of fixed ideas. By a devoted race and an historic church in Canada the *Quebec Act* is justly cherished, in the words

[1] *Shortt and Doughty*, i. 79. *Murray Papers*, i. 33.
[2] *Shortt and Doughty*, i. 79, 80, 231.

of Bourinot, as 'the charter of the special privileges which the French-Canadians have enjoyed ever since'—a 'Sacred Charter, granted by the King in Parliament to the Canadians as a Security for their Religion, Laws and Property'.[1] Other prepossessions have arisen from less authentic sources—the British traditions of the Revolutionary War where the *Quebec Act* is associated with the dauntless spirit of Carleton in the defence of Canada; or the loyalist traditions which have drawn a curtain across Canadian history at the Revolution, leaving the *Quebec Act* almost as far removed from its real context as though the thirteen colonies of the first Empire had belonged to another hemisphere.

The official defence of the *Quebec Act* fell to William Knox, whose intimate and confidential relations with Grenville, with Hillsborough, with Dartmouth, and afterwards with Germain, and North himself, made him, as Knox says of himself, 'a principal actor in the executive Government'—'the most important of all the subordinate offices of the State'—during the most critical stages of the American Revolution.[2] In the *Thoughts on the Act for making more Efficient Provision for the Government of the Province of Quebec*, and in a special and more guarded plea, *The Justice and Policy of the Late Act of Parliament . . . Asserted and Proved*, the *Quebec Act* appears as a measure of 'benevolence and humanity', of 'lenity and indulgence', framed upon 'the strictest principles of justice and humanity'. Oppression had been disastrous for Ireland. 'The effects of lenity' were now to be tried in Quebec.[3]

It is not easy to fit King George III into this picture with the 'four intolerable Acts' of the same session against the American colonies. Nor is it easy to recognize among the prophets of 'lenity and indulgence', the Solicitor-General, Wedderburn, who as Lord Loughborough in 1801 was so largely responsible for the King's stubborn refusal to implement Pitt's solemn promises to the Roman Catholics at the Irish Union. Perhaps it would be easier to credit Knox himself with 'benevolence and humanity' were it not that both his pamphlets in 1774 contain veins of vastly different matter, while his *Extra Official State Papers* published in 1789

[1] Haldimand to Germain, Oct. 25, 1780, *id.*, ii. 720.

[2] *Extra Official State Papers*, ii. 3; i. 19. Knox 'served as Under Secretary to every Secretary of State that has filled the American department, from its institution to its suppression' in 1782. *Id.*, i. 34.

[3] *The Justice and Policy* (London, 1774), pp. 29, 28; *Thoughts on the Act* (London, 1774), p. 32.

disclose still further the hidden principles of American policy which could not be avowed in 1774.

The apparent neatness and dispatch of French colonial government had always possessed a fascination for governors and a haunting menace for the northern colonies in America:

> 'The government of the French colonies (says Knox) particularly deserves our attention, and is worthy of our imitation; they take every precaution of a wise and prudent nation, to secure good order and government; a governor is appointed with a proper power, and a council established to give him assistance, as well as to guard the rights of the crown.... Without any of those pompous ideas of popular governments, which our countrymen are elated with, the people are happy.... Happy would it be for this kingdom, were such plans adopted for the government of our colonies, instead of that disorder and anarchy, that almost universally reigns in them....
>
> The noble personages who planned this bill, warily considered these material points; and in giving them a government, had the view of making a great and flourishing body of people happy; instead of creating in them a power of destroying their peace and tranquility....
>
> By giving the Canadians an assembly, we give them a power to oppose our own, we put in their hands a sword, that like the Bostonians they in turn may brandish (it) and put us at defiance.'[1]

Of all the provinces of the first Empire, Quebec alone met with Knox's approval. In 1774 he was convinced that if an Assembly were granted to Quebec 'in time Canada would be as over-run with patriots as Boston. . . . The northern colonies would have experienced a much greater degree of felicity, had their government consisted only of a governor and council'. In 1789, on the eve of the *Constitutional Act*, when at last an Assembly seemed inevitable, Knox was still opposed to 'fine spun theories, for promoting the happiness of the French Canadians by converting them into English Republicans'.[2]

II

But there is a more sinister vein in Knox which makes it difficult to avoid 'the imputation of motives' which the official defenders of the *Quebec Act* so sententiously deprecated in 1774.[3] The sort of

[1] *Thoughts on the Act*, pp. 14, 15, 37, &c.

[2] *Extra Official State Papers*, ii. 20. *Thoughts on the Act*, p. 13. *Extra Official State Papers*, ii. 6.

[3] In view of 'the considerations upon which that measure appears to be founded,' Knox contended in defence of the ministers that 'we have no right

Justice and Policy which Knox professed for Quebec ill accorded with the policy which Knox himself, above all the 'reinvigorated officialdom' of that generation, was known to advocate for the other colonies in America. The key-note of that policy, from beginning to end, was authority vindicated if necessary by coercion. When the *Stamp Act* was repealed Knox anticipated no results from America but '*addresses of thanks and measures of rebellion*'.[1] It was Knox speaking *ex cathedra* who admonished the American colonists, as we have seen, in 1769:

> 'If you do not avail yourself of the information I have given you, perhaps the people of England may be led by it to conceive more justly of their *Rights*, and of your *Intentions*, than they have hitherto done; and may compel you to submit, if they unhappily find no argument but force can induce you to obey.'[2]

With Grenville's approbation Knox became joint Under Secretary for the American Department under Hillsborough in July, 1770. Early in the following month, as we shall see, Carleton who had succeeded Murray in Quebec left for London with the chief features of the *Quebec Act* already fixed in his indomitable mind. The contrary policy of the Board of Trade in the *Report* of July, 1769, over the signature of Hillsborough himself, is heard of no more. When the *Quebec Bill* appeared, Knox himself in *The Justice and Policy of the Late Act* conceded that 'the inducement to adopt a plan of lenity and indulgence . . . was greatly heightened by a consideration of the avowed purpose of the old colonies to oppose the execution of the laws of *England*, and to deny the authority of the supreme legislature'. In the *Thoughts on the Late Act* he dropped less guardedly a hint that the Canadians if attached by religious and other privileges 'may be a security against the insurgents of the other parts of America; for in a case of exigency, a force can easily be raised from thence'.[3] A less wary apologist, though a member of the House, Thomas Bernard, pointed out that

to suppose their conduct to be governed by sinister or wicked motives.' *The Justice and Policy of the Late Act*, p. 6.

[1] 'I was sent for to a meeting of the opposition at Mr. Rigby's . . . the Duke of Bedford and several others desired to know my opinion of the effects which those Resolutions would produce in America. My answer was in a few words—*addresses of thanks and measures of rebellion.* Mr. Grenville smiled and shook his head, and Mr. Rigby swore by G–d he thought so, and both wished me a good morning.' *Extra Official State Papers*, ii. 26.

[2] *The Controversy between Great Britain and her Colonies Reviewed*, London, 1769, pp. 204–5. See above, p. 51.

[3] *The Justice and Policy of the Late Act*, p. 28. *Thoughts on the Late Act*, p. 28.

the Act would provide 'a politic check to the independence of our American children'—'a power of coercion over them'.[1] Sir William Meredith, a member of North's administration, while contending that the Act was 'consonant to justice, wisdom, benevolence and policy' hinted in no uncertain terms at 'the present state of Boston' and the possibility of 'a fatal necessity . . . to *coerce* America'.[2]

But it is unnecessary to go so far afield as Knox or Bernard or Meredith for the policy behind the *Quebec Act*. Even had the discussions which preceded the Act been as carefully guarded from posterity as they were intended to be from that generation[3] the correspondence of Carleton himself would be found to reveal the truth: sometimes with a suggestive wariness of phrase which that doughty champion found it necessary to use with a Shelburne or a Burgoyne, but usually when 'among friends' with a directness which became him like the scarlet of his soldier's uniform.

Whatever may have been the faults of Guy Carleton indecision was not one of them. At a period of grave and justifiable perplexity he had the signal virtue of knowing his own mind; and like the *enfant terrible* of the piece he sometimes declared it with a vigour disconcerting alike to his enemies and to his friends. Murray may have acted by instinct rather than by reasoned policy. There can be no doubt that his successor acted from downright conviction. For four years Carleton's policy in Quebec was directed with unwavering aim at one contingency. For four years more he laboured in London, by methods which we can only surmise, to impress his convictions upon the administration and to overcome the deliberate policy of the Board of Trade. When the hour struck it was Carleton's policy which prevailed. The contingency which he

[1] *An Appeal to the Public Stating and Considering the Objections to the Quebec Bill*, London, 1774, 54 f.

[2] *Letter to the Earl of Chatham on the Quebec Bill*, London, 1774, 35 f. This pamphlet was generally attributed to Lord Lyttelton, and was quickly reprinted in America as *A Letter from Thomas, Lord Lyttleton to William Pitt, Earl of Chatham, on the Quebec Bill*, New York, 1774. It seems clear, however, from internal evidence (p. 10) and from *A Letter to Sir William Meredith in Answer to his late Letter to the Earl of Chatham* (London, 1774), p. 21, that Meredith was the author.

[3] See Hillsborough to Carleton, Dec. 1, 1769, enclosing the *Report* of the Board of Trade, of July, 1769: 'This Report is sent to you in the greatest Confidence, and therefore you should be careful not only that no part of it is communicated to any other person, but that in conversing upon the subject of any Difficulties or Doubts that may arise, you do avoid the Appearance of their being other than the Result of your own Reflections; and I am particularly to desire that you will bring back the Copy of the Report with you, without suffering it to fall into any other hands whatever.' *Shortt and Doughty*, i. 377 n.

foresaw from the beginning was the same which Meredith hinted in 1774: 'a fatal necessity . . . to *coerce* America': a contingency complicated by the inveterate hostility of France and the presence in Quebec of an overwhelmingly French population. Expecting this he prepared for it. The *Quebec Act* was his measure of preparation, and he succeeded in 1774 in making it the measure of the British Government. The evidence for this is in Carleton's own letters, and Carleton himself would have been the last man to disavow their obvious import.

III

It is possible to find Carleton's convictions on the American situation within a few months of his arrival in Quebec and more than a year before his formal appointment as Murray's successor.[1] Up to this point Carleton's training and interests, like his experience in America, had been almost exclusively military. His earliest rôle had been cast at Quebec in intimate association with Wolfe himself in 1759. His greatest part was yet to be played upon the same stage sixteen years later—almost the only completely successful military rôle on the British side during the American Revolution. At the narrow beginnings of British history in Canada Carleton thus stands, like Quebec itself, guarding his charge with indomitable resolution. We are here concerned, however, with the work not of soldiers but of statesmen, and it becomes evident that Carleton's contribution to the gravest political problem that ever confronted the nation was the contribution not of the statesman but of the soldier.

In February, 1767, within a few months of Townshend's port duties on glass, tea, paints, lead, and paper, Carleton foresaw with unerring precision the military implications of British policy towards the American colonies. In discussing the importance of a chain of forts between Quebec and New York Carleton discloses in characteristic phrases that repay careful scrutiny the fixed idea which seems to have dominated his first administration in Quebec:

> 'The more I consider *the State of Affairs on this Continent*, more and stronger Reasons present themselves, and I am the more convinced, it is not only expedient, but indispensably necessary for the Interest

[1] Carleton was appointed Lieut.-Governor by Commission of April 7, 1766. Murray, though recalled on April 1, 1766, remained nominally governor until Carleton was formally promoted to that office in 1768. *Shortt and Doughty*, i. 276 n.

of Great Britain and His Majesty's Service, not only to keep these in good Repair, but to erect a *proper Place of Arms near the Town of New York, and a Citadel in or near the Town of Quebec*. . . . They will facilitate *the Transport of ten or fifteen thousand Men in the Beginning of a War*, from the one to the other, as the Circumstances require.

The natural and *political Situation of the Provinces of Quebec and New York* is such, as must for ever give them great Influence and Weight *in the American System*, therefore no Pains, Address, nor Expence too great to *root out Faction or Party*; to establish Tranquillity, and a *firm Attachment to His Majesty's Government*, at the same time it is equally essential to establish that security and Strength as can properly *curb and overawe*, should ever such arise, who by the Ties of loyal Subjects and honest Men, are not thoroughly bound to their Duty.

This Communication so established, will give *Security to the King's Magazines, till then precarious*, and doubtful who may avail themselves of them; will *separate the Northern from the Southern Colonies*, will afford an easy and advantageous Opportunity of *transporting His Forces into any part of this Continent*, and may prevent the greatest of all Inconveniences, *Delay and Loss of Time in the Beginning of a War*.'[1]

This theme is to be found recurring again and again throughout Carleton's correspondence until the forecast became an accomplished fact. Thus in November, 1769, in response to Shelburne's inquiry with regard to 'the right Administration of Government in Quebec' and 'the Improvement of its Civil Constitution', Carleton encloses a copy of the letter to Gage quoted at length above, and elaborated it 'with that Candor, which, I think, the King's Service requires'. 'I take it for granted', he observed, 'that the natural Rights of Men,[2] the British Interests on this Continent, and the securing the King's Dominions over this Province, must ever be *the principal Points in View, in forming it's Civil Constitution and Body of Laws; And that the last, is the Foundation of all, without which, other schemes can be little better than meer Castles in the Air*.' Carleton's observations are confined accordingly to the military situation. The fortifications at Quebec and Montreal were in ruins. 'The King's old subjects in this Province, supposing them

[1] Carleton to Gage, Feb. 15, 1767, *Shortt and Doughty*, i. 280. The italics are my own. Carleton on his arrival in Quebec had immediately taken sides with the faction against Murray; his relations with Gage are thus particularly cordial and unreserved. *Id.*, i. 277–9. Cf. *Murray Papers*, iii, pp. 186, 203, 208, &c.

[2] Cf. Carleton to Shelburne, Dec. 24, 1767, in which the question is raised how far British laws in Quebec were 'agreeable to the natural Rights of Mankind'. *Shortt and Doughty*, i. 289.

all willing, might furnish about five hundred Men. . . . *The New Subjects could send into the Field about eighteen thousand Men.* . . . As the common People are greatly to be influenced by their Seigneurs, I annex a Return of the Noblesse of Canada.' Among those who had returned to France were a hundred officers 'all ready to be sent back, in Case of a War . . . to stir up a People accustomed to pay them implicit Obedience'. Those in Canada could not be expected to defend a government which had 'deprived them of their Honors, Privileges, Profits and Laws', and had introduced instead 'a Deluge of new Laws unknown and unpublished'.

The preponderance of the French in Quebec, moreover, was certain to increase rather than diminish, since British settlers would normally prefer 'the more chearful Climates, and more fruitful Soil of His Majesty's Southern Provinces . . . so that, *barring Catastrophe shocking to think of*, this Country must, to the end of Time, be peopled by the Canadian Race'. What was this 'Catastrophe shocking to think of'? It could scarcely have been war with France, since a victorious France would still have left Quebec 'peopled by the Canadian Race'. The fortification of Quebec was thus of vital importance: it was 'not only necessary as Matters now stand, but *supposing the Canadians could be interested to take a Part in the Defence of the King's Government, a Change not impossible to bring about, yet Time must bring forth Events* that will render it *essentially necessary for the British Interests on this Continent*, to secure this Port of Communication with the Mother Country; as might easily be proved, were they not too remote for the present Purpose'.[1]

Without tracing this theme in detail it will be sufficient to note the growing strength of Carleton's convictions and the increasing bluntness of his address. To Hillsborough, whose appointment as first Secretary for the American Colonies in January, 1768, synchronized with his own as full governor of Quebec, Carleton could state his views without the necessity of official reserve. The letter of November 20, 1768, was marked 'Secret Correspondence':[2]

[1] Carleton to Shelburne, Secretary for the Southern Department, Nov. 25, 1767, *Shortt and Doughty*, i. 281–5. The italics are my own.

[2] Nov. 20, 1768, in reply to a letter of May 14 (not preserved in the *Q. Series*) inquiring about reports of an Indian and French revolt to be defeated by fire-ships. Carleton had 'not been able to make any discovery, that induces me to give credit' to such a plan 'after their experience in fifty-nine,' but 'I can have no doubt (he adds) that france, as soon as determined to begin a war will attempt to regain Canada, should it be intended only to make a diversion.' *Shortt and Doughty*, i. 325–7. The italics again are my own.

'Should france, begin a War in hopes the Brittish-colonies will push matters to extremities, and she adopts the project of *supporting them in their independent notions*, Canada, probably, will then become *the Principal scene, where the fate of America may be determined*. . . . Your Lordship must immediately perceive the many disadvantages Great Britain would labour under in a war of this nature; and on the other hand, how greatly *Canada might for ever Support the Brittish interests on this Continent, for it is not united in any common principle, interest, or wish with the other Provinces, in opposition to the Supreme-seat of Government*.'

Four months later, for reasons which will appear only when Carleton's policy in Quebec is brought into juxtaposition with that of the Board of Trade in 1769, Carleton requested leave to return to England. His influence there for four years is traceable by circumstantial rather than by direct evidence, but there can be little doubt that Carleton's review of his own policy as late as 1776 was correct. He refers Germain to the 'letters which lie in your Lordships office . . . particularly to one marked *secret* . . . to the Earl of Hillsborough; also of copies of my Letters to General Gage'. The letter to Germain is dated September 28, 1776, nearly a year and a half after the beginning of open hostility with the colonies at Lexington and *more than a year and a half before the outbreak of war with France*. In these dispatches, Carleton observed, 'and *indeed in all my political letters, I had a war of this sort constantly in view . . . and have not the least reason to change my opinion of these matters*'.[1] It would seem to be unnecessary to search further for Carleton's dominant motives in the *Quebec Act*. Many years afterwards he wrote that 'the Quebec Bill . . . took place at a time, when the Province was too much disturbed by the late rebellion to think of anything further than self defence, and immediate preservation'.[2]

IV

With this basic theme in view the details of Carleton's policy in the *Quebec Act* fall into place with complete unity of purpose. By December, 1767, a month after the letter to Shelburne quoted above, Carleton is prepared to make a recommendation with regard to the laws of the province. It is clear that the first consideration here is the position of the seigneurs. The French law upon which 'their Honors, Property, and Profits, as well as the King's Dues, in a great Measure Depended' had one supreme advantage. It had

[1] *Shortt and Doughty*, ii. 675–6. Italics are my own.

[2] Dorchester to Sydney, June 13, 1787, *id.*, ii. 866.

'established Subordination, from the first to the lowest . . . and secured Obedience to the Supreme Seat of Government from a very distant Province'. Carleton advised the repeal of Murray's ordinance of September 17, 1764, introducing English law, 'as null and void in its own nature, and for the present leave the Canadian Laws almost entire'. Accompanying this recommendation went the draft of an ordinance to re-establish seigniorial tenures of land retroactively 'without Interruption from the Time of the Conquest of this Country by the British Arms'.[1] The implications of French feudal tenures—the oath of the seigneurs, the exact accounting for their tenants, the obligation to appear in arms for the defence of their sovereign—were left to a later dispatch which reached England only after Hillsborough had become Secretary of State for the Colonies.[2]

When the British Government, bewildered by the absence of 'any specific or particular proof of any Grievances in Judicature', directed the governor, the Chief Justice, William Hey, and the Attorney-General, Francis Masères, to report formally 'whether the Canadians in particular are, or think themselves aggrieved', Masères prepared the masterly report which he afterwards published in 1772.[3] The vexed legal problem in Quebec lies outside the present survey, but Masères's report 'had not the good fortune to be approved by his excellency. Another report was thereupon drawn up by other hands agreeable to the governor's sentiments'.[4] This report the Government refused, by a vote of eighty-five to forty-six, to produce when the *Quebec Bill* was before the House of Commons,[5] and it is clear from Masères's criticism at the time that Carleton succeeded in overriding both his legal advisers and 'thought fit to mention only one method of settling the laws of the province, which he strongly recommends to his Majesty'. Carleton's original preference, it is clear, was for French law both criminal and civil, as urged by the seigneurs; with the exception, however, of 'the use of the Torture & the Punishment of breaking on the Wheel', and the addition of the 'Privilege of the Common

[1] Carleton to Shelburne, Dec. 24, 1767, *Shortt and Doughty*, i. 288–91. *Id.*, i. 292–4.

[2] See below, p. 119, and *Shortt and Doughty*, i. 299–301.

[3] *A Collection of Several Commissions, and other Public Instruments, Proceeding from his Majesty's Royal Authority, Relating to the Province of Quebec*, London, 1772. See *Shortt and Doughty*, i. 327–76.

[4] Maseres's postcript, *id.*, i. 369.

[5] Cavendish, *Debates on the Quebec Bill*, p. 94.

Law Writ of Habeas Corpus' and of trial by jury in capital offences.[1] Wedderburn and Hey, it seems, were responsible for the preservation of English criminal law,[2] but despite a bad half-hour which Carleton must have had on this topic at the bar of the House, British commercial interests in Quebec passed under the antiquated *Coutume de Paris*. The French civil law was subject to amendment by governor and council under the *Quebec Act*, but even this scanty concession was concealed from the Quebec merchants, and the governor's Instructions with regard to it were concealed even from the council. Where this measure of British law could give offence, the interests of the seigneurs must indeed have been paramount. It is reasonable to suppose that Carleton's enthusiasm for 'the Natural Rights of Men'—'meer Castles in the Air' (as that sturdy pragmatist had assured Shelburne) unless the King's dominion in Quebec could be secured—had less to do with the legal provisions of the *Quebec Act* than the prospect of re-establishing 'Subordination from the first to the lowest' and 'Obedience to the Supreme Seat of Government'.

V

Carleton's policy with regard to an Assembly—the most revolutionary phase of the *Quebec Act*—was the counterpart of his reliance upon the seigneurs. On one occasion he assured a group of petitioners in Quebec that he 'had no Objection to Assemblies in General'; but when they ventured to hope that he had no objection to a petition for an Assembly for Quebec in particular, Carleton replied that he 'had many Objections . . . it seldom conveyed the sincere Desire of the Subscribers . . . it had an Appearance of an Intention to take away the Freedom of granting or refusing the

[1] See *A Memorandum of things necessary for establishing Laws and Government in the Province of Quebec*, in Carleton's handwriting in the *Dartmouth Papers*, vii. 2352, *Pub. Arch. Can.*: 'First, to get rid of the Proclamation of 1763 . . . and to restore the old Law and Constitution. . . . 4thly To erect proper Courts of Judicature The nearer such Courts are to the Old ones in Form, the more agreeable they will be to the Inhabitants and more likely to have their Effect. . . . 6thly To abolish the use of the Torture & the Punishment of breaking upon the Wheel. 7thly To allow the Inhabitants the Privilege of the Common Law Writ of Habeas Corpus,' &c.

Cf. the Memorandum of Lotbinière at the time of the *Quebec Act*: 'Dans la demande qu'ils font de leur loix, il n'est nullement question d'en excepter celles qui regardent le criminel.' *Shortt and Doughty*, i. 562. Cf. also Carleton to Dartmouth, June 7, 1775: 'To render the Colony of that Advantage to Great Britain, it certainly is capable of, would require the reintroducing the French Criminal Law, and all the Powers of it's Government.' *Id.*, ii. 666.

[2] *Id.*, i. 536 n.

Request'. 'Tho' I had turned the Matter often in my Thoughts, (he continued) I could hit off no Plan that was not liable to many Inconveniences, and some Danger; That perhaps they might be more fortunate, and I should think myself obliged to them, if they would shew me one'. For nearly a year Carleton 'imagined, they had laid aside all Thoughts of the Kind', until one of the agitators who had formerly kept 'a small Ale House' in the north of Ireland, 'appearing zealous for the Presbiterian Faith', and having made a little money and 'gained some credit among People of his Sort' had turned patriot, and with the assistance of others 'egged on by Letters from Home' was at work again for an Assembly. 'The better Sort of Canadians (added Carleton) fear nothing more than popular Assemblies, which, they conceive, tend only to render the People refractory and insolent. Inquiring what they thought of them,[1] they said, they understood some of our Colonies had fallen under the King's Displeasure, owing to the Misconduct of their Assemblies, and that they should think themselves unhappy, if a like Misfortune befell them.'

In a more serious vein Carleton recorded his political faith without ambiguity:

> 'The British Form of Government, transplanted into this Continent, never will produce the same Fruits as at Home. . . . A popular Assembly, which preserves it's full Vigor, and in a Country where all Men appear nearly upon a Level, must give a strong Bias to Republican Principles; Whether the independent Spirit of a Democracy is well adapted to a subordinate Government of the British Monarchy, or their uncontrolable Notions ought to be encouraged in a Province, so lately Conquered, and Circumstanced as this is, I with great Humility submit to the Superior Wisdom of His Majesty's Councils.'[2]

If the truth were told of Carleton's honest conceptions of colonial government, even a council was not at all times well adapted for 'due subordination'. Upon his arrival at Quebec in 1766 Carleton had identified himself with the faction hostile to

[1] It must have been a well-informed wag who inquired of Carleton during his examination at the bar of the House of Commons during the discussion of the *Quebec Bill* whether 'any pains (had) been taken to explain to such persons the excellence of such a constitution, and the advantages that would arise from it'. Cavendish, *Debates*, p. 112.

[2] 'For my own part, I shall think myself Fortunate, if I have succeeded in rendering clear Objects, not allways discernable at so great a Distance.' Carleton to Shelburne, Jan. 20, 1768, *Shortt and Doughty*, i. 295–6.

Hillsborough was appointed Secretary for the Colonies the day after this letter was written in Quebec.

Murray by calling them together, as he afterwards explained, 'for private Information'. When Col. Aemilius Irving, in the interests of harmony, suggested to his fellow-councillors 'that it was accident & not Intention', Carleton retorted that it was nothing of the sort: 'let him explain his Reasons for so doing, He had no authority from me—But that there may be no further Doubt, I hereby make known to you, that I both have and will, on all Matters which do not require the Consent of Council, call together such Councellors as I shall think best qualified to give me Information: and further, that I will ask the Advice and Opinion of such Persons, tho' not of the Council, as I shall find Men of good Sense, Truth, Candor, and Impartial Justice. . . . After I have obtained such Advice, I will still direct as to me shall seem best'.[1]

After the *Quebec Act* Carleton took advantage of the second article of his Instructions fixing the quorum of the council at five to consult those only whose acquiescence could be relied upon.[2] Chief Justice Livius thus found himself virtually excluded from the council. When he protested, Carleton, whose own angry resignation had already been accepted by Germain, dismissed him (as the Board of Trade afterwards noted) with 'no complaint or imputation whatever . . . prefer'd against him in his Judicial Capacity'. At the inquiry which Carleton declined to attend, the Board made it clear that he had no right 'to select and appoint any such persons by name, as he shall think fit to make a Quorum. . . . There does not appear to us good and sufficient cause for displacing Mr. Livius'.[3] Much could be urged in extenuation of Carleton's conduct, but the governor's reasonableness in interpreting colonial government was not unlike Sir Anthony Absolute's: 'no one more reasonable, when I am not thwarted; no one more easily led when I have my own way.'

In truth Carleton's model for Quebec is to be sought far beyond the age of Tudor 'conciliar government'. Four months after advising Shelburne to 'leave the Canadian Laws almost entire' in order to re-establish French feudal tenures in Canada, Carleton urged the practical advantages of French feudalism:

> 'All the Lands here are held of His Majesty's Castle of St. Lewis, and nothing I am persuaded, would be so agreeable to the People, or tend

[1] *Shortt and Doughty*, i. 279.

[2] 'Acts of Legislation only excepted, (in which case you are not to act without a Majority of the whole).' *Id.*, i. 595.

[3] *Id.*, ii. 698–704. See *The Tragedy of Chief Justice Livius*, by Professor Burt in *Can. Hist. Rev.*, Sept., 1924, pp. 196–212.

more to securing the Allegiance of the New Subjects to His Majesty ... than a formal Requisition of all those immediately holding of the King, to pay Faith and Homage to him at his Castle of Lewis; The Oath, which the Vassals take upon the Occasion, is very Solemn and Binding, they are obliged to furnish what they here Term their Aveu et Denombrement, which is an exact Account of their Tenants and Revenues, and to discharge whatever they owe their Sovereign, and to appear in Arms for his Defence. . . .

The Canadian Tenures differ, it is true, from those in the other Parts of His Majesty's American Dominions, but if confirmed ... will ever secure a proper Subordination from this Province to Great Britain.'[1]

The response of the seigneurs to these prospects—the *habitants* who did not appear in these calculations unexpectedly developed opinions of their own, as Carleton afterwards discovered to his cost—is to be traced in petitions for the restoration of French law and in the memorial of 1773 foreshadowing with suggestive accuracy the chief features of the *Quebec Act*. 'It is easy to see', wrote Masères, 'that the foregoing petition . . . has been made the foundation of the Act'. It may be, as Professor Kennedy points out, that the petition was 'inspired from sources which Masères's Huguenot honesty least suspected'.[2]

VI

Meanwhile the Board of Trade had been wrestling with the problem to very different purpose. Whatever doubts may have been cited by Murray or Carleton in Quebec it was clear that the Board entertained none whatsoever. In a carefully drafted *Report* of September 2, 1765, and in their *Representation* of the same date, the Board reaffirmed 'the form of Government approved and Established in 1763'.[3] Murray's 'principal error' had been not indulging the French but denying them equal rights 'with the rest of His Majesty's Subjects'. The Board knew of 'no Law by which Roman Catholicks, as such, are disqualified from being Electors' for an Assembly.

The Instructions to Murray were repeated to Carleton in

[1] Apr. 12, 1768. *Shortt and Doughty*, i. 299–301.

[2] *Id.*, i. 504–11. *An Account of the Proceedings . . . to obtain a House of Assembly*, London, 1775, p. 131. *The Constitution of Canada*, p. 47.

[3] Providing for a 'complete Legislature' and courts as in 'Nova Scotia, the situation & Circumstances of which did, at the time of Establishing Courts of Justice therein (before the expulsion of the Acadians), bear a near Resemblance to the situation & circumstances of Quebec.' *Shortt and Doughty*, i. 237–48.

1768,[1] and in the following year a still more insistent *Report* was presented over the signature of Hillsborough himself and six other members of the Board. No more deliberate avowal of policy is to be found at any stage of this historic controversy. It was made in response to a petition of London merchants praying 'that a full Legislature may be speedily granted for that Province; and that a number of His Majesty's Roman Catholic Subjects there may be admitted into the Council and House of Representatives'. Among the appendices of the *Report* appear no fewer than eighteen documents, including Carleton's letters to Shelburne and Hillsborough, reports of the Attorney- and Solicitor-General, Carleton's *General State of the Canadian Noblesse*, and his draft ordinance for re-establishing French law and feudal tenures in Quebec. The Board affirmed that their recommendations were 'founded on the fullest Information'; that they were guided 'in those parts, that include great constitutional Questions, by the opinions of the ablest Lawyers in this Kingdom'; that 'no information necessary in this important consideration is wanting', and that 'the subject matter has undergone the most mature examination'. Nothing is wanting to bring the deliberate policy of the Board of Trade into direct juxtaposition with that of Carleton in Quebec.

The purpose of the Board in 1763 had been 'to extend to his Majesty's new Subjects those Privileges, which exist in the principles of a British Constitution'. Without such a constitution 'above eighty thousand brave and loyal Subjects, do. . . . Stand prescribed from every privilege, and denied every right, the possession of which can alone ensure their affection, and fix their attachment to the British Government'. To establish a 'complete legislative power' in Quebec it was now necessary to call an Assembly to which 'it is humbly conceived the Faith of the Crown stands fully pledged'.

That pledge committed the Board to perhaps the most tolerant and generous religious policy since the Reformation. The 'New Subjects' were to be admitted not only 'into the Council and House of Representatives, but also into the Courts of Judicature, and other Offices of Government'. The technicalities which had been held to bar Roman Catholics from these rights had already been abrogated in Grenada and were known 'both upon Antient precedent and late opinion of Law, to be a Matter entirely in His

[1] Cf. ss. 11 and 16 of Murray's Instructions with ss. 10 and 15 of Carleton's. *d.*, i. 185, 187, 304, 307.

Majesty's Discretion'. For the Assembly the franchise was to be extended to Protestant and Roman Catholic alike. In order to ensure representation of British commercial interests, the trading centres of Quebec, Montreal, and Three Rivers were to return Protestants only, this plan to be considered 'merely in the light of experiment'. Elsewhere Roman Catholics were fully eligible both for election and for office.

With regard to the Courts, the Board urged immediate action upon their previous *Report* of 1765 correcting the aberrations of Murray's ordinances.[1] For ecclesiastical affairs the Board drew up two series of recommendations which require no comment here beyond the fact that provisions 'affecting rights and property' were to be left for special legislation. The entire scheme required no Act of Parliament but could be put into immediate operation by royal prerogative as in other 'royal' provinces like Nova Scotia and New Hampshire. In emphasizing their 'most mature examination' of the entire problem—'the fullest Information' and the advice 'of the ablest Lawyers in this Kingdom'—it is clear that the Board had more in mind than praise for their own industry. In truth the import of Carleton's policy for Quebec was now unmistakable. In a letter which the Board added in an appendix, Carleton had already sought permission to 'go Home for a few Months':

> 'By being upon the Spot with the King's Servants, I might clear up to them many Points, and remove many Difficulties, which, at this Distance, can neither be so thoroughly discussed, or perfectly understood, as is necessary for the King's Service, whose Interests, in Regard to the Province, I really believe, I could more effectually promote and advance by a Residence of a few Months in London, than of so many years in this Country.'[2]

Carleton's uneasiness under the circumstances is easily under-

[1] *Id.*, i. 237–46. There was every attempt to safeguard 'any Rights or Claims' based upon the French régime: the Board advised that 'the several Courts shall admit and be Governed in their proceedings by the French Usages and Customs, which heretofore have prevailed in Canada, in respect to such property', and that 'to render these Provisions effectual, Care should be taken, that not only the Chief Justice, but also the puisne Judges should understand the French Language; and that one of those Judges at least should be well versed in the French Customs and Usages above mentioned.' *Id.*, p. 246.

Hillsborough who had been a member of the Board as early as 1763 wrote in 1768: 'I can take upon me to averr, that it never entered into Our Idea to overturn the Laws and Customs of Canada, with Regard to Property.' *Shortt and Doughty*, i. 297.

[2] Appendix No. 18, *Shortt and Doughty*, i. 392 n., 395.

stood: Hillsborough had informed him that the important business of Quebec was 'now drawing near to some conclusion'.[1] But the uneasiness of the Board is equally apparent. Perhaps it would have been still more so had they known what other influences were already in the ascendant against them. As early as March 6, 1768, it had fallen to Hillsborough as the new Secretary of the American Department, to confirm Carleton's scheme for French law and feudal tenures. 'His Majesty approves of every Sentiment.' Carleton's draft ordinance 'corresponds in almost every part with His Majesty's Opinions'.[2] It was clear that no time was to be lost. 'However satisfactory it might be', wrote the Board, 'to receive Governor Carleton's Sentiments upon many points', there was no justification for delay 'in a case of so great Importance, as to affect not only the security of this Colony, but with it, that of all His Majesty's other Dominions in America'.

Thus the most generous and comprehensive scheme hitherto projected for the government of Quebec was commended to the Crown for immediate execution.

The Quebec Act Passes

I

With the *Report* of July 10, 1769, the curtain falls upon British policy in Quebec, and the sequel is largely a matter of reconstruction after the fact. The *Report* of the Board of Trade was sent to Carleton under cover of the most carefully guarded secrecy. No part of it was to be communicated to any other person. In discussing 'any Difficulties or Doubts' he was to 'avoid the Appearance of their being other than the Result of your own Reflections; and I am particularly to desire (added Hillsborough) that you will bring back the Copy of the Report with you, without suffering it to fall into any other hands whatever'.[3] With the copy of the *Report* went the assurance that no action should be taken without Carleton's advice and presence in London.

Behind Hillsborough, now translated to the inner circles of royal influence as the first Secretary of State for the American Department, were already mustering the tacit forces of the Grenville tradition.[4] The mantle of Elijah had fallen upon Elisha. It is reasonable to suppose that the centre of gravity in colonial affairs

[1] Oct. 12, 1768, *Shortt and Doughty*, i. 325. [2] *Id.*, i. 298.
[3] *Id.*, i. 377, n. 1. [4] Cf. Knox's *Extra Official State Papers*, ii. 39–43.

was passing from the Board of Trade to the Cabinet and the Crown itself, and that the carefully matured policy of the Board was already in full retreat before the exigencies of state policy in America.[1] In 1769, as we have seen, William Knox, Grenville's chief protégé, had published *The Controversy between Great Britain and her Colonies Reviewed* for the purpose of 'bringing back the Colonies to their duty'.[2] In the following July, with Grenville's benediction upon him, he was installed as Under Secretary for the American Department under Hillsborough, with every mark of mutual understanding and confidence.[3] It was in the following month that Carleton returned from Quebec, and even the scanty evidence now available in the *Dartmouth Papers* indicates how close must have been the co-operation behind the scenes.[4] When the curtain goes up again Hillsborough is busy elsewhere, and Dartmouth, who had been President of the Board in 1765, is in the American Department; but Carleton's policy is in full possession of the stage, and the official apologist for the *Quebec Act*, as we have seen, is William Knox.

The progress of the Bill to its final form would be hard to trace,

[1] See the memorandum in the *Dartmouth Papers*, vii. 2353 endorsed *Opinion On the Government and Laws of Quebec* (n.d.): 'I think the Office that hath been devolved on the B. of T. of framing the Constitution of Quebec . . . was not properly speaking their original Business, It being a matter of general State Politics.'

Cf. also C. Greville to Dartmouth, July 18, 1774: 'I must tell you that the dissatisfaction among the Lords of Trade is general & it has been often said that if no other business but signing was expected that it would be unnecessary to attend.' *Dartmouth Papers*, vii. 2368. See also Cramahé to Dartmouth, Nov. 11, 1772: 'The Earl of Hillsborough, in his Letter No. 12, having signified to General Carleton, that . . . the General might for the future confine himself to one channel of correspondence, without transmitting to their Lordships Duplicates of his Dispatches, We have conformed thereto ever since and shall continue so to do.' *Q. Series*, 9. 51. 'Letter No. 12' does not appear in the *Q. Series*, but No. 13 is dated July 9, 1768. *Q. Series*, 5–2, p. 602.

[2] *The Controversy . . . Reviewed*, p. 207.

[3] 'However happy I should be to undertake an office under his Lordship, which so intirely corresponded with my views and habits, I could not think of making any engagement without first communicating his offer to Mr. Grenville, and receiving his approbation. The noble Earl replied, that he knew of my connection with Mr. Grenville before he sent to me. . . .

I liked the situation, and had the greatest respect and esteem for the principal, and wished much to be connected with his Lordship.' *Extra Official State Papers*, ii. 40, 42–3.

[4] Knox to Dartmouth, Apr. 30, 1774; Memorandum in Carleton's handwriting (n.d.); Memorandum in Knox's handwriting (n.d. but probably Apr. 30, 1774); Pownall to Dartmouth, July 17, 1774, &c. *Dartmouth Papers*, v. 2341; vii. 2352; vii. 2360; vii. 2369, &c.

and the task is perhaps unnecessary here. It was said in debate that 'no one has dared to avow *this Bill*—that it has been prolem sine matre creatam'; and Lord North himself refused to name its sponsors.[1] The Bill was introduced in the House of Lords on May 2, 1774, by Lord Dartmouth, whose well-known piety and benevolence, it is safe to say, covered vicariously a multitude of sins.[2] The debates remained unknown and unpublished for sixty-five years until the shorthand notes of Sir Henry Cavendish were discovered in the *Egerton Manuscripts* in the British Museum. The proceedings, in fact, from May, 1768, to June, 1774, had remained almost a sealed book, 'so strictly was the standing order enforced for the exclusion of strangers, and so rigidly were those persons punished who ventured to make public the speeches of the members'.[3]

For the *Quebec Act* in particular, the fugitive phrases that survived at the time indicate the widest divergencies of opinion. In official language the measure was based upon 'justice and humanity', and 'the sentiments and inclinations of those who are to be governed'. The King himself, having refused an answer to a petition presented by the Lord Mayor of London[4] because the Bill had not yet been 'presented for his royal assent', proceeded immediately to the Houses of Parliament and assented to the Bill, observing that 'it was founded on the clearest principles of justice and humanity'.[5] But the phrases which passed so unsuspectedly into historical currency for later generations could scarcely have convinced anybody in 1774 who was not already in agreement with North's fatal policy against the American colonies; and indeed it is

[1] *An Appeal to the Public Stating and Considering the Objections to the Quebec Bill* (Thomas Bernard), London, 1774, p. 56; *Debates of the House of Commons in the Year 1774, on the Bill for making more Effectual Provision for the Government of the Province of Quebec, drawn up from the Notes of the Right Honourable Sir Henry Cavendish, Bart.*, ed. J. Wright, London, 1839, p. 8.

[2] 'A Noble Man I hear of a very religious turn.' Murray to Ross, Dec. 4, 1765, *Murray Papers*, i. 289. Cf. Wm. Gregory's Memorial: 'Your Lordship's well known Character for being the Protector, Patron, and Advocate of Injured & Oppressed Innocence.' *Dartmouth Papers*, vii. 2381.

[3] Cavendish's *Debates*, p. iii. 'During the proceedings in the House of Lords on the three bills for the government of America, the members of the House of Commons . . . had been refused the usual admission behind the throne.' *Id.*, p. 169.

[4] 'Attended by several aldermen, the recorder, and upwards of one hundred and fifty of the common Council . . . supplicating his Majesty not to give his assent to the bill.' *Id.*, p. 3.

[5] *Ibid.* Cf. Knox's *Thoughts on the Act*, pp. 15, 32, &c: 'framed upon the strictest principles of justice and humanity.'

unnecessary to go beyond the sponsors of the measure itself for evidence that it marked a very fundamental reversal of colonial policy.

II

The first object of the Bill, in the words of Carleton's own *Memorandum*, was 'to get rid of the Proclamation of 1763 with the Commissions and Ordinances depending thereon and to restore the old Law and Constitution'.[1] By the *Quebec Act* all vestiges of British policy after 1763—the Proclamation so far as it related to Quebec, the governors' Commissions, all ordinances relative to civil government and justice, and 'all Commissions to Judges and other Officers thereof'—were specifically 'revoked, annulled, and made void'.[2] The 'old Law and Constitution' which Carleton so far succeeded in restoring was in effect 'a constitution such as the world never saw before'. 'With regard to state policy', said Burke, 'the only difference is, they will have George the Third for Lewis the Sixteenth'.[3] In 1763, 'the Benefit of the Laws of our Realm of England' had been promised to 'all Persons Inhabiting in or resorting to' Quebec, pending the calling of an Assembly. By the *Quebec Act* French civil law re-established alike the 'Honors, Property and Profits' of the seigneurs and the feudal obligations of the *habitants*; and it was not the fault of the seigneurs that French criminal law did not re-establish 'the use of the Torture & the Punishment of breaking upon the Wheel'.[4]

By Proclamation and Commission in 1763 'the King had immediately and irrevocably granted' an Assembly 'in like manner as in other provinces under the King'. By the *Quebec Act*, for the first time since the British constitution had been 'restored to its true Principles', a governor and council were to form by statute the normal legislature of a British province.[5]

In 1763 precise instructions were issued for 'the advantageous and effectual Settlement of our said Province' to be encouraged by 'Proclamation in all the Colonies in North America'. 'It is one object of this measure', said Wedderburn in 1774, 'that these

[1] *Dartmouth Papers*, viii. 2352.

[2] 14 Geo. III, c. 83. *Shortt and Doughty*, i. 572.

[3] Cavendish's *Debates*, p. 289.

[4] Carleton's *Memorandum, Dartmouth Papers*, viii. 2352; Lotbinière's *Choses Indispensables, &c., Shortt and Doughty*, i. 562. Lotbinière spoke 'tant en son nom, qu'au nom des Canadiens'. *Id.*, i. 564.

[5] Lord Mansfield in *Campbell* v. *Hall*, *id.*, i. 531; Lords of Trade to Lawrence, Mar. 25, 1756, *N.S.*, *A. Series*, 59. 22.

persons should not settle in Canada'.[1] But the *Quebec Act* was more than the reversal of Shirley's 'Great Plan'. It was the culmination of a slowly maturing policy in the inner circles of government with regard to the whole future of settlement in America. It is clear that Hillsborough, Carleton, and Knox were all opposed on general principles to the settlement of the hinterlands west of the Alleghany Mountains, and particularly, as it now appeared, to the extension of the boundaries of Quebec to the Ohio and the Mississippi as provided by the *Quebec Act*. When this extension was determined upon for other reasons, they insisted at least upon 'the french mode of Seigneuries . . . as corresponding with the whole scope & purpose of the Bill. . . . The Crown ought not to change those Tenures even when the Lands come into the hands of English subjects'. Knox is careful to add Carleton's significant hint that 'the Tenure by Seigneurie gives the Crown great power over the Seigneur' which would be lost if British grants of land were permitted in the Act. Dartmouth altered the Bill accordingly, and on the day before introducing it in the House of Lords assured Hillsborough that 'if it is not wished that British Subjects should settle that country nothing can more effectually tend to discourage such attempts'.[2]

During the debates official comment upon this phase of policy was very guarded, but Thomas Bernard in his published speech for the third reading of the *Quebec Bill*, stated with less restraint that the measure in its relation to the American colonies would have 'another good effect, to restrain and prevent their *back settlements*, where they would be beyond the reach of our controul; and will oblige them to cultivate the sea-coasts, where, so long as we command the sea, we shall always have a power of *coercion* over them'.[3] Knox in his *Thoughts on the Act* maintained that 'nothing

[1] Cavendish's *Debates*, p. 58.

[2] It had been Hillsborough's consistent policy to stop settlement west of the Alleghany Mountains; and even Knox on taking office under him had found 'no occasion to make his Lordship any representations upon the subject'. *Extra Official State Papers*, ii. 43. Hillsborough in fact resigned the seals of the American Department in 1772 on account of the projected plan of a separate government on the Ohio. *Id.*, ii. 44. The grant to Wharton, however, was not made. The Memorandum (n.d.) in Knox's handwriting in the *Dartmouth Papers*, vii. 2360, proving that Hillsborough, Carleton, and Knox were staunchly of the same opinion as late as April 30, 1774, is endorsed 'Lord Hillsborough's objections to the Quebec Bill in its present form'; the date is fixed by Knox's letter to Dartmouth in *Dartmouth Papers*, vi. 2341. See *Shortt and Doughty*, i. 551–4, and particularly the excellent notes.

[3] *An Appeal to the Public*, London, 1774, p. 55.

would prove more fatal to the authority of this kingdom over America' than the settlement of the hinterlands; the task of stopping it 'can only be done by giving a power in the governor of Quebec'.[1] In *The Justice and Policy of the Late Act* Knox is still more specific: 'the whole of the derelict country is, by the first clause of the act, put under the jurisdiction of the governor of Quebec, with the avowed purpose of excluding all further settlement therein'.[2] 'This is the border', exclaimed Wedderburn on the second reading of the Bill, 'beyond which, for the advantage of the whole empire, you shall not extend yourselves'.[3]

III

So much by way of deliberate reversal may be deduced from the official support given to the Bill in 1774. But in truth the ministers were not dependent upon debate for their majority; they carried through the main features of the measure with cool and sardonic resolution. Government alone had access to the reports of Carleton, of Wedderburn, of Thurlow, and of Marriott—the reports of the Board of Trade had long since been lodged in the recesses of state policy or were mentioned in debate only to be perverted.[4] All motions for papers were voted down by disciplined majorities: that for Carleton's report by 85 to 46, that for Thurlow's, Wedderburn's, and Marriott's by 85 to 45.[5] The *sanctum sanctorum* of state was open, said Burke, to the sponsors of the Bill; 'but the curtain is drawn upon us, and the door is shut'.[6]

[1] Settlements there were 'so contrary to those solid maxims of policy that penetrates into the future consequence of things, that it demands the greatest attention to prevent them'. *Thoughts on the Act*, pp. 29–30.

[2] 'And for the establishment of uniform regulations for the Indian trade.' P. 43.

[3] Cavendish's *Debates*, p. 58.

[4] See Bamber Gascoyne's speech in Cavendish's *Debates*, p. 93. Gascoyne, though a member of the Board (he had not signed the *Report* of 1769), was now in complete accord with the *Quebec Bill*. He opposed the vote for papers, and was one of the government tellers. *Id.*, pp. 94, 95.

Cf. Thomas Townshend, Jr.: 'Where are the members of that board of trade? Why have they gone from their opinions? Gentlemen who have signed their names to a report, should tell us why they now have differed from that report.' *Id.*, p. 231.

[5] *Id.*, pp. 94, 95. Cf. Dempster: 'My thanks to the gentlemen opposite, for allowing us any information upon this subject at all. . . . The administration have taken eleven years to consider of the subject; they have had it referred to the board of trade, and to the law officers abroad and at home . . . the only reason—why we are not to have the necessary light, is the time it would take to copy the reports.' *Id.*, p. 95.

[6] Cavendish's *Debates*, p. 172.

Baffled by the denial of material evidence the opposition had little at first to offer but general criticism—the arbitrary principles in the Bill, the 'sullen silence' of the government majority, the 'concurrence' which carried the Bill irresistibly forward. Five witnesses were permitted to appear when the House resolved itself into committee; but the evidence of at least two of them was not illuminating. The cross-examination of Dr. Marriott, the Advocate-General, and occasionally that of Carleton himself, can scarcely be read with gravity. The governor, as one member of the House sarcastically expressed it, was 'the most valuable witness I ever heard in my life. The general stood at that bar some hours, and now no gentleman is a bit the wiser'. At one stage the evidence reads like the story of the siege and sortie which formed one of the most brilliant exploits of that dauntless soldier less than two years later in the defence of Quebec. When the name of Le Brun was mentioned Carleton replied that he knew 'a great deal of him', and poured forth such a torrent of well-informed vituperation that the witness was abruptly 'ordered to withdraw' until the scandalized committee could recover its equilibrium.[1] The legal fencing of Marriott, the Advocate-General, on the other hand, was so adroit and nimble in its wit, so elusive and non-committal in its purport, that the ten pages of his evidence deserve to live as literature even if they contributed nothing to the matter under discussion. Colonel Barré, whose trenchant mind and incisive diction have brought him into the field as a candidate for the authorship of the *Letters of Junius*, admitted that 'there is no hitting this gentleman'. 'I cannot persuade myself to be out of temper with him. He was mounted very high, and pranced and pranced, and never moved from the place.' [2]

But the cool nonchalance of North and Wedderburn, and the unanimity of an invincible majority, inspired no laughter. Burke had returned to London too late for the second reading of the Bill; he solemnly protested that he approached it 'not only with my mind unprejudiced, but with a determination to avoid everything that had any shadow of passion in it';[3] but the evidence of Masères, Hey, and Lotbinière, and the inordinate haste of the government, drove home a conviction that some unexplained and sinister purpose lurked behind the Bill. Thus Masères maintained that 'the

[1] Cavendish's *Debates*, pp. 123, 112, 115–16.

[2] *Id.*, pp. 175, 239. Marriott's evidence, pp. 163 *et seq.*

[3] *Id.*, p. 233.

best method of giving satisfaction' to the Canadians was 'by retaining a system of English laws, with such alterations as it may be necessary to introduce'; and that an Assembly 'would be very agreeable to the Canadians, if Catholics were admitted into it'.[1] Chief Justice Hey stated that 'the body of the people are not at all dissatisfied with the conquest', though 'the higher part are'; that he had 'been unfortunate enough to differ with general Carleton' by recommending that British laws 'should be considered as the leading system of judicature'; that 'such a mixture might be made, as would be agreeable both to the Canadians and British subjects . . . and answer every purpose of state policy', though the seigneurs had 'risen in their demands of late, and hope to be gratified to the utmost extent of their desires'.[2]

Lotbinière on behalf of the seigneurs had pressed for French criminal as well as French civil law; he was 'in his own opinion much against' an Assembly; though the 'natural inclinations of the Canadians' were in favour of it, 'provided they were allowed to be a part of it themselves . . . if they had not expressed any desire for a legislative assembly, it was from having been informed, that, in that assembly, they would not be allowed as Roman Catholics, to sit'.[3]

In the face of this evidence the most mysterious features of the Bill—the boundaries, the insistence upon 'the Laws of *Canada*, as the Rule' for Quebec, the systematic indulgence of the seigneurs in conjunction with the coercive measures of the same session against the American colonies—began to wear a sinister and menacing aspect. By North's own admission the Bill was included among the measures which were designed 'to put an immediate stop to the present disorders in North America' and to make 'permanent provisions . . . for better securing the just dependance of the colonies'.[4] To that note the chief opposition to the Bill was pitched, and in the end perhaps no single measure of that whole cycle of coercion aroused more vehement defiance on both sides of the Atlantic than the *Quebec Act*. In 1779 Masères asserted that 'it had not only offended the inhabitants of the province itself, in a degree that could hardly be conceived, but had alarmed all the English provinces in America, and contributed more, perhaps,

[1] *Id.*, pp. 129, 132. Masères, whose distrust of the Roman Catholic Church was almost an obsession, preferred postponing an Assembly for seven years. *Ibid.*

[2] *Id.*, pp. 154, 156, 157.

[3] *Shortt and Doughty*, i. 562; Cavendish's *Debates*, p. 162.

[4] *Id.*, p. 13.

than any other measure whatsoever, to drive them into rebellion against their Sovereign'.[1]

IV

In truth no more fateful year is to be found in British history than 1774. It was the year of the *Boston Port Act*, the *Quartering Act*, the *Massachusetts Government Act*, the *Administration of Justice Act*, and of the first Continental Congress at Philadelphia. It was in 1774 that Vergennes became the Minister of Louis XVI. It was the year of Burke's *Speech on American Taxation*—just two weeks before the *Quebec Bill* was introduced—when the last vestiges of sound policy seemed about to vanish and 'all is confusion beyond it'. Deep and fundamental as the American issue had become there were those who still claimed that conciliation could yet keep it from becoming irremediable. Coercion, though proclaimed from the housetops by Knox and whispered anonymously by the King's ministers, had not yet resulted in that 'first drop of blood' which, as Chatham foretold, would make 'a wound of that rancorous, corroding, festering nature that it will straightway mortify the whole body'.

Thus the *Quebec Act*, which is now chiefly remarkable for its subsequent influence upon Canadian history and politics, belonged in its origin and in its context essentially to the age before the deluge. It was devised to preclude a 'Catastrophe shocking to think of'. Beyond all question, for weal or for woe, it was not without influence both upon the beginnings and upon the subsequent course of the American Revolution: though scarcely perhaps in the way its advocates intended. Chatham and Burke and Fox thus viewed the *Quebec Act* in a background then for the last time contemplated with hope by British statesmen—the background of an undivided Empire. Let it be conceded that this, the greatest issue of that generation or of any other, had the first claim upon the thought and allegiance of public men. And indeed the *Quebec Bill* was attacked not because it ignored the American situation but because, as the opponents of the Bill came to believe, it dealt with the American situation upon principles so reactionary that none thereafter could mistake their import.

'It is not right', said Fox, 'for this country to originate and establish a constitution, in which there is not a spark or semblance

[1] Quoted with approval by Wright, editor of the *Parliamentary History*, in the Preface to Cavendish's *Debates*, p. v.

of liberty.' It was 'a perfectly despotic government, contrary to the genius and spirit of the British constitution'. It carried with it 'the appearance of a love of despotism, and a settled design to enslave the people of America, very unbecoming this country. My idea is, that America is not to be governed by force, but by affection and interest'.[1] 'Am I sure', asked Burke, 'that this despotism is not meant to lead to universal despotism?'

> 'No free country can keep another country in slavery. The price they pay for it will be their own servitude. The constitution proposed is one which men never will, and never ought to bear.... By being made perpetual it is evident that this constitution is meant to be both an instrument of tyranny to the Canadians, and an example to others of what they have to expect; at some time or other it will come home to England.'

Burke's last word upon the Bill (June 10) was a warning that 'Canada will become a dangerous instrument in the hands of those who wish to destroy English liberty in every part of our possessions'.[2]

The boundaries fixed by the Bill were assailed as evidences of sinister and deliberate policy. 'I observe in this description of the frontier', said Dunning, 'a studied ambiguity of phrase. I cannot tell what it means; but I conjecture that it means something bad.' Burke spoke of 'a line of circumvallation' about the other colonies; and Colonel Barré suspected a design of securing 'a frontier at the back of almost all our capital settlements.... I suspect something behind which has not yet come out.... I look upon this measure as bad in itself, and as leading to something worse ... it carries in its breast something that squints and looks dangerous to the inhabitants of our other colonies'.[3]

But Barré's suspicion went deeper than this and it was not to be thwarted. At a midnight session, during which Burke in sheer physical exhaustion left the House in protest,[4] Barré forced from North an admission that 'by the passing of this bill' French subjects in Quebec would be put 'in possession of all the privileges

[1] Cavendish's *Debates*, pp. 61, 62.
[2] *Id.*, pp. 89, 290.
[3] *Id.*, pp. 16, 189, 42, 43. As already noted both Carleton and Hillsborough opposed the extension of the boundaries up to the end of April, and were reconciled to it only by the exclusion of British settlement and the uniform establishment of French feudal tenures. Carleton's plan was to operate between Quebec and New York, and thus to 'separate the Northern from the Southern Colonies'. See above, p. 112.
[4] *Id.*, p. 230: 'I have neither strength of body nor energy of mind, to proceed at this late hour.'

they before enjoyed', and could therefore 'serve the King of England, as officers and private soldiers, without taking the oaths, &c.'.[1] In tense and impassioned language Barré avowed 'a more serious and deeper detestation of this bill than before':

> 'I suspected throughout that there was some mischief in it, not avowed in the bill itself. A very extraordinary indulgence is given . . . calculated to gain the hearts and affections of these people. To this I cannot object, if it is to be applied to good purposes; but if you are about to raise a Popish army to serve in the colonies—from this time, all hope of peace in America will be destroyed. The Americans will look on the Canadians as their task-masters, and, in the end, their executioners. I smelt this business out from the beginning. . . . I wash my hands of this business. I here declare my solemn aversion to it. I know what you mean. *Liberavi animam meam!* I have foretold the thing. There is not a man in the government that means to deny it.'[2]

V

Other features of the Bill met a less critical reception. The House was disposed to accord the amplest recognition to the legal usages and custom of the French régime, but what was the meaning of the insistence upon French civil law instead of British as the basis of the legal system of Quebec?[3] Why was it deprecated by the Chief Justice and Attorney-General of Quebec before the bar of the House, and why was it promoted by Carleton—'the general officer' as Burke is careful to call him—in a report which the government refused to produce? It is worthy of remark that Burke supported the virtual 'establishment' of the Roman Catholic Church in Quebec by the legalization of tithe; stipulating, however,

[1] *Id.*, pp. 227, 228.

'Mr. *William Burke*.—Has the King the power of ordering the army to any part of his dominions ? . . .

Mr. *Baker*.—The difficulties thicken so amazingly, that it is almost impossible to go on with this bill. . . .' *Id.*, p. 228.

Lord Barrington on the government side afterwards contradicted North's view. *Id.*, p. 229.

[2] Barré's challenge was not met: 'The *Attorney-General*.—The single question is, whether this clause should stand part of the bill? . . . How the future condition of Canadian soldiers and officers can be made a part of the argument, I cannot see. . . .

Lord *Barrington*.—What the learned gentleman states is undoubtedly true. Whether the Canadians can or cannot be soldiers or officers has nothing to do with this clause.' *Id.*, pp. 228, 229.

[3] . . . 'In as large, ample, and beneficial Manner, as if the said Proclamation, Commissions, Ordinances, and other Acts and Instruments, had not been made.' *Quebec Act*.

that it must be a 'legal provision not an arbitrary provision' and must not be 'dispossessable at the King's pleasure'. 'I want as much of law as you please, and as little of the King's pleasure as possible'.[1] Wedderburn, on the other hand, made it clear that by the Bill 'all this indulgence (was) given subject to his Majesty's approbation. . . . So that all tithes are subject to be taken from them'.[2] While toleration as distinct from 'establishment' was not involved in the Bill, no more ardent appeal is to be found on either side than Burke's famous plea for that 'healing, Catholic principle': 'the thirsty earth of our own country is gasping and gaping, and crying out for that healing shower from heaven'.[3] No more tolerant conception of an Assembly, moreover, is to be found —even in the *Report* of the Board of Trade in 1769—than in Fox's challenge to North: 'Hitherto, I have not heard a single argument against the establishment of an assembly. . . . No one has urged the circumstance of the people of Canada being Roman Catholics as an objection to an assembly, and I trust I shall never hear such an objection stated.' North's reply was a question and a statement. 'Is it safe . . . to put the principal power into the hands of an assembly of Roman Catholic new subjects? . . . There is something in that religion, which makes it not prudent in a Protestant government.'[4]

But the core of the Bill was not tithe nor civil law nor Roman Catholic 'establishment' but arbitrary governance, and the use which the administration proposed to make of it in America. In that sense the real alternative to the *Quebec Bill* is to be sought not in the fierce denunciations of 1774—for it was too late to offer any concrete alternative but postponement till the next session—but the *Report* of 1769 which had seemed upon the point of acceptance before Carleton's return to England. In truth the bolt had already fallen, and the debates of 1774 were but distant thunders, full, nevertheless, of menace and of portent. Not even the strictest censorship upon the debates of both Houses[5] could prevent these reverberations from crossing the Atlantic. Chatham's 'Olympian thunders' descended wrathfully upon the third reading of the *Quebec Bill* in the House of Lords. The disconnected phrases that survive in the *Chatham Correspondence* must give but an imperfect

[1] Cavendish's *Debates*, p. 217.
[2] *Id.*, p. 55.
[3] *Id.*, p. 222.
[4] *Id.*, pp. 246, 247.
[5] See above, p. 124 and note 3.

impression of that 'piercing and terrible note'. No voice more potent than his had ever spoken to America. Tortured in mind and body, he appeared at Westminster, a shadow of the Great Commoner; but no more vehement or prophetic invective ever fell upon the central theme of the *Quebec Bill*. The Act would 'put the whole people under arbitrary power'. 'It was a most cruel, oppressive, and odious measure, tearing up justice and every good principle by the roots.' 'The bill established a despotic government in that country.' The whole temper of the measure was 'tyrannical and despotic'. The extinction of trial by jury was 'a very alarming circumstance', and he was 'a bold man who proposed such a plan'. In making the Roman Catholic Church under the arbitrary approbation of the Crown 'the established religion of that vast continent', the Bill was 'a child of inordinate power'. Turning to the bishops in the House of Lords he asked 'if any of that bench would hold it out for baptism'. In conclusion, states the report, 'he pathetically expressed his fears that it might . . . finally lose the hearts of all his Majesty's American subjects'.[1]

The Quebec Act in America

I

The burst of resentment aroused by the *Quebec Act* throughout the American colonies has sometimes been attributed to its association with the Coercive Acts of the same session against Massachusetts. The facts would seem to warrant no such discount. It is not difficult to account for the notoriety of the *Quebec Act* even among the 'intolerable Acts' of 1774.

The *Boston Port Bill* and other coercive measures of that year were admittedly temporary. The *Quebec Act*, as Burke pointed out, seemed to be the result of inveterate policy. After ten years of delay it bore all the marks of cold calculation—'an instrument of tyranny to the Canadians, and an example to others of what they have to expect'. Whatever hope the American colonist might retain in individual statesmen, or colonial agents, or the British public, it was impossible to mistake the temper and official policy of the King's ministers. Letter after letter in American newspapers denounced this 'military government', this 'detestable Quebec Bill, which is so evidently intended as a bridle on the northern colonies'.

[1] *Chatham Correspondence*, iv. 351–3.

'The Altar of Despotism is established in America!'[1] The Act was singled out in the *Suffolk County Resolves* as 'dangerous in an extreme degree . . . we are indispensably obliged to take all proper measures for our security'.[2] Alexander Hamilton in his *Remarks upon the Quebec Bill* marked the peril that menaced the colonies from an arbitrary government upon their frontiers, from a foreign law and an established Roman Catholic Church: he discerned two 'great purposes in contemplation—first, the subjugation of the colonies and afterward that of Great Britain itself'.[3]

The first Continental Congress met at Philadelphia scarcely more than two months after the *Quebec Bill* received the royal assent. In the *Journals* of that momentous gathering, the Act appears in every variety of protest—in the *Suffolk County Resolves* approved by the Congress, in the *Non-importation Association*, in the *Declaration and Resolves*, in the *Address to the People of Great Britain*, in the *Memorial to the Inhabitants of the British Colonies*, in the *Petition to the King*, and in the *Address to the Inhabitants of Quebec*. The Act was declared to be 'impolitic, unjust, and cruel, as well as unconstitutional, and most dangerous and destructive of American rights'. It resulted in 'erecting a tyranny there, to the great danger . . . of the neighbouring British colonies'. 'By the influence of civil principles and ancient prejudices', it was designed 'to dispose the inhabitants to act with hostility against the free Protestant colonies'. It was the culmination of the 'ministerial plan for enslaving us . . . that by being disunited from us, detached from our interests, by civil as well as religious prejudices . . . they might become formidable to us, and on occasion, be fit instruments in the hands of power to reduce the ancient free Protestant Colonies to the same state of slavery with themselves'. 'It is clear beyond a doubt, that a resolution is formed, and is now carrying into execution, to extinguish the freedom of these colonies, by subjecting them to a despotic government'.[4] Nor was this conviction less spontaneous in America than it was general, for the debates upon the Bill were, of course, unknown even to the British public. Thus in America as in Great Britain the most discerning minds of their day were moved to desperation. Chatham's fears

1 Quoted in Smith, *Struggle for the Fourteenth Colony*, pp. 80, 81, 82, &c., *q.v.*
2 *Journals of the Continental Congress*, ed. Ford, i. 35.
3 *Works*, ed. Lodge, p. 187.
4 *Journals of the Continental Congress*, ed. Ford, i. pp. 66, 72, 76, 87, 88, 99, &c.

had been but too truly prophetic that the *Quebec Act* 'might . . . finally lose the hearts of all his Majesty's American subjects'.

But the Act had a still more deplorable effect upon the American colonies. By opening the flood-gates of suspicion it brought all that was least worthy in colonial prejudice surging to the top. Never did Chatham more instinctively gauge the temper of New England than when he predicted the effect upon them of 'popery and arbitrary power'. 'The whole nation has taken the alarm', wrote Thomas Young to Samuel Adams. Gage wrote to Dartmouth that the Protestant religion was believed to be in danger—'They cannot be made to believe the Contrary'.[1] In the *Address to the People of Great Britain*, in strange contrast to the *Address to the Inhabitants of Quebec*, the Congress itself expressed its 'astonishment, that a British Parliament should ever consent to establish in that country a religion that has deluged your island in blood, and dispersed impiety, bigotry, persecution, murder and rebellion through every part of the world'.[2] When men like John Jay could draft so desperate an appeal to Britons it is easy to understand the fears of Cumberland County townsmen that the Act might bring back the days of Frontenac and 'introduce the French and Indians into our frontier towns'.[3]

II

In one respect at least the *Quebec Act* was still more disastrous, and in a sense perhaps decisive. Meredith's open letter to Chatham, published anonymously in 1774, had hinted at 'a fatal necessity . . . to *coerce* America'. It was reprinted almost immediately in New York and attributed to Lord Lyttelton.[4] The fears of a 'popish army' from the north to reinforce Gage in Boston ran like wildfire through the northern colonies, in many instances inspired by as clear an insight into the strategic importance of Quebec as Carleton himself had shown to Gage in 1767.[5] A well-informed observer at the Continental Congress wrote to Dartmouth from Philadelphia (September 25, 1774) that the fire which hitherto might easily have been quenched or controlled now

[1] Quoted in Smith, *op. cit.*, pp. 85, 88. For many similar extravagances see the same, pp. 80–93.

[2] *Journals*, ed. Ford, i. 88.

[3] Quoted in Smith, *op. cit.*, p. 86.

[4] *Letter from Thomas Lord Lyttleton to William Pitt, Earl of Chatham on the Quebec Bill*, New York, 1774.

[5] See Smith, *op. cit.*, pp. 81–6, and above, p. 112.

threatened a general conflagration. Up to the *Quebec Act* there had always been 'deliberate measures of petitioning previous to any opposition'. With the *Quebec Act* these were 'laid aside as inadequate to the apprehended danger and mischief, and now the people are generally ripe for the execution of any plan the Congress advises, should it be war itself'. The 'apprehended danger and mischief' was 'the idea of bringing down the Canadians and savages upon the English Colonies'.[1]

It was on the very morning the second Continental Congress met at Philadelphia (May 10, 1775)—ten days after the *Quebec Act* was to come into force and three weeks after Lexington—that Ethan Allen and the 'Green Mountain boys' took Ticonderoga. Brown's mission of the previous March on behalf of the Boston Committee of Correspondence had obtained rather more authentic news from Quebec than Carleton was likely to get from the self-interested seigneurs, and it is necessary, therefore, to discount the resolutions of both Congress and the Connecticut Assembly that the captors of Ticonderoga and Crown Point were already actuated by 'imminent dangers and calamities' from the north.[2] But when Brown presented the report of his mission (May 18) Congress declared that 'there is indubitable evidence that a design is formed by the British Ministry of making a cruel invasion from the province of Quebec, upon these colonies, for the purpose of destroying our lives and liberties, and some steps have actually been taken to carry the said design into execution'.[3]

A few weeks later the *Declaration on Taking Arms* was drawn up by Congress to be placed in the hands of George Washington. It contained the assertion, drafted by John Dickinson, the most moderate member of the Committee, that 'We have received certain intelligence that General Carleton, the Governor of Canada, is instigating the people of that province and the Indians to fall upon us'.[4] An observer who had 'spoken with many members of the Congress' afterwards wrote from Philadelphia that Congress was finally induced to support an invasion of Canada 'partly from assurances of a ready Reception by ye Canadians, and partly to

[1] Joseph Reed to Dartmouth, quoted in Coffin, *The Province of Quebec and the Early American Revolution*, University of Wisconsin, 1896, p. 482. See *Journals*, ed. Ford, i. 27 n.

[2] The captured troops had been sent into Connecticut. See 4, Force II. 570, quoted in Smith, *op. cit.*, p. 167; also *Journals*, ed. Ford, ii. 56.

[3] *Journals*, ed. Ford, ii. 55–6.

[4] *Id.*, ii. 152.

show the ministry that their Dependence on Canada is vain'.[1] In truth the plan 'long since Recommended'[2] by Carleton had come to grief, and when Montgomery and Arnold reached the frontier in the wake of the 'Green Mountain boys', they found themselves looking into a defenceless country.

In its effect upon the American situation, therefore, the *Quebec Act* proved to be a miscalculation. It had been associated by North and the King himself with other Acts 'to put an immediate stop to the present disorders in North America' and to secure 'the just dependance of the colonies'.[3] It proved to be not a deterrent but a violent irritant which did much to precipitate resistance by force in the thirteen provinces to the south and nearly lost a fourteenth, as we shall see, to the cause of the Revolution.

III

For Quebec itself the miscalculation was scarcely less disastrous. The Church responded loyally to the privileges accorded to them by the *Quebec Act*, and to the fear of vastly different treatment at the hands of the dour New Englanders. Less than a fortnight after the capture of Ticonderoga Bishop Briand addressed a *Mandement* 'To All the People of this Province' with an appeal against the attempt of those 'in revolt against their lawful Sovereign . . . to prevent you from opposing their pernicious design'. The government of His Very Gracious Majesty and 'the recent favours with which he has loaded us' warranted 'gratitude and zeal in support of the interests of the British Crown'. The *Mandement*, says Têtu, 'ensured to the British all the influence of the clergy', and there can be no doubt that the clergy adopted in many instances the most drastic measures to counteract the influence of emissaries from the south and to consolidate their own.[4] But the Church could not fight; and Carleton looked to the seigneurs to meet the obligations implied in the *Quebec Act*.

The day after his return to Quebec (September 18, 1774)

[1] John Ewing to Dr. Williamson (London), n.d., in *Intercepted Letters*, 1775–1777, *Col. Off. Records, C.O.* 5, vols. 40–2, p. 50. *Pub. Arch. Can.*

[2] Carleton to Gage, Sept. 20, 1774, in reply to Gage's proposal for 'a Body of Canadians and Indians . . . to form a Junction with the King's Forces in this Province'. Carleton added with regard to the Indians 'but you know what sort of people they are'. *Shortt and Doughty*, ii. 584. See below, p. 140.

[3] Cavendish's *Debates*, p. 13.

[4] Quoted in Smith, *op. cit.*, i. 210; Têtu, *Évêques de Québec*, 1889, p. 327. See the evidence cited in Coffin, *op. cit.*, p. 505 n. 2, &c. and Smith, *op. cit.*, pp. 196, 209, 210, &c.

Carleton received an inquiry from Gage in Boston for 'a Body of Canadians and Indians . . . to form a Junction with the King's Forces in this Province'. Carleton replied that the Canadians had testified 'the strongest marks of Joy, and Gratitude, and Fidelity . . . for the late Arrangements made at Home in their Favor', and that 'two, three or more Battalions' of them would be available for the plan which he himself had 'long since Recommended'. To Dartmouth a few days later Carleton wrote that 'All Ranks of People amongst them vied with each other in testifying . . . the Desire they have by every Mark of Duty and Submission to prove themselves not undeserving of the Treatment they have met with'.[1]

But the wish was father to the thought. Never were interested calculations more egregiously at fault than Carleton's reliance upon the old-world feudalism of Quebec. The governor, who had rested the weight of British policy in the *Quebec Act* upon the seigneurs and had believed only what he wanted to believe from their self-interested response, now discovered that a very important element had been left out of calculation. The 'due subordination' of the *habitants* was not forthcoming. The disillusionment came swiftly and convincingly, and it is unnecessary to go beyond the letters of the Chief Justice and of Carleton himself for the ironical retribution visited upon those who had put their trust in the traditions of French colonial government for Quebec.

The truth was that the hold of the seigneurs over the *censitaires* —largely a fiction even at the close of the French régime—had been reduced by 1774 almost to a shadow. French civil law, far from inspiring the *habitants* with 'Duty and Submission', soon filled them with suspicion and resentment. The seigneurs, wrote the Chief Justice, were 'too much elated with the advantages they supposed they should derive from the restoration of their old Privileges & customs, and indulged themselves in a way of thinking & talking that gave very just offence'. The *habitants* showed their resentment by 'every shape of contempt and detestation':

> 'What will be your Lordship's astonishment when I tell you that an act passed for the express purpose of gratifying the Canadians & which was supposed to comprehend all that they either wished or wanted is become the first object of their discontent & dislike. English officers to command them in time of war, & English Laws to govern them in time of Peace, is the general wish.'[2]

[1] *Shortt and Doughty*, ii. 583, 584.

[2] To the Lord Chancellor, Aug. 28, 1775. *Id.*, ii. 668 ff.

In May, 1775, Carleton at St. John's called upon 'the Noblesse . . . to collect their Inhabitants . . . but tho' the Gentlemen testified great Zeal, neither their Entreaties or their Example could prevail upon the People; a few of the Gentry, consisting principally of the Youth . . . formed a small Corps of Volunteers'. The *habitants* as a rule flatly refused to serve under their old masters.[1] The seigneurs did not always escape without personal violence. A few were made prisoners, sometimes with the help of the 'Bostonians'. When Ethan Allen appeared before Montreal his forces were 'two thirds Canadians'. Despite the best efforts of the seigneurs and 'every argument urged by the clergy' Carleton reported that 'the Canadian peasantry . . . not only deserted their duty but numbers of them have taken arms against the Crown'. 'The Rebels have been much more successful with them.' 'Had the present Settlement taken Place when first recommended', Carleton wrote ruefully to Gage, 'it would not have roused the Jealousy of the other Colonies, and had the appearance of more disinterested Favor to the Canadians.'[2]

Reluctant as Carleton was to face the facts, it was not long before the facts got the better of his prepossessions. His correspondence during this descent into Avernus is not pleasant to read. The *habitants* were 'the most ungrateful Race under the Sun', a 'wretched People . . . blind to Honor Duty & their own Interest'; a people of 'stupid baseness' and of 'blind Perverseness'. The 'Base Desertion of the Canadian Peasantry' was 'an unprecedented Defection without even pretending the least cause of Complaint'. There was 'nothing to fear from them in prosperity, and nothing to hope for when in distress'.[3] It will be observed that no blame is attached to the authors and direct beneficiaries of the *Quebec Act*. Carleton had not hesitated to rely upon 'the general Cause of the Attachments of Men, Self-Interest'[4] in dealing with the seigneurs; it would seem that the *habitants* like their betters were also human, and that even by the lowest standards of human conduct the invaders were likely to succeed where the seigneurs and the *Quebec Act* had failed. That the *habitants* or even the British settlers in Quebec were amenable to worthier motives seems never to have

[1] Carleton to Dartmouth, June 7, 1775. *Shortt and Doughty*, ii. 664.

[2] Carleton to Dartmouth, Sept. 21, 1775; Oct. 25, 1775; Nov. 5, 1775; Feb. 4, 1775, 'Secret'. *Q. Series*, 11. 261 ff., 267 ff., 274 ff., 290.

[3] *Q Series*, 11. 261, 267, 274; 12. 188, &c.

[4] Carleton to Shelburne, Jan. 20, 1768, *Shortt and Doughty*, i. 294.

appeared above Carleton's political horizon. Had the early successes of the invading army in securing the support of the *habitants* not been neutralized by almost incredible folly as the campaign proceeded, it is conceivable that the *Quebec Act* might have been no less disastrous in Quebec than in the thirteen colonies to the south.

IV

Meanwhile Dartmouth in Great Britain and Gage in Boston continued to rely upon Quebec. In the debates on a motion to repeal the *Quebec Act* (May, 1775) North now stated openly that 'if the refractory colonies cannot be reduced to obedience by the present force, he should think it a necessary measure to arm the Roman Catholics of Canada and to employ them in that service'.[1] In the previous September, as we have seen, Carleton himself was already upon the scene with the plan 'long since Recommended', and hopeful of 'two, three, or more Battalions'. 'The King relies upon the Loyalty & Fidelity of his Canadian Subjects', wrote Dartmouth in July, 1775, 'for their Assistance to suppress Rebellion.' Carleton was directed to raise 'a Body of 3,000 Canadians . . . to act as Light Infantry'. Three weeks later the news from Boston was more serious, and Dartmouth instructed Carleton 'that the number of Men to be raised in Canada, should be double what was first proposed'. It was 'His Majesty's Pleasure that instead of 3,000 Men . . . the number to be raised be 6,000'.[2]

A week later Dartmouth wrote that Gage was to return to England on leave; that Carleton was to have full command 'in Quebec and upon its Frontiers' with Howe 'in the Colonies upon the Atlantic'; if the two forces could effect a junction, the command of the whole was to devolve upon Carleton with the 'full appointments of Commander-in-Chief'.[3] A month later John Pownall, joint Under-Secretary of the American Department, wrote of 20,000 troops to be supplied by Catherine the Great of Russia: 'the greatest part of the Russians will be sent to Quebec'.[4] While Dartmouth was thus disposing of a Russian army and 6,000 hypothetical Canadians, Carleton found himself 'equally unprepared for Attack or Defence; Not six hundred Rank & File fit for Duty upon the whole Extent of this great River'.[5] Six months later, in the

[1] *Parliamentary History*, xviii. 681.
[2] *Shortt and Doughty*, ii. 667 n.
[3] *Q. Series*, 11. 198.
[4] Sept. 8, 1775, *Q. Series*, 11. 217.
[5] Carleton to Dartmouth, June 7, 1775. *Shortt and Doughty*, ii. 665.

ruins of the *Quebec Act* but with resolution still indomitable, he was defending the last square mile of British territory in Quebec.

The sequel belongs to the military history of the Revolution. *Silent leges inter arma*; though it is surely one of the ironies of Canadian history that Carleton's essay in military statesmanship should have been so far redeemed and sanctified by his heroic defence of Quebec that the *Quebec Act* has come to be associated with the incomparable courage of its author in the salvation of Canada. But in truth American policy had already entered upon a new phase. A month before the fall of Montgomery at the Près-de-Ville barricade Germain had succeeded Dartmouth as Secretary for the American Department, and there is discernible in the recall of Gage as Commander-in-Chief, of Legge from Nova Scotia, and finally of Carleton from Quebec,[1] the passing of at least one fatal project of coercion. The subjugation of the 'ancient British colonies' was not to be effected by 'Hylanders', Indians, 'Accadians', 'Germans, Neutrals and Irish' from Nova Scotia nor by Canadians and Indians from Quebec.[2] Carleton's worst enemies, and he had many of them, could scarcely have devised a harder fate than the association of his name with such a triumvirate.

But if ever an aberration of political judgement was incontinently expiated, Carleton must have expiated his at the hands of Germain. The first dispatch of the new Secretary began upon this ominous note. Carleton's own reports of 'unprecedented Defection' among the Canadians 'left no room for any other consideration but that of sending as early as possible a relief to the Town of Quebec'.[3] Thus instead of 6,000 Canadians on the march to 'suppress Rebellion',[4] it was now necessary to organize Burgoyne's ill-fated expedition for the spring of 1776, with 'a large Battering Train' and artillery, eight regiments of British troops, and 5,000 auxiliaries to be 'furnished by . . . the Duke of Brunswick and the Prince of Waldeck', in order to retake Quebec if necessary and secure the 'recovery of the whole Province'.[5] When the expedition

[1] Germain to Carleton, Mar. 26, 1777, 'Separate.' *Q. Series*, 13. 73 ff.; Carleton to Germain, May 22, 1777, *id.*, 13. 156, &c.

[2] See above, p. 80.

[3] *Q. Series*, 12. 1. See also *Q. Series*, 11. 318.

[4] Dartmouth to Carleton, July 24, 1775, *Q. Series*, 11. 182. Burke wrote to Rockingham on Aug. 23, 1775, of the British manufacturers beginning to 'snuff the cadaverous *haut goût* of lucrative war' in supplying provisions and clothing for 'the intended six thousand Canadians'. *Letters*, ed. Laski, p. 201.

[5] Germain to Carleton, Feb. 17, 1775, *Q. Series*, 12. 1.

finally marched south in 1777, Carleton was instructed to 'return to Quebec' leaving Burgoyne to 'proceed with all possible Expedition to join General Howe, and to put himself under his Command'.[1] The abrogation of a task which Carleton above all men in America was fitted to perform—a task which Carleton had made his own by ten years of unremitting anticipation—must have been gall and wormwood; and Carleton drank the cup to the bitter dregs, not without signs of impotent fury. But the iron must have entered into his soul when he was instructed to supply Burgoyne with the necessary handful of French-Canadians and Indian scouts; 'and I am happy,' added Germain maliciously, 'in knowing that your Influence among them is so great that there can be no room to apprehend you will find it difficult to fulfill His Majesty's Expectations'.[2]

Fortunately the deciding factor in the security of Quebec during the closing years of the Revolution was neither the statesmanship nor the magnanimity of the King's ministers. In the wake of Burgoyne's fatal surrender at Saratoga came the alliance between France and the thirteen colonies; and with the French alliance, followed a few months later by the alliance with Spain, the destiny of Quebec may be said to have passed to the ascendancy of another star. In this it can scarcely be doubted that the old French menace of colonial days—the menace which the colonies still discerned in the *Quebec Act* of Carleton and of Knox—was still dominant in the minds of Washington and of Franklin.[3] The implications of the Spanish alliance on the other hand were scarcely less decisive. Spanish fears of American aggression on the Mississippi were no more easily allayed than American fears of French power on the St. Lawrence; and thus it came to pass that the only basis upon which it seemed possible to keep the triple alliance in equipoise—Vergennes's formula of independence but no conquest—may have had more to do with the ultimate security of Canada than all the vigilance of that Swiss 'Chocolate Soldier' of Canadian history, Governor Haldimand, or the presence of British regiments on the St. Lawrence.

V

It is not always profitable to speculate upon the 'might-have-beens' of history. Could the magnanimous policy of the Board of

[1] Germain to Carleton. Mar. 26, 1777, 'Separate.' *Q. Series*, 13. 73.
[2] *Ibid.* For Carleton's angry reply of May 22, 1777, *id.*, 13. 156.
[3] Cf. *Writings of Washington*, ed. Sparks, i. 311–14.

Trade in 1765 and 1769 have done for Quebec what it did for Nova Scotia during the Revolution? Could it have succeeded better than Carleton's project of feudalism and coercion? In truth it could scarcely have succeeded worse. One lesson at least seemed clear from the darkest hours of Carleton's governorship: the surest way to antagonize the *habitants* was to rehabilitate the seigneurs; though it may be urged on the other hand that seigneur and Church together might have wrought more effectively in the cause of old France than in the cause of 'His Very Gracious Majesty King George the Third'.[1] It may be granted, moreover, that the French-Canadians with the exception of the seigneurs were unprepared for an Assembly in 1769. But were they better prepared in 1791 when the province of Lower Canada was segregated from the four or five other British provinces, and was granted an Assembly almost by acclamation?

In 1769 there was yet a prospect of retaining by 'large and liberal ideas in the management of great affairs' something of the 'grandeur and stability' which Benjamin Franklin had foretold for the British Empire at the close of the Seven Years' War. In 1769 the bitterness of the Revolution, the pledges of a reinvigorated feudalism to the seigneurs, the exploitation of the *habitants* in the interests of state policy, were all as yet in the future. In the future also was the menace which infected New England with ineradicable suspicion. And if political conditions were more promising in 1769, the promise of material progress was surely, as Burke said, the best and fairest in colonial history. In 1791 when an Assembly was finally granted, the only neighbours under British institutions were the scattered settlements of Nova Scotia, Cape Breton, Prince Edward Island, New Brunswick, and Upper Canada, in which disintegration rather than co-operation was the order of the day. In 1769 there were fifteen other colonies with nearly three millions of British subjects whose enterprise in the regions of the Great Lakes might have anticipated by half a century the settlement of central Canada. But these speculations are but figments of history, for they presuppose a possibility too vast for imagination itself to conceive—the possibility of an undivided Empire. On the other hand would statesmanship in 1769 have been worthy the name had it concerned itself only with the narrower and not with the larger vision?

[1] Bishop Briand's *Mandement*, Têtu, p. 327.

Would an Assembly in 1769 have led, as Haldimand afterwards stated and as Knox and Carleton no doubt instinctively felt, to the loss of the province to the Revolution? To men of little faith and of Knox's principles the answer was obvious. But it was not borne out by the history of Nova Scotia during the Revolution. If a 'strict regard to the rights of the People in this Province' could keep New Englanders in Nova Scotia 'Animated with the firmest attachment to the Mother Country . . . and dreading a Separation from her Government and protection, as the greatest political evil which can befall us or our posterity',[1] the conciliation of a primitive and conservative French population in Quebec ought not to have been impossible. 'Little, very little,' as Murray had written to the Board of Trade, 'will content the New Subjects.'[2] Lotbinière himself, the spokesman of the seigneurs at the bar of the House, had conceded that the 'natural inclinations of the Canadians' favoured an Assembly, 'provided they were allowed to be a part of it themselves'. Their apathy was due to 'having been informed, that, in that assembly, they would not be allowed as Roman Catholics, to sit'.[3] No more tolerant or magnanimous policy for Quebec had ever been devised than that of the Board of Trade in 1769. None could say of it as Carleton himself said of the *Quebec Act* in 1775 that it was wanting in 'the appearance of more disinterested Favor to the Canadians'. The propaganda in Quebec from the Continental Congress, moreover, was attributable in no small measure to the menace of the *Quebec Act* itself.

It may be urged that self-interest played no small part in the response of Nova Scotia. But could any play of legitimate self-interest in that province compare with the inducements that could be offered through the virtual monopoly of the lucrative fur trade in Canada? In that sense the extension of the boundaries to include the Great Lakes and practically the whole of the chief waterways system in North America would have subserved British interests as effectively under representative as under arbitrary government. It is one of the most remarkable facts of the Revolution that the much-maligned merchants of Quebec and even of Montreal remained so largely British. It was during the Revo-

[1] Reply of Assembly, in *Minutes of Council*, June 29, 1775, *Nova Scotia, A. Series*, 90. Address of Assembly to the Crown and Parliament of Great Britain, June 24, 1775, *id.*, 94. 11.

[2] *Shortt and Doughty*, i. 231.

[3] Cavendish's *Debates*, p. 162. See above, p. 129.

lutionary War that the Canadian fur trade began that phenomenal development which resulted in the North-West Company—within twenty-five years perhaps the largest commercial enterprise in North America. When Carleton, with his handful of men, made his final stand at Quebec, 320 of them were British volunteers and merchants whom Murray and Carleton had disparaged as having no abiding interest in the province.[1] Perhaps the highest tribute to Carleton himself after the successful defence of Quebec is to be found in their Address: the 'determined Resolution, steady Perseverance, and unshaken Constancy, which, during the tedious siege of this City, shone conspicuous in every part of your Excellency's Conduct'.[2] What must have been Carleton's reflections in forwarding that Address to Germain?

VI

Had the opponents of the *Quebec Act* been in power in 1774 would their policy for Quebec have been radically different? 'If it had fallen to Whig ministers to deal with it', writes Professor Coupland in his study on the *Quebec Act*, 'they would inevitably, after studying the facts, have drafted a very similar measure.'[3] With respect to many details that are sometimes regarded as though they were essential features of the Act this surely is the simple truth. The sudden reversal of French law and custom in Quebec in 1764 was almost universally condemned—by the Board of Trade, by Yorke and De Grey, by Thurlow and Mansfield, by Masères and Hey. With the exception of the cardinal feature of seigniorial tenures and the acceptance of French instead of English law 'as the Rule' and basis for the future, a practical compromise might have been much the same under any administration. With regard to religion, we have seen that Burke's defence of tithe itself was more generous than Wedderburn's; that Fox was both more generous and more tolerant of political rights to Roman Catholics than North; that Burke's plea for religious toleration was the most ingenuous appeal on either side.

But there is a difference in spirit; and when one compares the

[1] See Col. Allan Maclean's letter of May 28, 1776: 'The English Merchts. of Canada . . . were greatly soured by the preference, (which they insisted) was constantly given to the Canadians, and I will say that 320 British Militia of Quebec did their duty like brave men, many of the men, and all the Officers at their own Expence.' *Q. Series*, 12. 69.

[2] *Q. Series*, 12. 239.

[3] *The Quebec Act*, Oxford, 1925, p. 116.

comprehensive project of the Board of Trade in 1769 with that which supplanted it in 1774, the difference in time, in spirit, and in principle, becomes in truth unmistakable. Had French-Canadians, who have shown themselves perhaps the most politically minded people in Canada, been introduced into full British citizenship in 1769 in the spirit of magnanimous toleration, might not such a union at such a time have enriched Canadian history and Canadian politics for all generations to come? After the *mariage de convenance* in 1774 upon the basis of arbitrary governance, even the loyalist migrations—the forgotten step-children of the union—could be regarded by Church and seigneur as a violation of the spirit of the *Quebec Act*. And when these step-children proceeded to vindicate their right to the patrimony, can it be a matter of surprise that the step-mother began to reflect ruefully upon the inducements which the other contracting party had employed in 1774? Let it be remembered that whatever had been the attitude of the *habitants* who had not been consulted, the Church and seigneurs, as a whole, had resolutely 'played the game'. And thus representative institutions after 1791 were from the first but step-children in Lower Canada. In such a household, charges of self-interest and bad faith soon poisoned domestic relations; and when the other branch of the family in Upper Canada was brought in at the Union to readjust the balance, it is not difficult to understand the resentment of French Canada. Bitter and uncharitable though many of the judgements of Girouard and of La Fontaine may have been, who can deny that they had reason for their reflections, and that a nobler conception of the destiny of the two races under British institutions at the outset might have gone far to establish the golden rule of toleration and of compromise?

IV

NOVA SCOTIA AND THE SECOND EMPIRE

I

FOR the British provinces the American Revolution left 'the American question' still unsolved. It continued without intermission in Nova Scotia, it arose in the Assemblies of Prince Edward Island and New Brunswick after 1773 and 1785, and it was resumed in the Canadas after the *Constitutional Act* of 1791 almost where the Revolution had left it except for the false lessons that were drawn from that still incomprehensible disaster. The course of the second Empire for fifty years is thus not only reminiscent of the first but scarcely distinguishable from it.

The auguries at least for the old system were more favourable. The loyalists—30,000 in the Maritime Provinces and 10,000 in Upper Canada—could be relied upon, as William Knox reflected, to be 'abhorrers of Republicanism'. Many of them, as we have seen, had 'had enough of Assemblies'. Burke's 'unsuspecting confidence' was again in the ascendant. If the first Empire, as Knox maintained, had failed through lack of 'system', the second could now be systematized at leisure. The virtues of the old colonial system, it seemed, had sprung from the executive; the disasters, from the Assemblies and a Continental Congress. Carleton himself, now Lord Dorchester and Governor-General, could fortify the first; the disintegration of the remaining provinces seemed to forestall the others. Nova Scotia was broken into four fragments, three of which were never to be reunited. One was denied an Assembly altogether. Prince Edward Island, as we have seen, narrowly escaped the same fate. Knox proposed a fifth province on the St. Croix. Quebec was broken into Upper and Lower Canada. Permanent revenues robbed 'the power of the purse' of its terrors or transferred it bodily to the executive.

Not only the American Revolution but the French soon cast its shadow over colonial policy. Aristocracy and an established church—bulwarks against revolutionary Europe—were to be planted in the American wilderness. The good sense of Dorchester and the wit of Fox saved Canada from Pitt's scheme of an hereditary aristocracy as 'the true poise . . . of the constitution',[1] but with the strengthening of the councils 'the American question' trans-

[1] 'The sort of titles meant to be given were not named in the bill; he pre-

formed itself from a contest between the colony and the mother country into a contest between two sets of interests both within the colony, one claiming by virtue of appointment and the other by virtue of representation to control the executive. The issue was further localized by projects for an established church. The results here were quicker and more disastrous. 'Every attempt on the part of the Government to give pre-eminence to the Church', the staunchest of Anglican judges once observed in Nova Scotia, 'creates ten enemies for one friend'. In one province at least the Clergy Reserves jeopardized at last not only the future of the Church but the whole cause of authoritarian governance. Thus the second Empire which began with the same system as the first, with tried materials and with an ideal environment, ran almost the same course. In 1838 Robert Baldwin solemnly affirmed to Lord Durham that without responsible government the Canadas could be held by 'troops alone'. A few years later Howe wrote desperately to Charles Buller that the cause of reform would soon be championed 'by the Enemies of England, not by her friends'. The second Empire was saved at last by wiser counsels and better men. It was not saved without a conflict, but the conflict was parliamentary not military, and the victors were to be found on both sides of the Atlantic.

The course of this second Empire for fifty years is too vast a theme to be attempted here. Two rebellions in the Canadas and the most famous *Report* in colonial history are to be found in this period. But many of the problems which Durham found there, like the conditions out of which they arose, were abnormal and indeed unique in the second Empire. The 'proprietary' type of province they knew, and the 'royal' province they knew, but what were the Canadas? The first type survived in Rupert's Land and in some of the worst features of Prince Edward Island; the 'royal' type developed, upon the whole in 'harmony and moderation', in Nova Scotia and New Brunswick. But the old province created by the *Quebec Act* was a prodigy—a single province by statute in 1774 with a 'constitution such as the world never saw before'; two provinces by statute in 1791 with a constitution which could be abrogated altogether in one of them in 1838 for what Durham and Sydenham both conceded to be a 'despotism'; a united province again by statute in 1841, with problems indeed which defied solu-

sumed the reason was, they could not be named without creating laughter.' Fox in *Parliamentary Register*, xlvi. 391.

tion by any other expedient. Glimpses, nevertheless, of 'the great arcanum' of responsible government are to be found very early in the contest. First perhaps in point of time as in point of unwavering and incorruptible consistency, the Baldwins, father and son, reached 'the great principles' in their final form. Robert Baldwin's memorandum to Glenelg in 1836, enclosed in a still more urgent appeal to Durham two years later, remains the most accurate formula of responsible government up to that time.[1] It is to be found among the *Durham Papers*, and there can be no doubt that Durham had it before him when the *Report* was written, though his own apostolic ardour required perhaps no such stimulus. But Baldwin's indomitable 'principle' and Durham's *Report* alike received their vindication after the Union, not before it; and indeed the *Report* itself beneath its classic diction and consummate literary art scarcely conceals the political turmoil out of which it arose.

No such task in Canada ever challenged the resourcefulness of one man. All three of the major problems of Canadian history—race, responsible government, and confederation—clamoured at once for solution. Durham's plans for the last were abortive and had to be abandoned for a union of the Canadas. The first involved him in one of the most disastrous miscalculations in Canadian history—a prophecy which the French race in Canada resolutely set itself to falsify. Durham's incomparable project of responsible government became, in Charles Buller's phrase, 'the textbook of every advocate of colonial freedom'; but even this was based upon British analogies rather than upon the cogency of colonial conditions, for its context in the *Report* is the province of Lower Canada which by common consent was at that time ungovernable. All this, however, is a commentary not upon the most dynamic of colonial state papers but upon the conditions which Durham found in Canada. Thus while Nova Scotia and Canada were the first to force responsible government in its final form, there was a differ-

[1] *Durham Papers, Report of Public Archives*, 1923, 326 ff. Baldwin's memorandum to Glenelg was printed in *Brit. Parl. Papers*, Mar. 22, 1839 (41), 32 ff.

Baldwin states that 'as early as 1820 . . . some of the Leading Members . . . adopted the principles now contended for as a part of their political creed, and assumed it as necessarily pertaining as much to the provincial Constitution as to that of the Mother Country.' *Ibid.* Robert Baldwin in 1820 was 16 years of age. To his father, Dr. W. W. Baldwin, probably belongs the distinction of formulating adequately the 'principles' for the first time. See Miss Dunham's admirable study of *Political Unrest in Upper Canada, 1815–1836*, Longmans, 1927, p. 166 *et passim*. For Fairbanks's *Memorandum* of 1830 for Nova Scotia see below, p. 157.

ence between them in temper which reflected a vaster difference in historical background. What was the bearing of these two contests upon each other?

II

When Sydenham went to Nova Scotia in 1840 to adjust in person the relations between Sir Colin Campbell and his Assembly—perhaps the neatest of all the contests for responsible government—his secretary Murdock drew upon a long experience at the Colonial Office to draft a confidential memorandum for his guidance. Murdock noted the 'demand for a responsible Executive Council' from Nova Scotia, 'before the question was mooted in Upper or Lower Canada', but he was at a loss to explain the absence of that 'exasperation' which had marked the Canadian contest. 'The facts (he conceded) speak volumes . . . and it is extraordinary that these facts, notorious as they must have been, were never brought under the notice of the Government until 1837.'[1] Such were the traditions of decorum in Nova Scotia and the result. Murdock's own complacency in 1840, as we shall see, arose, it may be, from the same 'exemplary forbearance and moderation' still in evidence among the Nova Scotia reformers. The government, he added, 'could look with perfect confidence to the support of the People of Nova Scotia. . . . There is no disposition to carry out those views so far as to endanger the connection with the Mother Country.'[2]

The oldest Assembly of the second 'American empire' was also the first to win the formal concession of responsible government. It is a tradition that this achievement was largely due to the method; that the low road of moderation was shorter in the end than the high road of the Canadian 'Ultras'. Nowhere were the courtesies of official intercourse or the standards of honour in public life more scrupulously guarded than under the old Halifax 'Compacts'. The magnanimity and moderation of the Reformers belonged to the same tradition, and it was Howe's boast that responsible government was finally won without bloodshed, without a blow, without the breaking of a pane of glass. With that tradition the general conclusions of this essay will be found to agree, but it may be the more necessary to bear in mind from the outset the lesson of Murdock's insouciance in 1840. The Nova Scotia Reformers may have owed more than they were willing to acknowledge to the turbulence of the Canadian agitator.

[1] *Pub. Arch. Can., G. Series*, 265. 8. [2] *Ibid.*

To Howe and Uniacke it seemed that the cause of reform was altogether unnecessarily jeopardized not only by the Papineau and Mackenzie risings but by the uncompromising temper of the 'Metcalfe crisis'. On the other hand La Fontaine, whose opinions were seldom charitable, never acquitted Howe of self-righteousness and time-serving. Even Howe's open letter to Hincks in the Montreal *Pilot* failed to remove this bias. 'I have not more confidence in him', wrote La Fontaine, 'for all that'.[1] In truth, however, the two struggles, mutually obstructive as they seemed at times, were mutually helpful and indeed complementary. The methods were different, but so were the conditions. Each remedied the gravest defects of the other. The one was the first, the easiest, the most natural, and perhaps the most skilfully executed, of all the achievements of responsible government. The other was incomparably the most difficult, the most complicated, and by virtue of its very size and importance the most critical. Had it not been for the Canadian impasse the issue might have been won in Nova Scotia in 1840. Had it not been for Canada, on the other hand, Nova Scotia might never have been prepared to sacrifice cherished traditions in order to force the issue to a conclusion. The deluge of print in the *British Parliamentary Papers* after the Canadian rebellions bears witness in itself to a new interest in colonial policy. For the first time since the American Revolution it played a major part in British politics. The aim of this and the following essay will be to trace these two converging attacks upon the old colonial system. Both are essentially studies in parliamentary tactics. The armies were political parties—in the old Province Building at Halifax, in the House at Toronto, at Kingston, and at Montreal. Supported by the active counsel, as we shall see, of more than one British statesman the result transformed the second Empire and changed the whole basis of its unity.

'Moderation and Harmony'

I

The British temper of Nova Scotia was rooted in the traditions of the American Revolution. Many of these were indigenous, springing from pre-revolutionary sources in the New England migrations. Others were loyalist in their origin, and Murdock's note of a

[1] La Fontaine to Baldwin, May 25, 1844. *Baldwin Papers* (copies of originals in the Ontario Provincial Library), *Pub. Arch. Can.*, i. 15.

'natural sluggishness of the people' is not altogether complimentary. On the other hand, the freedom from 'political dissensions' was not, as Murdock thought, due to the 'remoteness from American institutions and habits'. The intercourse, in fact, was more friendly than appeared upon the surface. As local feuds subsided in the United States thousands of the loyalists had returned without compunction and 'remained Citizens of that Government.'[1] During the War of 1812 the sympathies of New England were notoriously pro-British, and the illicit commercial intercourse was lucrative to both parties. A joint address of council and Assembly in Nova Scotia bears witness to the 'proud and just spirit of their British ancestors' in 'our nearest neighbours in the United States'. In 1817 Dalhousie notes that 'the connection between the respectable inhabitants of this Province, and the States, is yet very intimate; scarcely is there a family that has not Fathers, Brothers, and near relations settled there'. This, however, did not imply 'the most distant doubt of the Loyalty of this Province.'[2]

The rescue of Nova Scotia from 'frontier' dependence upon New England becomes a commonplace in the pages of Haliburton and of Howe. It was perhaps the most solid ground which they had in common. But their methods were characteristically different. Haliburton's were imitative. British traditions of prestige and social intercourse were to be cherished with all the indiscriminate ardour of a Simcoe. Satire, however, is seldom convincing; and the satire upon American tendencies and what Haliburton regarded as their counterpart in Nova Scotia is put—somewhat unfairly—into the inimitable jargon of the Yankee pedlar Sam Slick himself. Haliburton may have confirmed some of his friends, but he confirmed also his opponents and he made no converts. Howe's remedy on the other hand was creative—not to imitate the British but to be British; not to emulate artificial standards but to rely upon the simple 'law that like breeds like'.[3] In stressing the self-respect and enterprise that accompany as well as produce self-government Howe was nearer to the genius of the race than Haliburton. Thus, like Elgin, and long before him, Howe sought the antidote to American republicanism in British self-government, and he had the same robust faith in its superiority. It is curious to find Haliburton the son of a pre-revolutionary New Englander and

[1] Dalhousie to Bathurst, Dec. 14, 1817. *A. Series*, 157. 159 (*C.O. 217*).
[2] *Id.*, 160. 59; 157. 110.
[3] Adderley, *Review of Colonial History*, 1869, p. 11.

Howe the son of a Massachusetts loyalist thus reversing the traditions of their origin.

In other respects Murdock's diagnosis was less faulty. From the problems of race and the worst issues of religion which convulsed the Canadas Nova Scotia was singularly free. The Clergy Reserves which Sydenham called 'the root of all the troubles of the province, the cause of the rebellion . . . the perpetual source of discord, strife, and hatred' had no counterpart in Nova Scotia. By 1828 scarcely more than one-fifth of the population of the province belonged to the Anglican Church,[1] and the bishop himself conceded that an endowment of crown lands would be 'worse than useless'. In 1811 the attempt to commute the quit rents for legislative support for the Anglican Church was rejected in the Assembly, even by Anglicans themselves, 'without a dissentient vote'.[2] Nor had the refusal of the Upper Canadian council for many years to countenance marriage by clergy other than the established churches of England and Scotland been repeated in Nova Scotia. Dalhousie himself took the orthodox view, but the Supreme Court broke through the practice, and a joint Address of council and Assembly found many of its ablest advocates in the Anglican Church. 'It can only be injured in the Province of Nova Scotia', they added, 'by the misguided zeal of its intemperate friends.' Brenton Halliburton, afterwards Chief Justice, in a masterly report once stated bluntly that 'every attempt on the part of Government to give pre-eminence to the Church creates ten enemies for one friend. . . . People on this side of the water are even more tenacious of religious equality than of political. . . . The generality of Churchmen themselves participate in it'.[3] Perhaps the fate of Bishop Inglis in Nova Scotia had something to do with Bishop Strachan's uncompromising tenacity in Upper Canada. Religious strife played no small part, as we shall see, in the politics of Nova Scotia, but there were cross-currents which neutralized its bitterness.

II

The economic conditions of the province were also less forbidding for many years than in Upper Canada. The population in 1828 was 142,548. It was not until the 'thirties that Nova Scotia was outdistanced in the race for second place among the

[1] Kempt to Huskisson, May 12, 1828. *A. Series*, 169. 55. The figures were 31,199 out of 142,548.

[2] *Id.*, 167. 151, 158. 'The Resolutions . . . were brought in by a Churchman.' *Id.*, 169. 49.

[3] *Id.*, 160. 16, 25; 169. 105 ff.

British provinces; though the union of the Canadas in 1841 naturally dwarfed every other province in British North America. In 1828 Sir Peregrine Maitland upon his arrival from Upper Canada was 'most grateful for the advancement to this Government as it is a proof of His Majesty's confidence and favor'. Distances were short and no point was more than a few miles from the sea. The roads, as Governor Kempt reported in 1827, were 'probably better than in any other Colony', with 250 miles of carriage roads in both directions from Halifax. 'Not a single case of bankruptcy has occurred in the whole Province for many years.'[1]

Agriculture, though primitive, had entered upon a new era with the publication of Young's *Letters of Agricola* (1818), in the *Acadian Recorder*. Dalhousie's interest in the agricultural progress of the province was unbounded. Available capital, however, found its way chiefly into the fisheries, the lumber trade, shipping and shipbuilding. In 1830 there were 1,321 ships owned in Nova Scotia, with a seafaring population of nearly 4,500 men. The Cunard shipping interests had their humble origin in Halifax, and in 1842 Bagot's genial friend Haddington—'Neptunus Britannicus', first Lord of the Admiralty—could already write of 'Cunarding it' across the Atlantic. The best traditions of the British Navy flourished at Halifax. Many a snug fortune had its origin in captured French or American ships put up at auction by the Vice-Admiralty Court—twenty-three on one accasion in a single day. Naval and military expenditures, too, wrought insidiously, as Murdock surmised, 'to produce an apathy, in regard to public events'.[2]

Provincial politics reflected these conditions and were frequently dominated by them. Halifax was long the only free port in the province; it was not until 1839 that a delegation from the Assembly—Herbert Huntington and William Young—vindicated at the Board of Trade the right to have free ports 'as many as the Assembly desired'. The banking interests of the province, the predominant mercantile interests with their British, West Indian, and foreign connexions, the garrison, the government, and the chief naval station in the North Atlantic were all concentrated at Halifax. At the meetings of the Legislature the 'stout yeomen of the counties' found their meagre fortunes and hard-driven thrift in constant contrast to the vice-regal state and wealth—much of it adventitious—which met them on every hand at the capital. Official circles, responding to the social standards of Government

[1] *Id.*, 169. 85; 168. 18.

[2] *G. Series*, 265. 8.

House, the garrison, and the navy, claimed the affluence and affected the exclusiveness of a governing class. For many years every member but one of the Executive and Legislative council lived in Halifax. Five of the twelve were at one time partners in the Halifax Banking Company. All but three belonged to the Church of England which comprised but one-fifth of the population. The most resolute opponent of responsible government in the council—himself at one time a Reformer in the Assembly—once observed in a confidential memorandum that 'our House, are comparatively poor men', whereas the Simondses and the Johnstons and the Cranes in the Assembly of New Brunswick were all 'men of considerable and some of them of large property'.[1]

In truth the social life at Halifax, graced at times by princes of the blood in the garrison or the navy, revealed tendencies both good and bad. A long train of periodicals from the *Nova Scotia Magazine* of 1789 to the *Halifax Monthly* of 1830 reflected the taste of the select circles to which they appealed. One of the first of provincial histories—Haliburton's *Historical and Statistical Account of Nova Scotia*—appeared in 1829. In its wake came the beginnings of a provincial literature. But there was another side to what Maitland called 'the highest class of society here'. More than one governor notes the straining after impossible standards; and James Stephen in one of his discerning minutes for Lord John Russell in 1840 has a true word about 'the extinction of Public Spirit in the effeminate passion for mere social and fashionable distinction'. In truth the real opinion of the province is to be found elsewhere. The Hollands in the *Acadian Recorder*, Jotham Blanchard in the *Colonial Patriot*, Joseph Howe in *The Novascotian* struck a truer note of native wit and robust local patriotism. From this source came the challenge to the old order.

III

Nothing but downright merit, however, could have commanded the respect so long enjoyed by the Executive and Legislative Council of Nova Scotia. In Upper Canada the two councils were separate—a fact which simplified immeasurably the objective of the Reformers. In Nova Scotia the same personnel discharged both functions. Appointed nominally 'during pleasure', they sat in effect for life. In more than one instance an office remained for

[1] *Pub. Arch. Can., C.O. 217* (photostat copies, after 1831, from the Public Record Office), 165. 693.

two or three generations in the same family. At the time of the famous 'brandy dispute' in 1830, Chief Justice Blowers had held office since 1788; the Treasurer, Michael Wallace, since 1802; the Attorney-General, R. J. Uniacke, and the Surveyor-General, Charles Morris, since 1808; Jeffrey, the Collector of Customs, since 1811. The normal tone of the Assembly and the press was respectful to the point of veneration, and it is easy to imagine the horror of the Levites when Howe laid impious hands upon the shewbread. The violence of their resentment was at least a measure of their sensitiveness to the slightest taint of public dishonour. To this must be added the sterling worth of Sherbrooke, Dalhousie, and Kempt. Whatever their subsequent fortunes as governors of Lower Canada they commanded 'unbounded confidence' in Nova Scotia. 'Everything continues to go on here', wrote Kempt in 1820, 'in the usual jog-trot way.' [1]

One result of this mutual confidence was very far-reaching—an assured access from all quarters to the governor and to the Colonial Office. In this the Speaker of the Assembly was upon as sure a footing as those who could write 'honourable' before their names. Thus, while the Upper Canadian Tories could pillory 'Goosie' Goderich for granting an interview to Mackenzie, and could deter even Glenelg from granting an interview to Robert Baldwin who had crossed the Atlantic for that purpose in 1836, the intercourse from Nova Scotia remained unbroken. R. J. Uniacke met Bathurst and Horton in 1826 as 'quite a veteran in the King's service', and left in the pigeon-holes of Downing Street the first serious project for a British Confederation.[2] Four years later, in 1830, Charles R. Fairbanks left with Hay at the Colonial Office an elaborate memorandum upon the Executive Council of Nova Scotia, anticipating Lord John Russell's famous dispatch of October 16, 1840, and containing a proposal of momentous import:

> 'The remedy is to be found in applying to the colonies the same principles on which the Government is conducted at home—and by seeking in the House *some at least* of the Advisers of the Executive. . . . Seats in the Executive Councils . . . can consequently be held only during pleasure. . . . It can hardly be questioned that the House of Representatives ought to possess powers similar to those exercised by the House of Commons. They have repeatedly claimed these as their rights and *will* exercise them.' [3]

[1] To Goulburn. *A. Series*, 161. 43.
[2] *Id.*, 167. 334 ff. See *Can. Hist. Rev.*, 1925, p. 142, ed. Trotter.
[3] June 1, 1830. *A. Series*, 172. 86 ff.; *C.O. 217*, 151. 257–282.

In this the Assemblyman could rely as confidently as the Councillor upon a sympathetic hearing at the Colonial Office: as Crane, Chandler, Simonds, and Wilmot from New Brunswick, Young and Huntington from Nova Scotia could attest. When Howe went to London in 1838 he sent in his card to Murdock at the Colonial Office without introduction and was taken in for a half-hour with Glenelg himself—a 'very affable intelligent grey-haired and brail (?) headed looking Scotchman', notes Howe in his diary; 'what passed not fit to put into Note Book which might fall into other hands'.

This freedom of intercourse, however, had also its seamy side in the interminable scramble for office and promotion. In Nova Scotia the game was played with almost quixotic chivalry, but the recurrence of the Speaker's name in that company is suggestive. No fewer than four of the Executive Councillors had passed through the Assembly and had earned the good graces of the Executive in the Speaker's chair. One of them was afterwards known to observe that the 'Supply of Patriots' in the Assembly was becoming 'greater than the demand, and they will thwart and embarrass the Executive Government because it cannot employ and reward them.'[1] It is easy to account for Sherbrooke's tactics with Papineau in Lower Canada. 'If a more turbulent and energetic individual at times arose', observes Murdock in his preliminary sketch of the Sydenham régime, 'it was easy by well-timed concession, to disarm his opposition, if not to secure his support.'[2]

Murdock's failure to detect the change in 1840 is thus easily understood, for S. W. G. Archibald was still Speaker of the Nova Scotia Assembly, and no more adroit and resourceful moderator ever officiated there. In 1825 he reminded Governor Kempt that his 'influence in the popular branch of the Legislature has ever been felt in support of the Executive Government'. A few years later, when his advice was sought upon the turmoil in Prince Edward Island, he added that 'Colonial Assemblies require to be moulded by men of good understanding and honest intentions ... otherwise they will produce little else than vexation'. When the conflict came with the Council on the 'brandy dispute' in 1830 Archibald's stand was correspondingly effective. 'No man in this Assembly', he could say truly, 'has exerted himself more than I have done to preserve the peace and order of the Colony, and no man has been more successful than myself in that particular;

[1] *A. Series*, 173. 14 (*C.O. 217*, vol. 152).

[2] Scrope, *Memoir of the Life of Lord Sydenham*, 1843, p. 117.

indeed, so far have I gone, that I have not escaped some censure'. An enraptured Assemblyman on that occasion exclaimed that Archibald's great speech 'would follow him as long as he lived, and would be looked back upon with pride by his children.'[1]

The traditions of 'honourable ambition', however, were not yet broken. Archibald himself became Attorney-General in 1830 and aspired higher—still without relinquishing the Speaker's chair. Stewart and Fairbanks, perhaps the most discerning of the early Reformers in the Assembly, in due time passed to their reward in the Executive Council and the Court of Vice-Admiralty. A few lines in Howe's commonplace-book must have done service many a time upon the hustings against some of his opponents, once his allies in reform:

> As Bees, on Flowers alighting, cease their hum
> So, settling upon Places, Whigs grow dumb.

For Howe, too, the honeyed trap was spread, and many a perplexed bureaucrat—Murdock among the number—thought that this was the remedy for the troubles of Nova Scotia in 1840. But he misjudged Howe, and, as we shall see, he misjudged the game that was afoot in the Assembly of Nova Scotia.

IV

The spirit and temper of the Nova Scotia Assembly had upon the whole run true to form since the recall of Governor Legge during the American Revolution. From 1818 until the Trade Acts of 1826 it was chiefly concerned with the commercial restrictions of the old colonial system. From 1826 to 1829 there was a memorable contest with the British Treasury and Customs Commissioners for the control of customs revenues. In 1830 the Assembly joined issue with the council in the 'brandy dispute', and fairly carried off the honours of the contest for both temper and moderation. All three were preliminary to the debates of 1834 with which the contest for responsible government may be said to open.

In the first of these, council and Assembly were in complete agreement. After the convention of 1818 with the United States, as John Young in his *Letters of Agricola* notes bitterly, 'the American flag waves triumphant in the port of Halifax' while provincial shipping was almost completely excluded from foreign trade.

[1] *A. Series*, 166. 133 (*C.O. 217*, vol. 144). Archibald to Kempt, May 12, 1828, *id.*, 169. 64 (*C.O. 217*, vol. 148). *The Novascotian*, April 1, 1830.

A joint Address of the council and Assembly 'as the senior British Government in the North American Colonies' invited 'all the Inhabitants of British America . . . to unite with us—not in factious or seditious murmurings', for 'faction and sedition meet no encouragement in this Province', but in an appeal to the 'confidence and assistance of the Mother Country':

> 'It is immediately necessary that the Colonies, in addition to the privileges they now enjoy, should be allowed the same freedom of trade with all the world which the people of the United States have acquired.'[1]

The work of Huskisson in substituting reciprocity for monopoly in the old mercantile system, the opening of Halifax and other ports to foreign shipping, and the Trade Acts of 1826 which provided virtually 'an unrestricted Traffic with all Countries' are features all too lightly stressed in the transformation of the second Empire. 'Had the administration of His late Majesty met the wishes of the North American Colonies fifty years ago with the same liberality', stoutly asserted the aged Uniacke in his *Proposal for Confederation* in that year, 'there cannot be a doubt that the separation of that Country from the British Crown would not have taken place'.[2] The direct influence of the Address of 1818 and of petitions innumerable from Nova Scotia would be hard to estimate, but the temper was exemplary, and in a province predominantly commercial perhaps no severer test could have been devised for it.

The second incident brought the Assembly and the British Treasury into direct conflict. Among other abuses the Acts of 1826 had abolished the fees of the customs officials, but by the instructions of the Customs Commissioners their salaries were to be paid directly from the revenues collected at colonial ports, thus violating, as the Assembly maintained, the *Declaratory Act* of 1778 which had placed the duties for the regulation of trade 'entirely under the controul, and at the disposal, of the Colonial Legislatures'. The new regulations, wrote Governor Kempt, 'excited a considerable sensation in this Colony'.[3]

During the session of 1826, the House, responding to an appeal to 'continue to be a Pattern to other Colonies for Moderation and Harmony in its Legislative Proceedings', restricted its protest to

[1] *Report of Committee* and *Address* in *A. Series*, 160. 59 ff.

[2] April 11, 1826, *id.*, 167. 337.

[3] *Journals*, Apr. 4, 1826; Kempt to Bathurst, May 14, 1826, *A. Series*, 167. 67 (*C.O. 217*, vol. 146).

an Address of 'temperate and respectful remonstrance against those infringements of the Constitutional Rights of the Assembly'. The next year they asserted 'with all deference and respect, but firmly and distinctly . . . that the appropriation of such Duties can originate only in this House', and proceeded to appropriate the customs revenues to the salaries of the officials, 'the rest to be paid to the Provincial Treasury'. The Bill passed unanimously. While it was under discussion, wrote the governor, 'the Legislative proceedings of the Sister Colony on the same subject were received by the Members of the Assembly, and I cannot be surprised that the People of this Province should feel, as they do feel, proud that a course has been pursued here strongly marked by a different Spirit.' 'No other Colony has made such an offer.' The Assembly was disposed to be 'liberal and moderate in all their Proceedings and thereby set a good example to the other Colonies'.[1] Two years, however, passed in silence from the Treasury, and finally in 1829 an exhaustive report upon the whole issue was drawn up by a committee of the House. The right was 'manifestly one which this House ought not, under any circumstances, to compromise or relinquish'. The report bears the signature of Charles R. Fairbanks. The following year, on the motion of Alexander Stewart, the House resolved to hold all customs officials 'personally responsible' for all disbursements other than those 'specifically directed by the Assembly of this Province'.[2] There is no evidence that the 'different Spirit' of Nova Scotia was deeply appreciated in Downing Street, but, though virtue had to be its own reward, the temper of the House had again been exemplary.[3]

With the 'brandy dispute' of 1830 one enters the orbit of reform. 'The restoration of harmony', Fairbanks wrote in his *Memorandum* of that year, 'is not to be expected until after very material changes of Men and measures.'[4] The details of the dispute have little interest here. In 1830 the Assembly discovered to their astonishment that a tax of 1*s*. 4*d*. on brandy since 1826 had

[1] *Id*., 167. 61; *Journals*, Apr. 4, 1826, Feb. 23, 1827; *A. Series*, 170. 48; 168. 42, 10.

[2] *Journals*, Mar. 23, 1829; Apr. 12, 1830.

[3] Cf. Maitland to Murray, July 7, 1830: 'The Assembly piqued themselves on doing handsomely in making a provision which had been so coarsely refused in a neighbouring Province and granted by none of the other Colonies, and I understand much mortification was expressed in the course of the last Session that nothing had since been heard of their Act.' *A. Series*, 171. 163 (*C.O. 217*, vol. 150).

[4] Fairbanks to Hay, June 1, 1830, *id*., 172. 86 (*C.O. 217*, vol. 151).

not been collected on account of a technicality. In re-enacting the Bill the Assembly 'spoke a language upon the Subject which could not be misconstrued'. At a joint conference both Houses were uncompromising, but the Bill finally reached the council only two days before the old revenue laws were to expire. The council, sensing deliberate discourtesy, rejected the Bill, and within a few hours the merchants of Halifax were clearing the warehouses 'without paying a single farthing to the Province'. The Assembly re-enacted the Revenue Bill, but the council refused 'to hold further communication with a Body of men, who had thus outraged the rules which regulate the intercourse of Gentlemen'. The province thus lost a revenue of £25,000. It would be hard to find a more quixotic reversal of 'the power of the purse'. The council, with salaries assured by permanent enactments, had 'cut off the supplies' because the Assembly had granted the Crown too much revenue. The Assembly had become the 'Guardians' of the province and the sponsors of 'the King's government'.[1]

Beyond a doubt personalities played no small part in the contest. Hartshorn, a sturdy old Quaker, and J. B. Uniacke, afterwards first premier of the province under responsible government, both reproached the Assembly with inviting the rebuff. But Archibald, the Speaker, carried an overwhelming majority of 31 to 5 against the council:

> 'This is not a matter of pence but of principle. . . . The rejection of a Revenue Bill . . . will form a new era in the History of the Province. . . . This is my native land, and my home . . . but if its freedom is lost . . . I would travel from it as far as the City of Destruction. . . .
>
> They have distracted the peace of a Colony, the most quiet and orderly within the wide circuit of His Majesty's realms. . . . A more peaceable and well disposed population than that of Nova Scotia do not exist. . . . Why then is it necessary to goad us into ill humour? . . .
>
> God knows I come with reluctance to this discussion and bring to it a melancholy mind.'[2]

The fact that the aim of the council was to 'preserve the Province from the domination of a Democratic faction' is a curious commentary upon the old order in Nova Scotia. To Sir George Murray himself, Wallace the Administrator of the province in

[1] *The Novascotian*, Apr. 1, 1830. *Statement* of council, July 1, 1830, *A. Series*, 171. 134 (*C.O. 217*, vol. 150). *Journals*, Apr. 13, 1830.

[2] Debates of Apr. 1 and Apr. 5 in *The Novascotian.*

Maitland's absence roundly charged the new temper of the Assembly upon the British Select Committee of 1828 and 'its hasty report upon Colonial affairs, without sufficient and impartial information'. The 'spirit of Faction and of Turbulence' had been 'encouraged by the success which has attended the workings of a similar spirit in other places'.[1] A new Assembly elected in the summer of 1830 passed the Revenue Bill a third time with resolution not to be mistaken, and the council without comment bowed to the storm. But again the oil was poured upon the troubled waters. Jeffrey, Archibald's friend, became Administrator, and Archibald himself became Attorney-General. Three years later both again reported 'the utmost harmony'. 'A more harmonious, and orderly, Session of the Legislature was never Witnessed in this Province.' Renewed harmony was ascribed to 'the good understanding . . . between the President of the Council, and the Speaker of the House'.[2]

V

The debate of 1834 on the functions of the council is the clearest forecast of responsible government up to that time, but it still belongs obviously to the old order. There is no concert as yet among the reformers. Upon several of the resolutions Huntington and Fairbanks found themselves in a helpless minority. 'On the main point', said Fairbanks, 'I differ most entirely.'

On December 8, 1832, Goderich had suggested, for Nova Scotia as for New Brunswick and Prince Edward Island, the separation of the Executive and Legislative Councils. Jeffrey with cool nonchalance replied in March 1833, that he had 'not deemed it advisable to bring the subject' even before the council on account of its 'tendency to disturb the peaceful state of the Colony'. When the debate in the Assembly became inevitable in 1834 Jeffrey informed the House—through the Speaker—of Goderich's dispatch in order that the Assembly should not be able to assume 'the whole merit of originating' the policy.[3]

The debate itself after three days of dispassionate discussion resulted in two innocuous resolutions,[4] but in the speeches of

[1] Wallace to Murray, May 10, 1830; *Statement* of council, July 1, 1830. *A. Series*, 171. 16, 125.

[2] *C.O. 217*, 155. 173, 183. From 1831 the Nova Scotia papers in the *Pub. Arch. Can.* are photostat copies of the Colonial Office records.

[3] *Id.*, 155. 145; 156. 437, 'Confidential'.

[4] For the separation of the councils and the opening of the debates of the Legislative Council to the public. *Journals*, Feb. 15, 21, 1834.

Stewart and Fairbanks, Blanchard and Doyle, as reported in *The Novascotian* by the hand of Joseph Howe himself, one detects at last a stirring in the tops of the mulberry trees. Nowhere, said Stewart, was there 'such a combination of power . . . except perhaps in the Borough of Cashel, in Ireland, where the Mayor of the Corporation was the Grand Papa, his twelve sons and sons in law the Aldermen and the twenty four Common Councilmen, so closely connected that they could not enter into the holy bonds of matrimony with the Aldermen's daughters'. Fairbanks, then Solicitor-General, recapitulated his memorandum of 1830 for the Colonial Office:

> 'In England the people operate upon the King through the Ministers, and these have seats in the Legislature. So far from this being the case in Canada, there the Assembly deprived Mr. Mondelet of his seat because he accepted the situation of an Executive Councillor. . . .
>
> Let the Executive Council be chosen . . . from both branches of the Legislature and from others unconnected with either. Let a part of them come here, Sir, to seek support to the measures of the administration; and when they cannot procure the sanction of the people's representatives to the measures they propose, let them either abandon them or resign. . . . The principles of the British Constitution ought to be in operation here as far as they can be introduced. . . . The present system cannot continue.'

A correspondent in Halifax sent this debate in *The Novascotian* to the Colonial Secretary as a timely warning of 'those political troubles which now distress the Canadas'; though one reformer at least in Nova Scotia regarded it, like Bob Acres's letter to Sir Lucius O'Trigger, as 'too civil by half'. Beyond a doubt it has a leisurely and academic air, unstirred as yet by the 'great winds of reality'. The manœuvres still suggest the mimic battles of condottieri. Stewart's popular influence was destroyed by his removal to the council. Fairbanks became Master of the Rolls and Judge of Vice-Admiralty, and the Assembly itself in 1835 barred him in both capacities from the House.[1] It was the vigorous press of Nova Scotia with its robust local patriotism and copious reports of British and Canadian politics that brought the vital issues of the day to bear upon the time-honoured proprieties of the old order. Even the quixotic 'brandy dispute' was less dramatic in its effect than the decision of the Crown in 1835 to challenge the freedom of the press in the person of Joseph Howe.

[1] *C.O. 217*, 158. 237.

Howe and 'the New Model'

I

The achievement of responsible government in Nova Scotia is known in Canadian history chiefly in the gargantuan biography of Joseph Howe. When Howe was at the height of his powers few could come within the orbit of his influence without symptoms of violent attraction or repulsion. Had he hoarded his abilities with the narrow intensiveness of mere talent he might have left a better record for consistency and personal advancement. But Howe's abilities were more than talent, and he poured forth his abounding energies with almost incredible prodigality. His name is perhaps the first in Canadian history to have inspired a cult. The traditions of his native province teem with cumulative reminiscences: how he looked in his speech on the resolutions of 1840 with his great head thrown back and the joy of battle in his eye; how he delighted a company on shipboard with his shrewd talk and his inimitable anecdotes; how he humbled himself 'like a little child' before the issues which he felt to be vital for his country and the Empire; how he loved his native province, its lovely valleys, the healing solitudes of its forests and of the sea; how he rambled to the remotest villages of the province, dignifying their humble life in the pages of *The Novascotian*, repaying their adoration with his own abounding confidence in their firmness and their intelligence, boisterously kissing their wives and playing like a school-boy with their children; how under the inspiration of one of his 'flashes', as he used to call them, he could toil with daemonic energy for days on end at an open letter to a British statesman, a confidential memorandum for an under-secretary, or one of his great speeches; how he could smite his enemies hip and thigh and forgive them, sometimes to his own undoing.

It would be easy to criticize Howe in detail. Compared with Robert Baldwin in Upper Canada, whose grasp of the principles of responsible government from beginning to end had the uncompromising precision of a Robespierre, Howe's early ideas were frequently instinctive and diffuse. His views in the Assembly in 1837 are substantially those of Fairbanks in 1834 or 1830. Hincks in Canada was a much abler administrator, a much shrewder partisan, ruthless in his methods, discreet and incisive in every emergency. Gifted with a suppleness which Howe's rugged and independent spirit could not emulate, Hincks easily outdistanced his Nova Scotian rival in the race for Imperial favours and the subtler accommodations of British bankers and contractors. In truth Howe's genius was too exuberant for precision. He spoke with great fluency and wrote with ease. It was the criticism of busy men like Grey and Elgin that he usually spoke and wrote too much; that his argument was too involved and his political judgement sometimes tainted with the cardinal sin of indiscretion. Much of this exuberance must have been habitual. The bulk of his writing was done week by week for his own day—for a public that was known to him in every mood and that forgave in turn his harmless extravagances, his abounding spirits, and his egotism.

But even in *The Novascotian* Howe seldom 'plodded like a man for working-days'. At his best the sheer exuberance of his thought and language, like Burke's, could transcend criticism with the ease and prodigality of genius. In a sense Howe is the Burke of the second Empire, for despite the contrast between his humble lot in Nova Scotia and Burke's in Georgian England both gave of their best to the same cause. Both saw its meaning for 'posterity down to remote generations'. In magnanimity, in prophetic insight into the workings of British traditions at their best, in the broad humanity which underlay a certain gorgeousness of language common to both, there was much in both that was 'meant for mankind'. In a sense the aberrations of both in later life—Burke's at the French Revolution and Howe's at Confederation—were reflexes of their early convictions. In the work which they had in common Howe's was the happier lot; for while Burke spent the profoundest intellect that ever busied itself with our politics in trying to goad even his own friends into activity on 'the American question'—spinning out 'the little slender thread of a peevish and captious opposition'—Howe's robust faith commanded a following without a parallel in the history of his native province. In truth his public was his own, for in a sense he created it. His articles in *The Novascotian*, and after 1830 his weekly *Legislative Reviews*, account for much of this mastery. But this was only half the story, for the confidence was mutual. After a certain 'Black Saturday' in 1850, in the throes of a bout with Grey and Hawes of the Colonial Office in London, Howe records in his diary the grim reflection, 'my countrymen have never failed me'. They had never failed him for the best of reasons. He had never failed them. In the *Howe Papers* is the note from Sir John Harvey (September 14, 1846) which proved to be the prelude to the first fully responsible government overseas. Upon the margin is a comment in Howe's meticulous handwriting: 'This was my first communication . . . from Gov't House, after my "proscription" and banishment therefrom for several years. During all that period I was a disaffected and dangerous man. Now I am my Sovereign's Representative's most excellent and talented friend.[1] I thank God, and the steadiness and intelligence of my countrymen for the change.'

II

Howe's early traditions were Tory, and another name or two, all too lightly esteemed, must be written here by way of prelude to the 'reform press' of Nova Scotia.

As early as 1827 Jotham Blanchard founded the Pictou *Colonial Patriot* to 'side with the most liberal system'. Blanchard's most immediate interest, perhaps, was the cause of Pictou Academy and the 'wee frees' against the Church of Scotland and the Anglican monopoly of higher education at King's. Behind Blanchard again was the rugged character of Dr. McCulloch, principal of the Academy, one of those apostolic worthies who live imperishably in the lives of younger men—of Blanchard himself, of Principal Dawson of McGill, of Principal Grant of Queen's, of Sir Adams Archibald, George R. Young, son of 'Agricola', and a host of others. One of Howe's innumerable biographers rates the most powerful of all the early influences upon his political thinking 'the strong personality of Thomas McCulloch'.[2] Blanchard was once burnt in effigy for his pains, but he lived to see *The Novascotian* also rated 'liberal' in politics. 'As regards yourself', wrote Howe a few months after the famous trial in 1835, 'I did hope to have fought under your banner for many a day.' But by 1835 Blanchard had become a 'suspicious and languid supporter' of reform while Howe had become the champion at once of a free press and of a people against 'those who have an interest in mismanaging their affairs'.[3]

Howe's family traditions were Tory, but his estrangement from Tory officialdom began early. His father was John Howe, staunch old Massachusetts loyalist, Postmaster-General, King's Printer at Halifax, and founder of the *Weekly Chronicle*. While still a 'printer's boy' with his father he had learnt 'the caprice of men in office', and with curious premonitions of 'something ahead' had

[1] The opening words of Sir John Harvey's note. *Howe Papers*, i. 158.

[2] *Pub. Arch. Can.*, *Johnson Papers*, p. 27.

[3] Howe to Blanchard, Oct. 26, 1835, *Howe Papers*, i. 2. *Pub. Arch. Can.*

waited for 'the glorious privilege of being independent'.[1] For seven years in *The Novascotian*, however, his political views were remarkably dispassionate. He joined issue with Blanchard against Papineau in Lower Canada. He once printed a spirited warning to the Assembly itself that if editors could be brought to the bar of the House, legislators could be brought by a free press 'before the bar of the public'.

But the menace to a free press came from another quarter. The famous libel case of 1835 was only indirectly concerned with provincial government, though the magistrates of Halifax, pilloried by Howe, were appointed and defended by the Executive Council. Howe's aged father had once been a magistrate, and Howe himself had served as a grand juror. Few could have known better the petty abuses of taxation and contracts under such a system. When a letter—by no means the first—appeared in *The Novascotian* on January 1, 1835, charging the magistrates with misconduct it was decided to prosecute the editor for criminal libel.

It is sometimes forgotten that the law of the day was almost undoubtedly against Howe; that his purely legal argument, as his biographer notes, was 'sufficiently curious'; that the Attorney-General, the official prosecutor, was none other than S. W. G. Archibald, Speaker of the Assembly; and that Howe in his own defence was permitted a latitude which the bench could never have accorded to a barrister. 'The lawyers were all very civil', Howe afterwards said, 'but laughed at me a good deal, quoting the old maxim, that "he who pleads his own case has a fool for a client". But the laugh was against them when all was over.'[2] His friends advised him to make his peace with the magistrates lest a worse thing befall him; but 'I asked them to lend me their books (Howe adds), gathered an armful, threw myself on a sofa, and read libel law for a week'. For Howe himself the cause and the crowded court-room must have stirred for the first time unsuspected depths in his faculty of appealing to his countrymen. The jury returned a verdict of 'not guilty', and Howe was borne home from the old Province Building upon the shoulders of his supporters. The magistrates resigned, 'smitten down in a day by this single speech'. But the Executive Council that had appointed them was not so

[1] 'We can never take the popular side...This while a boy I never liked and I know when a man I never could put up with.' Howe to his half-sister Jane, 1824. *Johnson Papers*, p. 16.

[2] Chisholm, *Speeches and Public Letters of Joseph Howe*, Halifax, 2 vols., i. 24.

easily to be regulated. For that struggle the meaning of Howe's libel case was his parting appeal to his supporters to teach their children the names of the twelve men who had established the freedom of the press in Nova Scotia.

III

Howe was now a marked man. He was returned for the county of Halifax in the elections of 1836, and within four years the Assembly then elected forced the neatest and most convincing demonstration for responsible government in the British provinces.

Howe's rise to the leadership of the Reform Assembly, though rapid and spectacular, was bitterly resented by the older leaders of the House, and it required a veritable revolt to drill the 'New Model' of 1836 into the 'Old Ironsides' of 1840. The Reformers in 1835 were scarcely a political party. 'They have the numbers it is true,' wrote Howe to Blanchard, 'but in knowledge, discipline, able leaders, everything in fact which ensures success in any struggle they have been and are miserably deficient.' The war must 'be carried on briskly' by a 'majority pledged to the people and kept in salutary awe of them'. With no 'pious horror of innovation' Howe soon put an end to the mimic battles of condottieri for 'honourable promotion'. 'In England', he said upon the hustings, 'one vote of the people's representatives turns out a ministry and a new one comes in. . . . In this country, the government is like an ancient Egyptian mummy, wrapped up in narrow and antique prejudices—dead and inanimate, but likely to last forever.'[1]

Howe's aggressive tactics were received on all sides with consternation. Four days after the opening of the session Alexander Stewart himself with polished sarcasm crossed swords with the young 'tribune', and became for many years the most implacable of his enemies. John Young—'Agricola'—counselled peace, but Howe drew up twelve resolutions in amendment and plunged into the fray with an almost uncanny mastery of parliamentary tactics. The council's reply to the twelve resolutions promised a repetition of the brandy dispute. Appealing to 'that decorum which regulates the intercourse of society' they ignored eleven of the resolutions, and under the thinly veiled threat of stopping the supplies demanded the rescinding of a phrase imputing to some of the councillors a disposition 'to protect their own interests and emoluments at the expense of the public'.

[1] *Howe Papers*, vi. 2. Chisholm, *op. cit.*, i. 104.

Howe's resourcefulness at this stage must have gone far to establish his reputation, for the opinion was now general in the lobbies that he had shot his bolt. After a long night's vigil he entered the House late in the debate with the *élan* of confidence in his manner. Rescinding not only one but all twelve of the resolutions in order to 'sacrifice neither the revenue nor the cause of reform', he followed up this demonstration of magnanimity by proposing an 'Address to the Crown on the State of the Colony'. What this cost in courage and in restraint was not apparent at the time, but four years later, at the time of his duel with Halliburton, he wrote to his sister that he 'would rather stand a shot than go through the "rescinding of the Resolutions" '.[1]

With the Address which Howe himself moved on April 13 the cause of reform passed beyond the grey walls of the old Province Building and entered a broader field. The reform press of Nova Scotia took it to every hamlet in the province. Its tone stirred the Colonial Office, as we shall see, to the most ingenuous response of that decade. Howe's vision was already ranging over a 'broader view'—the future of millions in every clime whose security and peace were to be 'sanctioned by the spirit and forms of the British Constitution'. In the midst of the debate came news of Lord John Russell's ten resolutions against responsible government in Lower Canada. If such, said Howe, were forever to be the views of the British Government, he would—go to England to live, where none could deny his birthright. Against such tactics and temper the doctrines of Lord John Russell himself could not in the end prevail. Three years later the Nova Scotia Reformers found themselves in command of the situation 'with the ball at their feet'.

IV

The Address of April, 1837, was a formidable indictment, and the astonishment of Murdock of the Colonial Office at its moderation is easily understood.

In religion nine of the 'Council of Twelve' belonged to the Church of England which comprised one-fifth of the population of the province. Two family connexions included five members of the council, and no fewer than five were at one time partners in

[1] 'There was more at stake than a limb, as far as I was concerned, more than a life as regards the Country, and I suffered a thousand times more.' *Howe Papers*, i. 14.

the Halifax Banking Company. For thirty years all but one had been residents of Halifax. In effect they and not the Assembly wielded the power of the purse, since the salaries of the chief government officials were paid by permanent enactment or from the casual and territorial revenues of the crown over which the Assembly had no control, while the revenues appropriated by the Assembly went to roads, bridges, schools, and other public services. Stoppage of supplies was thus a deadly weapon in the hands of the council. In the hands of the Assembly it merely recoiled upon themselves. In the brandy dispute the council had used it because the Assembly had 'outraged the rules which regulate the intercourse of Gentlemen', and the threat to use it again was enough to force the rescinding of the twelve resolutions. The Chief Justice as president of the Legislative Council helped to make the laws, as an Executive Councillor he helped to administer them, and as Chief Justice he interpreted them. The Legislative and Executive Councils—unlike those of New Brunswick, Upper Canada, and other provinces—had the same personnel, and in both capacities excluded the public from their deliberations. The Address closed upon a note which dominated Nova Scotian politics until responsible government was won:

> 'In England, the people by one vote of their representatives can change the ministry . . . here the ministry are your Majesty's Council, combining legislative, judicial, and executive powers; holding their seats for life, though nominally at the pleasure of the Crown. . . .
>
> We implore your Majesty to grant us an elective Legislative Council; or to separate the Executive from the Legislative Council . . . and, by the introduction into the former of some members of the popular branch, and otherwise securing responsibility to the Commons, confer upon the people of this Province what they value above all other possessions, the blessings of the British Constitution.'[1]

Glenelg's response confirmed that much-maligned statesman in the esteem of the Maritime Provinces. No name of that day in the Colonial Office—not even the third Earl Grey's—stands higher in their traditions. It was Howe's conviction that reform in Nova Scotia could have marched rapidly to its denouement had it not been complicated, and Glenelg himself overwhelmed, by the Canadian *débâcle*.[2] During the spring of 1837 a delegation from

[1] Chisholm, *op. cit.*, i. 154 f.

[2] Cf. the comment of 'J.S.' (James Stephen of the Colonial Office) in *C.O. 217*, 163. 135 ff.: 'not yet in a state for decision, nor even for discussion . . .

the New Brunswick Assembly—Wilmot and Crane—had arranged with Glenelg for the first time the amplest measure of reform hitherto conceded to a British province—the control of the lands and territorial revenues of the crown in return for a fixed civil list. The Assembly had acted 'in the most liberal and handsome manner', and Glenelg's response was acknowledged 'with hearts full of the warmest duty and gratitude'. Wilmot himself had moved for the 'full length portrait' of Glenelg which still adorns the Legislative Chamber of that province. The lieutenant-governor added his tribute to Glenelg's 'noble support' in changing the personnel of the Executive Council to command the 'entire confidence' of the Assembly—the first specific practice of responsible government, though the Assembly itself disavowed the enforcement of Howe's principle 'at all times'.[1] Years afterwards in Nova Scotia Glenelg's 'candour and frankness and liberality' inspired one of Howe's noblest tributes:

> 'A more accomplished scholar, a more accessible, amiable and ordinarily industrious nobleman than Lord Glenelg never held the seals. His published despatches display vigour and clearness of design, goodness of heart and habitual suavity of temper. . . . Yet Lord Glenelg was driven into a sort of incomprehensible disgrace. No man gave the old system a fairer trial; no man less deserved the fate to which it almost inevitably consigned its victims.'[2]

It was in June, 1838, that Howe called at the Colonial Office for the interview with that 'very affable . . . grey-haired and brail headed' Scotsman himself. Thus while Henry Chapman and the Lower Canadian reformers went to Roebuck whose 'talent and judgment' Howe profoundly distrusted, and while Baldwin and the Upper Canadian reformers went to Hume whose Ishmaelitish temper was perhaps the worst influence they could have enlisted in the British House of Commons, Howe and the Nova Scotia reformers dealt almost uninterruptedly with Glenelg, Normanby, Russell, and Grey, and confidentially with Charles Buller, perhaps the most gracious friend the British provinces ever had in Great Britain. Instead of a contest, as Hume and many of the Canadian 'Ultras' sometimes represented it to be, between the colony and

readiness of the Government to entertain and dispose of them whenever the occasion shall arise.'

[1] *Journals*, N.B., July 6–22, 1837, Appendix 1.

[2] Second *Letters to Lord John Russell*, in Chisholm, *op. cit.*, i. 612.

the 'baneful influence of the Mother Country', Howe never ceased to regard it as a contest between reform and vested interests on both sides of the Atlantic. It was this alliance, as we shall see, which finally prevailed in 1848.

V

The popular criticism of Glenelg, one of the shrewdest of his colleagues notes in his diary, was undeserved. 'He was not lazy; he was too scrupulous and critical as to what he wrote.'[1] Glenelg's kindliness, his responsiveness, his scrupulous justice, appear at their best in the Nova Scotia dispatches of April 30 and July 6, 1837.[2] But hopes of reform came to grief upon two obstructions—the powers of governor and council, and the Canadian *débâcle* which now dominated colonial policy, drove Glenelg from office, and in the end brought the Nova Scotia reformers to desperation in the attempt to salvage their cause from 'the two maddest rebellions on record'.

Glenelg's instructions of April 30 were peremptory. The councils were to be separated and reorganized 'in conformity with such advice as shall be deliberately tendered . . . by the Representatives of the People of Nova Scotia'. This was 'no reluctant concession': it was a 'peculiar pleasure' since the advice of the Assembly was 'dictated by more exact and abundant knowledge of the wants and wishes of their Constituents than any other persons possess or could venture to claim'. The crown lands and revenues had just been surrendered in New Brunswick for a fixed civil list. There was no reason why the same system 'should not be established in both provinces'. The alternative of an elective council, Glenelg assumed to have been 'thrown out by the Assembly rather as a possible compromise . . . than as expressing any fixed opinion'.[3] 'Neither the Chief Justice nor any of his Colleagues should sit in the Executive Council.' The dispatch closes with a 'sense of the

[1] Lord Broughton, *Recollections of a Long Life*, London, 1911, v. 97: 'His cousin, my friend Dr. Chambers, told me that he would get up early on a winter morning, light his own fire, and sit down to write a despatch.'

[2] *Journals*, 1838, Appendix No. 2; *Brit. Parl. Papers*, Aug, 27, 1839 (579), pp. 11, 27.

[3] 'Rather with the view of the possible compromise', in Glenelg's original draft. *C.O. 217*, 169. 91. Howe's early partiality for an elective council may have been due to conditions peculiar at this time to Nova Scotia. The two councils were still united, and both functions could thus be brought under popular control.

high claims which the Legislature of Nova Scotia have established . . . by a long and uninterrupted course of Loyal and zealous attachment to the British Crown'.

But the governor and his council had yet to be heard from. Sir Colin Campbell in Nova Scotia was the last of Wellington's officers to 'govern' the North American provinces. Like Colborne and Maitland and Arthur, Sir Colin was a gallant old soldier, but it cannot be said that any of them contributed much but obstruction to the solution of colonial government. In the end Sir Colin found himself in the toils of his advisers, to little purpose but their own. The Address of the Assembly had gone to Downing Street accompanied by thirty-four pages of *Observations* signed by every member of the council. Sir Colin's stubborn neglect of the instructions of April 30 'in direct violation of their avowed principles' stirred to exasperation the indulgent temper of Stephen himself at the Colonial Office. The governor was directed to publish the dispatches—a retribution 'which Sir C. Campbell has brought upon himself'.[1] Nine of the Legislative Councillors were finally selected from the counties—eight from religious denominations other than Anglican—and their sessions thrown open to the public. Four members of the Executive Council—Uniacke, Dodd, Huntington, and Dewolf—were chosen from the Assembly and could answer there for government policy.

This, however, was not responsible government. Huntington was at this time its only advocate in the Executive Council. The schedule of salaries for the proposed civil list, though drafted in Halifax, was to be presented to the Assembly as 'a specific proposition in detail . . . submitted *from home*', with the ingenious suggestion from Sir Colin that he 'should be authorized to explain to the Assembly, that, this proposition having received the deliberate consideration and approval of H.M. Government, no essential modification of its terms would be sanctioned'. In all this for many months it is easy to trace the Italian hand of Alexander Stewart. The schedule was finally received by the Assembly with 'execration'.[2] It was introduced by Uniacke and overwhelmingly defeated by an amendment moved by Huntington himself. When the dispatches were published it was found that

[1] Stephen's *memo.* upon Campbell's dispatch of August 26, 1837. *C.O. 217*, 163. 845.

[2] Campbell to Glenelg, Aug. 26, 1837, *Letter-Books* (Halifax) 115. 57. For Stewart's influence see *Memorandum* in *C.O. 217*, 165. 693, &c.

Glenelg at the outset had invited a deputation from the Assembly to discuss the civil list in London. 'Their Delegates', he wrote, 'will be received with all ... respect and confidence.'[1] But the wily councillors had held other views. In the end the schedule was withdrawn, and it was left to the first responsible government in the province, ten years later, to arrange a fixed civil list in return for the surrender of the crown lands and revenues.

More formidable than the council in Nova Scotia, however, was the reaction after the rebellions in Canada. From the time of the Ninety-two Resolutions colonial policy had been overshadowed by the uncompromising temper of Papineau. The minutes and memoranda upon the Nova Scotia correspondence attest its effect upon the cause of reform in the other provinces. While troops with bayonets on their muskets were moving to and fro in Lower Canada, responsible government, Stephen noted at the Colonial Office, was 'not yet in a state for decision, nor even for discussion'. The *motif* for Nova Scotia is more ingenuously worded: 'if conceded in any one Colony it must be granted in all.' What advice, asked Lord John Russell pertinently, would be given to a governor by 'a ministry, headed by M. Papineau'? The practice of Glenelg and much of the theory of Lord John Russell himself must have been dictated by that haunting spectre.[2]

From this *débâcle* the cause in Nova Scotia was salvaged chiefly by the unerring tactics of Howe. In May and July, 1835, Henry S. Chapman, then in London upon a confidential mission from the lower Canadian Assembly to Roebuck and the English radicals, had appealed to Howe for a simultaneous demonstration from all the colonies.[3] Howe's reply—one of his 'flashes', as he used to call them, written in October when he was barely thirty-one years of age—remained unknown for more than two years, but its publication in *The Novascotian* (December 21, 1837) in the midst of the Papineau rebellion now arrested attention on both sides of the Atlantic. In the temper of the Lower Canadian Assembly Howe

[1] Glenelg to Campbell, Oct. 31, 1837. *Id.*, 169. 211.

[2] *C.O. 217*, 163. 135; 169. 151. *Egerton and Grant*, p. 268. Glenelg commended the 'just delicacy' of Wilmot and Crane from the New Brunswick Assembly in waiving any 'peremptory rule' about the Executive Council in 1836 (*Journals*, Dec. 20, 1836—Mar. 1. 1837, Appendix, p. xvi). After Lord John Russell's resolutions for Lower Canada responsible government was 'inadmissible' for Nova Scotia also. The *motif* quoted above is in the original draft only.

[3] *Howe Papers*, i. 1, 5.

had surmised a determination 'at all hazards to precipitate a contest with the mother country'. To this end the redress of grievances 'was to be sought in a spirit the most uncompromising and offensive'. To these tactics the people of the Maritime Provinces were by tradition and by conviction overwhelmingly opposed. On the other hand they saw hope and promise in a constructive alliance with those in Great Britain who were 'struggling against the same enemies'. If their British allies, having established popular control for themselves then 'refuse to carry out in the colonies the principles they maintain at home', the British connexion might then be 'viewed very differently'. Meanwhile uncompromising obstruction was unfair and ungenerous. The magnanimity and breadth of view in this, the first perhaps of Howe's political 'flashes', cannot be conveyed by a paraphrase, but it was in the same spirit, as we shall see, that he and Charles Buller finally effected the historic alliance by which responsible government was effectually won. Both the tactics and the temper Howe made peculiarly his own. At their best they approach the insight and catholicity of Burke, and perhaps no reformer on either side of the Atlantic did more to sustain them at that level.

It was in the midst of this depression, in the shadow of the Durham 'fiasco' (as it seemed at that time) and three months before the counterblast of the *Report* itself appeared in the provinces, that the Nova Scotia Assembly determined to send Herbert Huntington and William Young to vindicate their cause at the Colonial Office.

VI

Herbert Huntington was the Robert Baldwin of Nova Scotia. Like Howe and Haliburton and a score of others in the public life of that province, Huntington came of New England stock, and he could trace his lineage to the Cromwells of the age of the Stuarts. Had he lived in those days, says Howe, like Oliver himself 'he would have drawn his sword against Charles as a necessity of his nature'.[1] His stalwart figure—'broad chest, a fine head, and an iron frame'—his sagacity, his inflexible principles and integrity, were characteristic, as Bourinot says, 'of the Hampden school.... No man in the legislature evoked more interest or confidence.'[2]

[1] Chisholm, *op. cit.*, i. 214 n.
[2] *Builders of Nova Scotia*, Toronto, 1900, p. 68.

'He never wasted a word,' adds Howe, 'but ran his thoughts, as men run bullets, into forms, compact, weighty and effective. . . . When out of health or out of humour, he was as moody and irascible as Oliver himself.'

No happier alliance could have been devised than that between Huntington and Howe. It was Huntington who acted as Howe's second in the duel with Halliburton. His good offices were still more valuable in the field of politics. When he died in 1851—like Charles Buller in the hour of assured success—his monument, a shaft of Shelburne granite, was raised in the Yarmouth churchyard by the Assembly which his inflexible spirit had inspired, and sometimes daunted, for twenty years. It was the first monument to the public life of the province. If Huntington was the Baldwin of Nova Scotia, Howe was the Hincks and Uniacke the La Fontaine. But these fanciful parallels must await an ampler survey.

In the reorganization forced by Glenelg Huntington had accepted office in the Executive Council believing that the same principles as 'at Home when circumstances render a change of Ministers necessary there' were now to be conceded for Nova Scotia, and that 'a Majority of the Councillors at least, would be chosen from those who profess what are deemed liberal political Principles'. To his astonishment he found the Reformers still in a minority in both councils. At this stage it was found that Durham's commission required an Executive Council of nine instead of twelve members. Huntington seized the opportunity of retiring from an impossible situation. When Glenelg confirmed the original appointments Huntington was again summoned to the council, but he refused to act without a radical change of policy and sent in his formal resignation.[1] From that time neither the wiles of Sydenham nor the entreaties of Howe himself could induce him to re-enter the Executive Council until responsible government was unequivocally conceded. Huntington's uncompromising precision, like Baldwin's, was perhaps open to the criticism that it impaired his political usefulness; but in the end, as we shall see, it was Huntington's doctrine and not Sydenham's that prevailed, and Howe himself was to become its prophet.

The decision of February, 1839, to send Huntington and Young to the Colonial Office was reached at the lowest ebb of reaction after the Canadian rebellions. The Durham mission had ended,

[1] Huntington to George, Sept. 28, 1838, *C.O. 217*, 166. 423.

it seemed, in a 'fiasco'. Four delegates from Nova Scotia—J. B. Uniacke, George Young, J. W. Johnston, and Mather Almon—had been appointed to meet Durham at Quebec, but they found him in the midst of the fatal quarrel with Melbourne and the British Whigs, and there is a tradition that at one stage he 'was overcome by his feelings, and had to retire for a little to a distant part of the room'.[1] Charles Buller distinguishes 'the Nova Scotia delegation in particular' as men 'not only of striking ability, but of a degree of general information and polish of manners which are even less commonly met with in colonial society'. But despite a very moderate paper by Howe, it seemed that the Reformers had shot their bolt.[2] The New Brunswick Assembly having reached their own immediate objective in 1837 hastened to 'repudiate the claim set up by another Colony' for responsible government 'at all times'.[3] Durham's *Report* had not yet appeared. Glenelg's resignation in February was ominous. In the Nova Scotia Assembly alone, it seemed, the Reformers still held an unbroken front.

One dramatic incident at least—another of Howe's 'flashes' in its origin but too spontaneous to have been premeditated—supplied Huntington and Young with spectacular credentials to the Colonial Office. In February, 1839, the 'Aroostook War' over the Maine and New Brunswick boundary had reached the point where American troops were being marched into the disputed territory. Amidst cheers that spread to the lobbies of the old Province Building and the streets of Halifax, the House voted £100,000 and called out the militia. 'Never have we witnessed such a heart-stirring scene,' wrote Howe in *The Novascotian*, 'nor ever before were such cheers heard in our House of Assembly.'

Huntington and Young were heralded at Downing Street by a private letter from Sir Colin that their grievances were 'imaginary, except to a few Demagogues'.[4] The appropriation for the expenses of the delegates was thrown out by the council because no provision was made for a similar delegation from the Upper House. In the end Huntington and Young sailed from Halifax at their own expense—'a forlorn hope', it seemed, in a desperate cause.

[1] Campbell, *History of Nova Scotia*, p. 325.

[2] *Sketch of Lord Durham's Mission*, Pub. Arch. *Report*, 1923, p. 358; *id.*, p. 126.

[3] *Journals*, 1837, 475 ff. Cf. Stewart's *Memorandum* in *C.O. 217*, 165. 693: 'Messrs. Crane and Wilmot, and indeed the whole House condemn the extreme opinions held by Mr. Howe and others in our Assembly.'

[4] *C.O. 217*, 170. 185.

VII

The story of the Huntington-Young mission, were it possible to trace it here, would illustrate, as no other incident perhaps of that time, the goodwill of the Colonial Office and at the same time the power of the old order in Nova Scotia. Without apprising Huntington of his intentions, Sir Colin appointed 'two Gentlemen as Delegates on the part of the Legislative Council'.[1] In sheer ability the governor's nominees had few equals in Nova Scotia. Lewis M. Wilkins, Sen., for twenty-two years Judge of the Supreme Court, was 'a learned lawyer' with scholarly tastes and 'old fashioned courtesy'.[2] Alexander Stewart was 'a practical man', as he once said of himself, adroit, ruthless, and resourceful. 'Having been one of the Whigs of our little Society, and one of their leaders in the House of Assembly', his was now perhaps the most implacable and pervasive of all the influences against them.

Normanby, who had succeeded Glenelg at the Colonial Office, laboured to reconcile the irreconcilable; advised the payment of the expenses of both delegations from the casual and territorial revenues of the crown; maintained that 'the liberality and gallantry' of the Assembly in the crisis over the Maine boundary would 'entitle them to every consideration which it is in the power of the Crown to bestow'; impressed upon the governor how 'desirable' it would be to have his Executive Council 'composed in a manner to command the co-operation [the word in the original draft is 'confidence'] of the Representative Branch'. Some of the caustic minutes of Labouchere and Stephen of the Colonial Office are less complimentary to the old order. The report of the delegates in the *Journals* of 1840 is a remarkable record of insight and resourcefulness. Much more was achieved than appeared upon the surface—practical reforms for the Post Office, bounties, a Land Bill, and free ports 'as many as the Assembly desired'. With quiet tact and firmness they penetrated through the Colonial Office to the Board of Trade, the Customs, and other departments of the government. There is a word for 'the courteous attention' and 'liberal views' of Labouchere and Baring—'this House may rely on both, in any future emergency'. To Charles Buller there were deeper obligations 'both for his personal recommendation which

[1] 'No hint of their appointment having been given by the Lieut.-Governor, though His Excellency held a conversation with one of us on the day we left Halifax.' Young and Huntington to Normanby, May 30, 1839, *C.O. 217*, 173. 7.

[2] Bourinot, *op. cit.*, p. 69.

smoothed our path, and for many valuable hints which were of essential service to us'. Both Huntington and Young returned with an abiding faith in the 'kindly and generous feeling' of the British public.

Their main mission, however, was foredoomed to failure, for it was at the close of their stay that Lord John Russell succeeded to the Colonial Office and officially disavowed the doctrine of Durham on responsible government.[1] Huntington and Young were present at Buller's trenchant speech on the *Re-union Bill* with its prophetic defence of Durham and its ringing challenge to the whole pontifical doctrine of Lord John Russell.[2] The delegates returned to Nova Scotia to find that Durham's *Report* had run like wildfire in *The Novascotian* to every village of the province. 'The remedy', exclaimed Howe, 'has two prime recommendations, being perfectly *simple* and eminently *British*.' The old system was 'now become contemptible in the eyes of every man of common understanding, who has no interest in keeping it up'.

The contest in Nova Scotia now passed quickly to its denouement, and Howe's share in it was perhaps the most finished and dramatic passage of his political life.

'Testing this Constitution'

I

The period from the publication of Durham's *Report* in 1839 to the arrival of Sydenham at Halifax in July, 1840, has the intensity of a pitched battle. The moves follow each other with such speed and precision that the strategy is apt to be lost in the tactics. Before Sydenham intervened with the avowed object of forcing a drawn battle it seemed that the rout of the old régime, horse, foot, and artillery, was inevitable. It was not the fault of Herbert Huntington that the attack was not driven home without quarter. But the work of Joseph Howe during these brief months was to give him a place among the first figures of the British Commonwealth, and beneath the spell of Sydenham's appeal Howe agreed to an armistice with the hope of strengthening Sydenham's hands in Canada and of establishing 'a rationally responsible government by degrees'. The prospect of 1840, it may be, warranted that hope. But Huntington was a true prophet, and it was only

[1] *Hansard*, 3rd Series, xlvii. 1254.

[2] 'Whatever decision he (Russell) might come to, he did not care a pin about it (a laugh).... Responsible Government would inevitably be established by the people themselves.'

after seven years of wandering in the wilderness that the Reformers entered the promised land.

There were three preliminaries of the crisis of 1840 in Nova Scotia. In June, 1839, Lord John Russell announced his Canadian policy, and his declaration upon responsible government was a challenge alike to the Durhamites in Great Britain and to the 'radical' reformers with whom Charles Buller was already in touch in Canada. Howe's four open *Letters to Lord John Russell* reverberated in reply throughout the reform press of Canada and the Maritime Provinces. The third preliminary was Lord John Russell's famous dispatch of October 16, 1839, making Executive Councillors removable from office, 'as often as any sufficient motives of public policy may suggest the expediency of that measure'. It was this dispatch, as we shall see, which turned the trench warfare between the Assembly and life-councillors into a war of movement; for in giving the governor complete command of the executive it brought him into direct juxtaposition with those who claimed the responsibility of that executive to the Assembly. Thus for the first time those elemental forces were brought into play which Buller in Great Britain, Hincks in Canada, and Howe in one of his old 'flashes' in Nova Scotia, all clearly foresaw would force responsible government in its final form.

These three preliminaries all belong to a broader field than Nova Scotia, and though one of them was the work of a Nova Scotian it will be possible here to touch them only in outline. While it was felt that Lord John Russell's doctrine in 1839, and indeed his whole Canadian policy, was the result of an obsession with the *impasse* in Lower Canada—'the measures which a ministry, headed by M. Papineau would have imposed upon the Governor'[1]—there was a note of finality in his speech, a cogency in his logic, which fell upon the Reformers in Nova Scotia like a bolt from Olympus. Re-affirming his own resolutions of 1837 against responsible government for Lower Canada, Russell joined issue with the most fundamental of Durham's principles:

> 'There is nothing in this report which has at all, in my mind, shaken the argument by which at the time I supported that resolution (of 1837). . . . It is in my opinion one of the most important points contained in Lord Durham's report and one on which I differ with him.'

A governor could not act 'in that high and unassailable position' which the sovereign occupied in Great Britain. 'He is a

[1] Russell to Thomson, Oct. 14, 1839, *Egerton and Grant*, p. 266.

Governor receiving instructions from the Crown on the responsibility of a Secretary of State.' To Thomson in Canada the Russellite doctrine was expressed in one terse question: 'Can the colonial council be the advisers of the Crown of England? Evidently not, for the Crown has other advisers, for the same functions, and with superior authority.'[1] Self-government was impossible because imperial logic predicated governance from Downing Street. 'Forced into a cleft stick,' said Howe, 'there was nothing left for us but to break it.' Thus while Huntington and Young were toiling with the Colonial Office, the Treasury, and the Board of Trade, through the summer of 1839, Howe in one of his daemonic 'flashes' of insight and of energy was straining at the cleft stick of Lord John Russell's Olympian logic.

By common consent Howe's four open *Letters to Lord John Russell* have been accepted as the colonial counterpart of Durham's *Report* and Charles Buller's *Responsible Government for Colonies*. To be grouped with these is to be enshrined in the political literature of the English language. Over both of these, however, the *Letters* had one great advantage. Howe's method was empirical, and he wrote with authority from the colonial point of view. In truth Lord John Russell's position was less vulnerable to frontal attack than to the sidelong approach of a nimbler adversary. The *Letters* were addressed to a British Minister, but the wealth of the imagery, the flexibility of the argument, and the vigour of the language all betrayed an appeal as wide as the political instincts of the race.

In this there was more of deliberation than appeared upon the surface. At Howe's interview with Glenelg in June, 1838, that 'brail headed . . . Scotchman' had invited frank advice upon the 'state of feeling in the Colony'. In January, 1839, Howe had described to him 'the bitterness of wounded spirits' after a 'mortifying and useless Session' overshadowed by the Canadian imbroglio and Glenelg's own reactionary dispatch of October 31:

> 'There is nothing left to us now but to endeavour to interest as many Members of the Imperial Parliament, and as large a portion of the Press in our cause as possible. The People of Nova Scotia will never rest satisfied with things as they are.'[2]

[1] *The Morning Chronicle*, quoted in Chisholm, *op. cit.*, i. 218–21; *Hansard*, 3rd Series, xlvii. 1287. October 14, 1839, *Egerton and Grant*, p. 267.

[2] 'I feel that it is due to the kindness received from your Lordship, and to my country, to avail myself of the permission given to write thus frankly.' *C.O. 217*, 169. 211; 171. 653.

For such an appeal few men of that day or any other had a surer touch; and none a serener courage. There was a time ten years later, after a passage with Grey and Hawes in London, when Howe —'tired and Savage' but undaunted by the 'enormous labour and fearful consequences'—nerved himself to 'fight an Imperial Government and agitate England. It will come to that at last.' The famous Southampton speech was a part of that grim resolve. 'My countrymen', he reflected, 'have never failed me'; and he adds in his diary how he longed for the long rides 'through the quiet wood roads' of his native province that he might think his own thoughts and prepare for the battle. Such must have been his dedication in September, 1839, for the *Letters to Lord John Russell*; and indeed the note of confidence in them is the note not of assurance but of assured mastery.

II

No summary could do justice to Howe's theme, but two phases of it contributed more perhaps to the winning of responsible government in Nova Scotia than any others, and both of them Howe made peculiarly his own.

The first of these was one of his 'flashes', and it was perhaps the first principle of his political life. Durham's *Report* with its sustained dignity was after all the work of a Briton reasoning from British analogies. The *ego quoque Romanus* of the Nova Scotian was charged with the political traditions of that province, and it enfiladed the lurking fear of separation which dominated the theory, if not the practice, of the Russell school:

> 'I have ever held, my Lord, and still hold to the belief, that the population of British North America are sincerely attached to the parent State; that they are proud of their origin, deeply interested in the integrity of the empire and not anxious for the establishment of any other form of government here than that which you enjoy at home. ... Why should we desire a severance of old ties that are more honourable than any new ones we can form? ... This suspicion is a libel upon the colonist and upon the Constitution he claims as his inheritance....
>
> The English rule is completely reversed on this side of the Atlantic. Admitting that in Lower Canada . . . such a policy may have been necessary; surely there is no reason why the people of Upper Canada, Nova Scotia, New Brunswick, Prince Edward Island, and Newfoundland, should, on that account, be deprived of the application of a principle which is the corner-stone of the British Constitution. . . .

Where is the danger?... What effect would it have upon the funds? Would the stocks fall? Would England be weaker, less prosperous or less respected, because the people of Nova Scotia were satisfied and happy? . . .

Can an Englishman, an Irishman or a Scotchman, be made to believe, by passing a month upon the sea, that the most stirring periods of his history are but a cheat and a delusion . . . that the principles of civil liberty, which from childhood he has been taught to cherish and to protect by forms of stringent responsibility, must, with the new light breaking in upon him on this side of the Atlantic, be cast aside as an useless incumbrance? . . . My lord, my countrymen feel, as they have a right to feel . . . that there is nothing in their present or their past conduct to warrant such exclusion. . . . Have we done anything to justify the alienation of our birthright? . . . The proudest naval trophy of the last American war was brought by a Nova Scotian into the harbour of his native town; and the blood that flowed from Nelson's death wound in the cockpit of the *Victory* mingled with that of a Nova Scotian stripling beside him struck down in the same glorious fight. Am I not justified, my Lord, in claiming for my countrymen that constitution, which can be withheld from them by no plea but one unworthy of a British statesman—the tyrant's plea of power? I know that I am; and I feel also, that this is not the race that can be hoodwinked with sophistry, or made to submit to injustice without complaint. All suspicion of disloyalty we cast aside, as the product of ignorance or cupidity; we seek for nothing more than British subjects are entitled to; but we will be contented with nothing less.'[1]

The logic of Lord John Russell's theory was less vulnerable, but here again Howe's reply was the logic of hard facts. The governor, said Russell, received 'instructions from the Crown on the responsibility of a Secretary of State'. 'Colonial government' thus resolved itself into a bicephalous hobgoblin, one head of which was the Secretary of State who was to 'decide', and the other the governor who was to govern. But whatever the logic of Russell's theory, there were two weak links in the practice. Hitherto the Secretary of State had not 'decided', and most certainly the governor had not governed. With thinly veiled impatience Howe overwhelmed these solemn fictions with merciless badinage as abstract 'nostrums by which the science of politics, like the science

[1] The *Letters to Lord John Russell* are in Chisholm, *op. cit.*, pp. 221–66; *Egerton and Grant*, pp. 191–252; Kennedy, *Documents of the Canadian Constitution* (Oxford, 1918), pp. 480 ff.

of medicine, is often disfigured for a time'. It was left to Charles Buller in his *Responsible Government for Colonies* in the following year, to trace the boasted 'responsibility of a Secretary of State' to its lair among the clerks in the attics of Downing Street. How could eight successive Colonial Secretaries in ten consecutive years 'decide' for a dozen different governors of varying abilities, in a dozen different colonies, each with the widest range of local problems and conditions? Mr. Mother Country resolved himself into the permanent clerks who knew the details of the business. Howe, too, has many a shrewd thrust for the complacency of an under-secretary talking for an hour or two to the prospective governor of what neither he nor the governor understands, and placing in his hands a packet of instructions 'of which half-a-dozen different readings may be given'.

But Howe's chief concern was the inflated impotence of the governor himself in the hands of his life-councillors. It would be little to the purpose to garble here the inimitable passages in which Howe imagines 'that after twenty or thirty years of military service, by which I have become disciplined into a contempt for civil business and a fractious impatience of the opinions of all beneath me in rank, Her Majesty has the right and graciously deigns to exercise it, of making me Mayor of Liverpool'. It was 'no fancy sketch; no picture, highly coloured to produce effect . . . it is a faithful representation of what occurs in some British colony almost every year'. The result was easily foreseen:

> 'He may flutter and struggle in the net, as some well-meaning Governors have done, but he must at last resign himself to his fate; and like a snared bird be content with the narrow limits assigned him by his keepers. I have known a Governor bullied, sneered at, and almost shut out of society, while his obstinate resistance to the system created a suspicion that he might not become its victim; but I never knew one who, even with the best intentions . . . was able to contend, on anything like fair terms, with the small knot of functionaries who form the Councils, fill the offices, and wield the powers of the Government. The plain reason is, because, while the Governor is amenable to his Sovereign, and the members of the Assembly are controlled by their constituents, these men are not responsible at all. . . . It is indispensable, then, to the dignity, the independence, the usefulness of the Governor himself, that he should have the power to shake off this thraldom . . . and by an appeal to the people, adjust the balance of power. Give us this truly British privilege, and colonial grievances will soon become a scarce article in the English market.'

But it would be as idle to attempt here a summary of the *Letters* as to speculate upon their ultimate effect. Their immediate effect is more easily traced, and much of this, at least, was not unforeseen. 'There is not an over-paid and irresponsible official, from Fundy to the Ottawa', wrote Howe, 'whose inextinguishable hostility I shall not have earned for the remainder of my life.' Sir Colin Campbell was instructed to offer seats in the Executive Council to 'some of the leading members of the House of Assembly'. He conceded that Howe was 'the head of the predominant party in the House'; but his appointment would be 'a most unwise and mischievous proceeding', for had he not 'published and extensively circulated, a series of letters, addressed to Your Lordship, advocating what is popularly called "Responsible Government"; and this, notwithstanding the declared hostility of Your Lordship and Her Majesty's Government to any such fundamental and pernicious change'?[1] Lord John Russell himself was not magnanimous. 'I should recommend the offer of a seat in the Executive Council to Mr. Howe,' he wrote in a memorandum of November 11, 'were it not that such an appointment at this moment might appear a sanction to the opinions of his recent publication.'[2]

III

Howe's *Letters* were dated September 18, 1839. On October 16, Lord John Russell's circular dispatch—in its results one of the most important that ever left the Colonial Office, though not in the way its author anticipated—supplied the third preliminary to a crisis in Nova Scotia.

Early in September Lord John Russell had taken over the Colonial Office. By common consent no stronger intellect or character was to be found at that time in the Whig party. The other link of 'colonial government'—the governor with his 'thraldom' to his life-councillors—was not so easily strengthened. Here, too, Russell's measures were heroic. In Lord Sydenham, as he will always be known in Canadian history, Russell sent as governor-general to British North America the ablest administrator who had ever left Britain on such a mission; and the dispatch of October 16 was designed to arm the colonial governor as never before to carry out his 'instructions from the Crown'.

[1] Campbell to Russell, Oct. 16, 1839, *Letter-Books*, Halifax, 115. 160.
[2] *C.O.* 217, 171. 433.

The terms of the dispatch were simple and precise. Custom had converted a seat in the Executive Council from 'a tenure at pleasure into a tenure for life'—with results which we have already seen in Howe's *Letters*:

> 'I cannot learn (wrote Lord John Russell) that during the present or the last two reigns, a single instance has occurred of a change in the subordinate colonial officers, except in cases of death or resignation, incapacity or misconduct. . . .
>
> You will understand, and will cause it to be made generally known, that hereafter the tenure of colonial offices held during Her Majesty's pleasure, will not be regarded as equivalent to a tenure during good behaviour; but that not only will such officers be called upon to retire from the public service as often as any sufficient motives of public policy may suggest the expediency of that measure, but that a change in the person of the governor will be considered as a sufficient reason.' [1]

But while the terms of the dispatch were explicit enough, its purpose was not so clear, and few documents have ever been more curiously misconstrued. In its Canadian context it must be examined in greater detail, but it was not designed to expedite responsible government as Howe understood it. Its purpose, in Russell's own phrase, was 'freedom of action' for the executive government.[2] The colonial governor could now break the net in which he had been wont to 'flutter and struggle' until he resigned himself to his keepers. He could now 'shake off this thraldom' to his life-councillors and resume the reins of government by commanding at will the services of those whose good offices might prove from time to time most useful for that purpose. Sir Colin Campbell in writing to Russell himself interpreted the dispatch of October 16 as 'not intended to sanction any fundamental change of the Constitution, but merely to strengthen the hands of the Governor by enabling him more effectually to control refractory Public functionaries'; and Vernon Smith of the Colonial Office adds the convincing comment that Sir Colin was 'right in his interpretation of Lord John's letter'.[3] The governor-general in Canada, as we shall see, expressed the same interpretation more discreetly, but Melbourne himself in the House of Lords was explicit. Government responsible to a colonial Assembly meant

[1] *Egerton and Grant*, pp. 270, 271.

[2] Russell to Thomson, Sept. 7, 1839, *Egerton and Grant*, p. 256.

[3] Mar. 1, 1840, *Letter-Books*, 115. 180; *C.O. 217*, 174, memorandum on Campbell's letter of Apr. 4, 1840.

government irresponsible to the Colonial Office. Russell's dispatch was intended 'directly to counteract the principle . . . and was properly understood by Sir Colin Campbell'. 'The opinion of this country and this government was entirely opposed to independent responsible government.'[1] Thus governance was to flow uninterruptedly, on the 'responsibility of a Secretary of State', through a governor who received 'instructions from the Crown'. The governor in turn could readjust the personnel of his Executive Council 'as often as any sufficient motives of public policy may suggest the expediency'. Under Lord John Russell at least the 'motives' were unimpeachable. 'The Queen's Government have no desire to thwart the representative assemblies of British North America. . . . They have no wish to make those provinces the resource for patronage at home.' In the colonies as in Great Britain there was to be a field for 'talent and character'. 'Affectionate attachment' was the 'best security for permanent dominion'.[2] But for all that, 'colonial government' meant governance, not self-government; and Lord John Russell's scheme of governance was to be as unimpeachable as his logic.

But the dispatch of October 16, 1839, could be put to another use which was to play havoc in the end with Lord John Russell's whole pontifical theory. For the first time it enabled 'the predominant party in the House' to determine, so simply and so conclusively that there could be no gainsaying the fact, whether the governor in the first instance, and in the last resort whether the British Government itself, was disposed to employ 'those who *enjoy the confidence of the people* and can *command a majority in the popular branch*'. 'The motives of public policy' might be Downing Street's, but the Executive Council was now the governor's, and he it was who must answer for its acceptability to the Assembly. This Howe in one of his old 'flashes' saw at a glance, and his political strategy until the recall of Sir Colin Campbell was perhaps the neatest and most brilliant constitutional procedure in that or any other province during the entire contest for responsible government.

IV

On February 3, 1840, Howe moved four resolutions in the Assembly culminating in the now classic formula that 'the Executive Council, as at present constituted, does not enjoy the confi-

[1] *Hansard*, 3rd Series, lv. 657.
[2] Russell to Thomson, Oct. 14, 1839, *Egerton and Grant*, pp. 268, 269.

dence of the Commons'. Two incidents lent precision to the stroke. In New Brunswick where harmony, at this time unparalleled in the American provinces, existed between the Executive Council and the Assembly, Sir John Harvey had referred to the dispatch of October 16 as 'conferring a new, and in my judgement, an improved Constitution upon these Colonies'. The construction which the Reformers placed upon these phrases was scarcely borne out by the context of Harvey's *Circular Memorandum*,[1] but no more opportune time could have been chosen to 'test the matter'. The governor-general in Canada had just announced the Queen's commands to govern 'in accordance with the well-understood wishes and interests of the people'. 'The Governor of the Province', exclaimed Howe, 'has the power to afford the remedy sought. It is only necessary for that Assembly to place its opinions on record, and the Governor will be bound to act on them.' The dispatch of October 16 had 'bestowed all that was required'. In a speech of great power and moderation Howe appealed to all parties to 'unite to give a constitution to our country.... The other colonies would follow her example'. 'Proud and happy that the commencement of these great changes should be laid here and that they should extend into all the British dependencies,' he foretold a 'form of government, which will, like the atmosphere, yield to every necessary pressure, preserve the balance of liberty, and yet expand with the growth of our posterity down to remote generations.'[2] The resolutions passed on February 5 by a vote of 30 to 12.

Sir Colin was now between the upper and the nether millstone. In truth he had been placed there by Lord John Russell himself, and in justice let it be added that he was powerless to escape. What the dispatch of October 16 was intended to effect he was in a position to know better than the Assembly. He replied truthfully that

[1] Harvey to Russell, Dec. 24, 1839, *N.B. Despatches Sent, C.O. 188*, vol. vii. The dispatch of October 16, 'while enlarging the powers of the Administrator of the Government, by leaving him free to choose his Counsellors and Office-Bearers', was designed to 'impose upon him a corresponding degree of encreased responsibility, as well towards the Queen's Government as towards the inhabitants of the Province . . . and above *all*, it has for its object to ensure for the Governor . . . the most cordial and sincere support, assistance, and co-operation, in carrying out His views and policy and those of Her Majesty's Government, on the part of every individual Member of the Provincial Government, whose tenure of office is now made dependent upon Him. . . . They will at the same time fully recognise the condition which . . . *dissent* from the views of the Colonial Government . . . must necessarily involve.'

[2] Chisholm, *op. cit.*, i. 269–93.

the decision of Her Majesty's ministers had been taken, and that he was not 'at liberty to adopt any other course. . . . Justice, however, to the Executive Council (he added loyally) leads me to say that I have had every reason to be satisfied with the advice and assistance which they have at all times afforded me.'[1] The issue lay, in fact, not with Sir Colin Campbell but with Lord John Russell. He it was who had forced—and afterwards approved without qualification—the 'determination not to assent to the Address of the House of Assembly, for the change of the Members of the Executive Council of Nova Scotia collectively, without the previous sanction of Her Majesty';[2] and his, as we shall see, was the sorry stratagem by which a well-nigh perfect demonstration of responsible government was finally frustrated.

The next step—the logical sequel of the first—Howe once referred to as 'the severest trial of my life. . . . I felt pretty much as a soldier would who should be called out on a firing party. . . . If ever I performed a task with a heavy heart it was that.' Nothing now remained but the recall of the governor. An Address was first voted to Sir Colin himself. Would 'those who still clung to power' permit the governor to be 'sacrificed to shelter them'? But the governor was still unable to establish so momentous a principle 'until Her Majesty's ministers shall have been consulted'. Upon the return of the Assembly to their chamber after this reply the Reformers took their last grim resolve for 'testing this Constitution'. Herbert Huntington, then as always perhaps the most resolute spirit in the House, gave notice of motion for an Address to the Crown for the governor's recall.

The Address was introduced on March 25 by Howe himself, who afterwards acknowledged 'the composition of every line of it'. The terms were not only moderate but magnanimous; but the argument was incisive and indeed unanswerable. Upon the word of the Colonial Secretary there was 'no surer way of earning the approbation of The Queen, than by maintaining the harmony of the executive with the legislative authorities'. Beyond this wisest and most moderate of dispatches it was impossible to penetrate,[3] but either the governor had violated his instructions or he had been

[1] Chisholm, *op. cit.*, i. 294.

[2] Russell to Campbell, Apr. 30, 1840, *C.O. 217*, 174. 275.

[3] 'I have thus cautioned you against any declaration from which dangerous consequences might hereafter flow.' Russell to Thomson, Oct. 14, 1839. *Egerton and Grant*, p. 269. This dispatch had just reached the Nova Scotia press.

instructed to withhold responsible government. 'Five-and-twenty stern men . . . voted for the whole address':

> 'In no portion of your Majesty's dominions, are the powers of the Crown and the rights of the people better understood. . . . Availing themselves of the influence which their loyalty, their intelligence, their firmness and their moderation, have acquired for them among the population of British North America, they will never cease . . . to vindicate and assert by every means in their power their rights as British subjects.'[1]

V

There was some consternation in Downing Street when the dispatches from Nova Scotia arrived in April, 1840. The memoranda, the minutes, the marginal notes, of 'Mr. Mother Country', must have inspired the wittiest of Buller's sallies had he known them.

> 'Of the two steps taken by the Assembly (wrote Sydenham from Canada) by far the most objectionable is the first:
>
> The demand for the removal of the Executive Council involves the establishment of this objectionable principle and I think could only be met when thus urged by a refusal. . . .
>
> I am not disposed to consider the Address of the House of Assembly for the removal of the Governor as a step so objectionable in theory as the other. . . . This course of an Appeal to the Throne . . . is the legitimate mode for the Legislature when it is unsatisfied with the Executive Government.'[2]

It might have surprised Sydenham to know that his chief had already condemned the Address for the governor's recall as 'a very unusual, irregular, and inconvenient proceeding' which he declined peremptorily 'to submit to Her Majesty'. More surprisingly still he had written to Sydenham *on the same day* that 'the Queen has remarked with pain' the demand for Sir Colin's recall.[3] To Sir Colin he wrote that the suspension of individual councillors was within the governor's powers. 'A total change in the composition of that Body is a measure of a very different nature. . . . I

[1] Chisholm, *op. cit.*, i. 307.

[2] 'This circumstance however undoubtedly complicates the question. To change the Executive Council would be to give up the principle for which we contend with regard to Responsible Government while to remove the Governor might . . . afford a triumph to a little knot of persons who certainly ought not to receive one.' Thomson to Russell, 'Confidential', Montreal, May 27, 1840. *G. Series*, 387. 209.

[3] Russell to Campbell, April 30, 1840 (approved draft), *C.O. 217*, 174. 275; Russell to Thomson, April 30, 1840, *G. Series*, 443. 23.

assume to Her Majesty's Government the responsibility of deciding whether the demand for such a change is in itself reasonable, and in what terms it ought to be met.' [1]

Here, then, was the very heart of the mystery, and the way in which Her Majesty's Government proceeded to meet 'the responsibility of deciding' must have appealed to Buller's sense of humour. Russell, Stephen, Vernon Smith, all conceded that Sir Colin's dispatches were hopelessly prejudiced and unreliable. Upon that of March 28 Lord John Russell himself left a note which must have startled the old governor had he seen it, and perhaps Russell himself had he reflected upon it: 'There is something untold. . . . The L. Govr. appointed Liberal Members, but put them in a Minority—They were out-voted in the Cabinet.' [2] The magic word was uttered! The Executive Council then was a 'Cabinet'. Huntington, representing a majority of 30 to 12 in the Assembly, had been outvoted 11 to 1 in the 'Cabinet'. 'Nothing can be done on this', notes Russell again, 'without much deliberation—But I cannot approve of the Lieutenant Governor's reckoning two thirds of the Assembly as "a few factious demagogues"—Let me have the despatches.' [3] Lord John Russell's reflections upon re-reading the dispatches can only be surmised, but it was obvious that 'a considerable change in the composition of the Executive Council is desirable'. It was equally clear that there was 'no ground whatever for believing that the Majority of the Assembly seek for any objects dangerous to the connection'.[4] But what was to be done with the governor? In the 'present circumstances of the Canadas' it was determined that Sir Colin must go.[5] To Sydenham, with his 'wand' and his 'star' and his magic touch, was to be entrusted the task of arranging the details upon the spot. Thus it was that Lord John Russell assumed the 'responsibility of deciding'; and the Ministers of the Crown, he added to Sir Colin Campbell, 'are relieved from the necessity of entering into many explanations'.[6]

[1] *C.O. 217*, 174. 275.
[2] *Id.*, 174. 309.
[3] *Id.*, 174. 323.
[4] *Id.*, 174. 275.
[5] Note by Vernon Smith: 'Lord John Russell wished an official letter to be written to Sir Colin Campbell announcing Lord Falkland's appointment in the "present circumstances of the Canadas".' *C.O. 217*, 175. 385. Before reaching Halifax Sydenham knew ('from your private letters') of Russell's plan for Campbell's recall. Thomson to Russell, July 27, 1840, *G. Series*, 184. Sydenham, in fact, had already suggested the same thing without compunction. Thomson to Russell, May 27, 1840, *G. Series*, 387. 209.
[6] *C.O. 217*, 174. 275.

It is on record that at the first levee of Lord Falkland, Sir Colin's successor—'within hearing of his Lordship and in the midst of a dozen of the Tories'—gallant old Sir Colin parted with Howe 'like a soldier and a gentleman'. 'You did what you thought was right', he said; 'you did it fairly and honorably, and I have no unkind feeling towards you.'[1] What reflections must have attended that honest hand-shake with Joseph Howe?

In Nova Scotia at least the contest was fairly won; and five months before Sydenham appeared there, like the god in the Greek play, to readjust the balance of victory, perhaps the greatest personal trophy of the contest had fallen to the Reformers. At the vote of want of confidence on February 5 the Hon. J. B. Uniacke, member of the Executive Council and long its chief defender in the Assembly, sent his resignation to the governor and joined the forces of reform.

James Boyle Uniacke's final stand was scarcely less dramatic than La Fontaine's in Canada. Both reached their final convictions during the same critical months of 1839–40.[2] Both became premiers—the first two premiers overseas under responsible government. Uniacke was the fourth son of R. J. Uniacke, the old 'Cumberland rebel' during the American Revolution, whose services as Assemblyman, Speaker, Attorney-General, and Executive Councillor filled the remarkable span of forty-eight years. At 76 years of age he could boast six sons who held his 'Character as the most valuable part of their inheritance'.[3] The eldest became Attorney-General and judge in Lower Canada; another became judge of the Supreme Court of Nova Scotia. Perhaps no family in Halifax inherited a more pervasive influence in the inner circles of government.

Uniacke's defence of the old order was instinctive, and much of his early repugnance to the new would not be difficult to justify. In truth there was a strain in Howe's manner to which Uniacke's polished and courtly address was a complete contrast; though there is perhaps no higher tribute than Howe's to Uniacke's 'noble form, easy deportment, graceful manners . . . a mind ever fruit-

[1] 'I am not without my own suspicions, however, that before he left Sir Colin had come slowly to the conviction that they had sacrificed him.' Howe to Sydenham, n.d., *Howe Papers*, vol. x.

[2] See below, pp. 256–62.

[3] Uniacke to Halliburton, Oct. 19, 1829 (*C.O. 217*, vol. 149). *A. Series*, 170. 261.

ful, a tongue ever eloquent, humour inexhaustible'. Uniacke resigned amidst the execrations of his set—the first formal demonstration of the principles of cabinet responsibility in Nova Scotia. 'From that hour', exclaimed Howe all too confidently in the Assembly, 'they might date . . . a constitution of which no power on earth could now deprive them.'[1]

The Coalition

I

For Sydenham as for Lord John Russell Howe's coup in Nova Scotia forced the first clear practical issue of responsible government in its final form.

Sydenham came to Nova Scotia after nine months of such success in the Canadas that his adroitness there passed into a proverb. The magic of his 'wand' must be examined in another context.[2] No more resourceful administrator perhaps ever came to Canada, but diffidence was not his besetting sin. A memorandum by Murdock, his indefatigable secretary, reflects inimitably, as we have seen, the sub-conscious mind of the Colonial Office upon the affairs of Nova Scotia. With this and the dispatches before him Sydenham wrote from Montreal on May 27—two months before his visit to Nova Scotia—with characteristic certitude:

> 'It is apparent to me that the present state of affairs there arises from no real grievance, but is the result of petty and personal ambition on the one hand and of a not over prudent management of affairs on the other. There exists . . . no impatience of British Sovereignty, no complaint of mismanagement at home, no financial distress. . . . Yet the Assembly by a large Majority have voted want of confidence in the Executive and have ultimately prayed for the removal of the Governor.
>
> I can attribute this state of things only to the cause I have mentioned.'

After nearly three weeks at Halifax Sydenham still professed the same opinion: the causes of dissension were 'those which I anticipated in my despatch . . . of the 27th May'.

But this infallibility was belied not only by the facts, but by the rest of his own dispatches. The case against the Executive Council was 'a just one'; and in Sydenham's deductions from this central truth are to be found all the fatuities which were soon to test, to the limits of his resourcefulness, his loyalty to the dominant creed of his chief in withstanding responsible government in its final

[1] Chisholm, *op. cit.*, i. 300, 295.

[2] See below, Chapter v, pp. 249 ff.

form. 'The removal of the Executive Council', as he wrote truly, meant 'the establishment of this objectionable principle.' The reason it was 'objectionable' and 'preposterous' was because 'no acts were assigned . . . as grounds': as though there could have been a clearer issue than responsible government itself and the civil list. The second, indeed, was carefully withdrawn from discussion by Sydenham himself. But what was to be done with Russell's dilemma? 'To change the Executive Council would be to give up the principle for which we contend with regard to Responsible Government while to remove the Governor might . . . afford a triumph to a little knot of persons who certainly ought not to receive one.' [1]

In truth the 'cleft stick' was now in the hands of the Reformers; and brilliant as may have been Sydenham's exploits in Canada his success in staving off 'this objectionable principle' in Nova Scotia may be regarded as the supreme test of his amazing tact and versatility.

II

Sydenham reached Halifax on July 9. It is not easy to trace the details of that memorable fortnight. The private letters between Sydenham and Russell are only partially in evidence, and revelations like the *Bagot Papers* or the *Grey-Elgin Correspondence* are seldom forthcoming. Sydenham's 'official' diagnosis, on the other hand, will be familiar to students of his political clinics in Upper and Lower Canada. There had been no personal quarrel, he wrote, with Sir Colin Campbell. 'The vote of the Assembly which affected him personally, was *I am afraid*, arrived at with the utmost reluctance and pain by most of those who concurred in it.' [2] The 'strong measures' of the Assembly, however, ought never to have been 'allowed to reach their present height'. Thus the disease was exceptional, and its malignancy was the fault of the physician. The hope of the future lay in hygiene rather than in surgery. In that sense Sir Colin's government was 'almost ridiculously powerless'. There was a 'total want of energy to attempt to occupy the attention of the Country upon real improvements'. The very consideration of these 'would divert men's minds from the agitation of abstract points of government'. Executive Councillors ought, therefore, to be in the Legislature in order to be 'instruments within

[1] Thomson to Russell, May 27, July 27, 1840. *G. Series*, 387. 209; 184.

[2] *Ibid.* The words in italics (my own) are suggestive. Had Howe's tactics been less magnanimous Sydenham's task had been easier.

its walls' for the governor's measures, 'or to defend his Acts or his policy'. 'If the proper direction be given to their labours, and due firmness evinced in controlling them, the Council will prove a very useful and powerful engine in the hands of the Governor.' In effect, as we shall see, the governor was to govern, and the Executive Councillors were to be the governor's 'placemen'—Sydenham's own phrase—diverting men's minds from awkward abstractions 'such as we have seen raised here'. In the Assembly as in the nursery, it would seem,

Satan finds some mischief still
For idle hands to do.

The necessary diligence could be exacted 'by no one but the Governor himself. He is in fact the minister.... There is I feel satisfied so much good sense amongst the People—so much respect and reverence for the Royal Authority, and so strong a desire for improvement, that he may Govern with ease to himself, and contentment to the people'.[1] Such was the Russellite creed in the hands of the shrewdest and ablest governor who ever tried to put it into practice.

In Nova Scotia as in Canada, however, Sydenham's real magic was always exercised *in camera*. 'I saw and conversed', he writes significantly, 'with men of all parties'; and there are few more engaging passages in Howe's life than the confidential interview in which he read to Sydenham the *Letters to Lord John Russell*; answering, as he thought, Sydenham's objections, and falling insensibly, it may be, beneath the spell of that remarkable personality. There is evidence, too, that the spell was reciprocal. But there were awkward possibilities in the Russellite creed which the subtlest charmer could scarcely dispel, charm he never so wisely. Hincks, who was a shrewder man than Howe, and as unscrupulous on occasion as Sydenham himself, had already seen this in Upper Canada. 'Privately His Excellency makes *the most liberal promises*', he wrote confidentially to La Fontaine. '*We think it policy to assume that Mr. T. is sincere.*'[2] In the end Hincks too,

[1] *G. Series*, 387. 209; 184; Scrope, *Memoir of the Right Honourable Charles Lord Sydenham with a Narrative of his Administration in Canada*, London, 1843, pp. 183–5.

[2] Dec. 4, 1839; Aug. 15, 1840. *La Fontaine Papers*, i. 31, 74. 'In Nova Scotia there is a Reform majority and yet notwithstanding Lord John Russell's celebrated despatch there has been no change.' 'We are all of opinion that Mr. Thomson has broken faith with us, and shamefully deceived the Reform party.... But the Reformers generally thought me too violent & too suspicious.' Hincks to La Fontaine, Jan. 30, May 2, 1840. *Id.*, i. 51, 59.

as we shall see, surrendered to the charmer. But Howe's faith was more ingenuous; though he, too, sometimes subdued his misgivings with a conscious effort.[1] In truth there are discrepancies which cannot be reconciled.

In 'confidential' and private letters to Russell Sydenham's adherence to the creed of his chief seems thoroughly orthodox. 'It has been my object', he wrote, 'carefully to avoid giving a triumph to the party which expressed want of confidence.' He had 'read people, parties, Assembly and all, a good lecture' in his reply to an Address from Halifax, and had taken that opportunity 'to place a decided negative upon the demand for what is called "Responsible Government" in the sense in which it is supposed to be used by the Popular party'. To confirm this report Sydenham enclosed a copy of *The Novascotian* with an article by Howe himself which would 'do away altogether with any difficulty on the score of his pamphlet'.[2]

But Sydenham's superlatives are not always warranted by the evidence. The article in *The Novascotian* (July 23) will be searched in vain for any recantation, on Howe's part, of responsible government. Howe's version of that memorable fortnight is vastly different: 'Before Mr. Thomson left Nova Scotia it was apparent that the old system was doomed and that Sir Colin would be removed. Expressions in his reply to an address from the people of Halifax were caught at as negativing this presumption, but those who had an opportunity of discussing politics with him could not be mistaken in the bias of his mind.'[3] Howe's private correspondence with Sydenham himself is more conclusive. Within three weeks he was writing warningly of the attempt of his enemies 'to make the whole affair bear the same appearance of trick and humbug as did the former Council'; though he himself was still hopeful of 'a strong but rationally responsible Executive', and ready 'to labour in all sincerity and good faith . . . to bring out the new policy discreetly'.[4] To Falkland Howe once wrote of a pledge to serve in the Executive Council for two years 'without fee or reward'.[5] Here, then, was Sydenham's pacification for 'a mighty storm in a very small ocean'—a curious response from the man

[1] Cf. Howe to Thomson, *Howe Papers*, vi. 22; x. 8.

[2] Thomson to Russell, July 27, 1840. *G. Series*, 184; Scrope, *op. cit.*, p. 185.

[3] Chisholm, *op. cit.*, i. 328. Annand's original edition was revised by Howe himself and was practically 'the work of his own hand'. *Id.*, i. vi.

[4] Howe to Thomson, Aug. 12, 1840. *Howe Papers*, vi. 22.

[5] *Id.*, x. 12.

whom Sydenham still represented to Russell as actuated by 'petty and personal ambition'. Elsewhere Howe stated to Falkland his *concordat* with Sydenham in precise and indeed unequivocal language. 'A Cabinet, composed of Heads of Departments, acting in harmony and possessing public confidence, was the ultimate object in view, as distinctly stated by His Lordship':

> 'When I consented to go into the Council, it was upon the distinct understanding with Lord Sydenham, that thereafter the House of Assembly was to possess and freely exercise its right, by a vote of want of Confidence or stoppage of supplies, to change the policy or dismiss the advisers of the Governor, subject of course to the restraints of the prerogative.... Relying upon this power in the popular Branch to produce ultimate harmony with the Executive, if the new arrangements were not satisfactory, I consented to go in.'[1]

The 'new arrangements' were that Howe and two of his friends including Herbert Huntington were to be invited to enter the Executive Council in a coalition under a successor to Sir Colin Campbell.

III

The Howe-Johnston-Stewart coalition in Nova Scotia was followed by a similar 'hermaphrodite administration', the Draper-Harrison-Hincks coalition in Canada after the Union—Sydenham's favourite expedient in both cases for making the Executive Council a 'useful and powerful engine in the hands of the Governor'. With Lord John Russell himself at the Colonial Office and Sydenham's mercurial genius thus successful in Canada, the two weak links exposed by Howe and Buller in the Russell theory seemed at last equal to the strain.

But there was already in Nova Scotia, and soon to be in Canada, a political dynamic strong enough to snap them both. 'We owe to party (writes Erskine May) most of our rights and liberties.... By argument and discussion truth is discovered, public opinion is expressed and a free people are trained to self-government.' From the Grand Remonstrance to the Reform Bill almost every great reform in British history had been the work of a political party. On neither side of the Atlantic was strong public opinion likely to function long without political parties, or a dominant party without power. It was the spectre of this historic tendency in British politics which haunted the Colonial Office and the death-

[1] *Howe Papers*, vi. 39, Apr. 3, 1843.

chamber, as we shall see, of Sydenham himself. What if discerning and disciplined political parties were to arise in these colonial parliaments as in Britain itself—not the 'voice of faction' but a 'body of men (in Burke's own phrase) united for promoting by their joint endeavours the national interest upon some particular principle in which they are all agreed'?

How Russell and Sydenham and Stanley and Gladstone and Metcalfe and Falkland, familiar as all of them must have been with the vital functions of party in British politics, could all have conceived it possible to blink the same tendencies in the colonies, must remain one of the mysteries of the Russell régime. Charles Buller, who had no small share in promoting such parties in both Nova Scotia and Upper Canada, gauged unerringly their functions and looked to them to vindicate the memory and principles of his chief. At the death of Durham, a broken and ruined man, in July, 1840, Buller consoled his daughter with this prophetic reflection. 'It does not matter very much', he wrote a few weeks later, 'what the Government repudiates and what it recognizes, for certain it is that in the Parliament of United Canada it has created a power from which no Government in this country will be able to withhold' the control of the executive.[1] The desperate shifts of Colonial Secretaries and governors to lay this ghost, to thwart the functions of party, to short-circuit them if possible by specious coalitions 'including all parties', and failing this to disparage their public spirit, now become for seven years the commonplaces of official correspondence. Sydenham's public censure of Baldwin in 1841 was more scathing, as we shall see, than his private libel upon Howe in 1840. In Canada the turmoil after the Union might put off the evil day, and this beyond a doubt was no small incentive to that measure.[2] But for better or for worse a sound political party after Burke's own heart was already in existence in Nova Scotia, and to say that the issues there were 'of no great magnitude' was merely to say that the province was of no great magnitude.

Now no man in British America had done more to create a sound political party than Howe. Upon the eve of 'the great

[1] Aug. 1, 1840. *Durham Papers*, xxvi. 501. *Sketch of Lord Durham's Mission*, *Report* of Pub. Arch. Can., 1923, p. 366.

[2] 'The whole system . . . must then be broken up and remodelled; and if for no other purpose than that the Union would be most desirable. . . . I am satisfied that if we fail in carrying it we may as well give up the Canadas at once, for I know no other means of governing either.' Thomson to Melbourne, Dec. 12, 1839. *Lord Melbourne's Papers*, ed. Sanders, Lond., 1889, p. 446.

election' of 1847 Howe left on record the aims that had dominated his political life: 'a healthy tone of public feeling, based on sound political knowledge, pervading not a class or a coterie, but the great body of the people; and an organized party in the Lower House, acting on general principles which the constituencies understood and feeling in honour bound to advance those principles until they should prevail.'[1] 'A more manly, public-spirited, united, and disinterested body of men', he was wont to say, 'were never exhibited by the legislative conflicts of any country.' With a resolute and disciplined majority of two to one in the Assembly it seemed that nothing could now stop the enforcement of responsible government in its final form.

Howe's failure to lead the party resolutely forward in 1840 carried consternation to many of his followers. His enemies said at once that he had sold his principles for office. His closest friends warned him of the 'curious cutting and carving' of his 'mangled reputation' by the rank and file of his own party.[2] In truth his decision looked like surrender. At best it was an ineffectual armistice when the state of the field, had he permitted his followers to stand to their guns, seemed to warrant an ultimatum. Scarcely three months had passed since Huntington had stood as his second in the duel with Halliburton; now, at the height of their intimacy, he withdrew his confidence, thrice declined Howe's adroitest inducements to take office, and held inflexibly to 'the good old cause'. So strained became the relations between them that common friends feared for their friendship,[3] and it was never perhaps quite unreservedly renewed. Howe, too, saw the dangers. 'Fully alive to the personal risk', he decided nevertheless to 'run all hazards'.[4] His reputation underwent its first eclipse, and nothing but the sheer strength of his influence enabled Sydenham, for the time at least, to carry the day. Where office itself was 'without fee or reward', and the price at once so obvious and so exacting, the urgency must indeed have been great. How was it to be explained?

There is much to be said for Howe's instinctive moderation. To Isaac Buchanan who tried to persuade him to enter the larger field by moving to Montreal Howe once wrote that he 'would not

[1] *Letter to the Freeholders of Nova Scotia*, Chisholm, *op. cit.*, i. 646.
[2] A. F. Ross to Howe, Pictou, Feb. 23, 1841. *Howe Papers*, i. 37.
[3] Cf. Stayley Brown to Howe, Yarmouth, Mar. 12, 1842. *Id.*, i. 69.
[4] Howe to Thomson, n.d.; to Huntington, n.d. *Id.*, x. 8, 39.

be sufficiently ultra' for Canadian politics.[1] Like Sydenham Howe distrusted stark theories and relied with great confidence upon the subtler accommodations of practice and experience. 'Responsible Government', he once wrote to one of his admirers in Upper Canada, 'is easily understood—to my mind it is a very simple affair—as simple as matrimony, but those husbands and wives get on the best, who respect each others' rights and say as little as possible about them.' 'It has always been my wish', he avowed to Falkland in 1843, 'that the new principles should be brought into operation without displacing or injuring a single person drawing his living from the public funds.' His magnanimity in the hour of success, in 1848, as we shall see, was in keeping with this generous impulse. But this alone would scarcely account for the armistice of 1840.

What then was the magic of Sydenham's 'wand', the burden of his appeal? It was Howe's belief that an obstructive and uncompromising temper in the Canadas had been responsible for the *volte face* of Glenelg in Nova Scotia, for his 'incomprehensible disgrace' in Great Britain, and for the counteracting firmness of Lord John Russell. The letter to Chapman and the columns of *The Novascotian* abound with these convictions. They had resulted in his earliest disagreement with Jotham Blanchard, and they coloured the whole temper of his mind towards Confederation. In 'the present circumstances of the Canadas' what would be the result of driving responsible government home without quarter, as Huntington stoutly advocated, in Nova Scotia?

To Falkland Howe once stated categorically his reasons for entering the coalition of 1840: 'being sincerely desirous to aid the introduction of the new system, and to lessen, if possible, the difficulties with which, at that time, the Governor General was beset.'[2] 'Your Lordship has a difficult task before you in Canada', Howe wrote to Sydenham himself. 'We will do our duty to you.'[3] To his followers in 1840 Howe appealed openly to support Sydenham in his great task, 'throwing the influence of Nova Scotia into the scale of Canadian politics, strengthening his hands, and giving the principles we value a wide circulation'. 'My pride and hope (he added) is that we shall make Nova Scotia, by her loyalty, intelligence and spirit, as it were, a normal school for British North America.'[4] Few more generous estimates of Sydenham's work are

[1] Aug. 31, 1844. *Id.*, vi. 72. [2] Apr. 3, 1843. *Id.*, vol. vi. [3] *Id.*, x. 8.
[4] Chisholm, *op. cit.*, i. 337.

to be found than Howe's in *The Novascotian* a few days before the news of his death at Alwington House: Howe had done his 'best to strengthen his hands' against the recurrence of that 'obstructive policy which had ended in open insurrection and the establishment of arbitrary power'. How far from just this was to Baldwin's inflexible 'principle', or to La Fontaine's austere 'constance', we must examine elsewhere; but in subordinating local tactics to the broader strategy Howe may perhaps be credited with more generosity than many of his critics then and since. In Canada in 1840 the Union itself was pending, and the approaching elections, as Sydenham well knew, were big with unknown possibilities. What if Howe were to lead an attack 'without quarter' in Nova Scotia? On the other hand, had the Whigs remained in power and had Grey instead of Stanley succeeded to the Colonial Office in 1841, it is conceivable that 'responsible government by degrees' might indeed have come in Nova Scotia like the dawn without those convulsions which afterwards distorted the contest in both provinces.

As it proved, Huntington's misgivings were amply justified; and indeed with six Tories and the implacable influence of Alexander Stewart in the cabinet three Reformers were not likely to leaven the lump. Uniacke, still a Tory on many issues, and James McNab, a relative by marriage of Howe himself, were induced to take office; but no inducement could prevail upon Huntington. *The Novascotian*, the *Recorder*, the *Register*, the *Times*, the *Yarmouth Herald*, and two of the three Pictou newspapers, gave the coalition their nominal support. To Huntington himself Howe wrote in praise of Falkland. The excluded members of the council 'died hard, but were in firm hands'. But Howe had given hostages, as every leader in a minority in a coalition must give hostages, to the enemy; and like Brown after Confederation, he lived, not to repent the deed but to pay bitterly for his magnanimity.

IV

The coalition of 1840 did not succeed, but the marvel was that it worked at all. Even in Canada where the Union tended to neutralize or confound the functions of the old parties Bagot was soon in the rapids, bending his 'back to the oar like a man', as Stanley had exhorted him, but utterly unable to stem the current. The second coalition of September, 1842, virtually forced the Tories from the council. In Nova Scotia the current was already faster, and there was still less discipline in the boat—much more of 'culling crabs, or backing water when they are wanted for "Hard all".'[1] If the cox, as late as 1843, could still report headway, it was because Howe in all his life had never rowed in better form.

In a sense the Sydenham régime had scarcely a fair chance. Until Sydenham's death and the fall of the Whigs from power in Great Britain—both in September, 1841—Howe's faith remained. The elections of 1840 had given the coalition a fluctuating majority. Huntington carried a vote against the government to reopen the civil list controversy but failed twice to carry want of confidence. Howe went to Canada for the opening of the first session after the Union, and returned with his misgivings of Canadian politics still unallayed even by Sydenham's amazing skill and resourcefulness. His own position, too, was anomalous. His role as Executive Councillor 'without fee or reward' was to be Speaker of the Assembly—a combination which sufficiently indicates what was expected of him. Not even S. W. G. Archibald at his best poured oil more sedulously upon the troubled waters. More than once he left the Speaker's chair to quell the storm by one of his Olympian speeches. *The Novascotian*, deprived of his versatile pen, quickly lost its hold upon the public except when Howe's unmistakable *élan* reappeared at intervals in a series of articles under a *nom de plume*. With his lips sealed by the confidences of the council chamber, his voice hushed in the Speaker's chair, his pen dry, his friends loyal but unconvinced, and the 'obstructive Press' doing its worst to goad him into speechless fury, Howe ruefully conceded that he had 'his hands full'.

The hope of 'the new system', however, lay with the new governor. With Lord Falkland Howe's relations at first were cordial to the point of intimacy. As Whig whip in the House of Lords during the 'thirties, Falkland must have got his knowledge of the game at first hand. Gifted with a famous name and handsome presence, married to a king's daughter, and liberal beyond Sydenham himself in his interpretation of 'the new system', he might have left a different reputation in Nova Scotia had his governorship continued under the auspices of 1840. Responding to such an intimacy Howe dedicated his abounding energies to the task of making Falkland's administration 'a bright page in the history of the Country'. 'Now is the winter of our discontent (he once quoted in a burst of enthusiasm) made glorious summer by the sun of Falkland.'

[1] Stanley to Bagot, May 17, 1842, *Bagot Papers*, ix. 60.

At the death of his brother—'the hardest blow (he wrote) I have ever had'—Howe was deeply touched by the governor's sympathy.[1] 'Your Lordship', he once added, 'has often in the frankness of personal intercourse tempted me to wish that the difference of rank which divides us were less.' With regard to policy Howe found Falkland's 'reliance upon the infinite superiority of the new system over the old almost as great and enthusiastic as our own'. Falkland once criticized—to Lord John Russell himself—the failure of coalitions to produce 'a regular steady Majority' in the Assembly.[2] When the *Bankrupt Bill*, a government measure, was lost, Howe outlined in strictest confidence a 'sketch of a party Administration', in order to 'protect your Lordship, our principles and myself.'[3] Falkland himself canvassed the retirement of Sir Rupert George from the Secretaryship; and Howe, whose name had been proposed for the Excise or the Post Office, did not hesitate, in one of the most intimate 'private and confidential' letters he ever wrote, to forecast the post which he finally occupied under responsible government in 1848:

> 'It is evident that the party through whose hands every detail of administration passes, is the best fitted to give views of the general "policy", and ready answers and explanations whenever they are required. With the knowledge I have of the temper of the House, and the friends I have there, and the facility which long practice has given me in speaking and writing I have the confidence to believe that if representing the Government there in that capacity I could do more good than in any other. . . . Every storm that rises satisfies me that some of our friends want more of nerve, tact and facility of resource, than they have, and that, all of us together have not more than is required. If appointed to the Secretaryship the study of my life would be the Country, its government, its legislation, and relations with the Mother Country and the surrounding Colonies. . . . To make this use of me would appear to be both sounder policy in your Lordship, and the Colonial Secretary, than to set me diving into Mail Bags or collecting Provincial duties.'[4]

Meanwhile Falkland wrote scathingly of '*the Society* of Halifax', their 'violent private enmities,' their insignificance in number and

[1] 'Your Lordship has ever been to me even more than a Brother.' *Howe Papers*, x. 4.

[2] Feb. 14, 1841, *Letter-Books*, 116. 33.

[3] 'Which nobody but your Lordship has yet seen, not even McNab, nor shall ever see, unless circumstances compel us to act upon it.' *Howe Papers*, x. 46.

[4] *Id.*, x. 12. Cf. the subsequent trouble of the Canadian Reformers with Metcalfe's son-in-law, Captain Higginson, 'the eternal Secretary'.

political influence, their isolation from their fellow citizens 'from a mistaken feeling of their own importance,' and the 'systematic opposition of some of the public functionaries in *conjunction*' with them, thus making the governor's 'social position . . . a difficult one.'[1]

The violent reversal of all these relations in the contest which followed must have owed much of its bitterness for both parties to the intimate knowledge of each other's vulnerability.

V

The dissensions with regard to 'the new system' were from the first irremediable, and the Reformers at the council table repeatedly invoked Falkland's best offices in vain to reconcile them.

The presence there of Alexander Stewart passed in itself for a living demonstration of his opinions. From the safe vantage ground of the upper chamber Stewart openly denied that any 'change had been made in the constitution'. 'Responsible government in a colony is responsible nonsense—it was independence. If the responsible government aimed at . . . were granted by a minister, he would deserve to lose his head.' Nothing but a formal declaration, forced through the council by the Reformers and sponsored before the Assembly itself by the Hon. E. M. Dodd—'the Doddean confession of faith'—could calm the speculations of the House upon the dissensions within the council chamber. The press was critical and sarcastic, and the Reformers themselves 'half believed that the Government was written down'.

In April, 1841, a more gracious personality than Alexander Stewart—a star of dire portent to Howe and his party—rose to the first magnitude in the Executive Council. Archibald was appointed Master of the Rolls, and James William Johnston succeeded him as Attorney-General. It would be hard to imagine more virtues in sharper contrast than Johnston's and Howe's. Their portraits hang in the old Province Building on opposite sides of the Speaker's chair, symbols of rival cults which still divide the political traditions of Nova Scotia. Howe's stormy countenance is clouded with tempest. Johnston's serene and finely chiselled features are sunk in meditative repose. An intellect of great range and power, trained to the law and unrelieved by fancy or imagination, was in itself a foil to the gorgeous exuberance

[1] Falkland to Stanley, Dec. 22, 1841; Sept. 13, 1842. *Letter-Books*, 116. 128; 117. 38.

of Howe's. Unostentatious like his name, but graced with that 'polish of manners' which had appealed to Durham and Buller in Quebec, Johnston moved with distinction in the most select circles of Halifax. But though his instincts were all Tory, his intellect, as a long series of reforms in Nova Scotia attests to this day, was almost as Liberal as Howe's. Howe himself so rated him in a confidential memorandum for Sydenham in 1840.[1]

The contrasts between the two were intensified by their associations. Johnston's finely wrought temper, aristocratic by instinct and by education, was combined with an incorruptible character of such austerity that scandal never marred its polished surface. Howe, a child of nature, with the pent-up energies of a volcano within his mind, moved in an atmosphere of boisterous self-confidence. Few surmised the existence of a secret chamber within that rugged spirit where Howe was wont to bow in humility and child-like simplicity at the great crises of his life. It was known that he had fought a duel,[2] that he had an illegitimate son, and that he was the choicest spirit in the province in that indefinable circle which Elgin once called 'the bhoys'. The stories of these escapades and a dozen others that were false were now set buzzing in every ear. Johnston, on the other hand, moved in a religious circle perhaps the most austere and pertinacious in the province. The Baptist traditions of Nova Scotia, like the Puritan traditions of New Eng-

[1] 'Liberal but opposed to Majority of Assembly.' Howe to Thomson, July 20, 1840. *Howe Papers*, vi. 18.

[2] The duel with Halliburton is thus referred to in a note which Howe left addressed '*To the People of Nova Scotia*': 'During the political struggle in which I have been engaged, several attempts have been made to make me pay the penalty of life for the steady maintenance of my opinions. . . . Well knowing that even a shadow of an imputation upon my moral courage would incapacitate me for serving my country with vigor and success hereafter, I feel that I am bound to hazard my life rather than blight all prospects of being useful. If I fall, cherish the principles I have taught, forgive my errors, protect my children.' To his wife he wrote: 'There shall be no blood on my hand'; Howe discharged his pistol into the air. To his sister he wrote less reservedly: 'I had been long impressed with the conviction that it would have to be done with somebody at some time. . . . So long as the party I opposed possessed all the legislative influence they did not much mind my scribbling in the Newspapers—when I got into the House they anticipated that *a failure* there would weaken my influence. . . . When however, they found I not only held my own against the best of them but was fast combining and securing a majority upon principles striking at the root of their monopoly, they tried the effect of wheedling, and that failing, resorted to intimidation.'

Howe declined subsequent challenges, refusing to fire himself and 'having no fancy for being shot at, by every public officer whose intellect I might compare with his emoluments'. *Howe Papers*, vi. 11, 12, 14.

land from which they sprang, were scarcely to be understood by the uninitiated, but Johnston was the flower of their creed and their champion, and they repaid him by a loyalty which bordered upon fanaticism.

A private dispute between Howe and a few of Johnston's co-religionists lit a long train of mischief. Private antipathies merged into public policy when a resolution to withdraw provincial grants from the four sectarian colleges of the province in favour of 'one good college, free from sectarian control, and open to all denominations', passed the Assembly by a vote of 26 to 21. The project ran counter to one of the strongest tenets of the Baptist tradition, and Johnston, who was a governor of their college, soon found an eager band of followers lecturing, preaching, and writing in his support. This was a kind of warfare in which Howe had no match in British America, and the very weight of his guns, charged as they were with every kind of ammunition from argument to ridicule, transferred sympathy—that of Falkland himself perhaps included—to his opponents. The governor discovered that he had 'relied too much on the prudence and forbearance of both these Gentlemen'.[1] In the end the issue of one provincial university appeared under the colours of a political party against the multiplication of sectarian colleges under the auspices of a coalition.

VI

A series of events, less personal in character, forced the governor in self-defence to rely increasingly upon the courtly counsels of his Attorney-General.

The return of the Tories to power in Great Britain in September, 1841, was followed by a rejuvenation of Toryism in the colonies. Howe's Tory colleagues now spoke without restraint, and many of their utterances were nicely calculated to compromise his waning influence with his followers. Falkland, too, soon found himself in difficulties. Howe warned him against more than one 'false move'; reminded him that 'the enemy know everything which passes in our camp'; and added the shrewd comment that 'Stanley, like most people, will approve what seems safe, *and has been shown to be successful*'.[2]

Falkland once ventured to discuss with Stanley the feasibility

[1] *Letter-Books*, 117. 122.

[2] Howe to Falkland, *Howe Papers*, x. 26.

of a full party government, and also the re-opening of the civil list controversy; with a prospect, as he thought, that 'it may in the course of the next year be definitely settled'.[1] Beyond a doubt the hope of an accommodation with Huntington lay behind this shrewd move, for Falkland was in a position to know what Stanley did not—that the casual and territorial revenues of the crown, which had warranted the nonchalant withdrawal of that issue from the Assembly by Campbell and Sydenham, were now for the first time unequal to the salaries charged upon them. The salaries were already in arrears. After a six years' contest with unpopular officials the Assembly professed no 'sympathy for the inconvenience'.[2] The power of the purse was now for the first time in the hands of the Assembly, and Huntington's terms were a homogeneous Liberal government and 'all the revenues of the country... under the control of the Assembly'.[3]

But any range of discretion was quickly terminated by Stanley himself. Refusing a parliamentary grant, he instructed Falkland to 'apply to the Assembly' for the salaries. Falkland replied bluntly that 'if this plan be followed the house will refuse any grant whatever': there was an 'invincible disinclination of the provincial parliament to act in conformity with Your Lordship's judgment in this particular'.[4] In the growing coolness thus developing between the governor and his Tory chief, Falkland, in desperation, approached Huntington for the third time.[5] Howe bent every art of advocacy to the task. But Huntington 'after many days' deliberation' still resolutely declined. Falkland's vexation was extreme, and indeed the ruin of the coalition to which he was perforce committed now seemed inevitable. 'From that moment', wrote Howe, 'I have not attempted to disguise my convictions that the Administration, as at present constituted, cannot go on a great while longer.'[6]

Other factors in the disruption of the coalition are more easily traced. In September, 1842, Howe had accepted the office of Collector of Impost and Excise.[7] The same month Baldwin and

[1] Oct. 3, 1842. *Letter-Books*, 117. 43.

[2] Aug. 18, 1843, *id.*, 117. 112.

[3] Falkland to Russell, Feb. 14, 1841. *Id.*, 116. 33.

[4] May 10, May 9, 1843. *Id.*, 117. 99, 96.

[5] The fifth time since 1838. Falkland's previous offers in February and December, 1841. *Howe Papers*, i. 33, 61.

[6] Howe to Falkland, April 3, 1843. *Id.*, vi. 39.

[7] 'I am quite sure that my having it in my power to name you . . . will not give you *half* the pleasure it has given me.' Falkland to Howe, Aug. 29, 1842. *Id.*, i. 84.

La Fontaine in Canada forced the Tories from the cabinet and quickly dominated a virtually party government under Sir Charles Bagot. It was not long before Falkland was loyally informed by Uniacke that 'an attempt to establish a party government would take place here', not by the Liberals but by the Conservatives themselves.[1] Stewart had approached Uniacke with a proposal 'to embark in the same boat with himself and Mr. Johnston, form a junction between the Tories and Baptists . . . and throw Howe overboard'. Howe too, ignorant of this cabal against him, was 'ready to come at once to the Canadian system', and to resign if necessary in order to give his colleagues 'a chance of trying the experiment'.[2] By the spring of 1843 the government was reduced to the lowest ebb of public confidence. Its members were 'openly and shamelessly intriguing against each other'. A section of the press began a savage attack upon Howe's personal character. Not a single newspaper in the province now supported the government. Even the heads of departments were hostile, like 'pursers and doctors, who having little or no perils to encounter, spend their time in starving and poisoning the crew'. Howe reported that his friends had 'abandoned the task in despair':

> 'There is something more required to make a Strong Administration (he wrote bitterly to Falkland) than nine men treating each other courteously at a round table. There is the assurance of good faith—towards each other—of common sentiments, and kindly feelings, propagated through the friends of each, in Society, in the Legislature and in the Press, until a great Party is formed . . . which secures a steady working majority to sustain their policy and carry their measures. . . . At the moment, although all the Members of the Council have some friends, the Government, as such, apart from your Lordship's personal influence, may be said to have none.'[3]

VII

The turning-point in Howe's relations with Falkland was reached at the close of the session of 1843. Driven to desperation by his instructions on the one hand and by Huntington's recalcitrance on the other, Falkland found himself committed in sheer self-defence to Stanley's favourite expedient of disparaging 'distinctions of local party'. Johnston, more discreet than Stewart, and well aware that the tide was now running in his favour, could

[1] Falkland to Stanley, Mar. 31, 1843. *Letter-Books*, 117. 80.
[2] Howe to Falkland, Apr. 3, 1843. *Howe Papers*, vi. 39; x. 30.
[3] Apr. 3, 1843. *Id.*, vi. 39.

well afford to acquiesce without reservations. With studied moderation he drafted a memorandum against 'a party Government in Nova Scotia' which was duly approved by Falkland and forwarded for Stanley's approbation.

This 'cross-ruffle' in the game must have stirred to their depths those infirmities of temper which Howe's enemies were now for the first time learning to exploit to his undoing. Goaded to fury by a provocative notice of motion that 'no Excise officer . . . should hold a seat in the popular branch', Howe threatened an amendment 'that the time has now arrived when the gracious intentions of Her Majesty with regard to these Colonies should be carried out in Nova Scotia by the formation of a Cabinet composed of heads of departments united in sentiment upon important public questions'.[1] Thus at last, whatever Howe might say to the contrary, was the gage thrown for a homogeneous party government. An angry interview followed at Government House, and Falkland's next dispatch to the Colonial Office, with all its interminable prolixity, scarcely conceals the fact that Johnston's star was now in the ascendant.

To the governor's reproaches Howe replied, with more truth than discretion, that he had proposed 'nothing which conflicts with the system I always understood it to be your Lordship's wish to introduce into this Province as early as circumstances would permit . . . the new system as contemplated by your Lordship and carried out in Canada'.[2] In a meeting of council, Howe, McNab, and Uniacke added bluntly that the House could 'have no respect for a body made up of individuals who were supposed to feel none for each other'. No longer now in a mood to make way for their enemies, and convinced that government measures could no longer be carried through the Assembly by a council which 'no man of any political sagacity' now credited with mutual confidence, the Reformers advised its reorganization in such a way as to command the confidence of the House.

As late as March 31 Falkland was still ready to face another session—the last before the election—with the old coalition, upon the understanding that if a new House pronounced 'decidedly in favor of a party Government it will then be my duty . . . to adhere

[1] 'Acting in harmony in both branches of the legislature and inspiring by the respect which its members entertain for each other respect and confidence in this house and throughout the country.'

[2] Howe to Falkland, Apr. 3, 1843. *Howe Papers*, vi. 39.

to that which is best capable of conducting the public business'.[1] This, it must be conceded, with Stanley in the Colonial Office and Metcalfe just assuming the reins of government in Canada, required no little courage; but in the midst of the bitterest exchanges between Howe and Johnston on 'the college question'—in Howe's absence and against his written advice—Falkland decided upon an immediate election as 'the only means by which I could hope to escape the necessity of immediately forming a Party Government'.[2] It was now too late to resign except upon the governor's undoubted right—at that time—to dissolve the House. Howe was 'trapped'. He had 'declared himself (so Falkland wrote to Stanley) in favor of a party Government from the Hustings'; but the ghosts of all his labours for the Sydenham régime now rose up against him.[3] 'Weary and sick at heart', his hands tied, the Nessus' shirt of office still upon his back, the pangs of resentment and wounded pride burning in his vitals, Howe found himself hoist with his own petard.

At first the Reformers thought they had won the day. But Falkland under the shrewd advice of his Attorney-General thought otherwise. Johnston himself, formerly in the Legislative Council, was now a member of the Assembly. His presence there 'to give greater strength to the Government than it has hitherto possessed in that branch' had been cited to Stanley as Falkland's final motive for an immediate election.[4] A few weeks later Johnston appears in the governor's dispatches as 'the leader of my Government'. Interpreting the election as 'adverse to the establishment of a Party Government', and without awaiting a trial of strength in the new House, Falkland appointed Mr. Almon, Johnston's brother-in-law, to the Executive Council with a seat in the Legislative Council vacated by Johnston himself. The appointment, 'after very mature deliberation', was intended as a demonstration in favour of 'a mixed Administration'; but this reason was barbed by another which Falkland added, no doubt for Howe's special benefit, in an open letter which he published over his own name in the newspapers: 'because . . . from his affinity to Mr. Johnston . . . his appointment would be looked upon by the public as a proof of my confidence in that gentleman.'[5]

1 Falkland to Stanley, *Letter-Books*, 117. 80.
2 Falkland to Stanley, Nov. 28, 1843. *Id.*, 117. 122.
3 *Ibid.*
4 *Ibid.*
5 Falkland to Stanley, Jan. 1, 1844, *id.*, 117. 141; Chisholm, *op. cit.*, i. 448.

The same day (December 21), four weeks after the Metcalfe crisis in Canada, Howe, Uniacke, and McNab resigned. It was clear that 'responsible government by degrees' was approximating by degrees not to 'the new system' but to the old. Many years afterwards when Grey was on the point of leaving office in England, Howe reflected upon his own plight in 1843. 'He has fortune (Howe notes in his diary), rank, and no family to support—no debts to pay. When I went out I had debts to pay—seven children to maintain—no fortune, and . . . a four years' fight for my good name against an infernal faction before me. He may wipe his eyes.' Thus ended for Howe the inglorious experiment of the Sydenham régime. Had Huntington been capable of malice towards his old friend what reminders must have passed between them as they began anew the task of reorganizing the fragments of their party in order to win back the commanding position of 1840?

'The Crisis'

I

In Nova Scotia as in Canada the resignation of the Reformers in 1843 was followed by one of the bitterest contests in the history of either province. It was Howe's opinion, recorded many years after his position as Provincial Secretary had given him access to the official correspondence, that there was 'a mysterious connection' between the two, and that Falkland in 'executing a coup d'état of his own' had burnt his bridges and identified himself with the Tory régime of Lord Stanley.[1] In the midst of the conflict the charge was made with less reserve. 'I retired with my party', wrote Howe in his scathing indictment of Falkland in *The Novascotian* of March 16, 1846; 'you held on when yours threw up the reins and changed your policy that you might hold your place.'[2]

The contrast between the Howe-Falkland correspondence of 1841–2 and the official dispatches of 1844 is in truth unmistakable. 'My present position', Falkland wrote a week after Howe's resignation, 'bears a remarkable similarity to that of the Govr. General of Canada.'[3] Henceforth Falkland's dispatches, like Metcalfe's, ring all the changes upon the approved Tory phrases of the day. Signs of party government which he had foreshadowed with com-

[1] Chisholm, *op. cit.*, i. 444, 445.
[2] Open letter in reply to the taunt of being a 'place-hunting mendicant'.
[3] To Stanley, Jan. 1, 1844. *Letter-Books*, 117. 141.

posure in March, 1843, were now 'instruments of mischief—by plausible and crafty demagogues'. The rights of minorities in such a system would be a 'nullity', and the sufferers—the Halifax 'Coterie', described by Falkland in vastly different terms two years before—would be driven to 'transfer their allegiance to any Country which would relieve them from subjection to such a domination'. The result 'would not only very soon be destructive of any Coalition but . . . loosen the ties which bind the Colony and the Mother Country'. 'Matters have arrived at a Crisis', he wrote in March, 1844, after one of Howe's speeches in the Assembly, 'at which that Gentleman and those who support him must triumph absolutely or . . . be resolutely excluded from office.' Nothing but 'decided interference on the part of the British Government' could now stop the process: Falkland suggested a written constitution by Act of Parliament. Otherwise 'the Governor . . . would become in effect elective'; he would be 'little else than the recording Clerk' of the Assembly; he would 'become utterly insignificant', and could 'without inconvenience be altogether dispensed with'; he would become a 'mere expounder and advocate on all occasions of the opinions of the majority of the elective branch'—'a mere Cipher under *their influence*'. Such were now the aims of the 'Ultras'.[1]

All this will sound strangely familiar to the student of the Metcalfe régime in Canada. But Falkland was shrewder in his tactics. He had not been Whig whip in the House of Lords for nothing. Metcalfe never descended to the level of Falkland's fierce vendetta against Howe or to the *gaucherie* of defending himself over his own name in the newspapers; but on the other hand the obloquy under which Falkland left Nova Scotia was scarcely a measure of his success. While Metcalfe was forced to descend into the arena in person in order to win the election of 1844 with the aid of Ryerson and the Methodists, Falkland had already snatched his majority of three by precipitating an election with the aid of Johnston and the Baptists. In a sense he had a less plausible cause and he fought with fewer weapons. The 'loyalty' cry which won the day in Canada was useless in Nova Scotia.[2] Not even Craskill, the

[1] Jan. 1, Mar. 2, 1844; May 29, 1845, &c. *Id.*, 117. 141, 155; 118. 103, &c.

[2] Cf. Adam Fergusson to Howe, Jan. 15, 1844: 'The Tories are stirring Heaven and earth to get up Addresses to Sir Charles belching "Loyalty, loyalty" and in his answers I think he acts disingenuously by receiving all they say, with reciprocal expressions indirectly accusing all who differ *with himself* of disloyal principles.' *Howe Papers*, i. 114.

Queen's printer, ever dared to level that 'antiquated blunderbuss' at Howe and the Nova Scotia Reformers. The term 'Ultras' found its way into Falkland's vocabulary, but in truth their views were so moderate by comparison that Howe himself once dropped the word 'blunder' in deploring the decision of Baldwin and La Fontaine to risk—and as it proved, to lose for more than four years—what had been so precariously won. Craskill in *The Morning Post* once tried to identify the demands of Metcalfe's retiring councillors with 'what Falkland is required to do by his opponents'. Howe was stirred from his customary banter to vehement denial:

> 'In the name of the ex-Councillors, on the house-tops, before Lord Falkland's face; aye, in the presence of the Queen herself; wherever and whenever this charge is brought against James McNab, James B. Uniacke and Joseph Howe, to our dying day, we will pronounce it a base, black falsehood, without a shadow of foundation; yes, and add, that no man knows better that it is so than the nobleman who thus instructs or permits his underling, to defame men, whom the plain unvarnished truth could not injure.'[1]

Despite the narrowness of his majority Falkland had disintegrated the most resolute Reform party in British America; and he never lost a vital division in the House.[2] His government, though it commanded a narrower majority, was stronger than Metcalfe's, and it lasted longer; and if Metcalfe's administration, as Gladstone maintained, might 'justly be regarded as a model by his Successors', there was a word of commendation too for Falkland's.[3] He finally left Nova Scotia at his own request, at the normal expiration of his term of office; and he was promoted to the governorship of Bombay.

II

One advantage at least Falkland had over Metcalfe in Canada. His Attorney-General was an abler parliamentarian and a far shrewder politician. Much of the tactical success of these four years it would not be amiss to attribute to Johnston. By 1846 there was truth in Howe's gibe that he governed Nova Scotia 'with as

[1] Chisholm, *op. cit.*, i. 519.

[2] 'Two or three recreant Liberals and all the "loose fish" voting with the Government.' Howe to Hincks in the Montreal *Pilot*, May 15, 1844.

[3] To Cathcart, Feb. 3, 1846, *G. Series*, 449. 330; Gladstone to Falkland, Dec. 23, 1845; Falkland to Gladstone, Jan. 31, 1846. *Letter-Books*, 118. 165. With humour which must have escaped Falkland, Gladstone wrote that further details were perfectly unnecessary. A single sentence selected at random from Falkland's interminable dispatches contains 317 words.

absolute an influence as Sir Robert Peel in England.'[1] There was something of Peel's hard, cool empiricism, too, in his method, and his was perhaps the only reputation which moved steadily forward throughout the Stanley régime.

The contest into which Falkland and Howe now descended soon became the chamber of horrors in the traditions of political decorum in Nova Scotia. Without giving ground in his own defence, Howe himself once wished it possible to 'blot out this disgraceful page from our Provincial history'.[2] Falkland's reflections when all was over can only be surmised, but if pride and an imperious temper, as his enemies maintained, were his besetting sins, bitterly must he have atoned for them. His new defenders in the Tory press were those who had never ceased to defame him, and his household, not always in the best of taste, during the Whig régime. Their comment had ranged from 'the bend sinister'—'not only . . . on his escutcheon, but on his heart'—to his private secretary who was accused of 'robbing a pawnbroker's shop to replenish his wardrobe'. The '*Society*' of Halifax which he had rated for their superciliousness now became his defenders, since he had made their cause his own; and not without a touch of malice did they contemplate the 'Whig taskmaster' and his 'Whig Premier' belabouring each other by proxy or otherwise in every political newspaper in the country.

For Howe, too, the situation had its ironies. The courtly seriousness of Johnston with his 'indictment against a joke' under his arm, turning a lampoon on *The Lord of the Bed-Chamber* into a state paper and passing solemn censures upon 'breaches of decency and good manners', could be countered by a squib or a pasquinade. By speech and pen Howe made the most of it, but though the smile of good humour was always upon his lips, the gall of bitterness frequently filled his heart. 'They have scorned me at their feasts,' he once exclaimed, 'they have insulted me at their funerals!' Women shunned him in the street. Much of the coarseness which disfigured his banter during this period was Gargantuan in its directness and its force, but he frequently contemplated the desolation wrought by his pen with real sorrow. 'I know him', he once said of Falkland, 'perhaps better than he does himself.' The wrath that worked like madness in the brain was the reflex of hopes, perhaps the most ingenuous that Howe ever indulged, for his native province, for the Empire, and for his own services to both.

[1] Chisholm, *op. cit.*, i. 588. [2] *Id.*, i. 506.

It cannot be necessary to explore this record in detail. Falkland demanded from Howe, Uniacke, and McNab the reasons for their resignations 'stated in writing'; in reply to which he not only 'answered those reasons', as he thought, but sent his letter to the newspapers for the benefit 'both of the people of the province and the members from the remote districts'.[1] Howe's rejoinder touched this *gaucherie* with great moderation, but it opened flood-gates of controversy which were never closed until Falkland left the province. Many of the governor's champions were volunteers. For several, however, the source of inspiration was never disputed—an army surgeon who was an intimate of the governor's household, the Queen's printer who had supplanted Howe's friend Thompson in that office, and a contributor to the New York *Albion* under the name of 'Scrutator'. There was truth in Howe's defence that he bore this defamation for four months—until May 6, 1844—before writing a single article against Lord Falkland; but he was unfortunate in his fame, for while the malice of his detractors was mercifully forgotten with their names, the tale of his own Rabelaisian humour in reply followed him as long as he lived.

Until the end of February, 1844, Howe once declared, he would have burnt his house over his children's heads 'to have saved or to have served Lord Falkland'.[2] On the 24th the governor made overtures to the three Reformers to re-enter a coalition; stipulating however certain conditions which all three declined 'in the most respectful manner'.[3] On February 29 Howe met by chance a close personal friend of Lord Falkland's and his own, and after mutual counsels entrusted him with a confidential note[4] to the governor. The proposal was to be delivered under pledge of secrecy, returned if not received, and burnt if rejected. The note was brought back unopened with a declaration by the governor 'in a towering rage' that thenceforth there was to be 'war to the knife' between them. That evening *The Gazette* printed a dispatch from Stanley that the governor would be supported in 'resisting the pretensions of the retired Councillors'. Howe always maintained that friendly relations were 'severed by rudeness which no gentleman can defend.'[5]

[1] Falkland to Stanley, Jan. 1, 1844. *Letter-Books*, 117. 141.

[2] Chisholm, *op. cit.*, i. 529.

[3] Falkland to Dodd, Feb. 24, 1844; Dodd to Falkland, Feb, 26, 1844. *Letter-Books*, 117. 160, 163.

[4] Published in Chisholm, *op. cit.*, i. 529. Howe suggested the retirement of two men, himself included, from either side, 'for the peace of the country'.

[5] *Id.*, i. 510.

For the political history of this period as for Howe himself the incident of February 29 was a turning-point. 'After that ill-judged publication in *The Gazette*', he afterwards said, 'the whole feeling of the Liberal party was changed.'[1] For more than three years the toil and restraints of office—'the ceaseless strife, heartless insincerity, and barren rewards of colonial public life'—had been borne with a fortitude at which Howe's enemies themselves sometimes marvelled. 'For three years and a half', he wrote as he plunged again into the fray in *The Novascotian* (May 1, 1844), 'we sometimes doubted our own identity.' From the Stanley régime he now drew the devastating lesson of the Canadian 'Ultras' that 'moderation and magnanimity are thrown away'.[2] Recalling the chivalry of the contest of 1840 when the antagonists 'saluted each other as the first volley was fired and drank at the same stream when the battle was over', Howe now launched upon a 'more barbarous style of warfare' which embittered his most cherished memories, coarsened his nature, and stained his name; lost him perhaps the first premiership under responsible government overseas in 1848, and in the end contributed not a little to fasten upon him the cardinal sin of indiscretion that barred him from the career he coveted beyond his native province.

III

The overtures of February were renewed in July, but Falkland's resentment had now a better excuse in the torrent of pasquinades and lampoons, mingled with trenchant argument of another sort, which issued from the press of *The Novascotian* and *Morning Chronicle*.

The July overtures were charged with mischief in every detail. Unlike those of February they were opened not through an intermediary but by a circular letter to Huntington, McNab, Uniacke Tobin, and Brennan—the last two with a special appeal to the Roman Catholics of the province—offering them seats in an Executive Council of twelve members with the express proviso, however, that Howe was to be excluded.[3] In the end all five declined—McNab and Huntington immediately, the latter for the sixth time, and the others after prolonged negotiations. In the follow-

[1] *Id.*, i. 530.

[2] Letter to Hincks in the Montreal *Pilot*, May 15, 1844.

[3] Stanley's permission to increase the numbers from nine to twelve had been given in February.

ing February when the House met, the correspondence was made public, together with a dispatch to Stanley in such glaring violation of confidence and (as it afterwards appeared) of fact that it threatened for a time to destroy the Liberal party.

Falkland wrote that 'the Opposition were ready for the exclusion of Mr. Joseph Howe, if I would consent to the formation of a Council of nine'. The details were to be arranged by Johnston after 'conference with Mr. J. B. Uniacke', while even Huntington and McNab were 'willing to reconsider their resolution'. Uniacke's final refusal was attributed only to the opposition of some of his followers.[1] The Opposition, added Falkland, had 'no acknowledged leader in the House (where, I believe, as well as in the country Mr. Howe's influence is greatly diminished)'. Howe's appointment would 'degrade the office I hold . . . and make Mr. Joseph Howe *de facto* Governor of Nova Scotia'. The issue had thus been reduced 'to a mere contest between myself and a political leader in the Province which I govern'. For the Reformers, as Howe wrote bluntly to one of his followers, the net result of the dispatch of August 2 would have been to 'fasten treachery on one Member—disloyalty on another—and poltroonery on all'.

The debate which followed, upon a series of resolutions moved by Uniacke himself and seconded by Huntington, was bitter beyond all precedent. Uniacke's scathing indictment of the dispatch in point of fact as well as faith was voted down by the government majority of three. Howe met the taunt of 'no acknowledged leader' by a stroke of magnanimity. 'Have they not?' he exclaimed. 'Then let there be no mistake about that point hereafter.' He acclaimed Uniacke the 'acknowledged leader' of a Liberal party. 'That gentleman and I', he added, 'started from different points in life, with different friends and adverse opinions; we contended in this arena till we understood each other and until the true principles of colonial government were developed by our collisions.'[2] The ominous reference in the dispatch to a 'private' correspondence with Stanley opened up vistas of influence that could never be reached through official channels. Like the ill-fated interview between Captain Higginson, 'the eternal Secretary',

[1] 'Mr. Uniacke . . . felt that if he accepted it alone he could bring me no efficient support, but must abandon his party and by acting independently divest himself of all political influence in the Assembly.' The dispatch, Aug. 2, 1844, is printed in Chisholm, *op. cit.*, i. 498 ff.

[2] *Id.*, i. 532.

and La Fontaine in Canada, Falkland's dispatch of August 2 did more perhaps than any other incidents in either province to discredit the whole Russellite theory of governance from Downing Street. But while the Higginson–La Fontaine interview had been egregiously misinterpreted in Metcalfe's dispatches, it had been made public only by Stanley himself in the British debates.[1] The publication of the dispatch of August 2 was aimed at close quarters and with deadly precision at the morale of the Reformers in Nova Scotia. 'An honest fame', exclaimed Howe, 'is as dear to me as Lord Falkland's title is to him. His name may be written in Burke's Peerage; mine has no record but on the hills and valleys of the country which God has given us for an inheritance, and must live, if it lives at all, in the hearts of those who tread them.'

> 'That my friends and colleagues ever consented to sacrifice or abandon me for thus defending them may be believed at the Colonial Office, on the assertion of an officer bound by every honourable consideration to tell the truth; but it has been flatly denied here and will not be believed by ten men who know these gentlemen from one end of the Province to the other. . . . I have no fears of forfeiting Lord Stanley's good opinion, when all the facts are put before him, and before I am many years older he shall, if God spares my life, have the means of judging fairly between Lord Falkland and Joseph Howe.'[2]

A few days later Howe broached to Charles Buller a plan 'to go to England in the Spring . . . to clear up the misrepresentations to my prejudice which I am certain have been made at the Colonial Office.'[3]

The last in this chapter of incidents, perhaps the most regrettable on either side, inflamed the contest and made it irremediable. Among the many projects for a railway to Quebec during the 'forties was one for which the Speaker of the Assembly, William Young—Huntington's colleague in the mission of 1839, and afterwards Chief Justice—and his brother, also a member of the House, were acting as solicitors. During the session of 1846 (February 21) there was 'brought down and read before the Speaker's face a dispatch in which he and his brother were referred to as associates of 'reckless' and 'insolvent' men. The sequel may be given in Howe's own words. The Speaker was 'for the moment powerless'; his brother was 'apparently stunned by the blow, and every-

[1] See below, p. 296.
[2] Chisholm, *op. cit.*, i. 531, 502.
[3] Feb. 28, 1845. *Howe Papers*, Letter-Book, 1839–1845.

body else seemed bewildered. . . . The Governor had smitten the Speaker . . . in his chair, before the whole House.' Howe leaped to his feet and spoke two sentences. The first was a protest 'against the infamous system . . . by which the names of respectable colonists are libelled in despatches sent to the Colonial Office, to be afterwards published here . . . without their having any means of redress'. The second was never forgotten against him. 'If that system be continued', he added, 'some colonist will, by-and-by, or I am much mistaken, hire a black fellow to horsewhip a Lieutenant-Governor.'[1] In a moment the House was in an uproar. The Speaker himself confessed that he was 'thunderstruck'. That evening all Halifax discussed the *lèse-majesté* with bated breath. Next day the House cleared the galleries and debated a vote of censure. Howe conceded that the case was 'quaint and eccentric and startling', like the prophet's 'when he compared the great king to a sheep-stealer'; but (he added) 'David let other men's wives alone after that flight of Nathan's imagination.'[2] But he had gone too far. The censure passed the House 29 to 20. The revulsion was felt even in the counties where Howe's support was strongest. With two scathing letters to Falkland he severed his connexion a second time with *The Novascotian* in April, 1846, and retired to his farm on the Musquodoboit. His parting injunction to Falkland showed wit and temper alike unrepentant: 'On one point (he wrote) your scribe has been correctly informed. I am about "to retire from the metropolis and turn up the soil of Musquodoboit". . . . But, hark ye, my Lord, in order that we may be good friends you had better keep your pigs out of my garden and not attempt to plant tares among my wheat.'

IV

In Nova Scotia as in Canada the bearing of this war of personalities upon the main issue of responsible government in its final form was more direct than either set of antagonists foresaw. It demonstrated the alternative in a form so forbidding that no colonial governor ever repeated the experiment.

It was the logical outcome of the Sydenham régime. If the governor was to be 'the minister' and go down in person into the market-place, he must expect the usages of the market-place not

[1] Chisholm, *op. cit.*, i. 594.

[2] *Letter to the Freeholders of the County of Halifax*, Feb. 23, 1846. *Ibid.*

without its dust and heat. To dominate two groups of men like Hincks, La Fontaine, Sullivan, and Baldwin in Canada, or Howe, Uniacke, Young, and Huntington in Nova Scotia—strong both of them in the confidence of their countrymen, and not without a consciousness of their own intellectual powers—required the mercurial genius of a Sydenham; and nothing is more certain, as we shall see, than that Sydenham himself must have failed, had he remained in Canada, to find in such men merely 'a very useful and powerful engine in the hands of the Governor'. To Metcalfe and to Falkland it seemed that to withdraw from the market-place, to 'hold the balance even', to 'remain neuter during the Contest and then distribute the prizes among the Victors', was to become a 'nullity', 'a mere Cipher'. It was left to Harvey and Elgin to discover what had escaped the Indian Viceroy and the Whig whip: that it was possible to build up a vast moral influence for good by shunning 'the néant of mock sovereignty' on the one side and 'the dirt and confusion of local factions' on the other—'an influence of suasion, sympathy, and moderation, which softens the temper while it elevates the aims of local politics'.[1] Thus while Falkland committed to an official dispatch the details of confidential negotiations obtained at second hand from interested advisers, and published the result to confound his enemies, Elgin followed a different practice. In tracing the Caron-Morin negotiations in 1847 he indicated his ministers by their initials in the privacy of 'secret' and confidential correspondence with his uncle. By this time Grey also, in the Colonial Office, had discovered 'the great *arcanum*'. 'You & the Home Government (he wrote) belong to neither party & have nothing to do with their contests. . . . This principle must be completely established in order long to preserve our connection with the Colony.'[2]

How far Falkland had fallen from this high estate is seen in his own dispatches. 'Duty (he wrote) did not admit of my remaining neuter';[3] and in taking sides he had identified himself with those whose interest it was to exploit his office in destroying their own enemies. It is not on record that Falkland's courtly advisers exerted their influence to withhold the dispatch of August 2 or the reflections upon the business associations of the Speaker. Having

[1] *Grey-Elgin Correspondence*, July 13, 1847; Walrond, *op. cit.*, p. 126.

[2] Elgin to Grey, Apr. 26, 1847, 'Secret'. Grey to Elgin, July 17, 1847, 'Private'. *Grey-Elgin Correspondence*.

[3] To Stanley, Mar. 2, 1844. *Letter-Books*, 117. 155.

taken sides in the contest the governor had no more 'escape from this thraldom' than had Sir Colin Campbell. If Howe was 'trapped' in 1843, so now was Falkland. 'He has quarrelled with one party', said Howe, 'and must rule by the other or throw up the reins and retire.'

The effect of the quarrel upon Howe was not so obvious. 'The war of the newspapers' has been left as far as possible in the background. That Howe in the end was content with the score is easily believed. 'Lord Falkland got his salary', he notes in recounting his financial straits during these years, 'but I think in other respects we are square.' 'But for the passages of arms between us', he wrote again to John Kent, his closest friend in Newfoundland, 'there were some tricks of fence I had not known. Besides, I now estimate at their true value some sneaking dogs that I should have been caressing for years to come, and lots of noble-hearted friends that only the storms of life could have taught me adequately to prize.'[1] A week after the vote of censure in the House he protested to Buller that Falkland's 'petty persecution of myself has more than restored to me the popularity I lost while a Member of his Government.'

In a sense this was true, for Howe's quarrel with Falkland was both less and more than statesmanship. It violated 'the principles', as we shall see, but Howe's sturdy independence appealed mightily to human nature, as the 'sturdy yeomanry' of Nova Scotia remembered to his credit. 'We would not allow the proudest duke that ever stood behind a throne', he once exclaimed, 'to play such antics in Nova Scotia without letting him feel that there was at least one person in the Province a little prouder than himself, and quite conscious that—

"The rank is but the guinea stamp—
A man's a man for a' that."'

'It is a trifle to damn a Nova Scotian's character', he added, in the same debate, 'but an unpardonable offence to hint that a nobleman wears a shirt.'[2]

But there was another side to the story. Every thrust at the governor stultified his own principles, for if the governor's advisers were indeed to be held 'responsible', the governor's own office must be kept sacrosanct. In Canada Baldwin had preached

[1] *Howe Papers*, Letter-Book, 1839–1845; *id.*, vi. 96.

[2] A reference to the first line of *The Lord of the Bed-Chamber*: 'The Lord of the Bed-chamber sat in his shirt.'

the same doctrine; but Baldwin practised it, too, with the inflexibility of a Robespierre. In Nova Scotia the two antagonists, with months of intimacy behind them, stood perhaps at too close quarters. The fiction was too thin, the facts too palpable. With instinctive pugnacity, incited by a challenge which could scarcely be put aside, and directed by an uncanny knowledge of the governor's vulnerability, Howe struck home with a recklessness that left his best friends aghast.

The colossal egotism, too, which afterwards proved his undoing was already in evidence. It had appeared in the feud with Johnston over the 'college question'—perhaps the most costly of his errors in tactics during the Falkland régime.[1] The rise of Uniacke to the leadership and eventually to the premiership in 1848 was not unrelated to these infirmities of temper. The unmeasured badinage of these years, 'rude and intemperate' as Howe himself confessed it to be, was scarcely more baleful for Falkland's prestige than for his own. A year after his retirement to his farm, 'like Cincinnatus to his plough', he wrote to his friend Leishman a revelation of the party—and of himself—which is surely unique. There is a scathing word for the lack of 'Party organization and action' except for 'the few bold fellows in Halifax and elsewhere'; for the 'bland and half apologetic smiles' towards the government benches; for the sympathy for himself which 'our *party* show . . . by going to dine' with Falkland; for their complacency, 'after boasting what they are going to do', in deciding to 'eat their leeks and do nothing':

> 'This sort of discipline, and moral tone never did and never will win any battle, martial or political. I have witnessed—deplored—struggled against it for three Sessions, and must confess I find but little honor to be won. . . . On the other side the organization is perfect —the leader uncompromising, the morale of the service active and elevated. We are a body of very honest and well meaning people, going to capture the Sepulchre, with "good intentions"—and we have to deal with pagans, who while they trust in the Prophet, know the value of close ranks, discipline and chain mail. . . . To break my own heart, while everybody else does what seems right in his own eyes, or does nothing, or does worse, is to waste life to very little purpose. . . . I must confess I am heartily sick of the service.'[2]

[1] 'The Liberals were somewhat weakened by a stupid sectarian prejudice among the Baptists.' Howe to Buller, Feb. 28, 1845. Letter-Book, 1839–1845. *Howe Papers*.

[2] 'It is now about twenty-seven months since we retired, during which I believe I have written as many quires. . . . With the exception of a few articles by George Young, and a few more by Doyle, not a man of our party in the House

V

Whatever Howe's own plight, however, the state of the party was not so desperate; and indeed his own letters to Charles Fisher of New Brunswick, to Isaac Buchanan and Adam Fergusson in Canada, and to the most valued of all his correspondents, Charles Buller in England, are still pitched as usual to the key of an abounding confidence in 'the cause'.[1] The issue was nearer to a solution than they thought.

The governor in siding with one party had made the triumph of the other, sooner or later, inevitable. The issue, Howe claimed in 1844, was 'already decided. The Liberals will have party government or ample justice; and the Tories can form no other.'[2] For a time Falkland deluded himself with Sydenham's project for 'a third and moderate party', but it was quickly ground to pieces between the other two.[3] The epitaph which Howe once volunteered for his rival was already true: 'Here lies the man who denounced party government, that he might form one; and professing justice to all parties, gave every office to his own'. 'All that we intend when we change the majority', he added, 'is to follow the example set by the other side.'[4] Falkland himself saw the handwriting on the wall. If he would not have a Liberal government, they could at least force him to have a Tory one, and thus in effect 'force . . . a party Government'. This 'Party aspect', to be sure, was less objectionable than 'the admission to the Council of men openly holding principles . . . destructive of any Coalition,' but in the end they 'must triumph absolutely'. 'The Crisis' could be met

has written a line. . . . Johnston, a fortnight ago, boldly stood up and defended Craskill (the Queen's printer). . . . When the Novascotian and Chronicle were assailed, not one Liberal in the House justified or defended me, and several timidly declared they never wrote in Newspapers. Is it then to be wondered at that of late, I should *study* and *not write*?

I attend twenty-four meetings. . . . While attending one of these, my friends combine with my enemies to give me a kick . . .

I often feel that I should be safer, and quite as useful, if I stood alone—and, if things go on as they have been going, I shall either take that position, or quit public life.' Howe to Leishman, 'Spring, 1846'. *Howe Papers*, vol. vi.

[1] Even the jeremiad to Leishman may have been written largely for effect at a committee meeting which Howe was unable to attend: 'If I went to the meeting, and told the Committee all this, it would not mend the matter—and might make things worse.' *Ibid.*

[2] 'Lord Falkland has done more to advance the development of this principle by his impolitic attempt to retard it, than all the agitators in Nova Scotia could have done in ten times the number of years.' Chisholm, *op. cit.*, i. 494.

[3] Falkland to Stanley, Jan. 1, 1844. *Letter-Books*, 117. 141.

[4] Chisholm, *op. cit.*, i. 541, 559.

by nothing short of a British Act of Parliament.[1] Thus was Saul, too, numbered among the prophets.

To such a pass, then, was 'colonial government' at last reduced; and perhaps no apter commentary than this of Falkland's could be found upon the theme of these essays and its swift denouement which we have now to trace. No Charter, no Act of Parliament, had marked the humble beginnings of the Nova Scotia Assembly in the 'royal' province of the first Empire. Reflecting for nearly a century the slowly changing 'conventions' of colonial governance, the relations between governor and Assembly, like those between the Crown and the House of Commons in Great Britain, were still undefined by Imperial legislation. The province now stood upon the threshold of self-government. The most distinctive of all these empirical adjustments was not to be denied. Governors and Assemblies in unbroken succession had met in the old Province Building. They were now to meet there, in a sense for the last time in the second Empire; for despite the humble surroundings and the simplicity of the change itself, a 'new and prodigious era' was about to begin.

Falkland himself had stated the unanswerable problem in the Whig days of 1842: since Nova Scotia, unlike Canada, had 'no constitution defined by act of Parliament', how was the governor to 'obey the instructions of his superior officer, the colonial minister' if the contest ever took the form of 'a party against a Governor'?[2] By 1846 Falkland and Howe, the governor and the Assemblyman, had moved to opposite poles of policy. For both of them 'the Crisis' had arrived—the one contemplating the *brutum fulmen* of an Act of Parliament, the other in the autumn solitudes of his Musquodoboit farm, chastened by reflection to a new discernment of the change in store for his native province.

With the main theme of Howe's second series of *Letters to Lord John Russell*, written *de profundis* during these months at Musquodoboit, we are not here concerned, but in more than one historic passage the mode of the coming Commonwealth is prophetically foreshadowed. 'We must be Britons', exclaimed Howe, 'in every inspiring sense of the word':

> 'You have no Act of Parliament to define the duty of the Sovereign when ministers are in a minority; we want none to enable us to suggest to a Governor when his advisers have lost the confidence of

[1] Falkland to Stanley, Mar. 2, 1844. *Letter-Books*, 117. 155.
[2] Falkland to Stanley, Aug. 1842. *Letter-Books*, 117. 30.

our colonial Assemblies. But what we do want, my Lord, is a rigid enforcement of British practice . . . the intelligence and public spirit of the people will supply the rest.'[1]

With the second *Letters to Lord John Russell* Howe's public life entered upon a new phase. There is a new incisiveness, 'a glint of steel'; a new note, too, of confidence, not without reason.[2] The letter to Leishman had marked the darkest hour before the dawn. The day had already broken across the Atlantic. In July, 1846, the Whigs under Lord John Russell had come back to power in Great Britain, with the third Earl Grey at the Colonial Office. In September, Buller acclaimed to Howe at last 'a Colonial Secretary who has sound views of Colonial Policy'. The change, as we shall see, came barely in time. Howe was 'devilish glad . . . to see the Whigs back', but his reply to Buller was not to be misunderstood:

'The men who drove the old Colonies to desperation, thought Jefferson, and Franklin, and Washington, very inferior to the merest drivellers by whom they were surrounded, and now we suppose the prevailing idea, at home is, that, though "there were giants in those days", the race is extinct. God send them all more wisdom—if this Whig Government disappoints us, you will have the questions I have touched discussed in a different spirit, ten years hence, by the Enemies of England, not by her friends.'[3]

Responsible Government

I

The most fortunate coincidence for Lord Falkland's administration in Nova Scotia was the date of his departure. A few weeks after the appointment of Sir John Harvey as his successor, a Durhamite succeeded to the Colonial Office, sharing, no doubt, Charles Buller's opinion that Falkland had 'certainly mismanaged matters . . . most miserably'.[4]

Measured by length of service and general popularity in the provinces which he administered Harvey was perhaps the most

[1] Chisholm, *op. cit.*, i. 613–14.

[2] 'The evils . . . from such a system North America has endured; but in her name, my Lord, I think I may be pardoned for desiring that it shall have an end.' *Id.*, i. 615.

[3] Buller to Howe, Sept. 10, 1846; Howe to Buller, Oct. 28, 1846. *The Correspondence between Joseph Howe and Charles Buller*, 1845–1848, ed. Chester Martin, *Can. Hist. Rev.*, Dec., 1925, pp. 316, 319.

[4] *Id.*, p. 316.

successful governor since the American Revolution. Without the brilliant personal achievements of Durham or Sydenham or Bagot to his credit it was his good fortune to govern four provinces in succession, in all of which his name is gratefully associated with reform. He had been a soldier under Abercromby in Egypt. He served as Adjutant-General and Governor's Secretary during the War of 1812. He was the hero of Stoney Creek. In Ireland he drafted a memorandum (1830) which the Colonial Office gave confidentially to Gosford for his Canadian mission.[1] His governorship of Prince Edward Island was too brief—scarcely more than a year—to restore harmony to that distracted province, but in 1837 he was transferred to New Brunswick to compose the quarrel between his predecessor and the Assembly, and to carry out, as we have seen, the most distinctive reforms effected up to that time in British America. In 1839 Harvey's phrase 'a new, and . . . improved Constitution' was appropriated by reformers throughout British America as an official estimate of Lord John Russell's dispatch of October 16. An unfortunate conflict with Sydenham in the 'Aroostook War' over the Maine boundary had led to his recall by Lord John Russell himself after one of the most regrettable incidents in colonial history. In Newfoundland he left behind in 1846 not only friends but defenders for the ordeal which now lay before him in Nova Scotia. It was his good fortune there, as we shall see, to preside over the first formal concession of responsible government overseas. When he retired in 1851, after nearly sixty years of public service, Howe referred to him with deep emotion as 'my venerable chief'. While it would not be true to say that Sir John Harvey conceived or indeed did much to effect the greatest of these reforms, his frankness, his 'imperturbable bonhomie', his obvious goodwill, were invaluable agencies in the process.

Harvey's appointment to Nova Scotia by Gladstone in Peel's administration was not at first sight reassuring. He was the last of the 'military governors'; and perhaps the most scathing sentence in Howe's second series of *Letters to Lord John Russell* was reserved for the 'rulers snatched from the tented field or the quarter-deck', to whom the British constitution appeared 'a prurient excrescence, defacing the articles of war'.[2] 'These Military statesmen', Buller agreed, were wedded to the 'notion of a Composite Ministry' under

[1] Harvey to Howe, Dec. 9, 1846. *Howe Papers*, i. 189.
[2] Chisholm, *op. cit.*, i. 619.

the delusion that they were 'the most useful instruments for themselves—not knowing that Coalitions always damage all engaged to them & fail all who lean on them'.[1]

In this respect Harvey, as it proved, was no exception; and his friend John Kent of Newfoundland, a reformer who had stolen the 'promethean fire . . . from Nova Scotia', was deeply concerned for his reputation. 'No person knows his weaknesses better than I do', he wrote to Howe. 'I should regret exceedingly if the success . . . of Sir Jno. Harvey in three Provinces were to meet a grave in Nova Scotia.'[2] But Kent agreed with Sir John that 'Coalitions . . . are absolutely necessary in the Colonies', thus confirming Buller's forecast and confirming Howe, too, in his unalterable conviction. He had learnt his lesson. Surely in vain is the net spread in the sight of any bird:

> 'The time for seduction, intrigue and splitting of parties (he replied to Kent) has gone by in Nova Scotia. Johnston can give Sir John no Coalition, for not a Liberal, will act with him. . . . Do not be much surprised if your old friend is victimized by the same influences which destroyed his predecessors. I shall do my best, as in duty bound, to serve him—he has a thousand good qualities, and is very civil to me, but I fear may not understand my countrymen, and may fail by relying on expedients which, however they may have answered elsewhere, are not suited to our meridian.'[3]

To Harvey's first overtures (September 14, 1846) Howe replied that the issue was now too momentous for compromise. 'Political principles and the rights of vast bodies of people are involved in the present struggle.' None but an apostate or a deserter could 'abandon or sacrifice these after a ten years' contest'.[4] Thus while Harvey's name in Nova Scotia might have ranked with Campbell's or Falkland's had Stanley or Gladstone remained at the Colonial Office, he was saved by a new spirit in Downing Street, and by his own pliancy of temper. When responsible government became inevitable he responded not only with goodwill but with a growing reliance upon his new advisers. They in turn responded with a loyalty surely unique in the British provinces; voting him an increase of salary, defending him against the Colonial Office itself, and associating his name with their own in the first achievement of responsible government.

[1] *The Howe-Buller Correspondence*, p. 320.
[2] Dec. 10, 1846. *Howe Papers*, i. 193. [3] *Id.*, vi. 96. [4] *Id.*, xxix. 20.

II

The various negotiations which began with Harvey's arrival in August, 1846, followed the well-beaten track of the Sydenham régime. In a memorandum addressed to Howe—his 'excellent and talented friend'—Harvey offered himself as 'a mediator and a Moderator between the influential of all Parties', with the plausible and familiar plea of eschewing 'any one Party' in order to command 'the support of all'. These views, added Sir John, he had 'expounded to the Home Government'.[1] But other views had already been expounded there to better purpose; for while Harvey and his councillors were exploiting for the last time the barren subtleties of a coalition, the Reformers, with Charles Buller as *liaison* officer, were perfecting their historic alliance with the British Durhamites, now in the Colonial Office. A special interest attaches to this confidential intercourse, for it predetermined not only the general principles but the tactics in detail for the impending change.

There were three courses open to the governor. His own preference for a coalition was never concealed. One alternative was an immediate dissolution of the Assembly. In the last resort he could await the general election—due in the summer of 1847—and thus allow 'the political clock to run down'.

It is clear that the Reformers themselves were not altogether in agreement. Howe's opposition to a coalition was now unalterable. 'With the members of the existing Council', reads the memorandum signed by Howe, Doyle, McNab, and George Young on December 17, 1846, 'we can enter into no political alliance until the people of Nova Scotia decide between them and us.'[2] In this the Reformers were supported without reserve by Charles Buller. 'I was delighted', he wrote to Howe, 'to find that you & your friends stood so firm against the Lt. Govrs. notion of a Composite Ministry.'[3] On the other hand Uniacke, who was in London in October, was still prepared to act in a coalition, not 'as a *wise* course but one which might aid a Governor disposed to act impartially.' 'I am aware', he added, 'that many contend for exclusive party government but I have misgivings as to its working in a small Colony like Nova Scotia but I keep these sentiments to myself and I shall urge a dissolution.'[4] In the end, as we shall see, the ranks

[1] Sept. 14, 1846. *Id.*, i. 158.

[2] Chisholm, *op. cit.*, i. 636.

[3] *The Howe-Buller Correspondence*, p. 322.

[4] Uniacke to Howe, Oct. 19, 1846, *Howe Papers*, i. 171.

of the Reformers proved invincible, and the policy which Huntington had advocated unceasingly for ten years came at last into its own.

The first alternative—an immediate dissolution—was advocated by all the Reformers. Howe suggested it to Buller and Grey as early as September 16,[1] and to Harvey himself two days later. Uniacke advocated it in London. It is clear that the situation was canvassed at the Colonial Office with every precaution against a false step at so critical a juncture. But the arguments against it were found to be conclusive. To act 'against the advice of his advisers for the time being' would be 'an extreme course, inconsistent with the usual course of representative Govt.'.[2] Buller might have added that a forced dissolution was strange doctrine from those who condemned the forced dissolution of 1843. But while the government must continue 'until they are beaten in the Assembly', the defection of two 'waiters on Providence' would leave them in a minority, and 'one hostile vote of the House would settle the matter'. More expeditiously still Sir John might force the resignation of his council in filling the vacancies at the council table. At the worst, added Buller, 'you will wait a year longer, but it will be a recognition of the Principle of Responsible Government . . . Ld. Grey's good intentions you may rely on. I do not think that even Ld. Stanley in his place could thwart you.'[3]

It is easy to see in this the theme of Grey's historic dispatch of November 3, 1846,[4] which undoubtedly passed through Buller's hands and two months later was placed in those of Elgin upon the eve of his departure for Canada. Thus were evolved, in Grey's own phrase, the guiding principles 'of general application to all colonies having a similar form of government'.[5] The transition from the second Empire to the Commonwealth is implicit in this dispatch. For the first time it authorized 'the fullest adoption of the principle of Responsible Government'. 'I have not the slightest fear', added Buller, 'but that Sir J. H. will show himself perfectly ready to entrust his Govt. to those who have the confidence of a majority of the Assembly.'[6]

[1] 'Dissolve our House, and you will have no more trouble in Nova Scotia for the next four years.' *The Howe-Buller Correspondence*, p. 318.

[2] Nov. 18, 1846. *Id.*, p. 320.

[3] *Ibid.*

[4] *Brit. Parl. Papers*, Aug. 10, 1848 (621), pp. 7 ff.; *Egerton and Grant*, 297 ff.; *Kennedy*, 570 ff.

[5] Grey's *Colonial Policy of the Administration of Lord John Russell*, p. 208.

[6] *The Howe-Buller Correspondence*, p. 320.

III

In this, however, Howe was the better prophet. Harvey's predilections for a coalition were soon allied with Johnston's indomitable resourcefulness in a desperate attempt to stave off the impending change.

The negotiations for a coalition were foredoomed to failure, and they are perhaps negligible here except as they reflect the traditional temper of the old order. Johnston's was perhaps the most masterly of rear-guard actions in the British provinces against the slowly enveloping forces of reform. It is easy to vindicate a successful cause. It is not so easy for another generation, inheriting the kingdom without a struggle, to deal justly by those who feared the change; who, identifying 'party government' with 'the spoils system', then at its worst in the United States, dreaded the crudities of the new order, and clung desperately to the studied decorum of the old. Responsible government has seldom raised at once the standards of public life. In Canada La Fontaine and Sullivan both resigned at last, in disgust with 'the tracasseries of Political life'. When Baldwin retired Elgin rated him the 'most Conservative public man in Canada'.[1] Hincks, who was as little troubled as any man in either province by 'squeamishness' in politics, once conceded that party spirit was nowhere in the world bitterer than in Canada. An austere Tory like Johnston, with no illusions about the humble 'affairs of this small colony', could bring as much of moderation, and perhaps of conviction also, to the conflict as 'the tribune' himself. Retreating warily, making a little ground and giving more, he stood at last with his back to the wall for the last session before 'the great election'.

With Harvey's views on a 'mixed government' in 1846, as with Falkland's in 1843, Johnston hastened to agree. Two vacancies in the council were already available for Reformers. Two Tory councillors—Almon and Dodd—agreed to make way for two others. The prospect of Johnston's relative making way for Howe's must have appealed to Doyle's sense of humour.[2] Harvey never plied his 'imperturbable bonhomie' with better will or with less effect. Howe retired warily to Musquodoboit in order to avoid all re-

[1] Elgin to Grey, June 28, 1851. *Grey-Elgin Correspondence.*

[2] 'That Mr. Almon should be willing to resign . . . we confess, does surprise us. The reason given for his elevation in 1843 was his "affinity" to the Attorney-General . . . the relationship still exists.' Howe, Doyle, McNab, and Young to Harvey, Dec. 17, 1846. Chisholm, *op. cit.*, i. 637.

sponsibility for the inevitable deadlock. Harvey followed him with assurances of Grey's appreciation for the *Letters to Lord John Russell*; with news of 'a communication from England which I should have been glad to show you'; with hopes of 'an early opportunity of doing so—indeed (he added) from the *present complexion of affairs you must I think be here shortly*'.[1] But in Howe's reply there is a new dexterity—'tricks of fence', as he wrote to Kent at the time, learnt from passages at arms with Falkland. He, too, had had 'a very interesting letter by the Packet' which had put him 'in possession of the views taken, at home, of affairs here'. If negotiations were to break down—'as I think they must', he added shrewdly—he would be ready to attend the governor, and 'a day or two will be sufficient to put matters right'.[2]

There were tricks of fence on both sides. The formal reply, signed by Howe, Doyle, McNab, and Young on December 17, was a masterpiece of advocacy. Johnston in the House refused to bring it down, while his own brief was spread with skill and resourcefulness upon the *Journals*. With studied poise he appealed to Elgin, then on his way to his great task in Canada, and drew from him a warning against the use of 'patronage and power' for the purchase of party support. Elgin himself, as we shall see, repeated in Canada, with Morin and Caron, the tactics of Harvey for a coalition in Nova Scotia.[3] A memorandum of January 28 for Harvey and the House was followed two days later by another for the Colonial Office. In the laboured exhaustiveness of his argument Johnston was once compared by Bourinot to Edward Blake:[4] no more formidable briefs were ever drawn for the old order in Nova Scotia. The province was but 'a small colony', its population scarcely more than 250,000, and its revenue only £80,000. The property qualification for the Assembly was only forty shillings freehold. A majority of the officers of government were not Executive Councillors, while a majority of the council held no office of trust in the government. There was 'no class born to fortune and leisure' for the exacting duties of public life. There was no departmental system, and the 'extravagant comparisons' with British usage had grown by 'vanity and self-interest', until

[1] Harvey to Howe, Dec. 3, 1846. *Howe Papers*, i. 186.

[2] Howe to Kent, Nov. 28, 1846; to Harvey, Dec. 7, 1846. *Id.*, vi. 96, 100.

[3] Elgin had an additional motive, however: 'to show the French that I do not distrust them'. Elgin to Grey, Apr. 26, 1847, 'Secret'. *Grey-Elgin Correspondence.*

[4] *Builders of Nova Scotia*, p. 77.

'unrestrained and unsound analogies' were 'calculated to give an air of burlesque and caricature' to the contest. Such were the results of 'a debasing agitation, calculated only to disturb the peace and retard the welfare of the country'. The entire council begged an 'authoritative declaration' from the Colonial Office.[1]

It was in reply to this request that the second of Grey's famous dispatches was written on March 31, 1847.[2] Thus at last was the reactionary gambit of 'coalition' graciously but firmly checkmated —Harvey's 'Private and Confidential' dispatch of September 15 by Grey's of November 3, and the classic memoranda of January 28 and 30, 1847, by that of March 31. All parties now agreed that 'further controversy was a waste of time'. The issue, as Grey now stated and as Buller had always maintained, now lay with 'the people themselves'.

IV

'The great election' of August 5, 1847, was followed with interest from Canada West to Bermuda. 'The effect will thrill through all British America', wrote a Reformer from New Brunswick. 'If Nova Scotia strikes the first blow I do believe that the next election in Canada will follow suit and it must have some effect here.'[3]

Harvey was now reconciled to the inevitable; but the skill of his advisers in the technique of elections was perhaps unexcelled at that time in British America. 'Close ranks, discipline and chain mail' were all in evidence, and behind them the shrewdest, coldest intellect in the province. The dispatch of March 31 remained unknown until six months after the election.[4] The Reformers charged their opponents with every resource of early-Victorian 'electioneering'—a fund in the bank, a schooner with liquid freight for the seaboard, placards and handbills without number, 'an organization and lavish expenditure never equalled in any former contest'. But compared with Sydenham's campaign in Terrebonne or with the by-election of April, 1844, in Montreal 'the great election' of August 5, 1847, was maintained by both parties upon a high level of public spirit. For the first time in British America the vote was polled in a single day—a Tory reform sponsored by Johnston himself. It was Howe's boast that the day

[1] *Brit. Par. Papers*, Aug. 10, 1848 (621), 16 ff., 18 ff.

[2] *Id.*, 29 ff.; *Egerton and Grant*, 302 ff.; *Kennedy*, 573 ff.

[3] Charles Fisher to Howe, June 12, 1847. *Howe Papers*, i. 238.

[4] 'Had they beaten at the Election, we should never have seen the Despatches at all.' *Howe-Buller Correspondence*, p. 325.

was won without a blow, without a drop of bloodshed, without the breaking of a pane of glass. It is on record that within three months he canvassed twelve counties, attended fifteen public dinners, and addressed sixty public meetings, not without 'great fun, particularly when there was opposition'. Only the note of desperation in his letter *To the Freeholders of Nova Scotia* betrayed the odds against them. 'I have never known you wanting (he wrote) in the hour of trial.' 'A million of North Americans' awaited the outcome:

> 'If you falter now; if, with the enemy before you, with the fruits of victory within your grasp, the highest privileges of British subjects to be secured or cast away by a single act, in a single day,—you show yourselves indifferent or undisciplined, I shall cease to labour, because I shall cease to hope.'[1]

The Reformers carried twelve of the seventeen counties with a resolute majority of seven in a House of fifty-one. Charles Fisher of New Brunswick, who was Howe's mentor in political finesse and knew more of the 'game' in many of the constituencies than Howe himself, was well satisfied with the results.[2] 'It is a glorious thing this election, for Nova Scotia and all the other colonies.... Canada will strike the next blow.' The cheers at Howe's home-coming to Musquodoboit 'could be heard for miles down the valley'; but beside his own fireside and in the austere household of the Huntingtons at Yarmouth there was a humbler exaltation of spirit: 'aye, it may be conceived (added Fisher), it can't be written.' Secure now in the inevitableness of responsible government in its final form Howe was content for a month to play 'with the children, and read old books to my girls'; he 'went into the woods and called moose with the old hunters, camping out night after night, listening to their stories, calming my thoughts with the perfect stillness of the forest and forgetting the bitterness of conflict'. The government clung to office for more than five months, 'true (Howe added ungraciously) to the instinct which guides the genus Tory everywhere'. The new House met on January 22, 1848.

Many of Johnston's 'old guard' had fallen by the way, but the survivors marched out at last with colours flying. For a moment, at William Young's election to the Speaker's chair, the old bitter-

[1] Chisholm, *op. cit.*, i. 645.

[2] 'Full more than I thought you would likely have.' Aug. 25, 1847. *Howe Papers*, i. 253.

ness reappeared. But on January 24 Uniacke moved, and Huntington seconded, the historic amendment to the Address embodying a direct vote of want of confidence—the first vote overseas, as Howe truly said, 'to turn out an administration and establish the Opposition in their places'. Thus was 'the *coup de grâce* constitutionally given' (January 25) by a vote of 29 to 22. The next day Sir John assured the House of his 'determination to give prompt effect to their wishes'. 'We were conscious', wrote Howe, 'of having achieved a Revolution without bloodshed'. On the 27th the old council resigned. The next day—January 28, 1848—Uniacke as premier was called upon to form the first formally responsible ministry overseas.[1]

V

The formal introduction of responsible government ran true to local traditions. There were still pilgrimages to Downing Street with 'every imaginable form of Protest, Petition and Remonstrance'. Sir Rupert George resigned his seat in the Executive Council but refused to surrender the Secretaryship of the province to Howe until the House, 'declaring the Office vacant . . . voted him an adequate pension, and gazetted him removed'. Johnston, too, reserved 'future claims to Professional advancement'.[2] The task of organizing the working departments of the government in a *Departmental Bill*, and of adjusting a fixed civil list in return for the surrender of crown lands and territorial revenues went rapidly forward. Though forced to form a ministry and carry their by-elections after the session began, the Reformers could soon boast the widest range of 'important public Bills' since the fall of the coalition. From an issue scarcely less than imperial in its scope and meaning, the province now turned to the prosaic work of self-government—roads and 'the railway question', schools and crown lands, the fisheries and trade with the United States. Johnston himself lived to be premier under the new régime; and thus the exaltation of spirit which had attended 'the fight for responsible government' faded at last into the light of common day.

[1] The first cabinet consisted of J. B. Uniacke (Premier and Attorney-General), W. F. DesBarres (Solicitor-General), Joseph Howe (Secretary), Herbert Huntington, L. O'C. Doyle, G. R. Young, Michael Tobin, Hugh Bell, and James McNab.

[2] Sir John Harvey 'without his knowledge' had already recommended him 'for Judicial preferment in another Colony'. Harvey to Grey, Jan. 29, 1848. *Letter-Books*, 119. 130.

The ultimate meaning of this 'Revolution without bloodshed' may be left to a later study, but there were two features of it which were distinctive of Nova Scotia. Against the evils of the American 'spoils system' which since the Metcalfe crisis in Canada had obsessed Grey and Buller and the best friends of the British provinces in Great Britain, Howe resolutely set his face. To one of his own patronage-mongering supporters he once wrote in this fashion:

> 'If you, or anybody else, supposed, that "responsible government" was to mean this—that the Members *responsible to a single County* were to compel those who are *responsible to the whole Legislature*, to do acts which they could justify upon no principle recognized in British communities . . . I never so understood it, nor would I yield up my judgement . . . to the best friends I have, or to the Representative of any County.'[1]

With Charles Fisher, in whose cast of mind there was more perhaps of Martha than of Mary, Howe once discussed the thorny problem of patronage in a spirit obviously inspired by the incomprehensible Metcalfe crisis in Canada:

> 'It is very simple . . . where a Governor is acting in good faith with his Council. If *he* or *they* desire to seek a ground of quarrel, this will answer as well as any other. . . .
>
> The Governor's only chance of safety would be in the general conviction that the collision had been forced upon him by the intemperance or arrogance of faction and then, as Shaftesbury was shattered in Charles the Second's reign, or Sarah of Marlborough in that of Anne, an exigeante, a corrupt, or an unmannerly ministry would be rebuked by the good sense of the people. . . . If wrong he is sure to be beaten, and must take back his old advisers or retire. Here is the check, and it is so stringent that a Governor with common sense who is treated with respect, will in all cases of importance ask the advice of his whole Council—in nine cases out of ten he will take it. . . .
>
> Here we have no difficulty nor can I imagine why there should be elsewhere. . . . Do not quarrel about abstract principles if in practice all goes well.'[2]

It is on record that during the three years and a half of the coalition when appointments were numbered by hundreds there was but one to which the governor raised the slightest objection, 'and that was the reappointment of an old servant'. With Sir John Harvey the relations of the new administration deepened into sympathy and affection. Thus was 'the sap . . . already beginning to circulate through the "girdled tree" '.

[1] *Howe Papers*, Private Letter-Book, vol. xxxiv. [2] *Ibid.*, Oct. 23, 1848.

In another respect the Nova Scotian achievement was distinctive. Happy in its priority, it was happier still in its moderation and in the confidential intercourse by which the local Reformers and their allies in Great Britain carried forward their common cause. The return of this intimate little group, pre-eminent for insight and harmony, to power on both sides of the Atlantic in 1846–7 was a coincidence of the first importance. In the midst of European revolutions of 'the 1848', when thrones were toppling in 'carnage and civil war', a British Queen, Howe remarked in the House upon the birth of the princess royal, was passing through no perils but those hallowed by maternal affection. 'Amid all these convulsions', added Buller, 'may *we* not think with pride and satisfaction on the establishment, & working of Responsible Government?' A fitting commentary upon this historic alliance is to be found in the words of those who guided it to success. 'We shall endeavour,' wrote Howe, 'following Sir John Harvey's example to cultivate, and diffuse through our society a kindlier tone of feeling. Of one thing you may be assured, we shall "keep within the ropes" ... Earl Grey's Despatches, clear as a sunbeam, breathe a spirit of generous confidence in our discretion and right feeling. He shall not be disappointed. It will be our pride to make Nova Scotia a "Normal School" for the rest of the Colonies.'

Passing unofficially through the Colonial Office Howe's instinctive goodwill brought from Buller a characteristic response in kind:

> 'I have been seldom so much gratified by any letter.... The wisdom & moderation of your views make me confident of the success, which I never mistrusted, of the working of Responsible Government.... This private exposition ... will have the best effects on the Colonial Office....
>
> When "advice" is needed, it shall be frankly given, & I am sure will be kindly taken. But it would be impertinence to offer any to those, who are acting so wisely: and I think I may give what is more useful than any counsels—namely an assurance of the confidence & kindliness with which your own generous policy is met here.'[1]

Relations with the Colonial Office were not always to remain at this high level. A series of mishaps, from 'the railway imbroglio' with Grey himself in 1852 to the Reciprocity negotiations and Confederation itself, coarsened the fibre of provincial politics and of Howe's own public life. Neither Buller nor Huntington lived to see this anti-climax. With Buller's lamented death in Novem-

[1] *Howe-Buller Correspondence*, passim.

ber, 1848, this essay may appropriately close. The theme with which it deals is aptly epitomized in the noble tribute paid by Howe in *The Novascotian* of December 25, 1848, to the memory of his friend:

'If the question had been asked a month ago, of the North American colonies, what English statesman they could least afford to spare, the almost unanimous answer of the best-informed men in the five Provinces would have been—Charles Buller. The last steamer brings the melancholy tidings of his death, and the sincere sorrow on this side of the Atlantic is as general as was the estimation in which the deceased was held.

There is something singularly sad in the death of such a man as Buller at the age of forty-one,—in the very flower of his days,—after the difficulties of early life had been surmounted and an honourable position had been attained, from which with practised and scarcely adventurous wing the highest elevations of imperial public life were fairly within his reach.

There is something, too, depressing in the reflection that another has been added to the list of able and distinguished advocates of colonial regeneration, who have passed from the stage of usefulness to the tomb, within a very few years.

Lord Durham, Lord Sydenham, Sir Charles Bagot, Charles Buller! With these men alive and holding high stations in England, North America would have had her advocates and friends, familiar with her wants and hopeful of her destinies, to appeal to, and to defend her interests, on all occasions. The grave has closed over them all, and we are scarcely consoled for their loss by the conviction that their works live after them and that the rights they advocated can never perish.

In the gradual evolution of general principles and in their practical application to the business of colonial government within the last ten years, Charles Buller, though inferior in rank and station to some of his fellow-labourers, exercised a vast and most beneficial influence. As secretary to Lord Durham, his talents contributed to the brilliant success which attended his Lordship's mission. When that great man was prematurely stricken down, Charles Buller in Parliament and in the press defended his memory and reasserted his principles. Out of office, he checked and restrained the party by whom Lord Durham was feared; in office, he gave to the present Ministry his counsel and his aid in perfecting that nobleman's colonial policy.

Contrasted with some others who take an interest in colonial questions, there was something safe, practical, and conciliatory in Buller's advocacy of North American interests. Unlike Hume, he never frightened or misled by counselling extreme measures; and instead of traversing boundless fields and generalizing like Molesworth, he stuck to the matter in hand and raised no difficulties, the facile removal of which was not proved to be as compatible with the dignity of the parent state as with the security of the distant provinces of the empire.

It was for this quality of his mind that we chiefly admired Buller. He never did violence to the antique prejudices of Parliament or feared to give honest counsel, when they seemed to require it, to the colonists themselves. There may be rising men in both Houses, of whom we know little; but of those we do know, there is not one, in the peculiar walks he chose, who can fill Charles Buller's place.'

V

RESPONSIBLE GOVERNMENT IN CANADA

I

THE contest for responsible government reached its climax in Canada. For many reasons its fate there was epochal for the whole Empire. Durham, in despair of a larger federal union, had recommended the fusion of the two Canadas, so that in sheer size and population the united province dwarfed all the others. At the close of Elgin's administration there were well over two millions of people in an area which Chief Justice Draper, a few years later, sought to extend to the Pacific. The issues, too, in Canada were beyond all comparison imperative. Whatever the Papineau and Mackenzie risings may have done or failed to do, they forced the problem of colonial government in its real proportions upon the best attention of the British Cabinet. A correspondent under Elgin once wrote that 'Canada ought to be *experimentum crucis* of all Governors. After governing Canada they can govern any country'.[1] The Colonial Office, tenanted, as Buller satirically pointed out, by nearly a dozen Secretaries in as many years, now demanded first-rate ability. Three Colonial Secretaries within ten years eventually reached the premiership, and some of the men sent to Canada were without exception the ablest who ever left Britain on such a mission.

On both sides of the Atlantic the effect of Durham's *Report* was dynamic—second only to the cogency of the events themselves. The interpretations put upon it varied with the political exigencies of the interpreters. To the colonial Tory it was, of course, anathema, and the attack upon it by the Select Committee of the Upper Canadian Legislative Council is classic.[2] Sir George Arthur, who reflected their views, regarded it as 'the worst evil that has yet befallen Upper Canada'.[3] Reformers, on the other hand, in Canada as in Nova Scotia, made it their gospel. Hincks, whose steadfast legend for the *Examiner* had been 'Responsible Government', always maintained that their programme was implicit in the

[1] In the *Grey-Elgin Correspondence*, Elgin to Grey, July 2, 1849. *Pub. Arch. Can.*

[2] *Egerton and Grant*, pp. 173–88.

[3] Arthur to Normanby, Aug. 21, 1839, *Brit. Parl. Papers*, 1840, Canada, Part II, p. 171.

Report—an opinion circumstantially confirmed by Buller's own letters and anonymous treatise on *Responsible Government for Colonies*, by Grey's steady advocacy during the Metcalfe crisis, and by Elgin's devotion to the Durham traditions as the household-gods of his Canadian mission.[1] On both sides of the Atlantic the *Report* was appropriated instinctively by those who disputed the pontifical doctrine of Lord John Russell.

But the *Report* was aimed not at North American opinion but at Melbourne and the British Whigs. By 1835 Durham had so far antagonized his father-in-law, the second Earl Grey, by forming 'bad connections' and by his 'folly' of advocating further reform, that he had been quietly read out of the Whig party by bell, book, and candle. Like Phaethon, 'Radical Jack' had aspired too far in driving the horses of the sun. He had encountered too the implacable and half-contemptuous distrust of Melbourne and Lord John Russell, the less calculating dislike of Poulett Thomson, and the malignant hatred of Brougham.[2] By his indiscretions and 'abundance of political courage . . . approaching to rashness' (as Hobhouse, his best friend in Melbourne's cabinet, set down in his diary)

[1] Hincks, Lecture on the *Political History of Canada, between 1840 and 1855*, Montreal, 1877, p. 9. Durham's attempt to delimit the *scope* of responsible government gave way to the empirical opportunism advocated by Elgin (see below, p. 318, and Chap. VI) but there is much to be said for the view that in *method*, Durham contemplated, as he himself wrote, 'administering the government on those principles which have been found perfectly efficacious in Great Britain'.

[2] Grey to Melbourne, Feb. 3, 1835, *Lord Melbourne's Papers*, ed. Sanders, Lond., 1889, p. 247. Cf. *id.*, p. 252, Lord Holland to Melbourne, Feb. 11, 1835: 'I see no use in Johnny (Lord John Russell) showing Grey's letter to Wellesley; there are expressions in it about Durham he would not like to be repeated.' See also Melbourne to Grey, 'Confidential', Jan. 23, 1835: 'I will have nothing to do with Durham.' Melbourne to Russell: 'It is very odd to me the terror Durham inspires.' 'Durham has so run at me in those letters of his, and I dislike him so much, that there is no course would please me so well as setting him at defiance; but . . . it would be said, "This was your intention from the beginning".' Melbourne to Thomson: 'You may call this submission to his insolence; but it is not much submission when you in fact say, "You have put yourself in a foolish passion and acted rashly; do think better of it".' *Id.*, pp. 235, 434, 435, 436, &c. See also Broughton's *Recollections of a Long Life*, v. 118, 161, 291, *et passim*: 'I found that our chief entertained a very unfavourable opinion of Durham; in fact he talked of him as a man on whom no dependence could be placed.' 'I did my best to give him (Durham) a more kindly feeling towards Melbourne and Russell; but he shook his head.' See also *id.*, v. 291 (at Durham's death in August, 1840): 'In his intercourse with his friends, he was by no means overbearing. . . . In fact, he did not attach so much value to his character, or opinions, as to give himself a sufficient amount of self-confidence in matters of importance.'

he had courted destruction in the toils of a relentless oligarchy. But his memory was yet to have its revenge upon them all. They themselves were now in the toils. As the meshes tightened, resistance became increasingly desperate. Stanley and the Tories, as we shall see, despaired of the Empire. The Whigs aspired to resignation, if not to hopefulness. But as the Durhamites well knew, the net could not be broken. 'Though such jays as Pou & Jonny (Poulett Thomson and Lord John Russell) may strut about with one or two of your feathers in their heads', wrote Buller in his last letter to Durham, 'all the world recognize the plumage as yours.... The ministers have pretended to differ from you. But what has their whole conduct been but a gradual though unwilling concession to your principles?' To Lady Mary Lambton a few days after Durham's death Buller added a prophecy of singular insight and conviction: 'If there is anything certain in the course of events, it is that the great principles, with which he has linked his name, will henceforth amid all the chances of party politics, & passing events, make good their sure & steady way'.[1] 'Whatever decision he might come to', Buller remarked again, on Russell's policy for Canada, 'I do not practically care a pin about it.... Responsible government will inevitably be established by the people themselves.' The contest in Canada is thus the story of the coercion of Lord John Russell's pontifical Whig logic—for Russell and Stanley, at the crisis, were in close personal agreement—by the still less fallible logic of events, until the whole position was conceded by the third Earl Grey in 1846. Between the administration of Lord John Russell as Colonial Secretary in 1839 and his premiership in 1846 lies the watershed between the second Empire and the Commonwealth.

II

Lord John Russell's theory has already been outlined in connexion with Nova Scotia where it was first brought to the test of practice. In the debate of June, 1839, he reaffirmed without qualification the resolution of 1837 that 'while it is expedient to improve the composition of the Executive Council . . . it is unadvisable to subject it to that responsibility demanded by the House of Assembly'. To Poulett Thomson—his colleague, his disciple, and eventually, as Lord Sydenham, the most adroit and resourceful

[1] *Durham Papers*, vol. xxvi, pp. 489, 501. *Pub. Arch. Can.*

champion his doctrine ever had in Canada—he wrote in terms which by all the canons of the old Empire were unanswerable:

'Can the colonial council be the advisers of the Crown of England? Evidently not, for the Crown has other advisers, for the same functions, and with superior authority.

It may happen, therefore, that the Governor receives at one and the same time instructions from the Queen, and advice from his executive council, totally at variance with each other. If he is to obey his instructions from England, the parallel of constitutional responsibility entirely fails; if on the other hand, he is to follow the advice of his council, he is no longer a subordinate officer, but an independent sovereign.'[1]

Thomson himself, whose veneration for Lord John Russell approached hero-worship,[2] refined still more confidently upon his chief's invulnerable logic:

'I am not a bit afraid of the responsible government cry. I have already done much to put it down in its inadmissible sense; namely the demand that the council shall be responsible to the assembly, and that the governor shall take their advice, and be bound by it. . . . I have told the people plainly that, as I cannot get rid of my responsibility to the home government, I will place no responsibility on the council; that they are *a council* for the governor to consult, but no more. . . . There is no other theory which has common sense. Either the governor is the sovereign or the minister. If the first, he may have ministers, but he cannot be responsible to the government at home, and all colonial government becomes impossible. He must therefore be the minister, in which case he cannot be under the control of men in the colony.'[3]

Sydenham's genius for administration and Lord John Russell's 'wise moderation'—the hall-mark of that remarkable man—saved this sterile logic for a time from disaster, and resulted, as Grey afterwards wrote, in 'the first attempt to give something like shape and consistency to these vague ideas'.[4] After all, Russell's caution, if not indeed his theory, was dictated by hard facts. What advice would be given to a governor by a 'ministry headed by M.

[1] Oct. 14, 1839, *Egerton and Grant*, p. 267.

[2] Scrope, *Memoir of the Life of the Right Honourable Charles Lord Sydenham*, Lond., 1843, p. iv: 'He exerted the last energies of his failing voice deliberately and emphatically to pronounce you "the noblest man he had ever the good fortune to know".' (Dedication to Lord John Russell.)

[3] Dec. 12, 1839, *id.*, p. 143.

[4] *The Colonial Policy of Lord John Russell's Administration*, Lond., 1853, i. 202. Cf., however, Adderley's *Review of 'The Colonial Policy of Lord John Russell's Administration' and of subsequent Colonial History*, Lond., 1869, pp. 24, 25.

Papineau'? Who could 'take upon himself to say that such cases will not again occur'? 'To recall the power thus conceded would be impossible.'[1]

There were other complications, however, which the Melbourne Whigs could adjust, as it seemed, to their own advantage. Long before Russell took over the Colonial Office it had been determined to unite the two provinces.[2] None saw more clearly than Thomson the ascendancy this would give to the governor-general. 'It will take time', he wrote to Melbourne in describing the chaos which prevailed in Canada upon his arrival, 'to remedy all this, but the Union will afford the opportunity, because the whole system . . . must then be broken up and remodelled; and if for no other purpose than that the Union would be most desirable. . . . I am satisfied that if we fail in carrying it you may as well give up the Canadas at once, for I know no other means of governing either.'[3] Thus the cards were to be reshuffled and, as many at first thought, the governor-general was to call the trumps. But Hincks and Baldwin, as we shall see, calculated the reshuffling of the cards to better purpose, and the game they were to play was peculiarly their own. Instead of 'swamping the French' and establishing the governor-general as a sort of 'patriot King' in the Canadas with 'still a fair chance', as Thomson hoped, 'of keeping them for a considerable time', the Union was destined to force responsible government in its final form and thus to make the institutions even of Lower Canada not only British as they had never been before, but British irrevocably. It was in the fertile brain of Francis Hincks, the first *liaison* officer between the Baldwin reformers of Upper Canada and the Lower Canadian French, that this shrewd counter-strategy originated. The bond of the alliance was the incorruptible character of Robert Baldwin. It was the strategy of these two which won La Fontaine to the Union and directed the shock-troops of a solid French *bloc* to the storming of the last stronghold of the old Empire. In the hour of his triumph Baldwin represented the French constituency of Rimouski where

[1] Russell to Thomson, Oct. 14, 1838, *Egerton and Grant*, p. 268.

[2] 'It is laid down by all as a fundamental principle that the French must not be reinstated in power in Lower Canada.' 'We are about to make a legislative union of the two provinces.' Melbourne to Russell, Dec. 23, 1838; Apr. 2, 1839. *Lord Melbourne's Papers*, p. 444.

[3] Thomson to Melbourne, Dec. 12, 1839, *id.*, p. 446. Melbourne's reply through Russell was characteristic: 'For God's sake tell him not to feel that, but to make the next best arrangement. If he suffers all "to be up" in his hands, all will be up with him and with those who sent him too.' *Ibid.*

—La Fontaine once assured him—'I speak the truth when I say that no one, nor Morin, nor myself, nor even Papineau himself, could be returned in opposition to you'.[1] It is a curious paradox that few contributed more to set these forces in motion than Poulett Thomson and Lord John Russell themselves.

It will be the aim of this essay to trace this train of policy through to conclusions which transformed the second Empire.

The Sydenham Régime

I

The mobility which the Russell-Sydenham régime imparted for the first time to colonial government may be illustrated by a rough metaphor from the chief Canadian industry of that day. When a 'jam' of logs blocks a Canadian stream in the spring 'drive' to the mills there is said to be a 'key-log' which holds the mass of timber in position against the current. With the location and removal of the key-log by the expert 'stream-driver', the whole mass thunders into motion and moves irresistibly with the stream. Lord John Russell's dispatch of October 16, 1839, may be said to have loosed the key-log of the old system and set in motion for the first time the elemental forces of representative government—forces which Sydenham had every confidence he could harness and control.

Hitherto the Executive Council, though appointed nominally 'during pleasure', was as immobile as a Canadian 'lumber-jam'. 'I cannot learn', wrote Lord John Russell, 'that during the present or the two last reigns, a single instance has occurred of a change in the subordinate colonial officers, except in cases of death or resignation, incapacity or misconduct.' Thus tenure at pleasure had become tenure for life. Thomson was instructed:

> 'to understand and . . . cause it to be made generally known, that hereafter the tenure of colonial offices held during Her Majesty's pleasure, will not be regarded as equivalent to a tenure during good behaviour; but that not only will such officers be called upon to retire from the public service as often as any sufficient motives of public policy may suggest the expediency of that measure, but that a change in the person of the governor will be considered as a sufficient reason for any alterations which his successor may deem it expedient to make.'[2]

The immediate purpose of this famous dispatch was not, as we have seen, that which the Reformers read into it. Sir John Harvey

[1] Nov. 12, 1844, *Baldwin Papers* (copies in the *Pub. Arch. Can.*), i. 92.
[2] *Egerton and Grant*, pp. 270, 271.

in New Brunswick had referred to it as 'conferring a new, and in my judgement, an improved constitution upon these Colonies'; and Howe claimed truly that 'it bestowed all that was required' to effect responsible government—if such were the intentions of the governor and of the British Government. The governor could now adjust the Executive Council to 'the well-understood wishes and interests of the people', and the philosophy of responsible government lies in the principle that by so doing the governor, like the Crown in Great Britain, would best consult British interests and his own. But he could also now adjust the Executive Council more directly to the 'wishes and interests of the people' as interpreted not by their representatives but by himself. This, as Sir Colin Campbell had demonstrated, might conceivably be a vastly different thing; and this, as we have seen, was the immediate purpose of the dispatch of October 16, 1839.[1] It was to add to the powers not of the Assembly but of the governor 'by leaving him free to choose his Counsellors'. It was to break the system which Howe had just pilloried in his second letter to Lord John Russell—the mortmain which Executive Councillors acting for life had almost invariably established over the administration.[2] It was to enable the governor to enforce the responsibility of his ministers not to the Assembly but to himself, to ensure the smooth and harmonious administration not of their policy but of his own, and to provide him upon the floors of the Assembly with a group of trained and subservient officials, sponsors for the governor's policy and eminently fitted to make it prevail.

This last refinement was Thomson's own peculiar contribution to the Russell régime. 'We do not derive from our officers', he wrote, 'that aid in the management of public affairs in the legislature which is absolutely indispensable', for it was one of the first duties of government to 'propose and submit to the legislature, with the full weight of its authority, whatever measures may appear to be called for for the good of the province, and the very consideration of which would divert men's minds from the agitation of abstract points of government.' Thomson proposed, therefore, to

[1] In writing to Russell himself Sir Colin had interpreted the dispatch as 'intended . . . merely to strengthen the hands of the Governor by enabling him more effectually to control refractory Public functionaries', Mar. 1, 1840. Governor's *Letter-Books*, Halifax. Cf. the memorandum of Vernon Smith of the Colonial Office upon Campbell's letter of April 4, 1840: 'he is right in his interpretation of Lord John's letter.' *C.O. 217*, vol. 174. See above, pp. 187 f.

[2] Sept. 18, 1839, *Egerton and Grant*, pp. 209 *et seq.*

utilize for that purpose 'the most influential members of either House—but especially those of the House of Assembly'; and secondly to stipulate that his ministers 'whom it may be desirable to make use of in that way, should be required, when necessary, to become members of the Assembly . . . in order to afford their assistance there'. Government was thus to 'acquire the necessary strength in the Legislature; and if the proper direction be given to their labours, and due firmness evinced in controlling them, the Council will prove a very useful and powerful engine in the hands of the Governor'. The regulation of October 16 would thus 'be of service' in explaining to those who had 'heedlessly adopted the cry of "Responsible Government", the extent to which Her Majesty's Government wish to go in administering affairs here according to the wishes of the People, and thro' persons having their confidence, at the same time that they reject a principle incompatible with Colonial Government'. In effect the governor's ministers were 'placemen', and Thomson did not hesitate to call them so and to use unsparingly his power over them.[1]

It has been necessary here, as Thomson himself once wrote, to 'recapitulate the principle' of his administration, for the astonishing fact is not only that he believed it feasible but that he put it into practice with almost magical success. The reason, as we shall see, belonged to that day and place. No environment was ever more favourable than Canada after the Union. No other system perhaps could have worked in Canada at that time, and no other man then living perhaps could have achieved what Thomson achieved for this country. Perhaps no man in Canada ever achieved so much of permanent good with such incredible speed. But his 'principle' of government was not of this order, for the wind blew upon that house and it fell. 'When I read Lord Sydenham's despatches', wrote Elgin in 1847, 'I never cease to marvel what study of human nature or of history led him to the conclusion that it would be possible to concede to a pushing enterprising people . . . such Constitutional privileges . . . and yet to limit in practice their power of self Government as he proposed.'[2]

[1] Scrope, *op. cit.*, pp. 183–5. Thomson to Russell, Dec. 6, 1839, *G. Series*, 387. 16. In the Upper Canadian debates on the Union in December, 1839, Thomson permitted his supporters 'the freest expression of opinion . . . whether placemen or not', and both the law officers on one occasion voted 'against the wishes of the Government'; but, he added, 'I should not for one instant have tolerated it under any common circumstances.' *G. Series*, 387. 27.

[2] Elgin to Grey, Apr. 26, 1847, 'Secret'. *Grey-Elgin Correspondence*.

II

Measured by standards of British public life Charles Poulett Thomson—Lord Sydenham as he will always be known—was perhaps the most distinguished statesman who ever came to Canada. He had sat in Parliament for fifteen years. For ten he represented Manchester, the centre of the most advanced economic thought in Great Britain. For five he was a member of Melbourne's cabinet as President of the Board of Trade at a time when economic issues were of prime importance. At the end of that period Melbourne rated him the ablest man in the government in public finance. In 1839 he declined the Chancellorship of the Exchequer in order to become Governor-General of British North America, while Lord John Russell—'beyond all comparison (thought Sydney Smith) the ablest man in the whole administration'—took over the Colonial Office. The brilliancy of Sydenham's success in Canada won him his peerage and the Order of the Bath. All this he achieved without the aid of rank or fortune before he was forty years of age. At his death he was barely forty-one.[1]

When Thomson came to Canada his eccentricities were perhaps better known than his abilities. A writer of memoirs once flippantly called him 'the greatest coxcomb I ever saw, and the vainest dog, though his vanity is not offensive or arrogant'.[2] In truth the frail physique and the countenance, singularly delicate and expressive, which looks out of Reynolds's portrait of him, accord but strangely with the daemonic energy which devoured the closing years of his life. His exuberant opportunism, his mercurial tact and versatility, his engaging address, his almost incredible powers of winning individuals to his service, became so notorious in Canada that he may be said to have founded a school. Sir John A. Macdonald and Sir Wilfrid Laurier, the first names in Canadian politics, were both his disciples. As Sydney Smith once said of Canning, he could 'leap about, touch facts with his wand and turn yes into no'. He had also an exuberant infallibility all his own. He may have made mistakes, but they were not self-confessed. He may have had his failures—and had he remained another session in Canada one failure at least would almost certainly have been catastrophic—but there is no hint of these in

[1] Shortt, *Lord Sydenham*, Makers of Canada Series, xv. 55 ff.; Scrope, *op. cit., passim.*

[2] Charles Greville, quoted in Morison, *British Supremacy and Canadian Self-Government, 1839–1854*, p. 77.

his official dispatches. Melbourne once referred to one of Thomson's private letters as 'desponding'.[1] We should like to see that letter.

Thomson came to Canada with a schedule of herculean labours, and he completed them on scheduled time—the Union to be carried through both provinces, the whole fiscal and economic life of the country to be revived, the government of the united province to be rescued from factions and committed to sound administration. The confusion which he found upon his arrival in October, 1839, was beyond description; but while it distracted the country it simplified not a little his own policy. For Lower Canada, he wrote, 'the best thing... would be a despotism for ten years more'; since the constitution there was already suspended, the 'despotism' enabled him to dictate by sheer authority a body of legislation which he believed 'the United Legislature, when it came, could not destroy', and which he afterwards assured Lord John Russell 'would have taken ten years of an Assembly'. Within two days he procured from his predecessor's Special Council, which he continued without alteration, a resolution in favour of the Union 'in terms so forcible', he reported, 'as to leave me nothing to say'. 'So far, therefore, as the Lower Province is concerned, I look upon the Union as settled.' But the prospects as he described them in the following March were not so promising for self-government. There was 'no such thing as a political opinion. No man looks to a practical measure of improvement . . . you might as well talk Greek to him. . . . The hand of the Government is utterly unknown and unfelt at present out of Montreal and Quebec, and not the slightest means exist of knowing what is passing in the rural districts.' More was passing there, as we shall see, than Thomson could have surmised; and to have imagined that the Union was to be 'settled' for Lower Canada by a summary despotism, or that the decision of the Special Council gave 'the greatest satisfaction to the Province generally', was one of Thomson's costliest miscalculations. There were some things, in Melbourne's sardonic phrase, which would 'not do in these days'.[2]

Thomson's classic descriptions of Upper Canada, less than three weeks after his arrival at Toronto and five days after the opening of the legislature, may also require modification, for the exuber-

[1] *Lord Melbourne's Papers*, p. 446.

[2] Scrope, *op. cit.*, pp. 149, 250. *Egerton and Grant*, p. 272; Scrope, *op. cit.*, p. 148. *Id.*, pp. 175 f. *Lord Melbourne's Papers*, p. 444.

ance of his private letters was sometimes second nature. In Upper Canada there was still an Assembly; success here, even with Head's 'loyal' majority, would be 'a more difficult matter':

> 'Then the Assembly is such a House! Split into half a dozen different parties. The Government having *none*—and *no one man* to depend on! Think of a House in which half the members hold places, yet in which the Government does not command a single vote . . . where there is no one to defend the Government when attacked, or to state the opinion or views of the Governor! . . . I am now more than ever satisfied that the Union affords the only chance of putting an end to the factions that distract the country; the only means of recruiting its finances by persuading Great Britain to help the Upper Canada Exchequer; the only means by which the present abominable system of government can be broken up, and a strong and powerful administration, both departmental and executive, be formed. And unless the people will assent to the general outline of it, and Parliament will then carry the details, upon which they would never agree, with a high hand, the province is lost. From all that I can hear or see, I would not give a year's purchase for our hold of it, if some great stroke is not given which shall turn men's thoughts from the channel in which they now run. . . .
>
> It is indeed a pity to see this province in such a state. It is the finest country I ever knew. . . . The climate, the soil, the water-power, and facilities of transport, finer than anything in North America. . . .
>
> I am sure it is the last and only chance . . . the state of things admits of no delays and no half measures.' [1]

With this conviction Thomson plunged at once into the task of carrying the Union through the Upper Canadian legislature. His message to the House stipulated equal representation for the two provinces, a permanent civil list, the amount to be settled by the Imperial Parliament, and the funding of the enormous Upper Canadian debt with that of the lower province. How the measure was carried through the council by a vote of 14 to 8, and through the Assembly after nearly a fortnight of bitter debate, Thomson describes in a series of private letters and two confidential dispatches to Russell in time for the opening of the British Parliament. 'I have done my business', he wrote. 'The Union is carried

[1] Scrope, *op. cit.*, pp. 150, 151. Elsewhere Thomson's verdict was less disparaging: 'I owe my success altogether to the confidence which the reform party have reposed in me personally, and to the generous manner in which they have acted by me. A dissolution would have been greatly to their advantage. . . . But they gave up all these considerations . . . and went gallantly through with me to the end.' *Id.*, pp. 161 f.

triumphantly . . . it now only remains for Parliament to do its duty, and pass the bill which I shall send home. It has not been without trouble, and a prodigious deal of management, in which my House of Commons' tactics stood me in good stead. . . . My ministers vote against me. So I govern through the opposition, who are truly "Her Majesty's".'[1]

Not content with the Union, Thomson drove through a settlement of the Clergy Reserves—'the root of all the troubles of the province, the cause of the rebellion—the never-failing watchword at the hustings—the perpetual source of discord, strife, and hatred.' Thomson's Bill passed the council 'without the change of a word', and the Assembly by 30 to 20. 'Ten members', he adds significantly, 'voted generously for me this time, though they may lose their seats by it.' The Act was torn to pieces by the House of Lords, and Bishop Strachan went farther and fared worse in 1854, but Thomson's exultation was pardonable. 'It is the greatest work that ever has been done in this country, and will be of more solid advantage to it than all the loans and all the troops you can make or send. It is worth ten Unions, and was ten times more difficult.' Thomson's official dispatch was still jubilant, but Elgin's comment upon it ten years later was less enthusiastic: 'He clearly admits that the Act is against the sense of the country and that nothing but his own great personal influence got it through—and yet he looks upon it as a settlement of the question. I confess I see few of the conditions of finality in measures which are passed under such circumstances.'[2]

III

The work of Sydenham—he was immediately raised to the peerage under that name—was pre-eminently administrative. It is impossible here to trace the multitude of his activities in this field or the desperate economic and social conditions he laboured to improve. Both are to be found in a final form for Canadian history in the pages of Dr. Shortt and of Professor Morison. Sydenham

[1] *G. Series*, 387. 27 f.; Scrope, *op. cit.*, p. 163.

[2] *Id.*, pp. 168 f.: 'He, therefore, entered into personal communication with the leading individuals among the principal religious denominations, and after many interviews succeeded in obtaining their support to a measure for the distribution of the reserves among the religious communities recognized by law, in proportion to their respective numbers.' Murdock in Scrope, *op. cit.*, p. 167. *Id.*, p. 169. Thomson to Russell, Jan. 22, 1840, *G. Series*, 387. 72–82; Elgin to Grey, July 15, 1850, *Grey-Elgin Correspondence*.

found the upper province 'overwhelmed by debt' contracted by the old Executive Council 'without the slightest effort on the part of the Government to warn the Assembly'. 'The finances', he wrote, 'are more deranged than we believed even in England. The deficit 75,000*l.* a year, more than equal to the income. All public works suspended. Emigration going on fast *from* the province. Every man's property worth only about half what it was.' The public credit was unequal to the completion of the Welland and Cornwall canals. The Lachine Canal, too, had yet to be built. Sydenham describes his own first journey to Toronto: 'A portage to La Chine; then the steamboat to the Cascades, twenty-four miles further; then road again (if road it can be called) for sixteen miles; then steam to Prescott, forty miles; then road twelve miles; then, by a change of steamers, into Lake Ontario to Kingston, and thence here. I slept one night on the road, and two on board the steamers. Such as I have described it is the boasted *navigation* of the St. Lawrence!' In his first venture above Lake Ontario, his boat—'the filthiest and vilest concern which ever floated on water'—was nearly swamped on the lakes. Finally in the Thames 'away went the rudder and tiller, both as rotten as touchwood'. Fortunately Sydenham was a good horseman, and on land 'made it out admirably'. Such was travel in viceregal luxury in 1840. But even the grim reports of Dr. Douglas, the quarantine officer at Grosse Isle, fail to depict the horrors of the fever-riddled immigrant-ships on the Atlantic or the desperate 'struggle with the wilderness' that went on in the backwoods of Canada.[1]

With Sydenham's genius for practical administration and a prospective British loan of £1,500,000 at his disposal to restore the credit of the province and complete the public works, much could be done to divert 'agitation upon theoretical points of government' to what Sydenham calls 'the real interests' of the province. Immigration by the St. Lawrence in 1839 had numbered 7,439. In three years it increased to 22,000, 28,000 and 44,000.[2] But his greatest reforms were in the administration of government. A system of municipal local government to absorb mediocre political ambitions, to test and train men of real ability for provincial

[1] Thomson to Russell, Dec. 15, 1839, 'Confidential', *G. Series*, 387. 28; Scrope, *op. cit.*, pp. 149, 141, 198; Douglas on immigration, *G. Series*, 390. 71–80.

[2] For Sydenham's able papers on lands and immigration see particularly *G. Series*, 387. 217; 389. 56, 112, &c.; Scrope, *op. cit.*, pp. 207 *et seq.*

politics, and to free the Assembly from the incessant jobbing that accompanied appropriations for 'every petty local job' in the province, had been an integral part of Sydenham's programme—'as much a part of the intended scheme . . . as the union of the two Legislatures, and the more important of the two'. When Lord John Russell omitted it from the final *Act of Union*, Sydenham's vexation was boundless,[1] but he forced it through the Special Council of Lower Canada—'off my own anvil'—and though the French sullenly refused to work it he used its establishment there to force it through the legislature for the rest of the province after the Union.[2]

Sydenham's description of the 'confusion and riot' of money-bills in the Assembly is classic. 'Every man proposes a vote for his own job; and bills are introduced without notice, and carried through *all* their stages in a quarter of an hour!' For the first time Sydenham 'got them into comparative order and decency by having measures brought forward by the Government, and well and steadily worked through'. By the *Act of Union* the initiation of money-bills was to be restricted to the executive: 'without the last', he wrote, 'I would not give a farthing for my bill.' For the first time it was possible to ask and to answer in the Assembly the question which was a commonplace of British politics: 'What course does the Government propose to pursue?'[3] Above all, Sydenham evolved the departments of the executive with an unfailing eye to results and to discipline. Thus in finance his eye fell upon Francis Hincks, the ablest financier of that generation in Canada and at one time perhaps the most implacable of his opponents.[4] Reforms like these, as Dr. Shortt truly says, were 'the very essence of responsible government in practice'. Without them it can scarcely be doubted that responsible government itself would

[1] *Id.*, p. 202; *Egerton and Grant*, p. 280. Sydenham's annoyance was the greater because he regarded it as a sort of innoculation against responsible government: the want of it had accounted for 'the readiness with which a demand for organic changes in the constitution has been received by the people'. *Ibid.*

[2] 'There could not have been the slightest chance . . . if it had not been already enacted for Lower Canada.' Sydenham to Russell, Aug. 28, 1841; Scrope, *op. cit.*, p. 252.

[3] *Id.*, p. 172. *G. Series*, 387. 28.

[4] See the interchange of letters between Hincks and Baldwin in the *La Fontaine Papers*, i. 96, and below, p. 269. 'A week before Lord Sydenham's death, in the last interview I had with him—he propounded Mr. Hincks's appointment to me.' Draper to Bagot, June 9, 1842, *Bagot Papers*, vol. ii. Murdock calls Hincks 'at one time Lord Sydenham's most uncompromising and ablest opponent.' Scrope, *op. cit.*, p. 267.

have courted discredit and disaster. Sydenham may not have been the first able governor but he was in effect the first premier in Canadian history. He may not have believed in Baldwin's or Howe's or Hincks's conception of responsible government, but he made it for the first time thoroughly feasible. In another sense he made it inevitable, for he taught the Reformers for the first time what good government was and thus prepared them for the Eleusinian mysteries of self-government.

IV

There was another side, it must be added, to Sydenham's administration. He had presided at the Board of Trade during that period of railway expansion when, as Elgin once observed, 'it is to be feared that, notwithstanding the high standard of honor in the British Parliament there was a good deal of jobbing'.[1] Sydenham's forays into 'practical politics' in Canada became a byword. In a sense his whole theory of colonial government forced him into it, for he was determined not only to avoid 'the great mistake' of all his predecessors who threw themselves 'into the hands of one party or the other, and became their slave', but to 'let them know and feel that I will yield to neither of them—that I will take the moderate from both sides—reject the extremes—and govern as I think right, and not as they fancy'.[2] This, as Adderley remarks, was perilously near Strafford's advice to King Charles, that 'a well-governed Parliament was the best instrument for managing a people'.[3] But the Baconian conception of parliamentary governance, while it might succeed for a time under a Strafford or a 'patriot King' like George III, was sure to encounter difficulties in Canada. After Sydenham's tour in Nova Scotia where, despite his exuberant self-confidence, his system, as we have seen, had the narrowest of its escapes, he travelled through Upper Canada with 'escorts of two or three hundred farmers on horseback at every place from township to township, with all the etceteras of guns, music, and flags. What is of more importance (he adds significantly), my candidates everywhere taken for the ensuing elections'.[4] In Lower Canada, where hatred of Union was at first almost in-

[1] Elgin to Grey, Nov. 1, 1850, *Grey-Elgin Correspondence*.

[2] Scrope, *op. cit.*, pp. 171 f.

[3] *Review of 'The Colonial Policy of Lord J. Russell's Administration', by Earl Grey, and of Subsequent Colonial History*, Rt. Hon. Sir C. B. Adderley, Lond., 1869, p. 28.

[4] Scrope, *op. cit.*, p. 199.

stinctive, more summary methods were employed. La Fontaine who had declined to join the administration never forgave—and Canadian politics for many a day never forgot—the means employed to defeat him in Terrebonne. Even Murdock, Sydenham's secretary, who contributes the Canadian section of Scrope's *Memoir* of Sydenham, can scarcely palliate the gerrymandering of Montreal. Bagot afterwards wrote bluntly of Sydenham's 'promise of the Loan and the bribe of the public Works'; and in truth Sydenham left behind him in Canada a legacy of 'places' and promises for no fewer than three of his successors to liquidate. One of his protégés was offered an accommodation in the West Indies. Another sought his reward from Bagot for 'services . . . in the way of elections in Lower Canada'.[1] The claims of a third found their way under Elgin to a full-dress debate in the House of Lords. In the famous by-election of April, 1844, in Montreal where 'bludgeon-men' from the Lachine Canal played a prominent part, the Reformers, to Metcalfe's chagrin, boasted of being 'apt scholars' of Lord Sydenham.[2] But it was Sydenham's 'business' to carry the Union, and he was 'resolved on doing the thing'. 'Small thanks', exclaims Carlyle, 'to the man who will keep his hands clean but with gloves on.'

Howe conceded in *The Novascotian* that 'there was, in fact, no alternative but to secure his majority, or throw aside all that had been done'. A fortnight before the elections Sydenham reported that he was 'under no uneasiness whatever'. Murdock gives the final results as 24 'Government Members', French 20, moderate Reformers 20, Ultra Reformers 5, Compact Party 7, doubtful 6, others 2. Meanwhile Sydenham had chosen Kingston as the seat of government, improvised buildings, and purchased 'about thirty acres in the heart of the Town at a very cheap rate . . . worth three times the sum which I gave for it'—'all this (he added) upon my own responsibility'.[3] The legislature of the Union met on June 13, 1841. The success of that session—Sydenham was to return to office in Great Britain at its close—is extolled in several of his most famous dispatches. To outward appearances it was spectacular, but to Melbourne and Russell Sydenham admitted that he

[1] Bagot to Stanley, Jan. 26, 1842, *Bagot Papers*, iv. 26: 'It was solely by his dexterity and exertions that two returns were effected, and three others in consequence of these two.'

[2] 'When constituencies were overawed by the introduction of bands of non Electors.' Metcalfe to Stanley, April 22, 1844, *G. Series*, 460. 312.

[3] *G. Series*, 390. 171; Scrope, *op. cit.*, p. 227.

had 'to fight the whole battle' himself, and it was 'a considerable pull on both one's adroitness and temper—particularly as I had "a ministerial crisis" on my hands on the very day of the meeting'. He had 'got rid of' his Solicitor-General.[1] The Solicitor-General was Robert Baldwin, and the 'ministerial crisis' was the first formal notice of an alliance between the Upper Canadian Reformers and the French under La Fontaine which was soon to make the Baconian system of governance for Canada thenceforth impossible.

V

Both Sydenham and Murdock have been unsparingly critical of Baldwin's conduct in June, 1841. 'Acting upon some principle of conduct which I can reconcile neither with honor nor common sense', wrote the governor-general, 'he strove to bring about this Union, and at the last having as he thought, effected it, coolly proposed to me, on the day before Parliament was to meet, to break up the Government altogether, dismiss several of his Colleagues, and replace them by men whom I believe he had not known for 24 hours. . . . I had been made aware of this Gentleman's proceedings for two or three days, and certainly could hardly bring myself to tolerate them. . . . I at once treated it, joined to his previous conduct, as a resignation of his office, and informed him that I accepted it without the least regret.'[2]

By every consideration of practical politics the abortive *coup* of 1841, as Sydenham stated bluntly, might have jeopardized 'the good Government of the Country, and have rendered all my efforts unavailing';[3] it was perhaps as fortunate for the Reformers themselves and for their cause as for Sydenham and the country that Baldwin was not called upon to form a government in 1841. But there was much beneath the surface that neither Sydenham nor Murdock could have known. The alliance with the French was not the product of twenty-four hours, nor was it 'within two or three days of the session', as Murdock states, that Baldwin 'entered into communication' with them. The conviction that the Union was inevitable and that it could be used to force responsible

[1] Scrope, *op. cit.*, p. 244; *Lord Melbourne's Papers*, p. 449.

[2] Sydenham to Russell, June 26, 1841, 'Confidential'. *G. Series*, 391. 265. For Murdock's view see Scrope, *op. cit.*, pp. 230 *et seq.* Baldwin had proposed the retirement of Draper, Sullivan, Day, and Ogden, all rated as Conservatives, and the substitution of La Fontaine, Morin, Hincks, and himself.

[3] *G. Series*, 391. 265.

government in its final form had been acted upon by Francis Hincks for more than two years. It had been reached at least two months before Lord John Russell proposed the Union in June, 1839, and four months before Sydenham himself had been appointed to effect it. The design was practically complete before Sydenham arrived in Canada. Thus for more than two years, three or four men, in discreet and confidential intercourse, had been labouring at the foundations. But despite the over-sanguine hopes of Hincks and Baldwin and Morin, the first session under the Union came upon them unprepared. The tactics in the end were crude and unavailing. It could scarcely have been otherwise. But the strategy remained, and remains, a landmark in the political history of Canada, and Murdock himself lived to see how far Robert Baldwin, whose whole political life from beginning to end was a vigil with an uncompromising conscience, could conform to the highest 'principles of political honour by which British statesmen are governed'.

Hincks's first letter to La Fontaine—on the subject of Durham's *Report*—was written from Toronto on April 12, 1839, without previous personal acquaintance.[1] In the *La Fontaine Papers* are to be found no fewer than thirty-four of his confidential letters from that date to June 29, 1841, and it would be hard to cite a better illustration of Lord Bryce's dictum that what passes for public opinion usually has a very select and intimate origin. So carefully guarded and confidential was this intercourse that it was carried on not by post but through the agency of trusted friends.[2] Nothing more discreet, more persuasive, more insinuating and adroit than these letters could have been written by Sydenham himself:

> 'The British party below (wrote Hincks) calculates as does Lord Durham on the French-Canadian party being destroyed in the United Legislature. This as I have always said might be the case as far as national objects are concerned, but if we all combine *as Canadians* to promote the good of all classes in Canada there cannot be a doubt that under the new Constitution worked as Lord Durham proposes, the only party which would suffer would be the bureaucrats. . . .
>
> I wish we could convince you, that a really responsible Executive

[1] 'Though I have not the honour of personal acquaintance with you.' *La Fontaine Papers*, i. 1.

[2] 'Like yourself I have so little confidence in our post office that I seldom send political letters in that way.' 'I dont like trusting the post-office with political letters.' May 14, May 26, 1839. *La Fontaine Papers*.

Council would accomplish all that we want. . . . As to the Union question, you should not mind Lord D.'s motives, but the effect of the scheme. . . . I am sure Lord D. from his speaking of not subjecting you to the British minority of Lower Canada understood well, that the Upper Canadian British would be your friends. N'importe. I am *sure* they will be.'[1]

With this clear theme and with convincing goodwill Hincks grappled patiently month by month with the developing details of the Union. It was not easy to convince a French-Canadian that a measure which outraged his instincts and many of his interests could yet be to his advantage. The funded debt, the irregularities of representation, the proscription of the French language, Hincks conceded to be 'monstrously oppressive and unjust'. Sydenham's grim fight for French rights against the 'Compact' Tories in both provinces was of course unknown. It seemed that he had no solution but Durham's for the question of race. But Hincks implored La Fontaine to let the Tories do the quarrelling with the governor-general. 'Pray do try not to quarrel with Mr. Thomson. Keep your enemies in the wrong and you will soon overthrow them.' 'Be assured,' he repeated, 'the Union is the only chance for us Reformers. I am glad to find that you are cautious in advocating it. I almost fear Le Canadien has said too much in its favour. Let the Tories fall into the pit of their own digging.' 'My confidence in a Union Legislature is unbounded. *We can not be beat.*'[2] With the mutual introduction of friends the circle slowly grew to include Cherrier, Morin, and Viger, Baldwin, Woodruff, Merritt, and Dunn. The meeting of Baldwin and La Fontaine, it is needless to say, was a turning-point in Canadian history, for Baldwin's character and 'incorruptibility' became the sheet-anchor of the alliance until responsible government was finally won.

VI

Baldwin's position, however, like Howe's in Nova Scotia, grew increasingly difficult. He had become Solicitor-General during the last session of the old Assembly, as a 'public pledge', he avowed, of a 'reasonably well-grounded confidence that the government of my country is to be carried on in accordance with the principles of Responsible Government which I have ever held'. After the Union he accepted a seat in the Executive Council but with a characteristic *caveat* to Sydenham that he 'had an entire want of

[1] *La Fontaine Papers*, Apr. 12, Apr. 30, 1839.

[2] Nov. 14, Dec. 4, 1839, *id.*, i. 27. 31.

political confidence in all of his colleagues except Mr. Dunn, Mr. Harrison, and Mr. Daly'.[1] Not content with this he served the same notice upon his Tory colleagues themselves—Draper, Sullivan (his own cousin), Day, and Ogden. A difficulty which his sleepless conscience had discovered in the oath of office under Head was now revived, and was referred by Sydenham to Baldwin himself and the Attorney-General as the law officers of the Crown! A collection of Baldwin's elaborate memoranda, usually in the third person, dictated by that uncompromising 'conscientious principle' which marked every gesture of his public life, would make a curious anthology.

By September, 1839, La Fontaine had begun to see hope in the Union. His consternation when Baldwin took office was allayed by Hincks. 'Come what will,' he wrote, 'I am anxious that you should believe what I know to be the case that Mr. R. W. Baldwin is *incorruptible*. He has taken office *solely from a sense of public duty*. . . . Depend upon it *all our liberties* must be attained by that measure no matter what may (be) its details.' 'I know you think we shall never get Responsible Government, that the ministry are deceiving us—granted—But *we will make them give it whether they like it or not*.' Slowly but surely La Fontaine's diffidence, his scepticism, his traditional Lower Canadian preference for direct action, gave way before Hincks's mastery of the indirect methods of responsible government.[2] A visit to Toronto at Hincks's invitation during the summer of 1840 further cemented the alliance.

As the Union approached Hincks plied his arguments with increasing effect—a judicious letter from Buller, the old files of the *Examiner*, above all 'the political integrity of Mr. Baldwin'. 'He

[1] Hincks, *Political History*, p. 19. Sydenham who had the most positive instructions from Russell to 'refuse any explanation (of responsible government) which may be construed to imply an acquiescence' beyond the Resolutions of 1837 (*Egerton and Grant*, p. 266) had refused to submit his dispatches to the Assembly; but he made to them the famous declaration that he had 'received Her Majesty's commands to administer the government of these provinces in accordance with the well-understood wishes and interests of the people, and to pay to their feelings, as expressed through their representatives, the deference that is justly due to them'. *Brit. Parl. Papers*, 1840, Canada, Part IV, p. 13. Had Baldwin seen the dispatches and Sydenham's private letters it is hard to believe that he would have taken office. Hincks held that it was good *policy* to 'be able to use the Gov. Gen's name *on our side* at the next election'. *La Fontaine Papers*, i. 55.

[2] *La Fontaine Papers*, i. 13, 55, 64. Cf. La Fontaine's insistence upon an elective Legislative Council, upon Baldwin as Speaker, upon stopping the supplies, &c.

only asks our confidence till the meeting of Parliament.' 'Be assured you have not a firmer friend. . . . If Mr. Viger, yourself, Morin, Girouard, Cherrier, and others were to exert yourselves, surely the people would see the necessity of Union.' In December, 1840, Hincks suggested in the strictest confidence that 'the accession both of Mr. Morin & Yourself to the Government would be indispensably necessary'. The governor must 'succumb to the House & take such a Cabinet as it will dictate. . . . We will teach him some truths of which he seems still ignorant.' With the elections of March, 1841, there is an added note of bitterness from La Fontaine; but Hincks, after a characteristic analysis of the returns, implored him not to retire from public life but to contest all doubtful elections, and summon a caucus of the party to act with 'the elements ready here for a Reform Cabinet'.[1]

A visit of Baldwin to Montreal in May confirmed the hope that the party 'will be kept united'. On the 26th Hincks thought 'Dunn and Harrison will go right and that Daly will join them. The dismissal of the Tory Councillors must be a sine quâ non but we do not agree as to the *time*, and the *mode*.' In confidence he expressed Baldwin's opinion and his own that they must act at the opening of the session, 'and if His Excellency will not do it, tender their resignation—This is the honest straight course'.[2] The denouement is briefly told. The evening of May 28 Hincks spent at the home of Baldwin where 'Dr. Baldwin (Baldwin's venerable father), Price, myself & Baldwin were decidedly for *not acting* under any circumstances with the present men. I see the danger to Mr. Baldwin's character in acting with them for a single day & be assured he does too.' By this time, however, little hope remained that Harrison, Dunn, and other moderates would 'come up to the mark'. In any event there could be 'no idea that the Govr. Genl. will come *to their terms*'.[3] And thus the *coup* of 1841 which Sydenham could 'reconcile neither with honor nor common sense' was in the last analysis an act of self-defence, actuated by 'the danger to Mr. Baldwin's character'!

In truth the first attempt to force a reform Cabinet with responsible government disintegrated into a fiasco in the hands of Syden-

[1] *La Fontaine Papers*, i. 84, 90, 78, 110, 120, 134, *et passim*.

[2] *Id.*, i. 148. 'I *think* Mr. Baldwin concurs with me but this is of course strictly confidential. It is almost dangerous to talk with Executive Councillors on such subjects.'

[3] *Id.*, i. 152.

ham's incomparable finesse—it was 'not even formidable'. Hincks carried the election of Cuvillier as Speaker, but by June 29 he confessed ruefully that he could 'hardly be surprised that the Lower Canadian members are disgusted at the conduct of our Reformers—I am so myself'. For Baldwin the die was cast: 'if he was sure of being deserted by the whole of Upper Canada he would stand by the Reformers of Lower Canada.' The full import of this did not at once appear, but Baldwin was to find it, as we shall see, after many days. Meanwhile Harrison—'safe', enigmatical, and cautious—though defeated by the Tories in his election, was deep in Sydenham's confidence. Dunn, too, and a dozen others responded to his forthright policy. As late as June 29 Hincks was still prepared to fight through the session. 'Our dictator will be gone before another and public opinion will bring the renegade Reformers back to their faith.'[1] But it was not long before he too surrendered to the spell, and Sydenham, a fortnight before his death, was prepared to name him Inspector-General for one of the most remarkable periods of public works, buoyant finance, and immigration in Canadian history.

The session was not to close, however, without a final attempt by Baldwin to impale the governor-general upon his great 'principle'. With all their stiffness and inelegance Baldwin's famous resolutions of September were perhaps the clearest forecast of responsible government hitherto formulated. While the governor was not 'constitutionally responsible to any other than the authorities of the Empire', the House had the constitutional right of holding his advisers 'politically responsible for every act of the provincial government of a local character, sanctioned by such government while such advisers continue in office'. Sydenham escaped the issue only by entrusting Harrison with alternative resolutions which did service on both sides during the Metcalfe crisis, and served for many a year to deepen the mystery of Sydenham's whole conception of responsible government.[2] Before the next session it

[1] Murdock in Scrope, *op. cit.*, p. 232. *La Fontaine Papers*, i. 142, 157, 151.

[2] Hincks always maintained that Sydenham's views underwent a decided change. *Political History*, p. 32. Cf. also Metcalfe to Stanley, Aug. 5, 1843: 'If Lord Sydenham did not intend this, he was more mistaken than from his known ability one would suppose to be possible; and if he did intend it, he, with his eyes open, carried into practice that very theory of Responsible Colonial Government which he had pronounced his opinion decidedly against.'

In any case Sydenham had no escape from Russell's peremptory influence. Cf. Thomson to Russell, Dec. 15, 1839, 'Confidential', *G. Series*, 387. 28: 'I am

was universally conceded that Sydenham's composite executive of moderate Tories and Reformers could not weather a vote of want of confidence. Baldwin's next attempt, as we shall see, was more successful.

VII

To outward appearances, at least, the long summer session of 1841 closed in a frenzy of achievement. The most difficult of Sydenham's measures, the District Council Bill for Upper Canada—'word for word after my ordinance for the Lower Province'—passed the combined opposition of Tories, Ultras, and jobbers by a vote of 42 to 29. 'I beat them all three', wrote Sydenham in one of the last of his exultant letters to his brother, 'to the astonishment of the spectators':

> 'I have brought the Assembly by degrees into perfect order, ready to follow wherever I may lead. . . . The five great works I aimed at have been got through—the establishment of a board of works with ample powers; the admission of aliens; a new system of county courts, the

bound to say that the representations which have been made in England, of the nature of that demand, are not exactly what I have found to be the case.'

Harrison's resolutions were as follows:

(1) 'That the most important, as well as the most undoubted, of the political rights of the people of this Province, is that of having a Provincial Parliament, for the protection of their liberties, for the exercise of a constitutional influence over the Executive Departments of their Government, and for Legislation upon all matters of internal Government.

(2) 'That the head of the Executive Government of the Province being, within the limits of his Government, the Representative of the Sovereign, is responsible to the Imperial authority alone; but that, nevertheless, the management of our local affairs can only be conducted by him, by and with the assistance, counsel and information, of subordinate Officers in the Province.

(3) 'That in order to preserve, between the different branches of the Provincial Parliament, that harmony which is essential to the peace, welfare and good Government, of the Province, the chief Advisers of the Representative of the Sovereign, constituting a Provincial Administration under him, ought to be men possessed of the confidence of the representatives of the people, thus affording a guarantee that the well understood wishes and interests of the people, which our Gracious Sovereign has declared shall be the rule of the Provincial Government, will, on all occasions, be faithfully represented and advocated.

(4) 'That the People of this Province have, moreover, a right to expect from such Provincial administration, the exertion of their best endeavours that the Imperial authority, within its constitutional limits, shall be exercised in the manner most consistent with their well understood wishes and interests.'

Journals of Assembly, Sept. 3, 1841, vol. i, pp. 480 f.

Baldwin's original resolutions as well are given in Leacock, *Baldwin, La Fontaine, Hincks*, Makers of Canada, vol. xiv, pp. 109–10. Professor Morison, it would seem, has given Baldwin's resolutions as those of Harrison. *Op. cit.*, pp. 119–21.

regulation of the public lands . . . and lastly this District Council Bill. . . .

What do you think of this, you miserable people in England, who spend two years upon a single measure?'

The establishment of common schools, the opening of vast regions of the province to new settlement, the return of public credit, the completion of public works with the projected guarantee of £1,500,000 from Great Britain, proved in themselves, as Murdock truly observes, 'the practical and most enduring monument' of his administration. One searches in vain in this crescendo of confidence for a false note, a sense of the danger that lurked beneath the surface not only for his own administration in Canada but for Melbourne's, then tottering to its fall in Great Britain. Was he 'whistling to keep their courage up' and his own? His letters to Melbourne and to Russell still spoke the language of infallibility. 'Send out as my successor', he implored, 'some one with House of Commons and Ministerial habits,—a person who will not shrink from work, and who will govern, as I do, *himself*. Such a man—*not* a soldier, but a statesman—will find no difficulties in his path that he cannot easily surmount; for everything will be in grooves running of itself, and only requiring general direction.'[1]

It would be idle perhaps to speculate upon Sydenham's reputation in Canadian history had he remained to administer the system which he now believed to be 'perfectly stable'—whether in truth a presentiment of political disaster already clouded his mind. There can scarcely be a doubt that his days were already numbered before the fatal fall from his horse on September 4, 1841. As early as April 10 an attack of chronic gout, the tenth in little more than a year, was nearly fatal—'the doctors thought me gone'. In May it was 'not gout merely, but fever, and horrible prostration both of mind and body. *In fact I have been done by the work and the climate united*, and God knows whether I shall see the other side of the Atlantic again!' In the midst of his 'ministerial crisis' he still hoped to 'get through triumphantly; unless my *wand*, as they call it here, has lost all power over the members, which I do not believe to be the case. But the excitement and worry are more than I can stand. . . . I long for September, beyond which I will not stay if they were to make me Duke of Canada and Prince of

[1] Scrope, *op. cit.*, p. 245; *Lord Melbourne's Papers*, p. 449.

Regiopolis.' It was Bagot's opinion, derived no doubt from Murdock himself, that Sydenham's 'health would scarcely have carried him back to England.' Wakefield during the Metcalfe crisis wrote that to his knowledge three governors—Durham, Sydenham, and Bagot—had been 'literally worried to death' in the turmoil of Canadian politics; but the testimony of that wily witness was never more unsafe than in 1844.[1]

Sydenham's greatest achievements concern only indirectly the theme of these studies. He was by common consent one of the ablest administrators in Canadian history. The secret of his success he once described to his brother and biographer. 'The people know that I am ready at all hours and times to do business, and that what I have once undertaken I will carry through; so they follow my star.'[2] Indirectly his administrative reforms—his 'wand' and his 'star'—expedited responsible government by bridging the gulf between the spirited but heedless agitation of the early 'thirties and the 'practical politics' of Hincks and Morin and Macdonald. It was as a minister that he founded a dynasty in Canadian history. As a governor he was in a sense the last of his line, for his 'wand', like Prospero's, was broken when he reported at last to Lord John Russell that his task was done.[3]

Two weeks before the death of Sydenham at Kingston on September 19, 1841, the Melbourne Whigs had fallen from power in Great Britain, and the Colonial Office had passed to Lord Stanley in the Tory administration of Sir Robert Peel.

Bagot's 'Great Measure'

I

Sydenham's successor belonged to a different school. Sir Charles Bagot's training had been diplomacy rather than politics; but if politics, as Lord Morley has maintained, is 'the art of the possible', Bagot's diplomacy proved to be statesmanship of the highest order. In his letters there is nothing of Sydenham's exuberant confidence. Modesty, suavity, 'temper and sound sense', sincere goodwill combined with perfect urbanity and an insinuating address, were strange weapons for the hurly-burly of Canadian politics. Bagot

[1] Scrope, *op. cit.*, pp. 257 f. Bagot to Stanley, 'Confidential', *G. Series*, 188. 158. Kaye, *Life and Correspondence of Charles Lord Metcalfe*, London, 1854, ii. 574.

[2] Scrope, *op. cit.*, p. 255.

[3] Aug. 28, 1841, *G. Series*, 391. 317.

once wrote that he had not the 'political courage' to make one of the most fateful decisions in Canadian history in defiance of his instructions; and Stanley, like many another unwary observer, friend as well as foe, was content to take him at his word. But few could undervalue Bagot's fine spirit with impunity. When the crisis came it was Bagot who spoke the language of mastery, and his courage flashed like a rapier. He transfixed Sherwood with a single thrust. La Fontaine he manœuvred into grateful acquiescence. The redoubtable Baldwin himself he kept at sword's point. Stanley and Peel, secure in the easy assurance of authority, were disarmed, to their utter astonishment, by a veritable feat of diplomatic fence. Even before his last grim adversary, Bagot brought his bright foil up to the salute with a serene gesture of 'Victory . . . on the Side of peace and Union'.

To his friend Lord Ashburton Bagot once described one of those vain men 'who mistake the most dogged obstinacy for firmness of character'.[1] Such a mistake could never be charged to Bagot, and his diplomatic experience had included a passage at arms with the Czar of Russia, a swift stroke in Canning's best manner with the Prince of Orange at the Hague, and the Rush-Bagot convention, the prelude to a century of peace with the United States. In the opinion of Hincks—and perhaps no man of that day was in a better position to judge—this was 'the very best school' for Canadian governorship. Bagot was not like Sydenham a 'party man', and he was not like Metcalfe inclined to 'paternal despotism'. 'The secret of Sir Charles Bagot's success', adds Hincks, 'was his *strict impartiality*.' His traducers who, even at his untimely death, represented him as 'incapable of detecting any intrigue, or resisting any pretensions' were strangely ignorant of their man. There was 'not the slightest evidence in support of their assertions'.[2] Egerton Ryerson, usually a more disinterested judge of men than of measures, credited Bagot pre-eminently with 'discrimination' and 'moral courage'.

The secret in turn of this serene 'impartiality' lay perhaps in a character which Hincks could only have surmised. The sallies of wit and playfulness in the *Bagot Papers* will never lose their charm. Bagot brought to Canada, as he said, only 'sexagenary vigour' of body, but his mind, to the last recorded syllable, spoke the language of perennial youth. The most intimate of these early friends,

[1] *Bagot Papers*, v. 42.

[2] Letter (by Hincks) signed 'A Canadian' in the Montreal *Pilot*, Aug. 16, 1844.

perhaps, was Lord Haddington, First Lord of the Admiralty in Peel's administration—the 'Neptunus Britannicus' of the *Bagot Papers*, 'the God of the Seas' whose vast bulk, like the apparel of his 'Amphitrite', was 'the amazement and admiration of all the Fishes'. Wellington and Wellesley—Bagot's uncles by marriage—Wharncliffe and Clarendon and Peel himself flit through the pages of the *Bagot Papers* for 'two or three days of duck shooting' at Drayton Manor or 'a turn . . . after the pheasants among the migglebugs.'[1] And when Stanley lays aside his official instructions for the intimacies of private intercourse he turns to the language of the river for his metaphor of Canadian policy:

> 'A stream you will have to pull against, do not doubt it; but . . . bend your back to the oar like a man, and above all, take none into your crew who will not bend their backs too, and who instead of pulling with you, will either be culling crabs, or backing water when they are most wanted for "Hard all".'[2]

II

In his Canadian policy Stanley had the advantage not only of Lord John Russell's experience but of his deliberate advice and support; but as late as October, 1842, Murdock doubted how far he was 'really alive to the true state of Canada, and to the necessity of governing through the Assembly'.[3] With invincible confidence Stanley set out to govern Canada from Downing Street upon the dictates of British public opinion. What would the British public think of an accommodation with 'men tainted with violent suspicion of treasonable practices'? How could Bagot's 'Great Measure' be commended in a public dispatch, as Bagot had implored, 'without running counter to public opinion in England'? How could the Queen declare 'her especial confidence in the "loyalty" ' of M. Girouard?[4]

Stanley's policy is thus ready-made, largely by the vociferous loyalty of Colonel MacNab and the Compact. Bagot was instructed 'to consult . . . (so far as may be consistent with your duty to your Sovereign and your responsibility to her constitutional advisers) the wishes of the mass of the community':

> 'The only Passports to your favor will be Loyalty to the Queen, attachment to the British connection, and an efficient and faithful discharge of Public Duty.

[1] *Bagot Papers*, ii. 10.
[2] *Id.*, ix. 60.
[3] Clarendon to Bagot, Oct. 9, 1841, *id.*, ii. 170; *id.*, ii. 676.
[4] Stanley to Bagot, 'Private', *id.*, ix. 186 ff.

... In Civil Matters, it must be your policy to seek to with-draw the Legislature, and the population generally, from the discussion of abstract and theoretical questions . . . to the calm and dispassionate consideration of practical measures. . . . You will endeavour to avail yourself of the advice and services of the ablest men, without reference to distinctions of local party, which upon every occasion you will do your utmost to discourage.'[1]

In this it is easy to recognize the policy of Lord John Russell and much of the phraseology of Sydenham; but the private letters make it very clear who were to be 'the ablest men' with the necessary passports to favour. Colonel MacNab dined with Stanley on the Queen's birthday. He was 'well-disposed and reasonable'. 'Although I am far from wishing to reestablish the old "Family Compact" of Upper Canada', added Stanley, 'if you come into difficulties, that is the class of men to fall back upon.'[2] Even British Whig influences were suspect. Murdock, Sydenham's indefatigable secretary, had remained in Canada. Bagot found him 'nearly the best man of business I ever knew'. 'I hope he is *not* a *confidential* adviser,' remarked Stanley, and proposed as Murdock's successor Captain Higginson 'fresh from the management of all the niceties of a Colonial Legislative Body' under Sir Charles Metcalfe in Jamaica 'where he had a very difficult game to play, and a very ticklish Legislature to deal with'.[3] Metcalfe and Captain Higginson were both to play their part in Canada in due time. Meanwhile Rawson, who had served under Gladstone at the Board of Trade, was to succeed Murdock, with added responsibilities as permanent 'Chief Officer of the Executive Government next after the Governor'.[4]

Bagot brought to his task in Canada, however, one prepossession of great moment: the French-Canadians must be taken magnanimously into the Union. As early as 1838 Melbourne, whose cool and somewhat sardonic estimates of men and measures were seldom at fault, had written that the French population must be given 'its clear weight . . . according to its numbers. Swamping them, or any devices by which the real power is given to a minority, will not do in these days.'[5] Bagot had expressed the same view to

[1] Oct. 8, 1841, *G. Series*, 445. 430 ff.

[2] May 17, 1842, *Bagot Papers*, ix. 60.

[3] *Id.*, iv. 154; ix. 60.

[4] Like Sir Rupert D. George in Nova Scotia. *G. Series*, 447. 128, 'Private'. Murdock would have remained had he been offered the same terms. Murdock to Bagot, Sept. 3, 1842, *Bagot Papers*, ii. 564.

[5] To Lord John Russell, Dec. 27, 1838, *Melbourne Papers*, p. 444.

Stanley before leaving England. There was advice to the same effect from unexpected quarters. Colborne, now Lord Seaton, wrote that the French could yet be 'recovered'. '*Au fond*', urged Sir George Murray, 'they are the most anti-Yankee, as also the most Monarchical portion of the population of the Provinces.' An official of Bagot's old post at Washington wrote earnestly that the recovery of their affections was 'a matter of the deepest political and Diplomatic importance'.[1]

Advice in Canada was equally emphatic. Murdock interpreted even the Sydenham régime as the prelude to conciliation. 'No half measures can now be safely resorted to.... That involves the admission of the French to a fair share of power.' 'The overwhelming importance of gaining the confidence—and removing the distrust' of the French was urged from the first by Draper, whom Bagot considered 'the most Conservative and perhaps the ablest' of his councillors. The convictions of Hincks and of Baldwin have already been noted, but none urged the inclusion of the French-Canadians into the Executive Council more persistently than S. B. Harrison, and in the end, as we shall see, none urged it with greater effect. Bagot afterwards stated that this was 'no new opinion on the part of the Council: they had advocated it with Lord Sydenham; and when it suited his policy, he had adopted it, but unsuccessfully' by offering a seat in the Executive Council to La Fontaine.[2]

III

One of the political realities in Canada beneath the 'thin veil' of Sydenham's success became apparent from the outset. It was everywhere conceded that the government could not command a majority in the Assembly. 'It was only by dint of the greatest energy', wrote Bagot, 'and I must add the unscrupulous personal interference of Lord Sydenham, combined with practices which I would not use, and your Lordship would not recommend, in addition to the promise of the Loan and the bribe of the public Works, that Lord Sydenham managed to get through the Session.'[3]

[1] *Bagot Papers*, ii. 144 ff., 88.

[2] 'I am convinced of the soundness of the views to which you had come in this matter.... After the Rebellion the Government had the option either of crushing the French and Anglifying the Province—or of pardoning them and making them friends. But as the latter policy was adopted, it must be carried out to its legitimate consequences.' Murdock to Bagot, Sept. 3, 1842, *Bagot Papers*, ii. 564 ff.; Draper to Bagot, May 18, 1842, 'Private', *id.*, ii. 373; Bagot to Stanley, Sept. 26, 1842, 'Confidential', *G. Series*, 188. 158.

[3] *Ibid.*

It is clear from Harrison's exhaustive analysis, to be noted presently, that two alternatives were placed before Bagot upon his arrival. One was 'to carry the French in a body with the Government;—to do which it was necessary to take in Mr. Baldwin'. To effect this, Draper with great magnanimity repeatedly tendered—and in the end, as we shall see, forced—his own resignation. But with Stanley's exhortations from the tow-path ringing in his ears this was scarcely the 'metaphorical crew' for Bagot's race at Kingston. The alternative was what Harrison called 'the principle of extension'—the old attempt to compose conflicting interests in the Assembly by including them in neutralizing proportions in the Executive Council.

Less than a month after his arrival in Canada Bagot startled Stanley by proposing Hincks as Inspector-General—the ablest financier, 'undisputably, and without any comparison, the best public accountant in the Country'. 'He is at heart radicalissimus', added Bagot, 'but he supported Sydenham's Government, and says he will support mine, and he has quarrelled with his friend Baldwin.'[1] Hincks's response, 'prompt, straightforward, and unconditional', raised him at once to a position which he never lost in Bagot's estimation. Overtures to Cartwright of the old Compact party, on the other hand, brought 'mere personalities'—nothing 'tangible, bold or statesmanlike'; and even Sherwood's final acceptance taxed Draper's most 'discreet diplomacy', and threatened, as Bagot wrote, to prove 'wormwood to Mr. Harrison, my *liberal* Colonial Secretary West'.[2] Meanwhile Bagot had appointed two French-Canadians to the bench, and had passed a month in Montreal, 'altogether the hardest I ever passed in my life (he remarked) showing my bienveillance towards them . . . thus smoothing my path hereafter'. Every attempt to disintegrate the French party by seducing individuals was abandoned: it could not win the party and would only ruin the man, who 'is then immediately in their eyes "Le Vendu"—and "Le Vendu" he remains'.[3] Such were the prospects when a confidential letter from Bagot to Harrison on July 2 drew from that cool and wary adviser a ruthless analysis which brought 'the policy of extension' down like a house of cards.

[1] *Bagot Papers*, iv. 255, 54. Hincks's name had been suggested by Sydenham a week before his death, but Draper 'in the last interview I had with him' had objected. Draper to Bagot, June 9, 1842.

[2] 'A very honest and valuable man.' Bagot to Stanley, *id.*, iv. 325 ff., 278.

[3] *Id.*, v. 22 ff.; iv. 325 ff.

Both Draper and Harrison—the right and left bowers of Bagot's council—were in agreement upon the necessity of admitting the French as a party. For Draper the advice meant his own resignation, and Bagot's tribute to Draper's magnanimity reveals the intimate sympathies between them. Harrison's personality, on the other hand, is somewhat elusive among the traditions of these eventful years. His wariness, his discretion, his conspicuous moderation, his dexterity, and above all a certain inscrutability, left him a somewhat mysterious but pervasive influence among his contemporaries.[1] The fact remains that Harrison's masterly letter of July 11 appears in substance—and much of it *verbatim*—in Bagot's first tentative project of 'the Great Measure' a fortnight later to Stanley.[2] In truth Harrison's influence is here unmistakable, and his role is nothing less than sponsor for the first demonstration of responsible government in Canada. 'The Government', he concluded, 'will be held to that doctrine whoever may form the administration.'[3]

Within a week Harrison's dispassionate analysis was confirmed by another from Draper.[4] Stanley himself had feared that 'this

[1] Even Hincks whose shrewd and somewhat cynical opinions are seldom at fault seems to have been mystified by Harrison: 'He is at heart a liberal.' 'I know he never commits himself on paper. . . . Harrison ought to tell us his intention *honestly*.' 'Harrison will be a spy & traitor in our Camp, always intriguing with weak men & trying to influence them.' 'Harrison . . . I think honest.' 'He will go no further than he can help.' 'I believe him really a liberal man.' Hincks to La Fontaine, *La Fontaine Papers*, i. 134, 161, 90, 124, 142, 110.

[2] 'Since I last wrote I have received a very sensible and proper letter from Mr. Harrison. . . . He puts aside all personal considerations, but urges strongly upon me the necessity of securing if possible, the assistance of The French as a Party—as indeed do Mr. Sullivan and Mr. Draper whom I consider as The Conservatives of My Council.' July 28, *Bagot Papers*, v. 22 ff.

[3] 'The principle of extension' had 'failed altogether'. 'It is absolutely necessary . . . to carry . . . the bulk of the French Canadian members. This moreover is nothing more than justice. . . . There is no disguising the fact that the French members possess the power of the Country. . . . The Government does not now command a majority in the House of Assembly ('the test of everything'). . . . Such will be made manifest at the very earliest period of the session. A vote of want of confidence will be brought forward and carried. . . . I who introduced and all who voted for the resolution of last session would be bound to bow to the decision of the House. . . . I do not for one moment suppose it possible to resort to the old system of Government irrespective of the views of the House of Assembly, because the consequences of such a course would be fearful in the last degree. . . . I therefore respectfully yet earnestly offer it as my advice to Your Excellency, that Mr. Baldwin and an individual of the French party, such as will answer the object, should be at once taken into the Government. . . . Not being in a situation to consult my colleagues on this point I am compelled to offer this as my individual advice.' Harrison to Bagot, 'Private and Confidential', July 11, 1842, *Bagot Papers*, ii. 412.

[4] July 16, 1842, *id.*, ii. 442.

chequering of black & white will not produce a harmonious grey'[1] —it seemed clear that the 'principle of extension' had hopelessly broken down. It stands to Bagot's credit that he was the first of British governors to reach and to act upon that conviction. His desperate attempt to convince the Colonial Office stands out in retrospect above all other incidents of the 'Great Measure' either in Canada or in Great Britain as perhaps the greatest of all Bagot's exploits in diplomacy.

IV

In one of the most intimate of his private letters Stanley had pictured Bagot 'in one of your Canadian rapids'. Never was there an apter metaphor. It was easy for Stanley at Brighton to signal 'Hard all'!—to bid Bagot stroke his crew against the stream, bending their backs to the oar like men. But the crew, responsive as they were, knew the river better than Stanley, and there is something of breathless interest in the adventure as Bagot pulls out into the current and rows for the rapids.

There is evidence that Bagot was not unprepared for the conclusions so emphatically agreed upon by Harrison and Draper.[2] But with the dispatch of July 28 one is conscious of a new sense of direction, a steadying of the nerves, a courage rising to the emergency. A few significant words had just been received in one of Haddington's most intimate letters: 'if sub rosâ as a friend I may venture to advise—I would say to you—take special care not to manifest that the course you are desired to take *at all* militates against your own judgment.'[3] The hint may supply a clue to much in the four or five inimitable dispatches in which Bagot feels his way warily towards the impending change.

In diplomacy, to be sure, Bagot was upon his own ground. The first of his virtues was a steady eye to the facts; and his letters, adroit and insinuating though they may be, depend upon hard facts for their truth and cogency. If he were to await an adverse vote in the Assembly, the majority flushed with success could make their own terms.[4] He would thus sacrifice his present councillors including four at least of the ablest men in the legislature; and such was the scarcity of ability for office that it would be impossible to

[1] April 1, 1842, *id.*, ix. 49.

[2] Cf. his letter to Stanley of July 10, concluding 'it is perplexing—infinitely perplexing.' *Id.*, iv. 325.

[3] *Id.*, ii. 348.

[4] Many of Bagot's phrases here suggest Draper's letter of July 16.

replace them. On the other hand, there was danger in the experiment of admitting Baldwin and the French as a party:

> 'I knew that I should make it in the very teeth of an almost universal feeling at home—possibly (if I were to venture to act in such a case as I should not be likely to do, upon my own opinion only) in opposition to a fixed and determined policy of your own—certainly in opposition to Lord Durham's recorded sentiments—and as certainly to Lord Sydenham's avowed practise—But I am nevertheless arriving fast at the perswasion, that the moment is come when this question must be determined one way or the other.'

To decide without Stanley's concurrence, he added, 'I have not the political courage'; for his decision 'a simple Yea or Nay would be sufficient'.[1] It is noteworthy at the same time that through Murdock and more subtly in his own letters to Stanley he hopes desperately for a free hand 'unfettered as to the course to be adopted towards the French'.[2]

But Stanley's 'simple Yea or Nay' reached Canada only after the crisis was over and 'after the power of acting upon it had passed away'. Stanley submitted Bagot's problem to Peel, and their joint deliberations were as characteristic of the old order as Bagot's were of the new. If the government party and Conservatives could not outvote 'the Radical and French Party', wrote Stanley, 'I own I fear the Union is a failure and the Canadas are gone'. Let Bagot carry on 'the game of multiplying these "Vendus" '.[3] Peel himself, wary but resolute, brought out of his treasure things new and old. Let Bagot not be disheartened by prospects of an adverse Assembly. The President of the United States and Louis Philippe in France were both contending successfully against popular majorities—'we know what George the Third did in 1783–4.' Bagot's policy must not be 'considered shabby' by the supporters of British influence: Peel little suspected that MacNab and his 'loyal party' were at that moment intriguing with the French in their own behalf. In offering their joint counsels 'in the strictest confidence' to Bagot, Stanley commended particularly 'the game of Divide et impera; and Peel's opinions are the more valuable upon this point, because he has had no inconsiderable experience in playing the game which he recommends'.[4]

[1] *Bagot Papers*, v. 22.   [2] *Id.*, ii. 564.

[3] 'I am not prepared to carry the notion of Colonial Responsible Government to such a length, and I cannot but recollect that we, as Ministers *here*, are a responsible Body, responsible to a public opinion, which in my judgement such a course would universally revolt.' Stanley to Peel, Aug. 27, 1842. *Id.*, ix. 143.

[4] *Id.*, ix. 151 ff.

V

Stanley's letter reached Kingston on September 21. The delay was a godsend, for less than a week before, Bagot had 'shot the rapids' and was already pulling with measured strokes towards the smooth water beyond.

The record of that week is a familiar story, and Bagot's incomparable letters of September 23 and 26 read like dramatic fiction. The Assembly had met on the 8th. It was clear that Baldwin, with the precision of a veteran, was massing his forces for the final assault. The tactics with Sydenham, seemingly so futile at the time, now provided the very resources of victory, for his ascendancy over La Fontaine and his followers was now irresistible. Bagot might dread the effect of Baldwin's name upon Downing Street and stipulate that he be 'brought in by the French Canadians ... to redeem their debt of gratitude to him'. But Bagot was not in the habit of blinking the facts: in his private letters it was Baldwin who was 'at the bottom of all'—'the actual and deservedly acknowledged leader of the strongest party in the House, *and in the Country*'.[1]

Two days before the Assembly met Baldwin was able to assure La Fontaine that even the Tories would 'join in a vote of want of confidence without conditions'.[2] The result both in the Assembly and upon the Executive Council would have been conclusive. On the 9th Bagot sent for La Fontaine. The negotiations which began on Saturday, the 10th, and dragged on until the following Tuesday, were charged with tension. On the 11th La Fontaine, who had been 'taken by surprise', indicated his terms—'four places in the Council, with the admission of Mr. Baldwin.' Bagot offered three, including Baldwin if 'brought in by the French Canadian party'. On the evening of the 12th the Executive Council urged Bagot to offer a generous but formal 'memorandum of terms'; otherwise 'they must resign'. But the terms stipulated pensions for two of the retiring councillors whose appointments had been of very long standing and 'non-political'. On the 13th La Fontaine 'expressed his gratitude, almost with tears in his eyes', but reported that 'Mr. Baldwin could not on principle promise to support' the pensions. At three o'clock

[1] *Id.*, v. 97; *G. Series*, 188. 158 ff. 'Confidential'. This letter was afterwards made 'Private'. *Id.*, v. 150.

[2] *La Fontaine Papers*, iii. 2.

on Tuesday Baldwin formally moved 'that confidence is not reposed in His Excellency's present advisers', and the crisis had arrived.[1]

The daring move which forced a compromise and finally effected the 'Great Measure' was a master-stroke of diplomacy. In anticipation of such a contingency Bagot's final terms to La Fontaine had not been marked 'confidential'. On Tuesday evening Bagot authorized Draper to read these terms to the Assembly, while he himself sat down to write for the mail which was then about to close, a terse note to Stanley which is almost incandescent with resolution and grim humour. There is a thrust for MacNab—'intriguing, slippery, unprincipled . . . but I shall keep faith. . . . Trust him I never will—He too has been making a Royal Speech, and it was delivered before mine—I enclose it for your amusement'.[2] There was a word of hope, too, for the French 'when They learn, as they are at this moment doing in the Assembly, How abundantly large an offer Their leaders have rejected, and the honest spirit in which that offer was made—The offer itself . . . will raise a prodigious outcry against me in certain quarters—I care not for this—morally I shall have gained by it. . . . I have no reason, even under present failure, to repent it—'[3] Diplomacy is here without gloves, and for once Bagot's fine temper is down to the naked steel. Bagot with his flashing rapier at Alwington House—Baldwin with his ponderous mace in the Assembly—little perhaps did either surmise how truly at that moment they were both vindicating the same cause.

In the Assembly Bagot's daring thrust went home: 'the effect was almost electrical.' The following morning the negotiations were renewed and finally concluded in a memorandum bearing the names of La Fontaine and Baldwin on the one side and Harrison on the other. Baldwin's motion was withdrawn and an address of 'unmixed satisfaction' with the new Cabinet (the word is Bagot's) was carried 55 to 5.[4] Difficulties disappeared as if by magic.

[1] *Journals*, Legislative Assembly, vol. ii, 1842, p. 8.

[2] A shrewd thrust at Stanley himself. The 'Royal Speech' was no doubt 'his own vaunts of loyalty and the extravagant and absurd demonstrations made to him in England. . . . Your Lordship has already some insight into his character.' *G. Series*, 188. 158 ff.

[3] 'But I have not the time to explain all this—I bespeak, till you hear from me again by the next mail, your confidence in the wisdom, and the necessity of the course that I have taken.' *Bagot Papers*, v. 97.

[4] *La Fontaine Papers*, iii. 19. *Journals*, Legislative Assembly, vol. ii, 1842, p. 23.

Thenceforth Bagot's letters are charged with deepening conviction:

'I am quite prepared to leave my justification . . . to the accounts of the success of my measure which will accompany its first announcement, and will follow it in quick succession.

I have united in my favor the mass of opinion—British as well as French—both in the House of Assembly and in the Country. . . .

Such has been my fixed perswasion founded upon the calmest and most careful observation of the State of Parties, and of the Colony since I arrived in it.—I found the Union was not completed—Sydenham had effected the fiançailles—the Marriage, as He very well knew, must be the work of His successor. . . . Upon my own responsibility I have decided—

If I have judged wrong . . . let me urge upon you the expediency of disavowing it by my public recall. . . . If on the other hand you acquiesce . . . I would ask you to give me all the assistance . . . in Your power. . . .

An Act of Amnesty . . . would effectually mark Her Majesty's adoption of my policy, and this I would most strongly recommend as a wise, and now a safe measure; and I would even solicit it, as the most acceptable mark of Her Majesty's approval.'[1]

VI

Bagot had still to reckon, however, with the minority in Canada and with Tory opinion in Great Britain.

In Canada the fury of the old Compact party burst upon his head in torrents of abuse. 'I am a "radical"', he wrote to Stanley, 'a "puppet"—an "old woman"—an "apostate" and a "renegade descendant of Old Colonel Bagot who fell at Naseby fighting for his King".'[2] There were awkward obligations to be broken. Four of the old councillors were to vacate office. One of them—Davidson—had held his post non-politically for many years. Two were absent, and Draper's magnanimous resignation alone was voluntary. Sherwood protested against measures 'concocted and matured' during his absence: Bagot's counter was swift and deadly.[3] In truth Bagot found little magnanimity on either side. A paltry pension or two would have paved the transition to the new system, but though urged by the old Executive and advocated by Hincks this solution came to grief upon the implacable 'principle' of Robert

[1] *G. Series*, 188. 158 ff., 'Confidential' and 'Private'; *Bagot Papers*, v. 131 ff.
[2] Oct. 18, 1842, *Bagot Papers*, v. 164.
[3] *Id.*, ii. 606; v. 116.

Baldwin—a characteristic of that great reformer and of the times in Canada which stands in unpleasant contrast to Howe's magnanimity in Nova Scotia.[1]

In Great Britain the odds were more desperate, and even the incomparable dispatches of September 26, 1842, won but a tactical victory. Stanley felt comment to be 'mere guess work', and gave Bagot credit 'unfeignedly, for being a better judge how to play the game than we can be here'.[2] Their private intercourse in the *Bagot Papers* is a revelation of British public life at its best—candid, scrupulously loyal, urbane. But Bagot was left under no delusions. 'A step which must have . . . immense effects upon the future government and destinies of Canada' had been taken 'on your own responsibility, and contrary to the wishes of the Home Government.' '*We do not disapprove* your policy', wrote Stanley after the formal decision of the cabinet; 'we are prepared to support it, and defend you.' But again and again recur the 'impressions at home', appearances 'to the public eye', the 'possible effect on other Colonies'. 'To us who know the dessous des cartes, the necessity is manifest enough'; to the public it must be '*demonstrated*'. A public approval, such as Bagot had solicited, would be 'running counter to public opinion in England'. If the Union could be accepted 'as a fait accompli which in the main has secured to them good government and the power of self-government . . . it would, I own (added Stanley), go a long way to reconcile me to the course which has been pursued'.[3] In private, one may believe, the comment in England was less charitable. The Duke of Wellington expressed his opinion with the characteristic vigour of a relative and an invincible Tory: 'What a fool the man must have been . . . and what stuff and nonsense he has written! and what a bother he makes about his policy and his measures, when there are no measures but rolling himself and his country in the mire.'[4]

In the Canadian Assembly Baldwin declared his 'great principle . . . formally and solemnly recognized by the representative of the crown'; but Bagot alone perhaps was in a position to appraise the net results of his 'Great Measure'. Unlike Stanley or Baldwin,

[1] See Hincks's *Political History*, pp. 25–7.

[2] *G. Series*, 459. 343 ff.; *Bagot Papers*, vii. 211, 'Confidential'; *id.*, v. 131 ff., 'Private'. *Id.*, ix. 177 in reply to Bagot's letter 'at night' of Sept. 13.

[3] *Id.*, ix. 180, 186 ff., 'Private'.

[4] Parker, *Life of Peel*, iii. 382–3, quoted in Morison, *op. cit.*, p. 250.

Bagot had in effect a double game to play. He was between two fronts and he was fighting against them both. Upon both he was substantially successful, but his success in both instances was curiously paradoxical.

In his role of moderator between Canadian radicalism and British toryism, Bagot's tactical triumph over Baldwin was the triumph of conservatism, and no effort was spared to make it so. The bold stroke in the Assembly was characteristic. There was no vote of want of confidence, no ministerial resignation, no new government. The new ministry was a coalition, not a party Cabinet. La Fontaine was first minister in 1848, but he was a leader of a racial minority in 1842. None saw this more clearly than Hincks. 'Mr. Lafontaine, Mr. Baldwin, Mr. Morin, Mr. Aylwin and Mr. Small', he afterwards wrote, 'became members of the old Government, six members of which retained their offices and their precedence, without concessions of any kind.'[1] How far the 'Great Measure' fell short of responsible government in its final form is apparent from the views not only of Stanley but of Bagot himself. 'The keystone of my policy', he wrote, 'was to admit the French as a part of, or an addition to, my old Council, and not to reconstruct my Council with Mr. Baldwin and the French as the staple of it.'[2]

Even had Bagot lived to administer his new policy in person there is evidence that the same issues of patronage which led to the resignation of Metcalfe's ministry in 1843 were already brewing, and that a crisis was averted only by 'the precarious health of the Governor General'. Here again the stumbling-block was Baldwin's implacable 'principle'; 'I advise you', wrote La Fontaine, 'to pass it over for this time.'[3] 'Party spirit', as Hincks remarked to La Fontaine, 'is about as bitter here as in any part of the world.' There was but too much truth in Bagot's emphatic conviction that the stakes of public life were 'men and not measures'. 'The struggles in this Country—*the main questions being now decided and settled*—are not so much for principle as for a share of power and place.'[4]

[1] *Political History*, p. 27.

[2] To Stanley, Sept. 26, 1842, 'Confidential', *Bagot Papers*, viii (M. 164), 229 ff.; *G. Series*, 188. 158 ff.

[3] 'I have made this remark—That every time the Government calls you to power, to have the advantage of your talents and influence, their first acts have a tendency to destroy that very same influence with your party.' La Fontaine to Baldwin, Nov. 26, 1842, *Baldwin Papers*, i. 118.

[4] *La Fontaine Papers*, i. 47. *G. Series*, 188. 158, 'Confidential'.

It can scarcely be doubted, therefore, that a complete 'Radical' victory in September, 1842, might have precipitated this petty conflict, might have postponed a magnanimous reconciliation between the races, and above all might have led to an undiscerning but disastrous reaction in Great Britain. It is conceivable that Bagot's victory for conservatism in Canada was thus a victory in the long run for moderation, for racial concord, and for responsible government.

Perhaps Bagot's victory over British conservatism was equally paradoxical. In one sense it was a triumph for racial reconciliation and, as Bagot himself did not hesitate to assert, for responsible government. 'I am prepared', he wrote resolutely to Sherwood, 'not to start at the discharge of Artillery which will be fired against this Great Measure, and when the smoke shall have cleared away, Victory, or I am much Mistaken, will be seen to be on the Side of peace and Union.'[1] He once rebutted Baldwin 'in the presence of M. Lafontaine for having travelled so unnecessarily and irregularly out of his record' in expounding his great principle, but to Stanley he wrote bluntly that 'whether the doctrine of responsible Government is openly acknowledged, or is only tacitly acquiesced in, virtually it exists'.[2]

On the other hand Stanley made it clear that he had nothing in his original instructions to 'retract or qualify'. The Government was committed to Bagot's 'great experiment'—neatly and conclusively committed—and no neater exploit of diplomacy stands to Bagot's credit than this. But the Government was not convinced. The governor himself is still the minister, 'supreme and irresponsible except to the Home Government'. Unlike the Crown in England which 'acts avowedly and exclusively on the advice of its Ministers', he must 'exercise over them a salutary authority, and an independent controul'. It is impossible to suppose that Metcalfe's mission was not intended to be a demonstration of Stanley's advice to Bagot stiffened by reaction from the imputations of 'surrender'. And thus while Bagot's victory over Canadian radicalism may have saved responsible government—chiefly perhaps from itself—his victory over British toryism may have precipitated one of the most unpleasant disputes in Canadian history, postponing the full achievement of responsible government for nearly five years.

[1] Sept. 17, 1842, *Bagot Papers*, v. 116. [2] Oct. 18, 1842, *id.*, v. 164.

VII

The weeks from the 'Great Measure' in September to Bagot's lamented death in the following May were full of poignant experiences—of painful expectancy for the dispatches from London, of 'incessant work and anxiety of mind', of demonstrations from a grateful people perhaps the most touching in Canadian history, and of abuse, virulent even for that day, from the Canadian Tories. Through the last, Bagot's growing faith carried him serenely. The private intercourse with Stanley, too, is altogether exemplary and infinitely honourable to both—'more comfort to me', wrote Bagot, 'than you can imagine'.[1] But the scores of addresses that poured in from both sections of the province were 'oil and gladness'. As the end drew near masses were said in the churches for his recovery. Thirty-five years later Hincks wrote that no governor—not even Elgin—was held in more 'grateful remembrance by the French Canadian population'.[2] Anonymously in the *Pilot*, Hincks was still more emphatic: 'Sir Charles Bagot was I hesitate not to assert the most successful Governor, that ever administered the affairs of any British Colony enjoying representative Institutions.' 'There never was a man acted a nobler part . . . or with more consummate Statesmanship. . . . Sir Charles Bagot was a much more profound Statesman than is generally imagined.'[3]

But the same shrewd observer adds a more poignant reflection. While Sydenham and Metcalfe had their peerages, their official biographies, and all the laurels that the British government could bestow, it was 'only in Canada that Sir Charles Bagot's sterling qualities are properly appreciated'. Despite the private letters of loyal support and sympathy from Peel and Stanley, Bagot must have felt his isolation from Tory opinion in England. Even to Haddington the news of September came 'like a clap of Thunder', and he was half inclined to wish that Bagot had gone down with colours flying, '*more Anglica*'. Hincks has recorded that 'in his last sad interview with his Ministers he more than once appealed to them "to defend his memory"'.[4] In his last letter to Peel he solemnly reaffirmed his faith in his 'Great Measure': 'looking back upon my Short administration of affairs here, and looking back upon it as my last act in this world. . . . I do assure you that,

[1] *Id.*, v. 247. [2] *Political History*, p. 29.

[3] Hincks in a letter signed 'A Canadian' in the Montreal *Pilot* of Aug. 16, 1844; *id.*, May 3, 1844.

[4] *Bagot Papers*, ii. 704. Hincks, *Political History*, p. 30.

up to this period, I have found no reason to regret my course.'[1] His last official letter, written an hour before Metcalfe's arrival, was an appeal to his council to work out 'what might remain to be done gradually and temperately and in the sober spirit of a constitutional Country. . . . My reputation is in your hands, I know that you will all protect it—I am too exhausted to say more'.[2]

The Metcalfe Crisis

I

Bagot's prophecy in his last letter to Peel that his 'Great Measure' would endure, required for its fulfilment a degree of magnanimity which his own 'strict impartiality' had already gone far to inspire. The personal regard for Bagot in the private letters of La Fontaine, of Girouard, of Morin, of Hincks, of Aylwin, was more than conventional confidence; it was 'affection, esteem and respect'. 'His uniform frankness and cordiality had so won upon his Ministers', wrote Hincks, 'that there was not one of them that would not have gone the utmost length in his power to meet and forward his views.'[3] The descent from this mountain of transfiguration to one of the most sordid political struggles in Canadian history took place within the space of eight months, and there was not a reputation on either side which did not suffer in the process.

It is not easy to approach Metcalfe's administration in Canada with an open mind. The fulsome pages of his official biographer—the antediluvian politics, the travesty upon the austere principles and character of Robert Baldwin—have left Metcalfe himself involved in the same narrow and invincible prejudices.[4] And so in

[1] *Bagot Papers*, v. 318.

[2] Bagot to Aylwin, Mar. 29, 1843, *Bagot Papers*, v. 325.

Cf. Murdock to Bagot, Oct. 18, 1842: 'I very much doubt how far Lord Stanley is really alive to the real state of Canada, and to the necessity of governing through the Assembly. . . . Will it not be the proudest satisfaction to feel that this success you have obtained not only without the support, but in spite of the discouragement of those who should have assisted you—and will it not attach the people of Canada still more firmly and generously to your Excellency to know that for their sakes you have taken on yourself this great responsibility and have braved the disapproval of your immediate Superior.' *Bagot Papers*, ii. 676 ff.

[3] *The Pilot*, Aug. 16, 1844. Cf. *La Fontaine Papers*, vol. viii, Cherrier to La Fontaine, Nov. 17, 1842; iii. 26, 30, &c. La Fontaine more than once intervened to temper the gaucheries of the Canadian press.

[4] *Life and Correspondence of Charles, Lord Metcalfe*, John William Kaye, 2 vols., Lond., 1854.

truth he was. But there is much to be said on the other side, and Kaye himself has not exaggerated Metcalfe's homely and simple virtues. No more resolute martyr to duty ever devoted to the Empire, as he conceived it, a lifetime of unremitting toil—from his departure for India at fifteen years of age, 'a prey to anxiety and dejection', to his last official appearance in Canada, in his darkened room, half-blind with cancer, volunteering to his Tory councillors to die at his post if they felt themselves unable to cope with their enemies without him.

Metcalfe came to Canada with a reputation for advanced liberalism in theory but with a genius in practice for rigid officialdom. The son of an East-India director, he had left England in 1800, and he returned to Fern Hill thirty-seven years later, the champion of honest administration at Hyderabad, the liberator of the Indian press, an administrator, as Gibbon Wakefield afterwards wrote, who appeared to love labour for its own sake. He had spurned the playing-fields at Eton, and it is on record that he spent his first week and a half in Canada without stirring from the house for exercise or relaxation. With a fortune of £100,000 he had looked forward, with a nabob's predilection, to a seat in the House of Commons, but in June, 1839, Normanby in Melbourne's administration had called upon him to undertake the government of Jamaica. His success there in conciliating an Assembly that was still resentful of Whig policy for the emancipation of the slaves—was such that Buller and Wakefield and Bagot himself regarded him as 'unicus homo' for the task in Canada.[1]

It was one of Metcalfe's infirmities however, that the kindliness and indulgence which he lavished in private life seldom graced his official intercourse. His benevolence to his intimate friends was boundless. His closest relatives—his sister Mrs. Smythe in England and the family of Captain Higginson, his secretary, who accompanied him to Canada—moved within a charmed circle of indulgent affection. Higginson himself came to be known in Canada as 'the everlasting Secretary'. But Metcalfe's public infirmities were in many respects the counterparts of his private virtues. He once described himself as 'from my infancy inclined to be a recluse'. The stiffness and reserve of his first encounter with Peel must have been characteristic.[2] His unfitness for parliamentary

[1] *La Fontaine Papers*, v. 8, 16, &c. *Bagot Papers*, iv. 295, 318, &c.
[2] Kaye, *Life*, ii. 432, 451.

life with its compromises and casual contacts was self-confessed. 'There is no chance', he wrote, 'for a man who is . . . totally disqualified to be a demagogue; shrinks like a sensitive plant from public meetings; and cannot bear to be drawn from close retirement, except by what comes in the shape of real or fancied duty to his country.' His Whig friends in England found him 'a little intractable', and reluctant to draw upon 'either the purse or the pride of the Nabob'.[1]

In Canada Metcalfe's official manner must have been unfortunate. He afterwards assured Stanley that he always took pains to suppress his 'feelings of disapprobation' against his councillors, though when the crisis came he admitted that there had always been an antipathy between them which prevented his 'sympathising with them'.[2] Long before the crisis of November, 1843, Metcalfe was popularly known in Kingston as 'Old Squaretoes'. Sullivan's name for him was 'Charles the Simple', and even Kaye admits that he was no 'tactician'. Bagot and Elgin, with that subtle alchemy in which both excelled, gave their confidence upon principle. Metcalfe did not subscribe to their principles, and his own downright honesty formed a barrier of reserve which seemed to imply a latent hostility from the outset. It was Dunn's conviction that Metcalfe was 'either stupid or cunning'. Adam Fergusson wrote to Howe in Nova Scotia of Bagot's engaging frankness: 'he knew mankind.' But at the first interview with Metcalfe he 'immediately saw his hostility' to responsible government from his '*sneering* emphasis upon the term'.[3] So much for the defects of the gubernatorial manner. Even Gibbon Wakefield whose opinions, like his quarrel with the Reformers at this time, are usually riddled with self-interest and personalities, wrote to Metcalfe's intimate friend Mangles in October, 1843, that there were 'some black clouds ahead'. Bagot's policy had proved completely successful, and the opposition had 'done little more than harp on the worn-out strings of disaffection and loyalty'. The attitude of the ministers before the country was exemplary—'no lies, no tricks, no shuffling, but many indications of honesty of purpose, to which they add a decorum and even dignity of manner, unexampled . . . in both divisions of the Province.' Metcalfe too was conscientious, single-minded, and 'as worthy of love and admiration, as you ever told me he was; but . . . the long habit of exercis-

[1] Kaye, *Life*, ii. 455, 357–8. [2] *G. Series*, 460. 111. [3] *Howe Papers*, i. 114.

ing a paternal despotism makes it difficult for him to comprehend the nature and consequences of the representative system. . . . I imagine it is this habit, combined with a strong sense of duty, which leads him to work like a slave at all sorts of matters of detail. . . . He might as well try to drink Ontario dry. . . . The faculty of quick rough-and-ready penetration—the clever attorney's faculty—has been absorbed in the nobler qualities.' Metcalfe would find it difficult to be a 'Governor of a *Parliamented* country', for no attempt 'to rule with his own hand' could possibly succeed. 'I have a profound conviction', added Wakefield, 'that such an attempt must utterly fail.'[1]

II

The province which Metcalfe had come to 'govern' was beset by tendencies still more dangerous and far less tractable. The beginnings of self-government have seldom moderated the elemental weaknesses of human nature. The crudities of Canadian politics, the turbulence of faction, the insatiable appetite for 'jobs', had grown with the hungry years of official exclusion. In urging 'the strictest impartiality' as the only safe rule for Metcalfe in Canada Bagot had conceded that nothing could be much lower or more discouraging than the character and moral standards of public life.[2] He had sought to exorcize the evil spirit by an appeal to magnanimity and 'the sober spirit of a constitutional Country'; but once the charm was broken, the evil spirit, finding the house swept and garnished, returned with seven other spirits more wicked than himself. Baldwin, the 'sea-green incorruptible' of Canadian politics, moved austerely in the rarefied atmosphere of his implacable 'principle'; but others were less squeamish, and with the deluge of Irish 'repealers' now pouring into the province, the turbulence of political life became a byword. Hincks subscribed bluntly to the principle that the distribution of patronage was one of the chief means of securing the active support of the friends of government and of weakening their opponents: 'A government that should neglect to avail itself of this power *could not long exist*.'[3] More pernicious than 'the universal thirst for

[1] Wakefield to R. D. Mangles, Oct. 11, 1843, in *A View of Sir Charles Metcalfe's Government of Canada*, by a Member of the Provincial Parliament.

[2] Bagot to Stanley, Feb. 23, 1843, *Bagot Papers*, v. 295.

[3] *The Ministerial Crisis, by a Reformer of 1836*, Kingston, 1844.

place', as Bagot called it, was the personal abusiveness of the press. Even in 1877 Hincks, who could speak with authority, stated that the public men of Metcalfe's day 'had to endure an amount of odium of which those of the present day have only a faint idea'.[1]

Many of these evils the ministers themselves were powerless to control or indeed to resist. La Fontaine, whose restraint Metcalfe himself conceded, was deluged with letters, some commending his moderation and some of a different temper. 'Je crains qu'il n'y ait parmi nous', wrote Cherrier, 'des personnes qui exigeront du Cabinet plus qu'il ne peut faire'. 'Je l'ai dit souvent,' he added, 'et je le repète, *le patronage* que vous avez à exercer sera souvent un écueuil pour vous, et cela parce que'il y a de gens trop exigeants.'[2] Worse than the embarrassment of the ministers would be the effect of faction upon the temper of British toryism. Gibbon Wakefield wrote to La Fontaine from London that there was an impression abroad of 'revolutionary or rebellious tendencies':

> 'Time is indispensable for the removal of this most false impression; and not only time, but patience and great moderation. . . . What you have most carefully to avoid is the giving of weapons to your enemies to wound you with *here*. . . . May you all bear in mind the saying of your illustrious namesake—" Patience et longueur de temps font plus que force ni que rage "! . . . It is but little more that the Imperial Government has to concede.'[3]

In such a setting, the prepossessions—both Stanley's and his own—which Metcalfe brought to Canada were charged with mischief. Kaye writes of his mission to 'rescue another colony from impending destruction'. Metcalfe himself wrote that he 'never undertook anything with so much reluctance, or so little hope of doing good'.[4] Buller and Wakefield, with a shrewd suspicion of domination from Downing Street, conveyed to Metcalfe a caution to exact 'stipulations' and 'certain powers to act'—there were 'essential steps . . . which . . . he ought to have power to take'. But this was not Metcalfe's conception of the Empire or of

[1] *Political History*, p. 35.

[2] 'Pour moi je ne craindrais rien tant que de nous voir exposés à perdre ce que nous avons gagné.' Feb. 12, 1843, *La Fontaine Papers*, vol. viii. *Id.*, Mar. 3, 1843.

[3] Jan. 2, 1843. *Id.*, v. 8 ff.

[4] *Life*, ii. 453. Metcalfe to Mangles, Jan. 22, 1843, *id.*, ii. 459. Cf. Metcalfe to Mrs. Smythe, Jan. 21, 1843: 'Never was a man dragged into public employment more against his will.' *Id.*, ii. 459.

colonial governance: 'it is impossible', he replied, 'to stipulate that they shall not control the Government of a colony'. In truth Metcalfe required no instructions from Downing Street with regard to 'the class of men to fall back upon' in Canada. It was not long before he was exhorting the Colonial Secretary himself to firmness in support of 'loyalty' against 'revolutionary opinions'.[1] The Queen's representative, he found, was required not to govern but to be a 'nullity'—merely a 'tool' in the hands of 'the Revolutionary party', distributing even the patronage of the Crown 'for the purchase of support and the confirmation and perpetuation of their own power and the reduction of that of Her Majesty's Government'. 'The men who can advance these pretensions', he added, 'must be reckless as to the consequences. . . . I therefore regard their faint profession of a desire to perpetuate their connexion of this Colony with the Mother Country, as utterly worthless.'

The inference was obvious. Majority or no majority, responsible government or no responsible government, 'the only thing certain is that I cannot yield'. 'I cannot submit, for that would be to surrender the Queen's Government into the hands of rebels, and to become myself their ignominious tool.' 'Whether my contest be with a malignant Minority, or with a Majority of the House of Assembly, or with the whole Colony run mad, my duty must be the same. I cannot surrender Her Majesty's Authority, or the supremacy of the Mother Country.'[2] There is much truth in Elgin's shrewd comment in 1852. 'The distinction', he wrote, 'between Lord Metcalfe's policy and mine is twofold. In the first place he profoundly distrusted the whole Liberal party in the province. . . . He believed its designs to be revolutionary. . . . And, secondly, he imagined that when circumstances forced the party upon him, he could check these revolutionary tendencies by manifesting his distrust of them, more especially in the matter of the distribution of patronage.'[3]

[1] *Id.*, ii, 454, 459. 'One of the difficulties . . . is want of confidence in the Firmness of Her Majesty's Government, on the part of those who have proved their desire to support Her Majesty's Authority.' 'No assurance that Her Majesty's Government will not ultimately . . . leave them to be sacrificed.' 'Distrust of the steady adherence of Her Majesty's Government.' 'Being the result of past experience, it can only be obliterated by consistent conduct of an opposite character.' Apr. 15, 1844, *G. Series*, 460. 302 ff.

[2] *Id.*, 460. 278 ff., 291 ff.; Kaye's *Life*, ii. 528, note.

[3] Elgin to Grey, Oct. 8, 1852, *Grey-Elgin Correspondence*.

III

The tragedies of history, it has been said, have frequently been the conflicts not between right and wrong but between right and right: and it may be added, between wrong and wrong. For sterling character dedicated to public duty there have been few peers of Metcalfe on the one side and Baldwin or La Fontaine on the other. It is impossible to read their intimate papers without the conviction that they were honourable men—'all honourable men'. Yet they met in Canada to impugn not only each other's motives but each other's honour, and to part in deadly enmity—an object lesson surely for more charity and magnanimity in interpreting those indefinable 'loyalties' which go to make up the British Commonwealth.

Beyond a doubt these mutual recriminations, however groundless, were made in good faith. Metcalfe is less prodigal than Head or Simcoe with such terms as 'rebel', 'republican', and 'Revolutionary party', but it is impossible to doubt his conviction that what he called 'British supremacy' was in peril. It is impossible on the other hand to discount the settled conviction in the *La Fontaine* and *Baldwin Papers*—the conviction of men whose honour survives the pestilential atmosphere of 1844 as unsullied as that of Metcalfe himself—that the governor or the governor's secretary was playing a double game by 'plotting against his ministry': that while solemnly subscribing to the resolution of September 3, 1841, he was bent upon using the patronage of the Crown on behalf of their political adversaries. La Fontaine once remarked bitterly that 'every time the Government calls you to power, to have the advantage of your talents and influence, their first acts have a tendency to destroy that very same influence with your party'.[1] As late as October 11, 1843, Wakefield himself had written of ministers 'dragged through the dirt of bearing heavy blame which they do not deserve';[2] and assuredly La Fontaine's suspicions would scarcely have been allayed had he seen some of the letters which Metcalfe was writing to Stanley within a month of his arrival in Canada. He was 'condemned ... to carry on the Government to the utter exclusion of those on whom the Mother Country

[1] To Baldwin, *Baldwin Papers*, i. 118.

[2] Wakefield to Mangles, Oct. 11, 1843, *A View of Sir Charles Metcalfe's Government*.

might confidently rely in the hour of need', and there seemed to be no remedy 'without setting at defiance the operation of responsible administration which has been introduced into this Colony'.[1]

> '*Now*, I conceive (he wrote in May), is the first time when the scheme of Responsible Government, as here construed, has come forward to be carried fully into effect in any colony. Lord Durham had no difficulty in writing at leisure in praise of Responsible Government. . . . For the greater part of (Lord Sydenham's) administration it had no existence, and was only coming into operation when he died. . . . Responsible Government, as understood by its extreme advocates, is said to be Sir Charles Bagot's policy; but . . . he had not the least intention of surrendering his power into their hands; and for the remainder of his time the contest was staved off by his illness. . . . Now comes the tug of war. . . .
>
> The sole question is, to describe it without disguise, whether the Governor shall be solely and completely a tool in the hands of the Council. . . . I must be prepared for the consequences of a rupture. . . . I cannot consent to be the tool of a party, and to proscribe all those who defended their party in the hour of need against foreign invasion and internal rebellion.'[2]

As the session approached suspicions multiplied. It is clear that the activities of Higginson—'the everlasting Secretary' who had come to Canada with a reputation for the 'management of all the niceties' of a 'ticklish Legislature' in Jamaica[3]—was deeply resented. 'It is notorious', wrote Hincks after the crisis, 'that . . . the Private Secretary has discharged more of the functions of a Minister of the Crown than any one of the really responsible

[1] Apr. 25, 1843, Kaye, *Selections from the Papers of Lord Metcalfe*, Lond., 1855, p. 407.

Cf. Metcalfe to Stanley, Apr. 24, 1843, *Life*, ii. 428: 'The Council are now spoken of by themselves and others generally as "the Ministers", "the Administration", "the Cabinet", "the Government", and so forth. Their pretensions are according to this new nomenclature. They regard themselves as a responsible Ministry.'

[2] Metcalfe to Stanley, May 12, 1843. *Life*, ii. 478 ff., 494. Cf. Metcalfe to Stanley, May 24, 1844, *G. Series*, 337 ff: 'Such a system of Government appears to me to be utterly inadmissible in a Colony . . . if for no other reason, because it might so happen that all the powers of the Government . . . might be surrendered to a disaffected Party hostile in Spirit to the Crown and the Mother Country.'

[3] Stanley to Bagot, May 17, 1842, *Bagot Papers*, ix. 60 ff. Higginson was afterwards made joint Private and Civil Secretary independent of the Legislature. *G. Series*, 460. 150.

Ministers.'[1] In May an interview between La Fontaine and Higginson was characteristically interpreted by Metcalfe to Stanley, and was recorded by La Fontaine in vastly different terms.[2] La Fontaine, it is clear, held that while the governor was not bound to accept the advice of his council, he was bound to ask it in order that they might resign if they 'did not choose to assume the responsibility of the act that the Governor wished to perform contrary to their advice'. This Metcalfe described—in terms which the Reformers read with astonishment when Stanley afterwards quoted them to the House during the crisis—as 'the complete nullification of her Majesty's Government. . . . Failing of submission to those stipulations, I am threatened with the resignation of Mr. Lafontaine.' Thus as early as May, 1843, are to be found the fixed ideas and indeed the very formulae endlessly reiterated throughout the Metcalfe crisis—the governor a 'reluctant and passive tool in the hands of a party for the purpose of proscribing their opponents', 'solely and completely a tool in the hands of the Council', 'the tool of a party . . . to proscribe all those who defended their party in the hour of need against foreign invasion and internal rebellion'. 'This question filled Metcalfe's mind', says Kaye: 'What . . . was to become of the Governor-General?'[3]

The tragedy of this was that there were more hopeful signs; though the healing of mutual confidence, to be sure, was scarcely to be wrought by men of little faith. Bagot had begged an amnesty for political offences as his only reward for the 'Great Measure'. Amnesty was granted, but its quality was strained. It was granted piecemeal and grudgingly, and not as Bagot himself most assuredly would have bestowed it, like the gentle rain from heaven. Metcalfe dutifully advocated 'entire forgetfulness of past offences against the State' as a 'healing measure in this Province', but he could not forbear adding that it was 'provoking to find that those who claim

[1] *The Ministerial Crisis, by a Reformer of 1836*, Kingston, 1844. Cf. La Fontaine to Baldwin, May 25, 1844, *Baldwin Papers*, i. 15: 'The idea of the Governor's Private Secretary intriguing with Members to defeat a Government Measure . . . !! I see nothing so revolting to the feeling of a man of honor—The fact is that the Governor, without perhaps being sensible of it, is completely under the influence of Capt. Higginson.'

[2] *Life*, ii. 493 ff.; Hincks, *Reminiscences*, Montreal, 1884, p. 93.

[3] 'At the nominal head of this Government-by-a-party in England was the wearer of a crown, who might be a child, a woman, or an imbecile old man, not expected to do, but to be—whilst at the head of this Responsible Government, or Government-by-a-party, in Canada, was one of the ablest statesmen that the mother country could send forth . . . for the post of the chief ruler of our North-American possessions.' *Life*, ii. 476, 480, 494.

amnesty for rebels and brigands, with whom to a certain extent they sympathised, are inveterate in their hostility to those who were faithful to their Sovereign and country'.[1] The death of Bagot in May, as Metcalfe himself reported, was 'lamented by all Classes . . . of this Province', but no attempt is visible to translate a common sorrow altogether unprecedented in Canada into healing for the deadly feuds of faction. The official tours of the province through which Bagot had laboured with incomparable humour in order to 'smooth my path hereafter'—'the pomps and circumstances attendant upon the great station (for such it is) of top-sawyer in these woods'—were dutifully undertaken by Metcalfe. 'I do not anticipate any particular public benefit,' he wrote, 'but something of the sort has been customary and seems to be expected, and possibly some useful information may be obtained.' Condemned to 'toil on to no purpose in the Slough of Despond', with 'no prospect of either public good or personal credit', Metcalfe prepared to meet the Assembly in September. As 'the tug of war' approached, hope failed, but duty remained. About him raged the feud between 'Tories and Family-Compact men' and 'Republicans and Rebels', 'the wars of the ins and the outs', the virulence of Orangemen and Repealers. 'I have made up my mind (he wrote) to utter failure. . . . Hope I have none, not even of escape.' 'I fear that the whole concern is rotten at the core.'[2]

IV

The long-expected crisis came on November 25. In the conflict which followed—probably the bitterest of its kind in Canadian history—the antagonists could scarcely have been more hopelessly at cross-purposes had they been dealing with completely different sets of facts.

The charges of aggression were mutual. Hincks and Girouard always maintained that Stanley had sent Metcalfe to Canada 'to overthrow Responsible Government'; and it is true that as early as May Metcalfe felt he 'must be prepared for the consequences of a rupture'.[3] Wakefield charged the Reformers with forcing the whole issue as a party manœuvre, but it must be conceded that

[1] *G. Series*, 188. 158; *id.*, 460. 47, 48, &c.; *Life*, ii. 494.

[2] Bagot to Grenville, Mar. 27, 1842, *Bagot Papers*, vol. iv; *G. Series*, 460. 40; *Life*, ii. 499, 500, 505.

[3] *Political History*, p. 29; Girouard to La Fontaine, Dec. 1, 1843, *La Fontaine Papers*, vol. viii: 'L'expression . . . des caprices d'un satrape délégué . . . Vous étiez trop vertueux!' *Life*, ii. 493.

his own letters suggest the contrary. As late as October 27 Wakefield himself had no objection to a 'Ministerial crisis . . . could I but be sure that the Governor General would pick well his ground of quarrel'. Two weeks later he wrote that 'Sir Charles will come to an open rupture with them ere long', and a fortnight later, on the very day of the crisis, he regretted that Metcalfe had had 'the opportunity of breaking with his Ministers on tenable ground, but seems to have let it slip. . . . I am unwilling to do him the bad turn of shooting the bird which I suppose him to be aiming at from behind the hedge. . . . But if he don't fire I must.'[1]

There can be no doubt also that Stanley, like Metcalfe himself, was 'prepared for the consequences of a rupture'. In a private letter which arrived only a few hours after the crisis, Stanley had shown an uncanny 'prescience of what was going on':

> 'On one point I am sure it is necessary that you should be firm—I mean in the disposal of Patronage. . . . If you let your Council take it out of your hands, they will at once strengthen a party already too compact and powerful, and tend to reduce your authority, as I doubt not they would desire, to a nullity. I believe this to be entirely in accordance with your views; and you may rely upon my support.'[2]

On the other hand it is clear that La Fontaine and Baldwin deliberately forced the issue and carried it through with complete confidence in their cause and its immediate success. Again and again Metcalfe assured Stanley that he 'always took pains to avoid' a quarrel; that he 'bore and forbore much rather than incur the evils of a rupture':

> 'Never I conceive did men act more wantonly to do mischief. Responsible Government was in full play. Politicians who came from the other Colonies were astonished at the extent to which it was carried. . . . I went along with them in the measures which they prepared to a degree which none perhaps but themselves approved. Things being in this state they suddenly make a demand of which the object is . . . the entire subserviency of Her Majesty's Government to their Party Views.
>
> Had the Leaders . . . been contented with the practical working of Responsible Government without the degradation of Her Majesty's Representative to the condition of a mere Tool in their hands the Country would not have been troubled with the present dispute. But

[1] Wakefield to Mangles, Oct. 27, Nov. 11, Nov. 25, 1843. *A View of Sir Charles Metcalfe's Government in Canada.*

[2] *Pub. Arch. Can., Metcalfe Papers,* p. 11. [Lent by the Earl of Derby, Knowsley, Lancs.]

that being their settled object they no doubt thought that the Time had arrived when by the aid of a large Majority in the Assembly they could accomplish it.'[1]

In truth the governor's obvious unpreparedness, his lack of tactical finesse, the long months of toil in reorganizing his council, and finally the sympathy which undoubtedly rallied to his support in his desperate struggle to carry on the government, all stand in contrast to the early confidence of the Reformers. 'Depend upon it', wrote Hincks, 'Upper Canada is perfectly safe. They must be begotten [*sic*] fools to think otherwise.' Dunn promised to bring Canada West against the governor 'like a clap of Thunder. . . . He must go to school again, and learn of the schoolmaster who is abroad in Canada.' 'Although an Oriental', wrote Derbishire, 'Sir Charles is not versed in the game of Chess, which requires that before making a move one should be prepared with its successor.'[2]

As it happened, the Radicals themselves might perhaps have improved their play by taking the longer view, for it was Metcalfe, as we shall see, who won the first game. Moderates like Harrison drew back and eventually dropped from the ranks. Sympathizers like Isaac Buchanan ranged themselves in open opposition, and, despite the best offices of Howe in Nova Scotia, were finally lost to the Reform party.[3] 'Cacodaemon' Wakefield, the 'arch-traitor', they affected to regard as no great loss—an egregious miscalculation belied by a whole train of Wakefield's wily strategy. But the alienation of Charles Buller was a disaster. No sounder or more pervasive influence for responsible government was to be found on either side of the Atlantic. Joseph Howe, too, in Nova Scotia, in an unguarded moment, dropped the word 'bungled'; and though he made amends handsomely in his letter to Hincks in the Montreal *Pilot*, he added that there had been 'no instance in three years' of a conflict over patronage in Nova Scotia. 'If you, having all this in practice, desire to press the theory to an inconveniently strict definition, you may be acting unwisely.'[4] 'Responsible Govern-

[1] Metcalfe to Stanley, Mar. 26, Apr. 15, 1844. *G. Series*, 460. 278 ff., 302 ff.

[2] Hincks to La Fontaine, Dec. 29, 1843; Dunn to La Fontaine, Dec. 22, 1843; Derbishire to La Fontaine, Mar. 25, 1844. *La Fontaine Papers*, i. 161 ff.; v. 22 ff.; vol. vi, &c.

[3] 'Why should you and Baldwin differ? If you and I agree, he and you ought not to be divided; and if Sir Charles Metcalfe is the man I take him for, a little tact and good temper would bring you all into line.' Howe to Buchanan, Aug. 31, 1844, *Howe Papers*, vi. 72.

[4] 'But of this the people of Canada are the legitimate judges.' *Speeches and Public Letters of Joseph Howe*, ed. Chisholm, i. 485.

ment,' he wrote to Buchanan, 'is a very simple affair—as simple as matrimony, but those husbands and wives get on the best, who respect each others' rights and say as little as possible about them.'[1] In Canada the Metcalfe crisis threw Egerton Ryerson and his responsive following into the arms of the governor, lost the bitterest election of that generation, sacrificed an overwhelming majority in the Assembly, and sent the Reformers into opposition for four years. What could have been the issue to warrant such an array of risks and political disasters?

Unfortunately the facts as well as the motives were drawn into dispute. There had been friction over three or four appointments —clerks of the peace of the Bathurst and Dalhousie districts, an aide to the governor, and rumours of the governor's favour elsewhere—though as Sullivan afterwards conceded, the actual 'appointments certainly were trifling'. On Friday, November 24, La Fontaine and Baldwin waited upon Metcalfe to demand that 'he should agree to make no appointment, and no offer of an appointment, without previously taking the advice of the Council; that the lists of Candidates should, in every instance, be laid before the Council; . . . and that the Governor General . . . should not make any appointment prejudicial to their influence'.[2] But the demand, wrote Metcalfe, 'clearly meant more than it verbally expressed'. It would have 'prostrated the Governor at their feet', reduced him to 'nullity', a 'tool' of faction. On the following day a discussion in full council 'elicited different views' of responsible government: the proposals were repeated 'over and over again', and the governor's 'refusal was each time followed by "then we must resign"'. Here at last was the tug of war; and that evening Metcalfe wrote to Stanley that with one exception the whole Executive Council had resigned.[3]

In truth the governor single-handed was no match at this sort of dialectic for the keenest minds on that particular theme anywhere to be found at that time—Baldwin with his implacable

[1] *Howe Papers*, vi. 72.

[2] Metcalfe's statement, in *Journals* of the Assembly, vol. iii, 1843, p. 182. According to Hincks, Metcalfe's system 'was calculated to destroy the political influence of the ministry, and they were compelled to . . . come to an understanding with His Excellency'. Hincks maintained that 'the Secretary should be a responsible minister', and that the lists of candidates should be deposited with him 'and not with the Private Secretary to the Governor'. *The Ministerial Crisis.*

[3] Metcalfe to Stanley, Nov. 26, 1843, *G. Series*, 460. 110; Metcalfe's draft of statement for the Assembly in *Life*, ii. 525.

'principle', La Fontaine's 'constance', the nimble shrewdness of Hincks, the wit of Sullivan. It is reasonable to suppose that Metcalfe's ingenuous arguments of Saturday claimed more than he was prepared to defend.[1] Anticipating a charge of opposing responsible government, and 'in order to counteract such an intention', he requested La Fontaine 'to put in writing the grounds of their resignation'. This was impugned by Metcalfe because it omitted the 'real grounds of their resignation'—the 'stipulation' that the 'patronage of the Crown should be surrendered to the Council for the purchase of Parliamentary support'. To Stanley, however, he observed less guardedly that La Fontaine's 'most disingenuous production' was based upon 'differences . . . which had been expressed in the freedom of conversation . . . and were therefore very unfairly used'.[2] Indeed how it was possible to avow the resolutions of 1841 with the reservations which Metcalfe habitually made to Stanley—not merely against a 'malignant Minority' but against a possible majority in the Assembly and if necessary against 'the whole Colony run mad'—is one of the marvels of logic. To La Fontaine the thing was inexplicable, and the terms applied to Metcalfe by the Reformers ranged from 'stupid' and 'simple' to 'cunning', 'hypocritical' and worse.[3] 'Bon Dieu!' exclaimed Girouard. 'Ces gens-là sont donc sourds & aveugles.'[4] Metcalfe's letters, too, official as well as private, were equally uncomplimentary. Baldwin was 'not scrupulous'; his professions of attachment to the mother country in the Reform Association were 'utterly worthless', while MacNab's 'gallant energy . . . in putting down Rebellion' deserved 'any reward that can be bestowed'. The explanations of the ex-councillors were 'gross misrepresentations'; their pretensions were 'monstrous',

[1] 'He did not disguise his opinion that these affairs would be more satisfactorily managed by and through the Governor himself, without the necessity of concord amongst the Members of the Executive Council, or obligation on their part to defend, or support in Parliament the Acts of the Governor.' La Fontaine's statement in *Journals*, vol. 3, 1843, p. 182.

[2] Metcalfe to Stanley, Nov. 26, Dec. 11, 1843, *G. Series*, 460. 110, 111.

[3] Cf. La Fontaine to Baldwin, Dec. 2, 1845, 'Private': 'Lord Metcalfe is gone!! Let his friends praise him as much as they please—But as to myself, I will always look upon him as a man who had no respect for truth, not to use a harsher word. I may forgive any thing but a lie.' *Baldwin Papers*, i. 81.

La Fontaine's personal estimates with a few conspicuous exceptions—Baldwin's 'noble character, public and private' among them—are almost uniformly uncharitable, sometimes egregiously so. Cf. *Baldwin Papers*, i. 15 ff., 24, 33, 64, 76, 90, &c.

[4] *La Fontaine Papers*, vol. viii.

and proceeded from 'inconceivable blindness or ignorance'. Metcalfe was willing to hope that La Fontaine was 'out of his Element in haranguing an Irish mob', and that Morin was not guilty of the 'grossly false' statements in the *Minerve* and the *Pilot*; but he had a different opinion of Hincks. 'Ruffianlike proceedings' would be met with firmness. The Tory press added that Hincks was a 'Villainous Liar', a 'Pennyless Vagabond', a 'Cowardly Blackguard', and a master of 'cool and steady villainy'.[1]

V

Into such a welter of vituperation the province now sank for the election of 1844. Daly who alone remained of the old executive was ill—a '*Parliamentary complaint*' one of his old colleagues uncharitably suggested—and it was necessary for Metcalfe to struggle on as best he could till the close of the session on December 9. A fortnight later Draper and Viger were added as 'a Provisional Council', and the 'staff work' of the governor's party—for so it soon came to be described—responded to new talent. 'Public Business', wrote Metcalfe in March, 'proceeds as well generally as if the Council were complete.'[2]

But the personnel of the new staff and their associates must have created consternation at Downing Street. Dunn describes the ubiquitous activity of Gibbon Wakefield 'who report says is the Governor General in fact and in deed.... He appears to have taken possession of the Public Office. I find him in and out the whole day long'.[3] Scarcely more than a year had passed since Stanley had denounced 'Cacodaemon' Wakefield to Bagot and had refused to see him in London.[4] Metcalfe's choice of French councillors, too,

[1] *G. Series*, 460. 291, 267, 365, 337, 300, 312; *Pilot*, Apr. 16, 1844.

[2] *G. Series*, 460. 126, 268 ff.

[3] Dunn to La Fontaine, Dec. 22, 1843, *La Fontaine Papers*, v. 22.

[4] Bagot, who coined the nickname, had shared Stanley's antipathies, and resented particularly the report that the 'Great Measure' was 'Cacodaemon's'. Wakefield, it seems, was prepared to 'admit the soft impeachment'. Cf. Bagot to Stanley, Sept. 26, 1842: 'Wakefield has been up here during nearly the whole period in which they (the negotiations with La Fontaine) were carrying on—but I have never seen him, or had any, the most indirect communication with him.' Oct. 12, 1842: 'He will endanger the complexion of my whole measure, and give colour to the report that, notwithstanding the scrupulous care which I took to avoid all communication whatever with him during my negotiations with the French Canadians, he was the real mover, and contriver of them all—Nothing, so far as I am concerned, can be more unfounded than such a notion.' Nov. 11, 1842: 'I wish you could contrive to keep him at home, or tell him that he is sadly wanted in Australia.' Dec. 27, 1842: 'I am rejoiced that you have resolved not to see Cacodaemon—Nothing will more effectually contradict the lie that he has been in my confidence, and that I desire to employ him—but it may be as

must have startled Downing Street. The first to be approached was Girouard[1] whose 'loyalty' Stanley himself had thought too questionable to appear in a mandamus from the Queen. Girouard had been in arms during the Papineau rising with a reward of £500 'offered and paid for his apprehension'. The appointment finally went to Viger whom Stanley had still more expressly barred because he had been 'imprisoned on a charge of treason', and was 'notoriously' wanting in loyalty and attachment to the British connexion.[2] It was September, 1844, before Metcalfe was able to announce a full Executive Council. No fewer than six candidates declined the office of Attorney-General of Lower Canada. Sherwood, Morris, and D. B. Papineau, brother of Louis Joseph himself, completed the strangest administration surely since the checkered and speckled and tesselated and whimsically dovetailed cabinet which Burke attributed to Chatham.

In the war of dialectics the Reformers were superbly armed, but the results were inconclusive. Wakefield's *Letter on the Ministerial Crisis* brought a chorus of rage from the Reformers—'Mensonge, déception, duperie, moquerie.' Viger's charges also in *La Crise Ministérielle*, that La Fontaine's public 'épice d'exposé' was a violation of their oaths of office as Executive Councillors, so far went home that La Fontaine had to apply more than once to Baldwin for precedents.[3] Egerton Ryerson barbed the accusation by citing the 'honourable and constitutional conduct of the ex-Counsellors in Nova Scotia'. Hincks, the most formidable journalist in Canadian politics, replied to Viger and the 'jugglery of Mr. Gibbon Wakefield'; and finally Sullivan and Egerton Ryerson entered the lists for mortal combat—adversaries as incongruous in their talents as Saladin and the Grand Master of the Templars.[4]

well not to affront him overly, as he is a vindictive, as well as subtle serpent, and like Col^l. Charteris—"would not give a fig for fortune if he could only get character."' *Bagot Papers*, iv. 255; v, 131, 150, 247, &c.

[1] Through Forbes. Girouard contemptuously sent Forbes's letter which was marked 'strictly *private* and *confidential*' to La Fontaine.

[2] Stanley to Bagot, Nov. 3, Apr. 1, 1842, *id.*, ix. 186, 49. Cf. Derbishire to La Fontaine, Feb. 12, 1844: 'I told him (Metcalfe) Lord Sydenham . . . was not an infallible guide as he had for instance kept Mr. Viger in gaol for 19 months.' *La Fontaine Papers*, v. 33.

[3] Girouard to La Fontaine, Dec. 1, 1843, *id.*, vol. viii; Dec. 23, 1843, Jan. 10, 1844, &c. *Baldwin Papers*, i. 52, 124, &c.

[4] *The Ministerial Crisis, by a Reformer of 1836*, Kingston, 1844. *Letters on Responsible Government*, by Legion, Examiner Office, Toronto, 1844. *Sir Charles Metcalfe Defended against the Attacks of his Late Counsellors*, British Colonist Office, Toronto, 1844.

Sullivan in the witty letters of 'Legion'—perhaps the most brilliant invective of the entire series—pierced every joint of his adversary's armour. Elgin once rated Sullivan 'a very able man, the readiest with his pen (perhaps a little too much so at times) that I ever encountered'.[1] Quarter was neither asked nor given. But much in the ruthless campaign of 1844 eludes the student of papers and pamphlets. Early signs favoured the Reformers. In April they won a by-election in Montreal, marked by bloodshed and by violence on both sides—a contest which filled many wrathful pages in Metcalfe's dispatches and drew a rejoinder from Hincks as late as 1877.[2] During the summer La Fontaine was stirred to new resentment against Metcalfe by evidences of the 'plotting against his ministers'—by further proofs of Higginson's devious activities, by Metcalfe's travesty upon the Higginson interview in the letter of May, 1843, which Stanley read to the House in the debate on the 'crisis', and by rumours of the promised Adjutant-Generalship to Sir Allan MacNab. La Fontaine little suspected that the last had been directed as early as July, 1842, by Stanley himself.[3] Metcalfe's paraphrase of the La Fontaine-Higginson interview was pronounced by Sullivan 'simply and manifestly untrue in fact. . . . Men will not patiently submit to have their meaning travestied even by Governors.'[4] The ardour of Baldwin's Reform Association was unexampled. Yet a chord was struck somewhere which vibrated into major harmony with the governor's party—a plea for 'moderation and loyalty'—and despite the evangelical rhetoric of *Sir Charles Metcalfe Defended* one is tempted to say that that chord was struck by Egerton Ryerson.

Ryerson's knowledge of constitutional law was chaotic, but he had few masters in his knowledge of human nature. Thus while Hincks and Sullivan had the cause which won in the long run, Ryerson had the case which won in 1844. Ex-councillors who habitually wrote and sometimes spoke of Sir Charles Metcalfe as 'Old Square-toes', 'the old squaw', 'the old woman', the 'old

[1] Elgin to Grey, Aug. 16, 1848, *Grey-Elgin Correspondence*.

[2] *G. Series*, 460. 312 ff; Hincks, *Political History*, pp. 34–7.

[3] Bagot determined to 'keep faith', though MacNab was 'rather damaged Goods'. *Bagot Papers*, v. 97, 150. Cf. Stanley and Hope to Bagot, July 4, 1842: 'He accepts with thanks, but with a reservation that it shall not be considered as a waiver of the great object of his ambition, which is a *Baronetcy*. . . . This is *the* object, which dangled before him will be more likely than anything to keep him quiet.' *Bagot Papers*, ix. 110 ff.

[4] *Letters on Responsible Government*, p. 80.

Hypocrite', and 'Charles the Simple', added little to their cause. Like Howe's badinage against Falkland in Nova Scotia, this disrespect brought speedy retribution. The charge that the resigning ministers by their public statements had outraged the proprieties was not dispelled by Hincks's blunt retort that they had a 'right to expect permission *to state everything necessary for their complete justification*'. Metcalfe's bearing, moreover, simplified the work of his defenders. 'I am guided', he wrote serenely to Stanley, 'by a sense of Duty which does not rest on speculation as to the issue, and would be equally imperative whatever that might be.'[1] He still played with Higginson's children, he still lavished subscriptions and hospitality, and he toiled like a galley-slave at the innumerable replies to Addresses on 'the crisis'.[2] Here was a governor after Stanley's own heart, bending his back to the oar like a man.

It is easy to decry the election of 1844 as a repetition of Head's desperate tactics in 1836. But there were differences as well as analogies. There was a difference between Head with his irresponsible rhetoric and Metcalfe with his 'hard-earned and hitherto unsullied reputation'. Head, in Melbourne's sardonic phrase, was 'such a damned odd fellow'.[3] The Canadian electorate, too, it is very certain, had grown in discernment: their verdict is not lightly to be dismissed. Nor can the governor's party be said to have monopolized the 'bludgeon-men' and the devious frauds and corrupt practices of the day. Metcalfe himself admitted that there were 'Irish ready for a Row on both sides', but it is clear from his dispatches that he had not outlived his old squeamishness of the Hyderabad Residency or the borough-mongering in England. In truth some of his opponents already boasted themselves 'apt scholars' of Sydenham's methods, and no doubt were quite able to take care of themselves.[4]

But Ryerson struck two notes which grew steadily in volume. For nearly a generation the Reformers had been assailing the 'old high party exclusion and domination' of the Family Compact.

[1] *The Ministerial Crisis*, p. 8. Mar. 30, 1844, *G. Series*, 460. 291.

[2] These were drafted with his own hand. Ninety-three were published in *Addresses Presented to Sir Chas. T. Metcalfe, Bart., G.C.B. . . . on the Occasion of the Resignation of his late Advisers; with His Excellency's Replies*, 1844.

[3] 'When he went to Lord Melbourne and asked to be allowed to justify himself, all the satisfaction he received was "But you are such a damned odd fellow".' *Lord Melbourne's Papers*, p. 423, note.

[4] Apr. 13, 1844, *G. Series*, 460. 300.

What was the claim of Hincks and Sullivan to the whole patronage of the Crown for party purposes but the 'old high ultra doctrine of party exclusiveness'? The voice was the voice of Jacob but the hands were the hands of Esau. In his *Address to the Reformers of Frontenac* Hincks stated bluntly that if the governor were to make appointments 'either without or against the advice of his responsible ministers . . . all the advantages of Responsible Government are lost'. Was this then 'the essence of Responsible Government'? With less than justice to Baldwin and his 'venerated father', Ryerson appealed to the record of Joseph Howe as 'the father of Responsible Government in British North America' against the unholy sacrifice of imperial prerogatives to the 'Moloch of party'.[1] For the appointment which had precipitated the crisis—the clerkship of the peace in the Dalhousie district which had been solicited by the appointee's widowed mother—Ryerson cited 'the orphan sisters at Bethany' and 'the son of the widow of Nain'. The Canadian radicals looked for victory in less time than it took Cincinnatus to subdue the Volsci. 'Canada owes all its evils', exclaimed Ryerson, 'to immoderate counsels and extreme men'.[2]

There was a more piercing note, however, to which Ryerson's immediate followers had once already responded. Let the members of Baldwin's Reform Association remember the Constitutional Reform Association of 1834. 'What took place in 1837 was but a preface of what may be witnessed in 1847.' The debates in the British Parliament lent colour to these nameless suspicions. With the second Papineau rising less than six years away Stanley 'could understand very well to what it might lead' if the governor were to become the 'mere machine of any set of men or party in the colony'. Lord John Russell himself supported Peel in stating bluntly that the 'power of patronage . . . was believed to be . . . necessary, if the time should arrive, to maintain the connexion between the two countries'. It was left to Ryerson to point the moral: the time might come for 'placing all administrative, and judicial, and militia offices of the country in the hands of those *only* who will maintain

[1] Howe stated in his *Letter to Hincks* that there had been 'no instance in three years' of a conflict over patronage; but Ryerson might have added Howe's dictum that if patronage in Canada were distributed to satisfy 'the Parliamentary majority in England, then you had better have a respectable despotism at once, without all the troublesome and expensive machinery of a representative government.' Chisholm, *op. cit.*, i. 484.

[2] *Sir Charles Metcalfe Defended, passim.*

the constituted authorities of the Empire'. Here was a reason with a vengeance for making Sir Allan MacNab Adjutant-General of the Canadian militia! Between these two desperate conceptions of patronage—the one as the tonic of party government and the spoils of faction, the other as the equally desperate expedient of men of little faith to safeguard their miserable conception of the Empire—many an elector must have gone to the polls in November, 1844, with Ryerson's words ringing in his ears: 'Are the people of Canada prepared for such a collision?'

VI

The election of 1844 was embittered by many other issues—the feuds between 'Repealers' and Orangemen, the removal of the seat of government from Kingston to Montreal in June, 1844, Metcalfe's reservation of the *Secret Societies Bill* against the Orange order, and Baldwin's *University Bill* for secularizing higher education. The last of these Bishop Strachan pronounced atheistical and monstrous 'without a parallel in the history of the world'.[1] But in the end Metcalfe attributed his victory to the 'loyalty and British feeling . . . in Upper Canada and in the eastern townships of Lower Canada'.[2] The election of Sir Allan MacNab as Speaker of the Assembly seemed at last to assure the right 'Class of men to fall back upon'. In December Metcalfe was raised to the peerage with Stanley's best official tribute to the 'zeal, ability, and prudence' tested and approved in the arduous duties entrusted to him. To distant appearances Metcalfe's success seemed complete. 'The favour of his Sovereign, and the acknowledgements of his Country', wrote Gladstone a few months later, 'have marked his Administration as one which . . . may justly be regarded as a model by his Successors'.[3]

But disillusionment was soon to reach every interest concerned in the Metcalfe crisis. In the end it closed in about Metcalfe himself, and with the Whig administration of 1846 it finally took possession of the Colonial Office.

Metcalfe's new council contrasted but sadly with the brilliant administration which Wakefield had described to Mangles less than a year before. Draper alone had administrative talent of the first rank—a match, as Metcalfe wrote, for half-a-dozen men[4]—

[1] Quoted in Kennedy, *Constitution of Canada*, p. 242.
[2] *Life*, ii. 564.
[3] To Cathcart, Feb. 3, 1846, *G. Series*, 449. 330.
[4] *Life*, ii. 550.

but the weakness of the government was self-evident. The confidence which begets leadership is a mutual thing, honestly earned on the one side and discerningly bestowed on the other. Not one of the new councillors commanded a following in the Assembly or in the country. Metcalfe himself must have swallowed many a bitter draft in the petty manœuvring which now fell to his lot. The Assembly, including Metcalfe's 'loyal' majority, voted unanimously an Address for a general amnesty: 'one of thanks for Her Majesty's clemency', wrote Metcalfe, 'would in my opinion have been more appropriate'. When the opposition moved to reinstate the French language in the legislature, Metcalfe, in defiance of his instructions, consented to allow Papineau, his Commissioner of Crown Lands, to disarm them by moving an Address to the same end.[1] Early in September Draper in despair opened negotiations through Caron to appoint La Fontaine to the bench and to take Morin into the council. But La Fontaine recognized Sydenham's old tactics and contemptuously declined. 'The same scene', he wrote 'is on the eve of being re-enacted, or I am much mistaken.... Lord Metcalfe is the Lord Sydenham and his successor will be the Sir Charles Bagot. Come what may, I desire above every thing to remain at peace with my own convictions.'[2] No surer prophecy was ever uttered. The truth was that Metcalfe, like Sydenham, had to be his own minister; and when the fatal disease which destroyed his right eye and finally his life had vanquished all but his indomitable will, the only recourse he had to offer to his perplexed councillors was to die at his post.[3] After he left Canada the ministry began to disintegrate. Elgin afterwards reported that 'notwithstanding the issue raised by Lord Metcalfe, they used patronage for party purposes with quite as little scruple as his first council'. The time came when even MacNab conceded that the Reformers were 'far superior to this —— Ministry!' In May 1847, MacNab, was ready for a *rapprochement* with Baldwin himself.[4] It devolved upon Lord Elgin—'the Sir Charles Bagot' of La Fontaine's prophecy—to close the Metcalfe régime by the dissolution of December, 1847.

For the Reformers, too, disillusionment followed the Metcalfe crisis. There was no little truth in Wakefield's charge that Baldwin

[1] Metcalfe to Stanley, Dec. 21, 1844, *G. Series*, 460. 391; *Life*, ii. 567.

[2] Caron to La Fontaine, Sept. 7 and 8, 1845; La Fontaine to Caron, Sept. 10. *La Fontaine Papers*, vol. viii.

[3] *Life* ii, 603.

[4] La Fontaine to Baldwin, May 13, 1847. *Baldwin Papers*, i. 64 ff.

and Hincks had tied the fortunes of Lower Canada to the chariot-wheels of Upper Canadian radicalism. La Fontaine protested, but his protests were paralysed by his gratitude. There are few nobler passages in Canadian public life than the friendship between Baldwin and La Fontaine; but after the election of 1844 in which even Hincks was defeated in his own constituency and the 'party completely routed', La Fontaine could not conceal the 'feeling of general disgust' in Lower Canada:

> 'Even the best disposed', he wrote bitterly to Baldwin, 'place little reliance upon the Reformers of Upper Canada. . . . Unless you are in power they are at all times (ready) to abandon you. . . . They cannot expect that Lower Canadians will continue to injure their own interest, by fighting for their cause which they have so shamefully abandoned. . . .
>
> As to myself I sincerely hope I will never . . . be obliged to take office again. . . . It seems as if duplicity, deceit, want of sincerity, selfishness, were virtues. It gives me a poor idea of human nature.' [1]

Hincks's characteristic comment in the *Pilot* was that 'so far as Upper Canada is concerned the people richly deserve a Tory Government'.[2]

Metcalfe did not live to see the extent of his own failure, though he must have felt its approach. He had come to Canada determined to know no parties but to deal justly with all. He embittered one party implacably in trying to control it, and his only recourse in the end was to identify himself so irrevocably with another that its defeat would have forced his own retirement.[3] Hincks once contrasted the addresses of universal welcome to Metcalfe in 1843 with the mingled execrations and partisan addresses of 1844. Metcalfe found the two races in unprecedented concord—such as Sydenham had despaired of and Durham had believed for that generation impossible. He left his name associated with theirs in French Canada without the extenuating plea of necessity. If there was one passion above another which animated Metcalfe's forty-three years of public service it was his devotion to the Empire as he conceived it; but in rallying 'loyalists' against a 'revolutionary party' in Canada he risked another rebellion, and four years later his 'loyal' supporters in Montreal burnt down the parliament buildings, pelted the Queen's representative with rotten eggs, and signed a manifesto for annexation to the United

[1] Sept. 23, 1845, 'Confidential'. *Id.*, i. 76 ff. [2] Nov. 16, 1844.
[3] Metcalfe to Stanley, *Life*, ii. 571, note.

States. There are few more mendacious words, even in an epitaph, than Macaulay's lines upon Metcalfe's tomb in Winkfield Church: 'In Canada ... he reconciled contending factions to each other and to the Mother Country.'

If this must be said of Metcalfe, it was surely a tragedy that he ever came to Canada or that he did not live to try again; for in his disillusionment at the end he had almost done for himself what others had failed to do for him—convinced himself of the inevitableness of responsible government. In one sense his own party demonstrated it willy-nilly, and his own offer in 1845 to make way, if necessary, for La Fontaine and Baldwin was but a part of that demonstration. Its inevitable corollary was the policy of Grey and Elgin, for it proved, as perhaps nothing else could have proved, the truth of Buller's prophecy that 'Responsible Government would inevitably be established by the people themselves'.[1]

It is conceivable that Metcalfe might have demonstrated responsible government in a better sense had his lot, either before or after his Canadian experience, fallen elsewhere. To Joseph Howe, whose robust and unerring instinct had cast aside 'all suspicion of disloyalty ... as the product of ignorance or cupidity', it seemed that Metcalfe might have responded to 'a little tact and temper'—'a judicious friend to the principles, having the confidence of all parties, and no interest in the matter.'[2] Assuredly no governor ever had more to say categorically in support of responsible government. 'With moderate Men', he wrote to Stanley, 'I see no impossiblity in carrying on the Government ... on the principle of Responsible Government'; but with immoderate partisans who 'will not be satisfied without trampling on the Crown, and reducing the Governor to the condition of a mere Tool in their hands ... the undertaking is perfectly hopeless.'[3] There may have been much truth in Wakefield's shrewd remark that Metcalfe, accustomed from long habit to 'exercise his own mind upon everything', was 'provoked into wishing for more control than would satisfy him if they left him a reasonable share'. At one time Metcalfe himself caught a fleeting glimpse of the great arcanum that 'opposition to the Council need not be regarded as opposition to the

[1] In the debate on the *Re-Union Bill.* Cf. Grey in *Colonial Policy*, p. 206: 'The Governor, by his rupture with one party, was placed ... in the power of the other.... The danger of his position was fully understood by Lord Metcalfe.'

[2] Howe to Buchanan, Aug. 31, 1844, *Howe Papers*, vi. 72.

[3] May 24, 1844. *G. Series*, 460. 337 ff.

Governor',[1] but it fell to other men of greater faith—and it is but fair to add, with Metcalfe's bitter experience to guide them—to lead the way to a wiser policy..

ELGIN'S 'GREAT EXPERIMENT'

I

With the departure of Metcalfe in 1845 the direct influence of Canada upon the official acceptance of responsible government by the Colonial Office came to an end; for the brief period of Cathcart's governorship under Gladstone merely confirmed the false estimates of the Metcalfe régime, and before Elgin arrived in Canada in 1847 there had come a new heaven and a new earth. In July, 1846, the Whigs under Lord John Russell had come back to power in Great Britain. The Colonial Office, moreover, passed not to Lord John Russell himself with his Olympian Whig logic but to the third Earl Grey who, though a Whig, was at least unashamed of his Radical affiliations. The name of Durham was to come at last into its own. Grey himself was his brother-in-law. Elgin was his son-in-law, and Elgin's administration in Canada began in 1847 with the conviction, as he wrote to his young wife, that 'the real and effectual vindication of Lord Durham's memory and proceedings will be *the success of a Governor-General in Canada who works out his views of government fairly*'.[2] Behind Grey stood the sound and resolute support of Charles Buller and Benjamin Hawes.[3] No worthier names than these are to be found behind British colonial policy during the second Empire, for in the end their work was to transform governance into self-government, and the second Empire itself into a Commonwealth of self-governing Dominions.

Among those who contributed directly to that change, no governor, and perhaps no single individual, in the esteem of posterity, stands higher than Elgin: 'his name is almost the first.'[4] But it is clear that the new policy was shaping itself long before Elgin was

[1] *Life*, ii. 485.

[2] 'Depend upon it, if this country is governed for a few years satisfactorily Lord Durham's reputation as a statesman will be raised beyond the reach of cavil.' *Egerton and Grant*, p. 312.

[3] Jan. 3, 1844: 'I dined at Lord John Russell's. . . . Buller who sat next to me, was very reserved, and appeared to have grown into a greater man than I left him in 1842. Palmerston whispered to me afterwards that Buller and Ben Hawes entertained a project of making Howick leader of the party, or a leader of a party.' *Recollections of a Long Life*, Lord Broughton, vi. 89.

[4] Morison, *op. cit.*, p. 189.

appointed to Canada, and it had already entered upon its final phase before Elgin left England. Early in September, 1846, Buller had written to Howe of Grey's 'sound views of Colonial Policy', though the good results were not to be achieved all at once until he could 'find Governors to carry his views into effect'. Again on November 16, a week after Elgin's marriage to the daughter of Lord Durham and more than two months before his arrival in Canada, Buller wrote of 'the fullest adoption of the principles of Responsible Government' in the instructions to Sir John Harvey in Nova Scotia to 'entrust his Government to those who have the confidence of a majority of the Assembly'.[1] Harvey's instructions, adds Grey, were intended to establish 'principles of general application to all colonies having a similar form of government'. Upon this point, indeed, Grey's own record, revised by Elgin himself, must be conclusive:

> 'As Lord Elgin . . . did not leave this country . . . till the month of January, 1847, I had the opportunity of communicating with him very fully . . . with respect to the line of conduct to be pursued by him, and the means to be adopted for the purpose of bringing into full and successful operation the system of constitutional government which it seemed to be the desire of the inhabitants of British North America to have established among them. . . . The best explanation I can give of these views, and of the principles which have guided our whole policy towards the North American Colonies, will be afforded by an extract from a despatch . . . to Sir John Harvey, the Lieutenant-Governor of Nova Scotia, on the 3rd of November, 1846. . . .
>
> The despatch . . . was communicated to Lord Elgin previously to his proceeding to Canada; and, in conformity with the principles there laid down, it was his object . . . to withdraw from the position into which Lord Metcalfe had, by unfortunate circumstances, been brought . . . and to make it generally understood that, if public opinion required it, he was equally ready to accept their opponents as his advisers, uninfluenced by any personal preferences or objections.'[2]

With Grey's dispatch—'clear as a sunbeam'—for his guidance and with the closely knit circle at the Colonial Office staunchly behind him, one of the wisest and most gifted of men undertook

[1] *Correspondence between Joseph Howe and Charles Buller, 1845–1848*, in *Can. Hist. Rev.*, Dec. 1925, pp. 316, 320.

[2] Grey's *Colonial Policy of the Administration of Lord John Russell*, pp. 208, 209, 214.

the mission to Canada. He was barely in time, for the measure alike of Elgin's task and of his achievement was the peril from which the province was saved in 1848.

II

Elgin's name is a household word in Canada, and it seems unnecessary to dwell upon the superlative gifts of heart and head that made him, in temper and in spirit, the most prophetic figure of the Commonwealth. As a fellow-student of Gladstone who once awarded to him the palm for 'the natural gift of eloquence', he inherited something of the hard empiricism of Sir Robert Peel, the instinctive distrust of doctrinaire theories which the Peelite shared with the Benthamite Liberal of the next generation. As member of Parliament for Southampton Elgin had seconded the resolution which led to the fall of Melbourne and to Peel's premiership in 1842. He had followed Metcalfe as Stanley's appointee in Jamaica. His name was suggested for Canada by Queen Victoria herself. 'He was at that time', wrote Grey, 'personally altogether unknown to me.'[1] His appointment to Canada by a Whig administration, like Metcalfe's by the Tories, was thus a tribute alike to the man and to his mission.

In Canada Elgin's genial spirits, his reputation as 'the most effective speaker in the province', his youth and robust health, all contrasted with the elderly valetudinarianism of his predecessors. His political views were equally robust, for above all British statesmen of that generation Elgin was a man of faith; and 'faith, where it is sincere', Elgin himself was wont to say, 'is always catching'. Five years later he could boast that he had 'imparted this faith, more or less thoroughly' not only to all his Canadian ministers but to many a sceptic in England, Bagot's old friend Wharncliffe among the number.[2]

Elgin's first year in Canada was not spectacular; yet it was the key to all the rest, for without it, as he afterwards maintained, the rest would never have been possible.[3] He found his ministers 'struggling for existence Catching at straws—living from hand to mouth', and several of them 'playing rather fast and loose' with their colleagues. With candour and goodwill he advised them to meet the Assembly at once with a bold and practical programme; but 'too weak or too wanting in pluck for this . . . they smile and

[1] *Colonial Policy*, i. 207. [2] *Egerton and Grant*, p. 331.
[3] Elgin to Grey, Mar. 17, 1848, *Grey-Elgin Correspondence*.

shake their heads'. Draper had no policy to offer, he added, but to 'turn my back upon the French & to go all lengths with the exclusively British party'—to become a 'partisan Governor, at the head of a British Anti-Gallic party—a position alike repugnant to my principles & inconsistent with my Professions'.[1]

Elgin began by convincing his ministers that they might 'with perfect safety' confide their political difficulties to him—confidences which Elgin honoured even with Grey himself by indicating his ministers by their initials. With their complete approval he undertook to renew negotiations with Morin and Caron which Draper, to do him justice, had already tried in vain. In these overtures it is clear that Elgin was discharging more than a perfunctory duty. Like Bagot before him he was inclined to doubt the permanency of the 'unnatural alliance between the Baldwin & French factions'—a doubt which the closing chapter of La Fontaine's public life and indeed the whole career of John A. Macdonald went far to justify. With the concession of responsible government the instinctive conservatism of French Canada would be left free to reassert itself.[2] So careful was Elgin, however, to preserve his own 'strict impartiality' that in the end La Fontaine himself was given to understand that 'the invitation to the *French Canadians* to take office *contained no exception*'.[3]

The overtures came to nothing, for the Reformers already saw the ball 'rolling to their feet', and were prepared to bide their time. But Elgin's chief object had been achieved—'not the formation of a mixed administration . . . but to show the French that I do not distrust them'.[4] Here was the 'unsuspecting confidence' —'something to trust to'—which Burke and Chatham had invoked in vain. With equal candour Elgin turned to the reconstruction of his ministry under Sherwood and Cayley. The government weathered the session of June, 1847, by the narrowest of margins, but during these early months of his administration, long before any change in policy was openly discernible, Elgin had struck the key-note of a new Empire. He had laid the foundations

[1] *Id.*, Mar. 2, 1848; May 18, 1847, 'Secret'; Feb. 24, 1847, 'Secret'.

[2] *Id.*, Feb. 24, 1847, 'Secret'; Mar. 27, 1847, 'Secret': 'I believe that the problem of how to govern United Canada would be solved if the French would split into a Liberal & Conservative Party and join the Upper Canadian Parties bearing the corresponding names. . . . The national element would be merged in the political.'

[3] La Fontaine to Baldwin, Apr. 11, 1847, 'Private', *Baldwin Papers*, i. 70.

[4] Elgin to Grey, Apr. 26, 1847, 'Secret', *Grey-Elgin Correspondence*.

of a lasting tradition in Canada and had established with Grey himself an ascendancy hitherto unequalled in colonial administration:

> 'My course . . . is I think clear & plain. . . . I give to my Ministers all constitutional support frankly and without reserve, & the benefit of the best advice . . . that I can afford them in their difficulties. . . . I have never concealed from them that I intend to do nothing which may prevent (me) from working cordially with their Opponents. . . . That Ministers and oppositions should occasionally change places is of the very essence of our Constitutional system, & it is probably the most conservative element which it contains. By subjecting all sections of politicians in their turn to official responsibilities it obliges heated partizans to place some restraint on passion. . . . It is indispensable that the head of the Government should show that he has confidence in the loyalty of all the influential parties with which he has to deal.'
>
> 'I have always said to my advisers (he afterwards wrote) "while you continue my advisers you shall enjoy my unreserved confidence; and *en revanche*, you shall be responsible for all acts of government".'[1]

Grey's confidence in turn was given as frankly and as unreservedly to Elgin as Elgin's to his ministers. The letter quoted at length above, Grey pronounced to be 'as clear & complete an account of the proper duties of the Governor of such a Colony as it is possible to write'.[2] A month later (July 19) Grey was prepared to accept Elgin's conclusions on local issues 'from what you tell me of them' without the pretence or even the concern of understanding them in detail. In the intimacies of the *Grey-Elgin Correspondence* it became a practice to consult the requirements of their respective constituencies by suggesting to each other what to put into their official dispatches. It is clear that the 'great experiment', as Elgin called it, was to be a concerted policy. For Canada itself one rule was imperative. 'You & the Home Government', wrote Grey, 'belong to neither party & have nothing to do with their contests. . . . This principle must be completely established in order long to preserve our connection with the Colony.'[3] The rest of Elgin's administration was but the application of this principle. The first-fruits were naturally the formal concession of

[1] *Id.*, Elgin to Grey, May 27, 1847, 'Private'. Elgin to Cumming Bruce, Sept. 1852, *Egerton and Grant*, p. 333.

[2] June 16, 1847, 'Private', *Grey-Elgin Correspondence*: 'Your letter has interested me exceedingly & I most entirely concur in every word you say.'

[3] *Id.*, July 19, 1847, 'Private'.

responsible government in its final form. A second series of problems tested the efficacy of the 'great experiment' during one of the gravest crises since the American Revolution. A third served to reduce the vexed issues of 'loyalty' and the British connexion, of relations with the United States; and of self-government in Canada, to a series of practical conceptions upon which the whole subsequent history of Canada is scarcely more than a commentary.

III

The first of these, after a contest which had convulsed colonial government for twenty years, proved to be almost commonplace in its simplicity.

The formal concession of responsible government in Canada was made to a political party which Elgin, as we have seen, believed to be factitious and unnatural—an alliance which after coming into power with the largest majority in the history of the Union disintegrated within three years. 'Responsible Government', wrote Elgin, 'is the only subject on which this coincidence is alleged to exist'; and unfortunately responsible government though the greatest of issues was not a measure but a method. Beyond this there were 'half a dozen parties' dominated by all sorts of 'affections and antipathies, national, sectional and personal'. All were intent upon 'making political capital out of whatever turns up'. Public life was thus 'so occupied with personal squabbles that the bent of men's opinions on graver subjects can hardly be conjectured'. Still less adaptable was the gregarious inertia of French nationalism. The British Reformers, Elgin wrote bluntly,

> 'have at least some notion of fair play in carrying out the principles of Govt. which they advocate. But with the French generally it is far otherwise. They adopt at second hand the political dogmas of the English Liberals.... But they are unwilling to admit—I might almost say they seem incapable of comprehending—that the principles of constitutional government must be applied against them as well as for them—and whenever there appears to be a chance of things taking this turn, they revive the ancient cry of nationality, and insist on their right to have a share in the administration, not because the party with which they have chosen to connect themselves is in the ascendant, but because they represent a people of distinct origin.'[1]

In Canada, therefore, there were to be found few of those instinctive affinities which had drawn Howe and Harvey and Buller

[1] *Grey-Elgin Correspondence,* Elgin to Grey, Apr. 26, Apr. 27, May 27, June 28, 1847, 'Private & Confidential'.

together for the first responsible government in Nova Scotia. Elgin himself, with the thrifty reluctance of the true Peelite to forgo an urgent practical programme, offers the prosaic comment that 'this change of Government occurs at an inconvenient moment'. There were compensations in new talent and a strong party able to carry out its policy: 'the difficulty will be to get them to agree'.[1]

After the narrow margin of the government in the session of 1847 the news of the reform victory in Nova Scotia was interpreted as the handwriting on the wall. The word went out that the governor 'not only would take no part in the elections but would take good care that the elections should be free from government influence'. 'Is it true,' asked La Fontaine, 'and is there sincerity?'[2] In December the ministry, correctly judging the rising tide to be against them, advised a dissolution before it should be too late. With Hincks absent in Great Britain Elgin was inclined to believe a ministerial victory possible, and La Fontaine 'would have preferred another session' before a final struggle at the polls.[3] But the result was the overwhelming defeat of the government. The constituency which had defeated Hincks's every exertion in 1844 now elected him in his absence. The new house met on February 25. Morin was elected Speaker by a vote of 54 to 19. On March 3 a vote of want of confidence moved by Baldwin was carried, 54 to 20. The following day the ministers resigned in a body. On March 7 Elgin sent for La Fontaine and Baldwin:

> 'I spoke to them (he wrote) in a candid and friendly tone. Told them that I thought there was a fair prospect, if they were moderate and firm, of forming an administration deserving & enjoying the confidence of Parliament,—that they might count on all proper support and assistance from us. La Fontaine's manner, (to whom Baldwin seemed desirous to yield the first place) is naturally somewhat stiff, but he soon thawed, and our intercourse has been entirely frank & satisfactory.'

Thus quietly and without ostentation the first avowedly responsible government in Canada came into being on March 11, 1848. The comment of the British press, Elgin noted bitterly, was still 'plough written' and undiscerning, but Grey's support was all that could have been desired. 'There is no middle course', he wrote,

[1] *Id.*, Elgin to Grey, Jan. 22, 1848.

[2] La Fontaine to Baldwin, May 13, 1847, *Baldwin Papers*, i. 64.

[3] Elgin to Grey, Dec. 9, 1847, 'Private', *Grey-Elgin Correspondence*; La Fontaine to Baldwin, Oct. 29, 1847, *Baldwin Papers*, i. 126.

'between this line of policy, & that which involves in the last resort an appeal to Parliament to overrule the wishes of the Canadians.' Even if it were necessary to include Papineau himself, he added, 'in spite of his manifesto I should not object if his being included... should be insisted upon by the leaders of a party which can command a majority'.[1] Concession could scarcely go farther than this, for Papineau had returned to Canada in 1847 with a manifesto which Elgin had described as charged with republicanism, hatred of the British connexion, and distrust of responsible government. In the general elections Papineau had been returned by acclamation, and this last foray into Canadian politics was but one of the ingredients of the perilous situation which Elgin now turned to encounter as the second phase of his 'great experiment'.

IV

Walrond has applied to Elgin the praise which Melbourne once bestowed upon another famous diplomatist of his day: 'My Lords, you can never fully appreciate the merits of that great man. You can appreciate the great acts which he publicly performed; but you cannot appreciate, for you cannot know, the great mischief which he unostentatiously prevented.'[2]

In Canada as in Europe 1848 was a prodigious 'year of trial', attended, as Elgin wrote, by the most incongruous complications. Many of these were economic. Others were racial—some indigenous to Canada, and others imported with the tens of thousands of plague-stricken immigrants from Ireland during the famine. Across the border the Hunters' Lodges and the Irish Republican Union were exploiting a presidential election in order to visit the woes of Ireland upon Canada. In Canada itself, Papineau, fresh from republican agitation in France upon the eve of 'the '48', appeared like a stormy petrel above the elements of confusion.

The economic background in Canada was doubly irritating. The struggle for responsible government had presented the usual aspect of the debtor 'frontier', in the popular theory, against the credit centres of population. But the imperial approach to responsible government had also been economic, and the movement for free trade, for which Grey could boast that he had voted consistently since 1827, had wrought 'nothing less than a revolution' in the relations between Great Britain and her colonies. Thus

[1] Grey to Elgin, Feb. 22, 1848, 'Private', *Grey-Elgin Correspondence*.
[2] Walrond, *Letters and Journals of Lord Elgin*, Lond., 1872, p. 63.

those imponderables of colonial policy—the spirit and political aptitudes of Britons at home and abroad, the discerning of which has proved at all times the surest index to statesmanship—were now freed from many of the devious interests of the first Empire. Grey and Newcastle were still imperialists for free trade, but they affirmed too the benign imperialism which Burke had contemplated, directing the destinies of colonies 'as from the throne of heaven' for their own salvation.[1]

But if the repercussion of free trade upon colonial policy in Great Britain loosed the bonds of mercantilism and struck a chill through the faith of the old Empire, its effect upon the colonies themselves was doubly operative. In the first place it destroyed much of the glamour, and exposed the less creditable motives, of the old order; for if Lord John Russell, whose austere probity was beyond question, could so easily console himself for the dissolution of the Empire once it was demonstrated that it did not pay, what was to be said for the sedulous loyalty of lesser breeds when profit was openly avowed?[2] More directly still, the fiscal changes in Great Britain wrought havoc with colonial prosperity. The colonies lost their advantages in the British market. The British connexion took on a new aspect. 'Distress (wrote Grey) is usually the parent of political discontent.'

In Canada this distress was directly chargeable to the British connexion. By Peel's *Canada Corn Act* of 1843, which Grey almost alone in Great Britain had consistently opposed, wheat and flour from Canada were admitted to Great Britain at a nominal duty in consideration of a provincial duty of 3*s*. a quarter on wheat from the United States. American wheat thus poured into Canadian mills for the British market, and much of this buoyant prosperity was reflected in the politics of the Metcalfe régime. For Elgin and his 'great experiment' the conditions were exactly reversed. By the Act of 1846 the whole basis of this lucrative trade was swept away. The capital invested in Canadian mills, warehouses, docks, canals, and ship-yards, was almost destroyed. Elgin's remedy for this must be noted presently, but without redress of some sort it was clear that 'both home and foreign trade

[1] Grey's *Colonial Policy*, i. 6, 13: 'The authority of the British Crown is at this moment the most powerful instrument, under Providence, of maintaining peace and order in many extensive regions of the earth, and thereby assists in diffusing among millions of the human race, the blessings of Christianity and civilization.'

[2] Cf. Knox, *Extra Official State Papers*, ii. 54.

would be benefitted by the severance of the connexion'.[1] The crisis was not to pass, as we shall see, without a startling revulsion in the 'loyalty' of Canadian Tory vested interests, and a manifesto for annexation to the United States.

There was a second element of peril in 1848. The prosperity of frontier communities depends largely upon the steady influx of immigration. Grey himself was a convert to Gibbon Wakefield's school, and his letters are filled with projects for systematic colonization by regiments of prospective settlers to be employed in public works until fitted for pioneer conditions. More promising still was the able and constructive policy of R. B. Sullivan. But the Irish famine of 1847 deluged the province from the seaports to the western frontiers with 100,000 immigrants attended by all the horrors of disease and destitution. The quarantine stations became plague centres for the entire community. Elgin took advantage of a brief absence of Lady Elgin to 'run down to Grosse Ile and see with my own eyes'. A shipload of tenants from the Irish estates of Lord Palmerston after the closing of the quarantine stations, filled the cup of exasperation in Canada to overflowing. 'France and Ireland are in flames', wrote Elgin, 'and . . . nearly half the population of this Colony are French—nearly half of the remainder Irish. . . . The events which are succeeding each other with such dread rapidity in these two important countries, are producing a groundswell even here.' To the accompaniment of placards and public meetings it was stated that '50,000 Irish were ready to march into Canada from the United States at a moment's notice'.[2] With less than his usual composure, Elgin wrote of 'Guy Fawkes Papineau, actuated by the most malignant passions, irritated vanity, disappointed ambition, and national hatred . . . waving a lighted torch among these combustibles'. 'Lord John Russell was a deceiver and Responsible Govt. a delusion and a snare.'[3] For many weeks Elgin searched the French press in vain for a frank disavowal of Papineau's virulent propaganda. In the midst of these alarms Elgin was 'required to accept as advisers persons who were denounced very lately by the Secretary of State and the Govr. General as impracticable and disloyal'.[4] 'You will, I think, admit',

[1] Elgin to Grey, Apr. 9, 1848, 'Private', *Grey-Elgin Correspondence.*

[2] *Id.*, Elgin to Grey, April 26, 1848; July 18, 1848.

[3] *Id.*, Elgin to Grey, May 4, 1848; Jan. 22, 1848.

[4] 'In these sentiments however I have never either overtly or covertly expressed concurrence.' *Id.*, Elgin to Grey, Feb. 5, 1848.

he added three months later, 'that if we pass through this crisis without explosions, it will be . . . an encouragement to persevere in a liberal and straightforward application of Constitutional principles to Govt.' [1]

V

Elgin and Grey never doubted that the day was saved by the timely granting of responsible government. In this their own share was beyond calculation. It is on record that when Grey's dispatches to Sir John Harvey appeared in the Canadian press 'even Papineau . . . was staggered, & for a moment admitted that Perfide Albion might be sincere'.[2] But in truth Canada was saved not in London but in Montreal, for Elgin had better allies than he knew. Faultlessly as his own part had been played, it was upon Baldwin and above all upon La Fontaine—the 'rebels and republicans' of desperate Tory invective—that Elgin now fell back in the hour of need. It was Baldwin who met Papineau upon his own ground in the caucus of the party[3] and carried an Address of 'loyalty and attachment to the British connexion'. Papineau was unable to find 'in the most liberal Assembly ever elected in Canada an individual who would second his amendment'. 'If I had adopted the views which I inherited,' Elgin wrote advisedly, 'a declaration of this nature at the present time would have sounded like the blast of a trumpet through the Union.' [4]

The duel with Papineau however was fought by one of his own race and language. The crucial debate of January, 1849, was to prove that Papineau had returned to a Canada that knew not Joseph. The new constitution of the province, he cried, was 'false, tyrannical and calculated to demoralize its people'; it was 'conceived by statesmen of a narrow and malevolent genius'; its results would be 'ruinous and disastrous'. But the central figure of Canada was now La Fontaine, and there can be few incidents more climacteric in Canadian history than La Fontaine's speech, said to be the greatest of his career, vindicating in the French tongue the advantages of responsible government against 'the fluctuating constitutions of France'; vindicating also that early

[1] *Id.*, May 4, 1848.

[2] *Id.*, Elgin to Grey, Feb. 5, 1848.

[3] On March 1 to consider the Address in reply to the Speech from the Throne in which Elgin, in order to force Papineau's hand, had attributed 'the blessings of Peace' to patriotism and a 'State which is both just and powerful'. *Id.*, Elgin to Grey, Mar. 2, 1848.

[4] *Id.*, Mar. 2, Mar. 17, 1848.

prophetic insight of Hincks and Baldwin and Harrison and Bagot without which such a climax as this might have been forever impossible. In the midst of 'the astounding intelligence from Europe' Elgin had resolutely 'committed the flag of Britain to the custody of those who are supported by the large majority of the representatives and Constituencies of the Province'. For the benefit of those 'whose vocation it is to invent wrongs for Ireland', he enclosed a list of the five Irishmen, four Frenchmen, one Englishman, and two Scotsmen in his Executive Council; and one of Metcalfe's old councillors, he added, had congratulated him 'more than once on the seasonable change of administration'.[1]

In Great Britain, too, Grey quoted the presentment of the Grand Jury of Montreal: the peace and tranquillity of Canada 'dans les troubles et le feu des révolutions . . . est due à la forme de notre Gouvernement, et surtout à la sagesse, à l'habileté et à la fermeté des hommes appelés par le Représentant de notre Souverain à le faire fonctionner'. 'Nor have I any doubt whatever', he wrote to Elgin, 'that you are right in your belief that by acting on the very different policy of Lord Metcalfe (which you know I never approved) you would have got into inextricable difficulties.'[2] At the close of 'this year of trial' Elgin's deliberate conviction may be left in his own words:

> 'Looking then calmly at the state of feeling and parties both here and in the States, and at all that has occurred during the last twelve months, with the utmost desire to see things exactly as they are, I have no hesitation in expressing my conviction, that if I had failed in conveying to the leaders of the Liberal Party here . . . an impression of my perfect sincerity and fairness—if I had not (having thus prepared the ground) allowed constitutional principles to have full scope and play . . . we should by this hour either have been ignominiously expelled from Canada, or our relations with the United States would have been in a most precarious condition.'[3]

VI

Responsible government was now implanted in Canadian soil, and its future was to depend not upon nice adjustments of British policy but upon its own organic growth. It must suffice here to note

[1] *Grey-Elgin Correspondence*, Mar. 27, May 4, May 10, 1848.
[2] *Colonial Policy*, i. 216–17. Apr. 14, 1848, *Grey-Elgin Correspondence*.
[3] *Id.*, Nov. 30, 1848, 'Private'.

briefly in conclusion two or three of the transformations wrought by Elgin's 'great experiment' in the political outlook of Canada.

In the first place it broadened and transformed the whole conception of 'loyalty' and the British connexion. In Stanley's opinion 'the Canadas are gone' if the governor with the prestige of Downing Street behind him were to fail to keep 'the party of the connexion' in the ascendant.[1] Nothing could have been more fatal than this, for the party of the connexion, entrenched in place and power, relied upon Downing Street in direct proportion to their unpopularity in Canada, and they accumulated unpopularity in Canada in proportion to their reliance upon Downing Street. Now Elgin was not blind to the value of 'romantic loyalty', though he found it 'fast waning in Canada',[2] but none did more to break the old rampant Tory monopoly of it which had flourished under Head and Metcalfe. He did this not by discrediting them but by allowing them to discredit themselves; and it stands to his lasting credit that the shame which they brought upon themselves and upon Canada did not distort his outlook or deter him from winning them to a better cause.

The story of the *Rebellion Losses Bill* and the burning of the parliament buildings at Montreal is too familiar to require repetition. The Bill itself for the payment of rebellion losses in Lower Canada was based upon a unanimous address under Metcalfe. 'Having taken the measure of the late Conservative Government', wrote Elgin, 'we are proceeding to reappoint their own Commissioners . . . with instructions which place upon the Act the most restricted and loyalist construction of which the terms are susceptible! Truly if ever rebellion stood on a rickety pretense (he added) it is the Canadian Tory rebellion of 1849.'[3] The Bill had passed by overwhelming majorities, both British and French; but the Tory opposition, then 'very low in the World', exhausted every expedient 'of menace, intimidation and appeals to passion' to have 'the Metcalfe game . . . played over again', and to force the governor to a *coup d'état* as the leader of a 'loyal' party. To have reserved the Bill would have invited this conclusion. To have dissolved the House would have stultified responsible government. Grey and Elgin were in agreement from the first, and Elgin had fixed upon his course nearly two months before the Bill was presented to him

[1] Stanley to Peel, Aug. 27, 1842, *Bagot Papers*, ix. 143.
[2] Elgin to Grey, Mar. 14, 1849, *Grey-Elgin Correspondence.*
[3] *Id.*, June 17, 1849.

on April 25, 1849. When he left the House, however, 'persons of a respectable class in society, pelted the carriage with missiles which they must have brought with them for the purpose'. A mass meeting, summoned by printed notice, broke the windows of the parliament buildings while the House was in session, 'set fire to the building and burnt it to the ground'. Five days later brickbats were substituted for rotten eggs, and Elgin narrowly escaped with his life in the streets of Montreal. The Tory press alternated 'the vilest calumnies' with almost unbelievable petulance.[1] Military officers regarded the governor and his ministers as 'little better than rebels and do no small mischief by talking in that sense', while the rioters welcomed the troops, 'cheering on their approach and dispersing with "God save the Queen".'[2] *The Patriot* predicted a similar welcome for Elgin in Upper Canada. Both the Chief Justice and the Bishop were conspicuously absent from Elgin's reception in Toronto. The British League, 'furiously loyal' in the same sense, and Sir Allan MacNab's Hamilton *Spectator*—'loyal tories *pur sang*'—joined forces against the governor with the Tory commercial interests of Montreal advocating annexation to the United States.

Meanwhile British Tory opinion was 'not less unscrupulous & violent than that in Canada', and the Whigs were scarcely more hopeful for the connexion. With the death of Buller in 1848 it seemed that Grey on one side of the Atlantic and Elgin on the other were the only British statesmen who had not bowed the knee to Baal. Peel and Graham, Stanley and Gladstone, obsessed with the mechanics of colonial government, saw no interest in preserving the colonies—an opinion which Grey found prevalent in the House of Commons even 'in the highest quarters. . . . Nor do I find some members of the Cabinet free from it. . . . It is the existence of this feeling which is to me by far the most serious cause of apprehension for the future.'[3] On February 8, 1850, Lord John Russell himself made his long-awaited speech with 'the sting in the tail'—a forecast of independence which Elgin in anger and vexation deplored as 'one of that class of prophecies which work their own fulfilment'.

Elgin's rejoinder is the best known of all his published letters.

[1] 'Since I changed my Govt. no fête or Party that I have given has ever been noticed by one of them.' *Grey-Elgin Correspondence*, Nov. 1, 1849.

[2] *Id.*, June 11, Aug. 20, 1849.

[3] *Id.*, Grey to Elgin, Mar. 22, May 18, 1849.

Its most poignant passage must have gratified Grey. It turned upon the man whose protestations of loyalty Metcalfe had pronounced 'utterly worthless' but whose influence Elgin now held to be 'of more importance to the connexion than three regiments':

> 'Baldwin had Lord John's speech in his hand. He is a man of singularly placid demeanor, but . . . I never saw him so much moved. "Have you read the latter part of Lord J. Russell's speech?" he said to me. I nodded assent. "For myself," he added, "if the anticipations therein expressed prove to be well founded, my interest in public affairs is gone for ever. But is it not hard upon us while we are labouring through good and evil report, to thwart the designs of those who would dismember the Empire, that our adversaries should be informed that the difference between them and the Prime Minister of England is only one of time?" '[1]

The truth was that under responsible government both loyalty and the connexion were to be defined in Canada without 'rescripts from the Colonial Office'. For better or for worse Canada must be taken for what it was, with 'the establishment of the relation between them and the mother-country on the basis of mutual affection'. Upon this both Grey and Elgin were agreed. The old ideas of 'a Colonial Empire for the purpose of exercising dominion or dispensing patronage' or as a 'hot-bed for forcing commerce and manufactures' had been abandoned and renounced. Canada was to be retained 'neither by the golden links of protection, nor by the meshes of old-fashioned colonial office jobbing and chicane'. 'The advantages of the connexion to both parties must in future be of a very different kind.'[2] Positive influence and direction were still in order,[3] but even here the spiritual values were paramount. Grey on his side wrote of the blessings 'of Christianity and civilization', of the 'authority of the British Crown . . . at this moment the most powerful instrument under Providence, of maintaining peace and order in many extensive regions of the earth', and of moderating the excesses of faction. Elgin, too, with the eye of faith saw countervailing values in Canada. How far these values on both sides were removed from the mere mechanics of administration Elgin was prepared to demonstrate. Henceforth all provincial

[1] *Id.*, Jan. 28, Mar. 23, 1850; *Egerton and Grant*, 323 f.

[2] Elgin to Grey, Mar. 23, 1850, Nov. 8, 1849, Walrond, *op. cit.*, pp. 119, 102; Grey to Elgin, May 4, 1848, *Grey-Elgin Correspondence*.

[3] Grey, for instance, refers repeatedly to the possible necessity of disallowing 'that silliest of all silly policies, the meeting of commercial restrictions by counter restrictions'. *Grey-Elgin Correspondence*, *passim*.

parties, cliques, and interests must 'bow before the authorities of Government House, Montreal, rather than those of Downing Street'. Unlike Durham and most of the Radicals, Elgin saw it was impossible to draw 'a line of demarcation' between Imperial and provincial interests. 'I see nothing for it but that the Governors should be responsible for the share which the Imperial Government may have . . . with the liability to be recalled and disavowed.'[1] He was prepared to contemplate a time 'when it may be expedient to allow the Colonists to elect their Governors', while Great Britain should be 'represented in the Colony by an Agent. . . . If your Agent was well chosen and had a good status I am not sure but that the connexion might be kept up under such an arrangement quite as well and as profitably for England as under the present.'[2] At the same time none, then or since, has seen more clearly the vital and invaluable functions of the Crown in the practical working of responsible government. 'One thing is however indispensable (he added) to the success of this or any other system of Colonial Government. . . . You must allow them to believe that without severing the bonds which unite them to Great Britain they may attain the degree of perfection and of social and political development to which organized communities of freemen have a right to aspire.' Not without faith was this to be avowed in 1850, but Elgin, as we shall see, remained long enough in Canada to find much of this faith magnificently vindicated.

VII

A second change of vital importance owed not a little to Elgin's own robust faith in British institutions. He believed that responsible government could transform the whole pathology of relations with the United States—a distemper of British policy which was far more prevalent than many were ready to admit. The dread of annexation was scarcely less than an obsession. Grey and Elgin himself before his departure for Canada shared it, and Lord John Russell advocated a union of the British provinces that 'they might be likely to become an independent state instead of being merged in the Union'.[3]

Now Elgin was quick to see that whatever was sincere in the annexationist movement culminating in the famous manifesto of

[1] Walrond, *op. cit.*, pp. 111, 114.

[2] Elgin to Grey, Mar. 23, 1850, *Grey-Elgin Correspondence*, omitted in Walrond, *op. cit.*, p. 116, and subsequent editions of this famous letter.

[3] *Id.*, Grey to Elgin, Aug. 8, 1848.

1849 was fundamentally economic—a 'trade wind' of variable velocity. There were other ingredients—vestiges of the old idea of keeping Canada 'English even at the expense of not being British', Tory opposition to responsible government under 'rebel' auspices, and the sort of bravado which usually attends political irresponsibility. 'Whether merchants be bankrupt, stocks depreciated, roads bad, or seasons unfavourable—annexation is invoked as the remedy for all ills imaginary or real.'[1] Even the economic motives, however sincere, were not always sound. 'The political economy of Mr. Merritt', wrote Grey, 'is certainly of the lowest order.'[2]

Elgin dealt with annexation in three ways. For the 'sincere convictions' of annexationists he had economic remedies to propose—'*free navigation and reciprocity trade with the States are indispensable.*'[3] Elgin's economic gospel, culminating in the most brilliant of his diplomatic achievements, the Reciprocity Treaty of 1854, lies beyond the scope of this essay, though it may be noted that his insistence upon it invited criticism from apostolic free-traders like Grey, and that prosperity in fact did return to Canada long before it was consummated. The more flagitious aspects of annexation Elgin assailed without compunction. His ministers dismissed the militia officers, magistrates, and Q.C.s who signed the manifesto of 1849, and beyond a doubt the removal of the capital from Montreal—'this hot bed of prejudice and disaffection'—where the whole agitation was concentrated was regarded by Elgin as one of the chief factors in the speedy collapse of the movement.[4]

[1] *Id.*, Elgin to Grey, Mar. 14, 1849.

[2] Referring to a protectionist letter from Merritt to Elgin, Oct. 24, 1849. *Id.*, Nov. 30, 1849.

[3] *Id.*, Mar. 14, 1849. The repeal of the Navigation Laws was not forced through by Grey until 1849.

[4] *Id.*, *passim.* 'You find in this city I believe the most Anti-British specimens of each class of which our community consists. The Montreal French are the most Yankeefied French in the Province—the British, though furiously anti-Gallican, are, with some exceptions, the least loyal—and the commercial men the most jealous annexationists which Canada furnishes. It must, I think, do great mischief to the members who come from other parts of the Province.' (Sept. 3, 1849.) 'I believe that if we had returned (to Montreal) this complex iniquity would have worked the desired result—and that the annexation mania would have spread rapidly through U.C. . . . The removal of the seat of Govt. was absolutely necessary to keep it right.' (Oct. 25, 1849.) 'Their journals (six out of seven were anti-ministerialist) are the only authorities on Canadian affairs ever quoted either in the U. States or in England. . . . The allegation, that Canada is ruined, that the people are generally disaffected to Great Britain and that the local government is imbecile or traitorous becomes established as a truism in the Public mind.' (Nov. 1, 1849.)

But there was a third and in Elgin's opinion a more fundamental remedy. It was the demonstration of responsible government together with the removal of the seat of government from Montreal which led 'under Providence . . . to the check which the desire for annexation has received'. But for this 'the annexation cry would have run over the country like wild fire'.[1] Evidence to the same effect could be multiplied from the *Grey-Elgin Correspondence*. Stanley suggested 'amid cheers' of Tory followers that Grey 'had already established a Republic in Canada!'

> 'Now I believe, on the contrary (wrote Elgin), that it may be demonstrated that the concession of Constitutional Government has a tendency to draw the Colonists the other way. . . . It habituates the Colonists to the working of a political mechanism which is both intrinsically superior to that of the Yankees, and more unlike it than our old colonial system.[2]
>
> The faithful carrying out of the principles of constitutional Govt. is a departure from the American model, not an approximation to it. . . . Of the soundness of this view of our case I entertain no doubt whatsoever. . . . The fact is that the Yankee system is our old Colonial system with, in certain cases, the principle of popular election substituted for that of nomination by the Crown.[3]
>
> When a people have been once thoroughly accustomed to the working of such a Parliamentary system as ours, they never will consent to revert to this clumsy irresponsible mechanism.'[4]

It is unnecessary to follow Elgin into his good-humoured—and never malicious—criticism of the American system, but he once remarked that he seldom failed to carry his point; and his converts included his old colleague at Merton, Sir Edmund Head, Sir Henry Bulwer, British plenipotentiary at Washington, and Grey himself. With this sheet-anchor to windward he embarked fearlessly upon the most favourable commercial relations it was possible to get with the United States. Though not at first without misgivings, he reached finally the conviction that it was commercial restriction not commercial intercourse which generated the desire for annexation. In that sense reciprocity, far from leading to annexation was its most effective antidote.[5] In the Reciprocity

[1] *Grey-Elgin Correspondence*, Dec. 17, Dec. 10, 1849. [2] *Id.*, Dec. 17, 1850.
[3] *Id.*, Nov. 1, 1850. [4] Walrond, *op. cit.*, p. 121.
[5] This was clearly seen by both Canadian and American annexationist papers like the *Courier*, *Herald*, and *Witness* of Montreal, and the New York *Tribune*, which consistently opposed reciprocity. Cf. *Grey-Elgin Correspondence*, June 11, July 2, July 23, Nov. 8, 1849; Jan. 28, 1850, &c. 'Shrewd persons among the

Treaty of 1854 which was due in no small measure to Elgin's ceaseless advocacy with the Colonial Office and diplomatic skill at Washington he did not hesitate to carry his creed fearlessly into practice. The refinements of this theme which are later to be found in the speeches of Cartwright, Mowat, and Fielding, or in Edward Blake's masterly letter to the electors of West Durham, are not to be found in Elgin's letters; but for the fundamental faith which underlies a British Dominion on this continent—a Canadian nation with an undefended frontier and the kindliest of relations with the United States[1]—Elgin may well be numbered among the first of the major prophets. 'To render annexation by violence impossible, and by any other means as improbable as may be', he once defined as 'the polar star of my policy'. 'I have been possessed (I used the word advisedly, for I fear that most persons in England still consider it a case of *possession*) with the idea that it is possible to maintain on this soil of North America, and in the face of Republican America, British connexion and British institutions, if you give the latter freely and trustingly.'[2] Yet his popularity at Buffalo, at Boston, and at Washington, and with visiting Americans in Canada, was prodigious. Despite the over-clever pages of Oliphant it was won without malice and without chicane; and it was enhanced rather than impaired by his robust faith in his own cause.

annexationists perceive that their game is up if reciprocity is procured.' 'The annexationists are moving heaven & earth at Washington to prevent the passage of the Reciprocity Bill.' The Southern States at first opposed the Bill fearing it would lead to annexation of 'free' territory to the Union, but sounder views soon prevailed and Elgin found them his chief allies in 1854.

[1] To Grey's plaints of military expenditure for the defence of Canada Elgin once replied with a touch of impatience: 'Only one absurdity can be greater, pardon me for saying so, than the absurdity of supposing that the British Parliament will pay £200,000 for Canadian Fortifications. It is the absurdity of supposing that the Canadians will pay it themselves ... £200,000 on Defences! and against whom? Against the Yankees. Your own kindred a flourishing swaggering people who are ready to make room for you at their own table. ... You are just as little able to cope against the power of the States with 5,000 men as with 3,000.' (Dec. 17, 1849, *Grey-Elgin Correspondence*.) In a second letter of the same date Elgin with characteristic humour and goodwill referred to the United States as 'a community ... which never makes a bargain without getting at least twice as much as it gives ... a community the members of which have been within the last few weeks pouring into their multifarious places of worship to thank God that they are exempt from the ills which afflict other men.'

[2] Walrond, *op. cit.*, pp. 161, 126. Cf. Elgin to Grey, Dec. 17, 1849: 'I have deprived the advocates of annexation of every pretext which could grace or dignify rebellion ... they are compelled to put forward ... reasons which never would tempt a man to shed his blood or to risk his fortune except as a speculation.'

VIII

Responsible government was the beginning, not the completion, of self-government; and its greatest task like that of Elgin himself was the political education of the Canadian people to what he called 'national and manly morals'. The whole problem, as he saw it, was to 'carry on the war here long enough to allow the principles of Constitutional Government and the habits of mind which it engenders to take root'.[1]

A correspondent in Upper Canada told the simple truth: 'Canada has all along been its own worst enemy. Its factions have been its curse.' Elgin's own faith sometimes wavered. Extremists were 'rabid and unreasonable'. The worst phases of French nationalism and Upper Canadian radicalism were alike forbidding.[2] If one had 'no notion of fair play', the other was prone to 'plunge at once into the most reckless opposition'. Demagogism was rampant, and 'with a thousand other mutual suspicions and repulsions, it is hardly possible to touch any part of this rickety machine without bringing the whole about one's ears'.[3]

The only effective political education here was of course self-education, but the value of Elgin's example was beyond calculation. 'My business', he once said, 'is to humanize—not to harden. At that task I must labour, through obloquy and misrepresentation if needs be'.[4] His whole term in Canada was a series of object-lessons. He found the French embittered and almost proscribed. Before he left, it was his boast that 'on one point all are agreed. We must have done with this habit of abusing the French, we must live with them on terms of amity and affection. Such is the first fruit of my policy'. 'Who will venture to say', he asked in a more famous passage, 'that the last hand which waves the British flag on American ground may not be that of a French Canadian?'[5] He lived, too, to see 'symptoms of a blush rising on the cheek' of the Montreal Tories. In truth their conduct could not be contemplated without shame and without profit. Less than three years after the Montreal riots a general election took place in Canada without

[1] *Grey-Elgin Correspondence*, Nov. 1, 1850. Cf. Grey to Elgin, *id.*, May 18, 1849: 'The main object of our policy ought to be to support the hopes & courage of the Canadians until their natural advantages begin to tell.'

[2] 'Candor compels me to state that in these respects the conduct of the Anglo-Saxon portion of our M.P.P.'s contrasts most unfavourably with that of the Gallican.' *Id.*, Aug. 2, 1850.

[3] *Id.*, July 2, 1849.

[4] Walrond, *op. cit.*, p. 96.

[5] *Grey-Elgin Correspondence*, July 9, 1849; May 4, 1848.

stirring an issue on '*the connexion with England, the Union of the Canadas . . . or the Governor General*'. Elgin dined in Toronto with Morin on one side, MacNab on the other, and with Papineau among his guests. For the famous visit to Boston in 1851 Elgin was invited by 'the Montrealers . . . by an unanimous vote of the Corporation *to go* with them'.[1]

All this Elgin did not hesitate to attribute to constitutional government fearlessly and justly carried out. On at least one occasion he had 'stood literally alone'. In that sense responsible government was not a reward but a remedy. By concentrating the fury of the rioters upon himself and avoiding bloodshed he had 'left the door open', as he wrote at the time, to those who should one day say, 'he has only been carrying out fairly the principles of responsible Government'. If this, as Professor Morison has finely said, was the most heroic thing he did in Canada, his magnanimity too was heroic. He was too great a man to keep a grudge. At his farewell to Montreal in 1854 he recounted with deep emotion the memories which he expected to carry with him from Canada: 'And I shall forget—but no—what I might have had to forget is forgotten already; and therefore I cannot tell you what I shall forget.'[2] At the same time this 'moral victory', though chivalrously addressed to the highest motives of human conduct, had a less exalted faith to work upon. After the riots in Montreal he travelled unattended through Upper Canada, meeting 'the bhoys' on their own ground. A single touch of superciliousness here would spoil the picture; but it is not to be found. The truth was he had faith in this people. At Niagara he once dined 'in the presence of 6 or 700 substantial Upper Canadian Yeomen, a body of men not easily to be matched'. It was 'a glorious country'. Whether for 'knowledge of man or nature' there were materials here for 'the future of Nations'. Thus while he could not fail to see the worst, Elgin looked also for the best and found it.

No man was ever more successful in raising the level of magnanimity and public life in Canada by the simple expedient of taking men at their best. Baldwin's character too made a profound impression upon Elgin. Their relations showed 'the most sincere esteem', and though Baldwin's resignation in 1851 in disgust at his desertion by the Clear Grits on 'the chancery question' was a bad sign of the times, Elgin still believed that 'the sacrifice of

[1] *Id.*, Dec. 19, July 5, Sept. 11, 1851.
[2] *Id.*, Apr. 12, 1849; Morison, *op. cit.*, p. 227; Walrond, *op. cit.*, p. 167.

office by such a man for the sake of principle may do good'. La Fontaine was a gentleman. One of his 'excellent speeches'—on the Clergy Reserves in 1850—was 'admitted on all sides to have been one of the most able and statesmanlike ever made in the Canadian Parliament'. Lord John Russell himself suggested a baronetcy; and though La Fontaine too, like Baldwin and Sullivan, retired in disgust with the 'tracasseries of Political life', he left an abiding influence upon Canadian politics. Hincks, in Elgin's opinion, had 'more energy than all the Canadian Statesmen I have yet had to do with put together'. In the controversy with the British Treasury over the *Currency Bill* Grey himself conceded that 'Hincks has much the best of it'.[1] Here and there a commercial report, an article from the press, or a lecture which Grey had time to read, did 'infinite credit to Canada': the province stood 'very high among the nations of the world in the scale of intelligence'. With the return of prosperity the phenomenal growth of the country was in itself imposing. Assessable property in Upper Canada had more than trebled in twenty years. The population of the united province was nearly two millions and a half. Faith of a very material order was not difficult in a community like this.

Upon the personnel of parties responsible government naturally acted as a dissolvent. It had long been the fashion of governors and the Colonial Office to disparage 'party'; as though political issues did not create parties on this side of the Atlantic, and as though the most vital issue for the Commonwealth were not at that time responsible government. In truth if ever there was a party, in Burke's sense, in Canada before Confederation, united for promoting the national interest upon some particular principle upon which they were all agreed, it was the band of Irish and French and British Reformers who united in defiance of a score of minor divergencies of interest, in order to force responsible government. The danger came, as it always comes, when the 'principle' was finally vindicated. The bonds of 'party' are then dissolved, and all the latent tendencies towards 'faction' begin to reassert themselves during that critical period of flux and flow before new issues can force a realignment.

Now while Grey saw that 'the system now established in Canada is that of Party Government, that is to say government by means

[1] *Grey-Elgin Correspondence*, July 5, 1851; June 28, 1850; May 17, June 13, 1851, &c.

of parties',[1] both he and Elgin welcomed the disintegration which responsible government itself was sure to bring. The form which it took, however, was not that which Elgin and Bagot had anticipated. Both correctly foresaw that the French would be 'rescued from a false position into which they had been driven', and would become 'essentially a conservative element in the Canadian compound'; but the truth was that Canada under the Union was much too complex for clearcut policies. It was necessary to hobble forward upon the twin crutches of 'double majorities' and coalitions.[2] In 1850 Elgin had compared 'the party of which Mr. Baldwin is at the head . . . a party liberal though conservative of the Institutions of the Country', to Lord John Russell's party in Britain, beset by Radicals and held together by Tories. But as the Clear Grits gained in momentum, the old reformers themselves became conservative. La Fontaine's last great speech carried him almost into the arms of the Tories. 'Il faut jeter l'ancre de la Constitution', exclaimed Baldwin; and when he resigned in 1851 Elgin regarded him as the 'most Conservative public man in Canada'.[3] Power passed to 'practical politicians' who were not squeamish as to methods—to coalitions and 'perpetual ministerial crises' culminating in dead-lock and Confederation.

In a sense also Elgin's fine conception of his own office was transitional. The fundamental change was permanent. He was to be a 'moderator between parties, the representative of interests which are common to all . . . as distinct from those which divide them into parties'. We have seen how shrewd and kindly and wordly-wise was his advice, and how cautiously he trod the 'somewhat narrow and slippery' path between 'the *néant* of mock-sovereignty' on the one side and 'the dirt and confusion of local factions' on the other.[4] But the governor-generalship of Elgin is not that of to-day. The help which he gave to his ministers was perhaps too material to please their opponents, and it was poor comfort to know that he would have acted with equal goodwill towards themselves. Thus John A. Macdonald carried forward into Canadian politics a tradition that Elgin was more than just to

[1] *Colonial Policy*, p. 33.

[2] *Grey-Elgin Correspondence*, Aug. 2, 1850. It is interesting to note that Baldwin who had opposed the former as certain to 'perpetuate distinctions . . . and sap the foundation of political morality' (*Baldwin Papers*, i. 100) commended the second under Hincks in 1851.

[3] *Id.*, Nov. 22, Mar. 23, 1850; June 28, 1851.

[4] Walrond, *op. cit.*, p. 96. *Grey-Elgin Correspondence*, July 13, 1847.

the Reformers; and it is curious to recall that Baldwin and La Fontaine themselves had objected to the name of Buller as Metcalfe's successor because 'he would be disposed to take an active part himself, like Lord Sydenham, in our politics'.[1] Elgin was wont to say that in Jamaica he had 'not half the power I have here with my constitutional and changing Cabinet'. In 1862 he compared his powers as Governor-General of India unfavourably with the 'amount of influence which I exercised over the march of events in Canada, where I governed on strictly constitutional principles, and with a free Parliament'. It was to be 'an influence, however, wholly moral—an influence of suasion, sympathy, and moderation, which softens the temper while it elevates the aims of local politics'. As the scope of responsible government slowly broadened and deepened, this too, like the governor's relations with his Cabinet and with the Colonial Office itself, was profoundly modified. But the neutrality of the governor-general and his capacity of 'acting with such Ministers as the Constitution may impose upon him' had been 'the great Constitutional Principle' which Elgin had come to Canada to inaugurate. 'It is the practical illustration of this principle', he wrote, 'which will bring the theory of Constitutional Government in a Colony from the region of chimeras into that of facts.'[2]

[1] La Fontaine to Baldwin, July 26, 1845, *Baldwin Papers*, i. 96.

[2] Walrond, *op. cit.*, pp. 125, 126. Elgin to Grey, July 26, 1851, *Grey-Elgin Correspondence*.

VI

THE COMMONWEALTH AND ITS COROLLARIES

RESPONSIBLE government has been the most dynamic achievement of Canadian politics, and the Commonwealth may fairly be said to have begun when the principles were conceded which made it inevitable. More than a score of British provinces and Dominions have since passed from governance to self-government. Scarcely less dynamic than the change itself has been the method, for nothing has been more serviceable than this in enlarging the scope of responsible government to include all the attributes of nationhood. The resulting change from the second Empire to the Commonwealth has transformed the whole basis of its unity.

In the old province of Canada both the method and the change itself were quickly overshadowed by other issues. The decade from the MacNab-Morin administration of 1854 was filled with kaleidoscopic coalitions, all of them revolving about the axis of racial dualism. The system of 'double majorities' to include both races, was the last device of desperation. At its best it meant duplication of offices and expenditures, from 'the double-barrelled premiership' downward; at its worst it sanctioned the racial dualism and led to 'creeping paralysis and deadlock'. The escape from this 'chronic sectional hostility and discord' came only through Confederation.

This also tended to obscure both the method and the true import of responsible government. The essence of federalism is the bond which defines the relationship between the constituent provinces and the federal government; and since this, by its very nature, is a 'written' instrument, it came to be associated not only with the series of statutory 'constitutions'—the *Quebec Act*, the *Constitutional Act*, and the *Act of Union*—which had already complicated the evolution of self-government in Canada, but with a 'written constitution' like that of the United States. There has been a tendency to regard the *British North America Act* of 1867 as the 'constitution of Canada'. The conflict between federal and provincial powers in sections 91 and 92 of the Act bulks almost as large in our constitutional law as the issues of state rights in the United States. Thus Lord Bryce refers to 'the Canadian Constitution' as having been 'prepared by a group of colonial statesmen in 1864 and enacted in 1867 by a statute of the British Parliament'.[1] Dicey remarked, on one occasion, that the phrase 'a Constitution similar in principle to that of the United Kingdom' in the preamble of the *B.N.A. Act* of 1867 would be correct if instead of 'Kingdom' were written 'States'. One of the most trenchant critics of constitutional anomalies in Canada once proposed a constituent convention with parliamentary sanctions to 'draft an amended constitution',[2] upon the principle that Canada was 'given the right to govern itself by the *British North America Act* of 1867'. Others have found a transition from the second Empire to a 'third' in the Great War, or have attributed more recent developments to sudden and inscrutable impulses.

The historical approach to these tendencies leads to a very different origin and a vastly different procedure. The normal evolution from governance to self-government in the second Empire is to be sought not in the written statute but in those unwritten 'conventions' which came to govern the relations between Crown, councils, and Assemblies in the old 'royal' provinces. In that sense the most fundamental part of our constitution—both provincial and federal—is not, and never has been, 'written'. It is the result of a process which began long before the *B.N.A. Act* of 1867, and has since developed almost independently of that great measure. It is to be found in the change from Lord Russell's early conception of 'Colonial government' to that of Charles Buller and Lord Grey; and recent developments are found to be scarcely more than corollaries of principles that were vindicated seventy-five years ago. The method, too, has been distinctive; and it still remains the most useful yet devised for implementing the equality of status now conceded in theory among the nations of the British Commonwealth.

The 'Unwritten' Constitution

The method of attaining responsible government followed very naturally from the British analogy.

Nearly four centuries of parliamentary development had taken place in Great Britain before the Grand Remonstrance in 1641 demanded ministers whom 'the Parliament may have cause to confide in'. Another century and a half passed before that project was

[1] *Modern Democracies*, ii. 459.

[2] 'Just as our statesmen in 1867 drafted the British North America Act.'

achieved by empirical methods so gradual in their operation that even in the early nineteenth century they had scarcely been reduced to a body of political doctrine. Peel, as we have seen, could cite to Stanley the parliamentary tactics of Louis Philippe and the President of the United States: 'we know (he added) what George the Third did in 1783–4.'[1] It was Peel nevertheless who dictated to Queen Victoria the personnel of her ladies-in-waiting.

In the primitive Assemblies of the 'royal' provinces, this British Constitution, vital, growing, indeterminate, was veritably planted in Canadian soil. There, too, its living principles defied definition in the 'written' statute. 'You have no Act of Parliament', wrote Howe to Lord John Russell, 'to define the duty of the Sovereign when ministers are in a minority; we want none to enable us to suggest to a Governor when his advisers have lost the confidence of our colonial Assemblies.'[2] Falkland found to his dismay that the process was inevitable, and that nothing indeed but a British statute could stop it.[3] Responsible government was thus an 'unwritten' thing achieved not by Act of Parliament, British or Canadian, but by a new practice:

> 'It needs no change (wrote Durham) in the principles of government, no invention of a new constitutional theory to supply the remedy. . . . It needs but to follow out consistently the principles of the British constitution, and introduce into the Government of these great Colonies those wise provisions by which alone the working of the representative system can in any country be rendered harmonious and efficient.'
>
> 'This change might be effected by a single dispatch containing such instructions.'[4]

It remained for Durham's own brother-in-law to demonstrate this truth in the dispatch of November 3, 1846, to Sir John Harvey in Nova Scotia, enjoining, in Grey's own phrase, 'principles of general application to all colonies having a similar form of government'.[5] Under Grey's instructions the governor ceased to be, like Sydenham, the 'minister'; in time he ceased to be, like Elgin, the political mentor of his 'Cabinet'; he ceased to attend, after the

[1] Cf. Stanley to Bagot, Sept. 1, 1842: 'He has had no inconsiderable experience in playing the game which he recommends.' *Bagot Papers*, ix. 151.

[2] Chisholm, *op. cit.*, i. 613–14.

[3] See above, p. 225.

[4] *Report*, ed. Lucas, ii. 278, 280.

[5] *The Colonial Policy of the Administration of Lord John Russell*, p. 208.

manner of Sir Edmund Head, their meetings; on July 1, 1927, he ceased to correspond officially with the Dominion Office except through his responsible ministers. This position, analogous to that of the Crown in Great Britain, has also been reached not by Act of Parliament, nor by the terms of a 'written' constitution, but by usage and 'convention'.

While it is true moreover that responsible government was concerned primarily with the control of the executive, it has been the key, as Hincks and Durham saw from the outset, to the control of everything else. It has been used more than once to vindicate autonomy in legislation. To British protests against the Canadian tariff schedule of 1859, Galt replied effectively that 'Her Majesty cannot be advised to disallow such acts unless her advisers are prepared to assume the administration of the affairs of the Colony'. In truth responsible government so far tempered the legislative supremacy still vested technically in the British Parliament that critics of this anomaly are hard put to it to devise a satisfactory substitute. Nor is this the result altogether of negative virtues of restraint. For speed and flexibility, the technical supremacy of the British Parliament has proved a godsend in more than one emergency. Sir Edmund Head in his first project of a British American federation in 1854 foresaw its strategic value in escaping the wilderness of ratifications which had jeopardized the Constitution of the United States.[1] It is safe to say that the Canadian Confederation could never have been effected in its present form had it not been possible to carry the *B.N.A. Act* of 1867, as Macdonald wrote, 'per saltum'. No fewer than six amendments to the Act, moreover, have been sought by the same procedure, and the most flexible method of self-amendment hitherto projected would be initiated in the same way. If the *Colonial Laws Validity Act* and other 'vestigial anomalies' of the second Empire remain, it has been because the spirit of the Commonwealth, discernible throughout the whole era of responsible government, robbed them long since of their danger, and made forever impossible the fatal policy which stirred the first Empire to suspicion and revolt—the triple menace of imperial Acts, administered by imperial officials, and enforced in imperial courts without juries. Such has been the range of those unwritten 'conventions' by which responsible government was effected three generations ago.

[1] Head's *Draft of a Memorandum . . . sent privately to Lord Grey*, 1854, *Head Papers, Pub. Arch. Can.*

Its Scope Indeterminate

The range of powers now exercised by responsible ministers warrants a second corollary. The scope of responsible government has never been successfully defined, and indeed no attempt has ever been made to define it by legislation. The historic phrase appears in no statute. The principles of responsible government are unknown to administrative law. The 'conventions' of the system, as Lord Grey wrote in 1850, 'stand on the faith of the Crown';[1] and it may be added, on the faith of the Houses of Parliament. The range of power, both direct and indirect, claimed by responsible ministers has steadily and inexorably expanded. It will suffice to examine very briefly three or four instances of this expansion.

It is well known that Lord Durham himself, the apostle of responsible government, conceived it possible to reserve three or four spheres of government for imperial control:

> 'The constitution of the form of government,—the regulation of foreign relations, and of trade with the mother country, the other British Colonies, and foreign nations,—and the disposal of public lands, are the only points on which the mother country requires a control.'[2]

The fate of these reservations is instructive. Not one of them has survived intact, and at least one of them was still-born in the *Report* in which it was recommended. Gibbon Wakefield's project for imperial control of public lands in the interests of imperial land-settlement was incompatible with the first principles of responsible government in Canada, since it was the control of public lands, and particularly the issue of clergy reserves, which had forced the larger issue in its acutest and most convincing form. Of all the reservations conceded by Durham this was the first to go by the board. The administration of crown lands by locally responsible ministers followed as the first-fruits of responsible government.

Durham's second reservation has disappeared more slowly. The regulation of trade was an integral part of the mercantile theory under which British colonization in the early eighteenth century

[1] When the Assembly of Prince Edward Island wished to make a Civil List Bill contingent upon the granting of 'responsible government'. Grey to Bannerman, Jan. 31, 1851, *Journals*, 1851, Appendix D.

[2] It is fair to add that Durham's argument is addressed to the Melbourne Whigs who were not prepared to concede the responsibility of ministers even for local administration, and that Durham, as the context shows, does not necessarily regard these reservations as immutable in his project of responsible government.

was supposed to flourish, and the importance attached to it could be illustrated in profusion from the documents of the period. Governor Murray in Quebec was forbidden 'upon any Pretence whatever, upon pain of our highest Displeasure' to assent to 'any Law or Laws for setting up any Manufactures and carrying on any Trades, which are hurtful and prejudicial to this Kingdom'.[1] The American Revolution 'knocked the bottom out of the much-vaunted mercantile system', since it was found that trade with the independent states of America was vastly greater than trade with dependent colonies. Reciprocity was substituted for monopoly in the mercantile system, but even the abolition of the corn laws and the adoption of free trade in Britain meant 'the triumph of free trade and not of freedom'. Grey himself refused to concede the issue: 'the question . . . was nothing less than whether the Imperial Government . . . should abandon the authority it had always exercised of regulating the commercial policy of the whole Empire, and should permit every separate colony to legislate without restriction on commercial subjects. We came to the conclusion that this change could not be acquiesced in.'[2] Hincks, then Canadian Inspector-General, in introducing his budget in 1849, took the view that a differential protective tariff for Canada would be tantamount to a declaration of independence.

Ten years later imperial fiscal control was supplanted after a memorable passage at arms between the Duke of Newcastle, Secretary for the Colonies, and the Hon. A. T. Galt. Galt's tariff schedule of 1859 brought the well-known protest from the Sheffield manufacturers to the Colonial Office. Denouncing the Canadian fiscal programme as 'indecent and a reproach' to the well-considered British policy of free trade, they maintained that 'Her Majesty's Government has a right to demand that what revenue is needed shall be raised in some other way'.

Galt's memorable reply carried with it the deliberate opinion of the Canadian cabinet:

> The Government of Canada acting for its Legislature and people cannot, through those feelings of deference which they owe to the Imperial authorities, in any manner waive or diminish the right of the people of Canada to decide for themselves both as to the mode and extent to which taxation shall be imposed. . . .
>
> '. . . . Responsibility in all general questions of policy must be to

[1] *Shortt and Doughty*, i. 200.

[2] *Colonial Policy of Lord John Russell's Administration*, i. 284.

the Provincial Parliament by whose confidence they administer the affairs of the country. . . .

Her Majesty cannot be advised to disallow such Acts, unless her advisers are prepared to assume the administration of the affairs of the Colony irrespective of the views of its inhabitants.'[1]

The negotiation of trade regulations with foreign countries was more difficult to effect because Canadian ministers here encountered that veritable Cerberus of state at that time, the permanent staff of the Foreign Office. The various stages, however, from Galt's own negotiations with the French consul ('no official correspondence could take place') and the very subordinate part played by Hincks, Merritt, and Chandler in Elgin's Reciprocity Treaty with the United States, to Sir Charles Tupper's mission to France in 1893, Sir Wilfrid Laurier's in 1907, the Hon. Mr. Fielding's in 1922, and the Hon. Mr. Lapointe's to Washington in 1923, might be described by the formula already employed. Within a steadily broadening horizon of Canadian policy—a horizon bounded not by legislation but by the legitimate interests of the Canadian people—the Crown has come to act, 'in fact, if not always in form', upon the advice of Canadian ministers.

A third reservation was of course taken for granted in 1839—the control of foreign policy with its implication of defence both naval and military. The development of British provinces from comparative defencelessness to self-defence and finally to offensive warfare on no mean scale in the Great War requires little detailed illustration. The Trent affair, the defeat of the Militia Bill, the pessimism of official British opinion with regard to the defence of the British American provinces, all preceded Confederation and in the end expedited that great measure. The first Riel Insurrection in 1870 was dealt with by a joint British and Canadian force commanded for obvious reasons of policy by a British officer, Sir Garnet Wolseley. The Riel Rebellion of 1885, however, was quelled by a purely Canadian force under Canadian command, and it was perhaps significant that in the same year Sir John A. Macdonald not only declined to assume any responsibility for the war in the Soudan, but suggested a new basis for reciprocal defence. Writing to Sir Charles Tupper, then High Commissioner in London, Sir John used language that was not to be mistaken:

'Our men and money would, therefore, be sacrificed to get Gladstone and Co. out of the hole they have plunged themselves into by

[1] *Egerton and Grant*, p. 350.

their own imbecility. . . . The reciprocal aid . . . should be a matter of treaty entered into and settled on a permanent basis.'[1]

During the South African War British troops were withdrawn from garrison duty in Canada and significantly again Canadian troops were enlisted for service in South Africa. During the Great War half a million men were enlisted, and during the closing months of the war conscripted, for service on the western front. The Canadian force was equipped, paid, and controlled by the Parliament of Canada.

The repercussion of this upon external policy was to be expected. Complete control of the military and naval resources of Canada, and above all of the fiscal resources upon which both depend, can never in the long run be divorced from responsibility for the way in which such resources are to be used. Without pursuing at this stage the development to the peace conference and beyond, it will be conceded that here also the range of responsible government has long since passed the limitations contemplated by Durham in 1839.

The last reservation—the form of the constitution—has yielded to local control least rapidly of all in theory but no less effectually perhaps in practice. Certain 'written' elements in our constitution have been, and still are, Acts of the Imperial Parliament, but even the *Union Bill* of 1840 was drafted by Chief Justice Stuart of Lower Canada, and it went to London with the support of the Upper Canadian electorate. The terms of the *B.N.A. Act* of 1867 were almost exclusively the result of Canadian statesmanship, though it must be conceded that had its final enactment depended not upon the British Parliament but upon a constituent convention or a two-thirds majority in the provincial legislatures, the Canadian Confederation as we know it would never have come into being. The far-reaching amendment of 1871 (as in 1875, 1886, 1907, and 1915) was drafted in Ottawa and passed so perfunctorily in London that it was regarded then and since as a measure of domestic legislation. If present tendencies hold it can scarcely be gainsaid that statutory amendment to the 'written' part of our constitution may come, in practice, to be as easy as in any federal constitution in the world; far easier than in the United States or Australia; perhaps too easy rather than too difficult. It is thus seen that all of Durham's reservations have gone by the board in whole or in part, in practice if not in theory. The range of responsible government

[1] *Correspondence of Sir John A. Macdonald*, ed. Pope, Toronto, 1921, p. 338.

has steadily and automatically expanded with the legitimate interests of the Canadian people, and the flexibility of this process will invite the same jealous regard for local responsibility in whatever sphere those interests may come to be engaged.

A Third Corollary

These two corollaries will support, perhaps, a third: that the *B.N.A. Act* of 1867 made no fundamental difference whatever in the practice of responsible government, though Confederation naturally quickened its operation and in the end added immeasurably to its scope.

Had Sir John A. Macdonald's frank preference for legislative union prevailed, another simple *Union Act* would have provided for the fusion of powers already enjoyed by the provincial legislatures. For reasons that are well known it was necessary to fall back upon the federal plan, with the result that certain powers only were fused into a national federal government while other powers continued in the several provinces. Far from originating or even amplifying 'responsible' self-government, the *B.N.A. Act* of 1867 thus divided between federal and provincial governments the aggregate of self-government already enjoyed by the original provinces.[1] That division is of the essence of any federal system, and it was effected necessarily by a 'written' instrument. The ultimate value of Confederation in multiplying the resources of the British provinces, broadening their interests, and increasing their momentum towards full pan-Canadian nationhood, was of course beyond calculation; but the *B.N.A. Act* of 1867 left the ratio between governance and self-government at that time undisturbed. The cardinal principles of responsible government remain unchanged; there is still no attempt to define the range of its operation; that range continued to expand with greater inevitableness than ever and by the same methods.

Let us illustrate very briefly each of these points.

The cardinal principles of responsible government are safeguarded in the *B.N.A. Act* of 1867 in a very characteristic British way: by a phrase which, if it were to appear in the Constitution of the United States, would mean exactly the reverse of the practice which it warrants in Canada. Section 9 of the Act provides that 'the Executive Government . . . is hereby declared to continue and be vested in the Queen'. Behind this phraseology lie two centuries

[1] *B.N.A. Act*, 1867, s. 12.

of history and 'unwritten' convention from Pym and Hampden to Walpole and Chatham and Rockingham and Addington and Durham and Elgin and Joseph Howe.[1] What sections 9 and 63 really mean is that by these unwritten conventions the Crown is bound in honour to act upon the advice of ministers responsible to the Dominion and provincial legislatures. The very terms of the *B.N.A. Act* of 1867 would be incomprehensible without this unwritten law and custom of the constitution.

The second point scarcely requires illustration. It is one of the most remarkable features of the venerable instrument of 1867 that the relationship between the Dominion and Great Britain as well as that between the Dominion and foreign countries is left so largely undefined. There is not a word about the appointment of the Governor-General, whether he is to be appointed upon the advice of British or (as in the case of the Lieutenant-Governors of Provinces) of Canadian ministers. Similarly in section 9—'the Executive Government . . . is hereby declared to continue and be vested in the Queen'—there would seem to be nothing repugnant to the widest action of the Crown, international as well as internal, upon the advice of Canadian ministers. It is now more than sixty years since Sir John A. Macdonald declared that 'we are standing on the very threshold of nations'; that 'we are fast ceasing to be a dependency, and assuming the position of an ally of Great Britain' in a world-wide 'confederacy'. Not less memorable than the written federal bond of the Dominion was the faith in the cogency of time and of the unwritten conventions of a constitution 'similar in principle (as the preamble to the *B.N.A. Act* of 1867 states) to that of the United Kingdom'.

The continued broadening of 'responsible' self-government since 1867 by this method could be illustrated in great detail. Two developments only may suffice: the rapidly narrowing functions of the Governor-General and the rapidly expanding responsibilities of Canadian ministers in external affairs.

Three centuries of change in the functions of the Crown in Great Britain have been effected in the functions of the Governor-General in the Dominions in less than three generations. In 1841 Sydenham advised Melbourne to send out as his successor a man 'who will govern, as I do, *himself*'.[2] Sydenham claimed that his system was 'perfectly stable' and that 'everything will be in

[1] For the provinces, cf. *B.N.A. Act*, 1867, s. 63, &c.
[2] Sydenham to Melbourne, *Lord Melbourne's Papers*, p. 449.

grooves running of itself'. At the Imperial Conference of 1926 it was agreed that the Governor-General was to hold 'in all essential respects the same position in relation to the administration of public affairs in the Dominion as is held by His Majesty the King in Great Britain, and that he is not the representative or agent of His Majesty's Government in Great Britain or any Department of that Government'. This whole transformation has taken place within the lifetime of men now living.

The withdrawal of Sir Edmund Head from the presidency of the Canadian Executive Council during the 'fifties reflected the growing power and joint responsibility of the Canadian cabinet. After Confederation the same tendencies prevailed, despite the vastly increased prestige of the Governor-General. In 1876 Lord Carnarvon, the Colonial Secretary, in seeking to standardize instructions from the Colonial Office, authorized the Governor-General to preside in person over the Canadian cabinet with power to accept or reject their advice. It fell to the lot of Edward Blake to vindicate anew the doctrine of cabinet responsibility in Canada. In 1875 for the last time the prerogative of pardon was exercised by the Governor-General upon his own responsibility. Thenceforth it was to be exercised only upon the advice of the Canadian cabinet and the Minister of Justice. After Blake's state paper the Governor-General no longer reserved certain Canadian Bills upon the instructions of the Colonial Office. By the *B.N.A. Act* of 1867, section 15, the command-in-chief of all naval and military forces in Canada, like the executive government itself, 'is hereby declared to continue and be vested in the Queen'. The Dundonald incident in 1904 made it clear that the Crown in Canada must act upon the advice not of the British War Office but of the Canadian Minister of Militia. The functions of the Governor-General in Canada have thus steadily approached those prescribed by custom and convention for the Crown in Great Britain, and since July 1, 1927, his official contacts with Great Britain have been through his responsible ministers.

The broadening of the range of responsible government in external affairs is perhaps more spectacular, though here again the most fragmentary illustrations must suffice. Four years after Confederation Sir John A. Macdonald signed the Treaty of Washington as one of the British plenipotentiaries—the first Dominion minister to sign a British treaty. The mission itself, in Sir John's blunt phrase, was 'bungled . . . from beginning to end', but Macdonald's share in it has been pronounced 'the finest chapter in the history of Canadian diplomacy'. Sir Charles Tupper's share in forcing through the Franco-Canadian Treaty of 1893, and Sir Wilfrid Laurier's in 1907, have already been mentioned. 'Without revolution, without any breaking of traditions, the time has come when Canadian interests are entrusted to Canadians. . . . A treaty has been concluded with France—a treaty which applies to Canada alone, which has been negotiated by Canadians alone.'[1]

With Canada's participation in the World War the scope of responsible government crossed irretraceably the boundaries of the Dominion, and a nation was launched upon the high seas of world politics. It is well known that Sir Robert Borden, the Hon. Arthur Sifton, and the Hon. Mr. Doherty were given 'full powers' as plenipotentiaries at the Treaty of Versailles, though the Crown acted upon the advice of British ministers, and the Canadian order-in-council was apocryphal. The treaty, however, bears the Canadian signatures and was ratified by the Canadian Parliament. By signing the Peace Treaty the Dominions became members of the League of Nations, 'and their position', adds Sir Robert Borden, 'as to membership and representation in the assembly is in all respects the same as that of other signatory members'. Canada has since been elected to a non-permanent seat in the Council of the League. A series of precedents from the Washington Disarmament Conference of 1921 to the Locarno Conference of 1925 has recognized the direct responsibility of Canadian ministers for the external relations of the Dominion. In 1908 a treaty adjusting certain points of the boundary between Canada and the United States was signed at Washington by Lord Bryce as plenipotentiary of the British Government. On February 24, 1925, a new treaty modifying and completing the same boundary, was signed by the Hon. Mr. Lapointe in the name of His Majesty 'in respect of the Dominion of Canada'.[2] In 1926 a comprehensive technique for treaties, based upon that of 1923, was devised by the Imperial Conference, providing for consultation within the Commonwealth, and 'full powers issued in each case by the King on the advice of the Government concerned'. The point has now been reached where the self-governing Dominions, in the historic words of the

[1] Sir Wilfrid Laurier, Sept. 26, 1907, Porritt, *Fiscal and Diplomatic Freedom of the British North American Dominions*, p. 202.

[2] *La Situation Internationale du Canada*, par L'honorable M. Ernest Lapointe, Montreal, 1928, p. 10.

Imperial Conference of 1926, are to be regarded as '*autonomous Communities within the British Empire, equal in status, in no way subordinate one to another in any aspect of their domestic or external affairs, though united by a common allegiance to the Crown, and freely associated as members of the British Commonwealth of Nations*'.

Anomalies of the Commonwealth

It would be easy to prove that these dynamic principles which have been evolved empirically by statesmen in the field of politics conform neither to the theories of the jurist nor to the letter of administrative law. Though unanimous that 'equality of status' was a constitutional right, the Imperial Conference of 1926 was also agreed that inequality of function was still to be found in practice:

> 'Equality of status, so far as Britain and the Dominions are concerned, is thus the root principle governing our Inter-Imperial Relations. But the principle of equality and similarity, appropriate to *status*, do not universally extend to function.'

In all three functions of government, executive, legislative, and judicial, anomalies abound. Despite the agreement at the Imperial Conference—by statesmen who are in a position to implement that agreement in practice—that in the making of treaties 'the plenipotentiaries for the various British units should have full powers, issued in each case by the King on the advice of the Government concerned',[1] there are jurists who reserve an ultimate responsibility for British ministers, thus implying still the doctrine of Lord John Russell in 1839 that Dominion ministers cannot be 'advisers of the Crown of England . . . for the Crown has other advisers for the same functions, and with superior authority'.[2] British legislative supremacy also has been apparent in the *B.N.A. Acts*, in the *Commonwealth Act*, in the *South Africa Act* of the British Parliament; and even the provisions for self-amendment in the last two are still interpreted as British statutes. Has the British Parliament which had power over the cause, power also over the effect? For the oldest of the Dominion federations, the *B.N.A. Acts* can still be amended only by other Acts of the British Parliament. The Canadian Parliament cannot legislate for Canadian ships upon the high seas. Beyond the three-mile limit a Canadian ceases to be

[1] *Imperial Conference*, 1926, Summary of Proceedings, Ottawa, 1926, p. 19.

[2] *Egerton and Grant*, p. 267. Cf. Keith, *Responsible Government in the Dominions*, Oxford, 1927, I. xiii.

amenable to Canadian law. *The Colonial Laws Validity Act* of 1865, passed primarily to validate 'colonial laws' that are not repugnant to British statutes, implies the invalidity of those that are: and its repeal would raise problems as well as solve them. The British *Merchant Shipping*, *Naturalization*, and *Copyright Acts* still over-ride Dominion legislation. Since the *Act for the Regulating the Privy Council and for taking away the Court commonly called the Star Chamber*, passed by the Long Parliament in 1641, there has been no normal appeal in Great Britain to committees of the Privy Council. The Judicial Committee of the Privy Council—now regulated of course by statute—still survives as a court of appeal for the Dominions. Without disputing the doctrine roundly laid down by Lord Morley that no right is worth a straw apart from the good that it brings, it may be noted that Sir Edmund Head, Elgin's successor in Canada in 1854, emphatically rejected the jurisdiction of the Judicial Committee of the Privy Council in his secret project of that year for a federation of the British Provinces. Can such 'vestigial anomalies' be reconciled with 'equality of status'?

This general remark may perhaps be made with regard to them: constitutional right may march far in advance of administrative law, but like the Pied Piper of Hamelin it has the sovereign faculty of drawing administrative law to follow in its footsteps. The Report of the Imperial Conference on Inter-Imperial Relations, unanimously adopted on November 19, 1926, may resemble the Petition of Right and the Declaration of Rights in providing in itself no administrative law, and in adding nothing altogether new perhaps to current conceptions of constitutional right. But a political principle which is once conceded to be a constitutional right seldom fails to find its way in the end into administrative law; and the Report of 1926—'une reconnaissance par des égaux et des associés d'un état de choses accepté par tous'—can scarcely fail to prove a forecast of this historic procedure. The 'skill of jurists', writes Lawrence, 'toils far behind the constructive ingenuity of statesmen'.[1]

In truth the process from governance to self-government, as we have seen, has been the work not of jurists but of statesmen. It has been easy at every stage for the jurists to confound the statesmen with inconsistencies and antinomies. Familiar passages will occur from each cycle of this historic development. 'I do not enter into these metaphysical distinctions', exclaimed Burke at the most

[1] Hon. Ernest Lapointe, *La Situation Internationale du Canada*, p. 6.

critical stage of the American Revolution. 'I hate the very sound of them. . . . If intemperately, unwisely, fatally, you sophisticate and poison the very source of government, by urging subtle deductions, and consequences odious to those you govern, from the unlimited and illimitable nature of supreme sovereignty you will teach them by these means to call that sovereignty itself in question.' In America, too, the same insight into the subtle relations between human nature and sound policy had led Benjamin Franklin to remind the greatest of colonial governors that 'in Matters of General Concern to the People . . . it is of Use to consider as well what they will *be apt* to think and say, as what they ought to think'. Franklin's letter of 1754 became at once a melancholy proof of political insight and the most prophetic forecast of the Revolution.[1]

During the second cycle of this trilogy, Lord John Russell's theory of 'colonial government' was stated with unanswerable logic, and it was applied by the ablest of his governors in terms equally satisfactory to the jurist. The Executive Council was 'a *council* for the governor to consult, but no more. . . . There is no other theory which has common sense'. The governor 'must therefore be the minister, in which case he cannot be under the control of men in the colony'.[2] The answer to this came not from the jurist but from the humble statesmanship of Howe and Huntington in Nova Scotia, and of Harrison, Baldwin, and La Fontaine in Canada. The same Assembly which Sydenham had so confidently 'managed', forced his successor, in defiance alike of Lord John Russell's theory and of Stanley's instructions, to accept as 'ministers' those who could 'command a majority in the representative branch'. 'Whether the doctrine of responsible Government is openly acknowledged or is only tacitly acquiesced in,' wrote Bagot bluntly, 'virtually it exists.'[3] Let it be repeated that both in Nova Scotia and in Canada, responsible government was finally won not by spectacular feats of advocacy but as Buller had foretold, by the inexorable discipline of political parties upon the floors of the provincial Assemblies.

The era since responsible government has been increasingly dominated by the statesman. Aside from the dark page of Irish history—'now a page that has been turned'[4]—and the heady

[1] Franklin to Shirley, Dec. 4, 1754, *Correspondence of William Shirley*, ed. Lincoln, i. 103.

[2] *Egerton and Grant*, p. 280.

[3] Oct. 18, 1842, *Bagot Papers*, v. 164.

[4] Sir Cecil Hurst in *Great Britain and the Dominions*, Harris Foundation Lectures, Chicago, 1927, p. 13.

course of South Africa, leaping into self-government like Minerva full-armed from the head of Jupiter, the coming of the Commonwealth has been the result of empirical adjustments reached, upon the whole, in a spirit of mutual confidence. The key to this unprecedented harmony is not far to seek. The control which responsible ministers had won over local administration gave them, 'in fact, if not in form', control over everything else. Jurisprudence has yielded to politics. More than thirty of these landmarks—one for every three years—could be cited to illustrate the patient adaptation of legal theories to political realities. The formulae of jurists have been powerless to circumscribe the accommodations of statesmen. While the jurist, obsessed with time-honoured theories of sovereignty and prerogative, has seen change in every adjustment, the statesman, concerned only with the practice of responsible government, has seen no change except in the scope of its application; and the same process which seems unnatural and irregular to the one has all the inevitableness and infinite adaptability of nature itself to the other. The ministers of the Crown in the Dominions have been held responsible wherever the vital interests of the Dominions have been involved: responsible too for safeguarding those novel interests that are sure to arise with the growth of sentient nationhood. To expect a people trained to these 'forms of stringent responsibility' to relax them precisely where their dearest interests may come to be involved would be to expect to 'see the streams turn back upon their fountains'.[1] It is reasonable to suppose that similar 'conventions' will continue to accommodate the vital forces of the British Commonwealth to each other, and that the statesman rather than the jurist will continue to have the casting vote.

The Proceedings of the Imperial Conference of 1926—a gathering of statesmen with no fewer than seven sources of responsibility—bear witness to this dominating influence in the sections relating to the Position of Governors-General,[2] to the Operation of

[1] Howe to Lord John Russell, *Egerton and Grant*, p. 248.

[2] 'In our opinion it is an essential consequence of the equality of status existing among the members of the British Commonwealth of Nations that the Governor-General of a Dominion is the representative of the Crown, holding in all essential respects the same position in relation to the administration of public affairs in the Dominion as is held by His Majesty the King in Great Britain, and that he is not the representative or agent of His Majesty's Government in Great Britain or of any Department of that Government.' *Summary of Proceedings*, Ottawa, 1926, p. 14.

Dominion Legislation[1] and to Relations with Foreign Countries.[2] The adjustment of many such anomalies has been simplified by the fact that these have been governed by the 'unwritten' conventions of the constitution, and nothing more spectacular has been required in each instance than a single concerted action discerningly devised to form a precedent for the future. Constitutional problems of this nature can thus be solved one at a time, each upon its own merits, each in the order of its importance or practical expediency.

And not only are specific adjustments more easily made by this historic method but they are more effectively consolidated and conserved. It is true that usage and custom require time to settle down into recognized convention or precedent; and perhaps that is why this method has seldom appealed in times of revolution to headlong and inveterate reformers in a hurry. There is a cumulative conservatism in the end, however, which can be very nearly irrevocable. Lord Byng commanded Canadian troops at Vimy Ridge, but he never commanded Canadian military forces as Governor-General of Canada as did Murray and Dorchester, Brock and Colborne. No Colonial Secretary will ever again determine how a Canadian Minister of Finance is to balance his budget. There is something altogether more permanent about these conventions of the constitution than there would be about the repeal of a certain section in a written statute and the enactment of another. It is easier to plant an oak tree than to build a cottage, yet in the fullness of time it will be easier to pull down the cottage than to tear up the oak tree by the roots. The growth of such a political organism may not be very rapid or spectacular but it is apt to be remarkably steady.

The project of the Imperial Conference for a 'Committee with terms of reference' to deal with more difficult anomalies may be expected to move steadily forward in the same direction, though many of these problems, without a doubt, will tax alike the temper of the jurist and the resources of the statesman. To those meanwhile who see in this 'constructive ingenuity' of statesmanship

[1] 'We propose that it should be placed on record, that apart from provisions embodied in constitutions or in specific statutes expressly providing for reservation, it is recognized that it is the right of the Government of each Dominion to advise the Crown in all matters relating to its own affairs.' *Id.*, p. 15.

[2] Cf. the report with regard to Procedure in Relation to Treaties, *id.*, 17 ff.: 'The plenipotentiaries for the various British units should have full powers issued in each case by the King on the advice of the Government concerned.' *Id.*, p. 19.

some latent principle of mischief unless 'all the preliminary details . . . all the technical difficulties which have their origin in the long history of our Oversea Dominions' can be classified and settled beforehand, Lord Balfour has replied with scathing emphasis:

> 'Can anything be more legal and less statesmanlike? I cannot even put myself in the frame of mind of the noble Lord on the subject. . . . You might as well consider all the causes of divorce before you decide upon the problems of matrimony. . . . My view most strongly is that the British Empire is now a more united organism than it ever has been before. . . . Nothing, as I believe, can increase the feeling of solidarity more than the sense that that solidarity depends on the complete sense of free equality. . . . If International Law has not the sense to get over (these difficulties) we must manage as best we can.'[1]

The Basis of Unity

The unstinted recognition of Dominion nationhood by British statesmen has been termed the most signal act of self-abnegation in modern history. Were its purpose purely negative much might be said for this conclusion. But this is only half, or less than half, of the meaning of responsible government. To the jurist or the centralizing imperialist self-government has ever been a process of disintegration. The concurrent process of integration through what Burke called the communion of the spirit—'wild and chimerical' as that seemed in 1775 to 'mechanical politicians . . . who think that nothing exists but what is gross and material'—is a subtler and in the last analysis a much profounder conception. The pearl of great price here is mutual confidence, and it is not to be created by the mechanics of government. 'The very idea of subordination of parts', exclaimed Burke, 'excludes this notion of simple and undivided unity.' In the ceaseless friction generated by subordination during the second Empire, the harmony of what Burke called 'the spirit of the constitution' was seldom audible; 'but to men truly initiated and rightly taught, these ruling and master principles, which, in the opinion of such men as I have mentioned, have no substantial existence, are in truth everything, and all in all.' Lacking at once the narrower intensiveness of sheer separatism and the ardour of imperialism, this conception of the Commonwealth may be based upon nothing more spectacular than a sense of common weal. Fitted by its very catholicity for the

[1] *Journal of the Parliaments of the Empire*, January, 1927, pp. 15 f.

environment in which a League of Nations is seeking (in the words of the Covenant) to 'promote international co-operation and to achieve international peace and security . . . by the prescription of open, just and honorable relations between nations', the Commonwealth is in itself a microcosm of international statesmanship, and its most exemplary virtues are those which are capable of being projected into international relations. In phrases now historic, the *Report of the Inter-Imperial Relations Committee* of the Imperial Conference of 1926 outlines the scope of these creative forces:

> 'No account, however accurate, of the negative relations in which Great Britain and the Dominions stand to each other can do more than express a portion of the truth. The British Empire is not founded upon negations. It depends essentially, if not formally, on positive ideals. Free institutions are its life-blood. Free co-operation is its instrument. Peace, security, and progress are among its objects. . . . And though every Dominion is now, and must always remain, the sole judge of the nature and extent of its co-operation, no common cause will, in our opinion, be thereby imperilled.'

It would be idle to assume that this vision of constructive statesmanship has guided the development from governance to self-government in the British Dominions. To many—at one time or another, perhaps to all—who wrought materially in that cause, the dust and heat of the local struggle beclouded the larger vision. The Adamses and the Papineaus were from the outset intransigent. A fierce love of liberty as they understood it drove the Gourlays and the William Lyon Mackenzies into sheer despair and defiance. For the Girouards and the La Fontaines the waters of Marah never lost their immemorial bitterness. In 1838, Baldwin, contemplating a province to be held 'by troops alone', almost despaired of his 'great principle'. Howe, in the flight of his mind the loftiest and most adventurous of the Reformers, was at times 'tired and Savage' with the prospect. Reflecting upon the policy that 'drove the old Colonies to separation', he once foresaw even in Nova Scotia the rise of 'a different spirit' dominated 'by the Enemies of England, not by her friends'; and he could never speak of the 'dark days' without a tremor. For many who inherited a happier outlook the integration of spirit which has accompanied the disintegration of government has been not only a by-product or an afterthought but a mystery.

Projects of a centralized or materialistic Empire, on the other hand, have taken forms without number; and the defects of vision, of temper, and of motive, long survived to discredit more magnanimous projects of the Commonwealth. For William Knox at the beginning of the second Empire, the leading principles of colonial policy were to be 'the *permanency* of their connection with this country' and 'the advantage to be derived from them'. Their prosperity was to be 'encouraged only as far as it may consist with these two; for it would be much better (he added) to have no Colonies at all, than not to have them permanently connected with this country, and subservient to the increase of its maritime strength and commercial prosperity'.[1]

The shifting devices of colonial policy—for a colonial aristocracy, for vested interests in the councils, for an endowed church, for casual and territorial revenues ample enough to wrest the power of the purse from the Assembly, for subtler methods of disarming opposition by official favour—were commonplaces of the second Empire. So also were the benevolent intentions of the younger Pitt, of Dalhousie, of Gosford, and of Lord John Russell. As mercantilism gave way before Huskisson's great reforms, and the traditional 'bonds of Empire' were finally loosed in the repeal of the corn laws and in free trade, self-interest and faith in the Empire alike decayed. Huskisson was content to regard the colonies as 'free nations, the communicators of freedom to other nations'. How far the official acquiescence of Great Britain in responsible government was simplified bythe commercial doctrines of *laissez-faire* can only be conjectured. Had the older creeds prevailed, the rise of well-nigh irresistible political parties in Nova Scotia and in Canada might have resulted, not in less conclusive demonstrations of responsible government but in more resolute obstruction from Great Britain; and this in turn might have embittered the whole subsequent history of the British provinces. On the other hand it is well to remember that the repeal of the corn laws meant 'the triumph of free trade and not of freedom'. Grey's zeal for free trade was scarcely less pontifical in its outlook and its temper than Knox's for the mercantile subserviency of the second Empire. With the trend towards protection in the colonies, commercial subordination was still the order of the day.[2]

By the middle of the nineteenth century, however, the worst

[1] *Extra Official State Papers*, vol. ii, Appendix xiv, p. 48.

[2] Cf. Grey's strictures in the *Grey-Elgin Correspondence* against 'that silliest of all silly policies, the meeting of commercial restrictions by counter restrictions'. See also his policy on the New Brunswick bounties in *Grey-Elgin Correspondence*, Oct. 25, 1850.

devices of the old order had passed away. Elgin renounced scathingly, as we have seen, the discredited projects of 'a Colonial Empire for the purpose of exercising dominion or dispensing patronage', or as a 'hot-bed for forcing commerce and manufactures'. The connexion was to be safeguarded 'neither by the golden links of protection nor by the meshes of old-fashioned colonial office jobbing and chicane'. The net result of these shallow expedients from beginning to end was unfortunate. The positive results were negligible. The indirect results were positively dangerous, and other traditional 'bonds of Empire' that were less objectionable shared the same fate. In almost every instance the procedure has been the same. Friction rather than cohesion resulted from many of these 'bonds', until they threatened to destroy more than they safeguarded. When they reached the point of jeopardizing the 'unsuspecting confidence', which Burke regarded as 'in truth everything and all in all', they were cast aside by common consent, and normal relations were again resumed. None could now be found to advocate the reinstatement of the Governor-General to the presidency of the Canadian cabinet, of the Colonial Office to the control of fiscal legislation in Canada, of the instructions formerly issued for the reservation of Canadian Bills, or of the British War Office to the control of the Canadian militia. When viewed in retrospect it is hard to discover virtue in these 'vestigial anomalies', and it is a truism of Canadian politics that whatever the traditional views of political parties, the policy of Dominion ministers in practice has had the appearance of unbroken continuity. Of the seven or eight successive party administrations since Confederation, not one has failed to enlarge the bounds of Dominion autonomy. Macdonald and Tupper, Blake, and Laurier, Sir Robert Borden, the Hon. Arthur Meighen, and the Hon. W. L. Mackenzie King have all responded instinctively, in practice, to the same national impulses. The coming of age of the 'great lubberly boy' of 1850, as Elgin humorously described the Canada of that day, has had all the steady growth and adaptability of the slow processes of nature.

But while the integration of spirit which underlies the moral unity of the Commonwealth has been largely a by-product or an aftermath of self-government, its growth has been no less spontaneous and natural than the more elemental forces of the second Empire. With a rooted distrust of the mechanics of government, the most discerning prophets of the Commonwealth have relied consistently upon a single constructive principle which is cohesive not by virtue of 'exquisite policy' but in the very nature of things. 'Like breeds like'; and there are likenesses that are no less fundamental than race or language. 'The free Greeks', exclaimed Adderley, 'bred only free colonies, which "homed off" from them as New England did from us. . . . Unnatural treatment may alienate them—*tamen usque recurret natura*.'[1] Lord Morley's formula is to be found in the words of Matthew Arnold: 'What attaches people to us is the spirit we are of, not the machinery we employ.'[2] Lord Balfour's historic dictum is still more broadly catholic in its scope:

> 'The British Empire . . . is held together far more effectually by the broad loyalties, by the common feelings and interests—in many cases, of history—and by devotion to great world ideals of peace and freedom.
>
> 'A common interest in loyalty, in freedom, in ideals—that is the bond of Empire. If that is not enough, nothing else is enough.'[3]

Separated from this in time by the whole range of two Empires is the incomparable insight of Burke. Too often perhaps have the Speeches on America been quoted for their rhetoric rather than for their wisdom. 'They compose', Morley once exclaimed, 'the most perfect manual in our literature, or in any literature, for one who approaches the study of public affairs, whether for knowledge or for practice':[4]

> 'My hold of the colonies (said Burke) is in the close affection which grows from common names, from kindred blood, from similar privileges, and equal protection. These are ties, which, though light as air, are as strong as links of iron. Let the colonies always keep the idea of their civil rights associated with your government. . . . Deny them this participation of freedom, and you break that sole bond, which originally made, and must still preserve the unity of the empire. Do not entertain so weak an imagination as that your registers and your bonds, your affidavits and your sufferances, your cockets and your clearances, are what form the great securities of your commerce. Do not dream that your letters of office, and your instructions, and your suspending clauses, are the things that hold together the great contexture of this mysterious whole. These things do not make your government. Dead instruments, passive tools as they are, it is the spirit of the English communion that gives all their life and efficacy to them. . . .

[1] *Review of "The Colonial Policy of Lord J. Russell's Administration"*, p. 11.
[2] *Recollections*, p. 129.
[3] *Journal of the Parliaments of the Empire*, Jan., 1927, p. 16.
[4] *Burke*, London, 1888, p. 116.

All this, I know well enough, will sound wild and chimerical to . . . those vulgar and mechanical politicians . . . who think that nothing exists but what is gross and material. . . . But to men truly initiated and rightly taught, these ruling and master principles, which, in the opinion of such men as I have mentioned, have no substantial existence, are in truth everything, and all in all.'

This doctrine, assuredly, is not to be traced in apostolic succession from Burke to Balfour, but it recurs repeatedly from every round of practice. It is to be found in the pages of Howe even during the 'dark days'. Baldwin and La Fontaine acted upon it less instinctively, but with conviction born of bitter experience. In Gibbon Wakefield it may not have been altogether without guile; but in the gracious spirit of Charles Buller—the Ariel, surely, of that political tempest—it was to be found in its sprightliest and kindliest form. Lord Durham with his robust opportunism and his 'abundance of political courage, sometimes, perhaps, a little approaching to rashness',[1] had a more pragmatic outlook upon the Empire. The third Earl Grey—in some respects a baffling figure, passing into permanent eclipse after six eventful years of incandescence at the Colonial Office—accepted a less arduous philosophy for the British provinces: 'the establishment of the relation between them and the mother-country on the basis of mutual affection.' 'The main object of our policy', he wrote to Elgin, 'ought to be to support the hopes and courage of the Canadians until their natural advantages begin to tell.' To Lt.-Gov. Campbell of Prince Edward Island, Grey had already outlined a deeper conviction: 'In the present state of political Society, and with the free Institutions which now prevail in the Mother Country and Colony alike, mutual goodwill can constitute the only real tie between them.'[2]

In the pages of the *Grey-Elgin Correspondence* this spirit of the Commonwealth is to be found not only in the making but almost in its final form. The death of Buller in 1848 left Elgin and Grey—one on either side of the Atlantic—almost alone among the British statesmen of that day in the belief that a new and constructive principle would arise from the concession of responsible government. Surrounded on all sides by men of little faith, they kept their own, at times, only with a conscious effort. None, then or since, ever jettisoned with less compunction the 'vestigial anomalies' of dependence or subordination from the old Empire.

[1] Broughton, *Recollections of a Long Life*, v. 291.

[2] Dec. 27, 1849, *G. Series* (P.E.I.), 284. 281, *Pub. Arch. Can.*

Durham's reservations, as we have seen, were the first to go. There could be no 'line of demarcation' between imperial and provincial interests: 'I see nothing for it but that the Governors should be responsible for the share which the Imperial Government may have . . . . with the liability to be recalled and disavowed.' The time might come 'when it may be expedient to allow the Colonists to elect their Governors', leaving the British Government to be 'represented in the Colony by an Agent. . . . If your Agent was well chosen and had a good status I am not sure but that the connexion might be kept up under such an arrangement quite as well and as profitably for England as under the present.'[1]

At the same time none saw more clearly the vital functions of the Crown in those invaluable 'conventions' which make up the practice of responsible government. The vital problem too of integration—the communion of the spirit—was dealt with upon an analogy which must have appeared, like Burke's, somewhat 'wild and chimerical' to 'mechanical politicians', but which has proved so apt and discerning in practice that it may still bear the scrutiny of cold and deliberate calculation. With kindly feeling and good-humour Elgin wrote that the 'great lubberly boy' was coming of age. Never was he likely to feel more sensitively the surviving restraints of his minority. Never, it is true also, were blunders of tact and judgement likely to prove more costly; for though the exercise of parental authority had often been arbitrary and short-sighted, there had always been the saving prospect hitherto of re-establishing confidence and goodwill before the bonds of authority should be finally abrogated. With goodwill and a sense of humour, however, permanent estrangement ought to be the last normal eventuality of a well-ordered family, unless domestic relations were egregiously mismanaged. Even these might yield to concord if sought, after Burke's formula, not in the 'juridical determination of perplexing questions; or the precise marking the shadowy boundaries of a complex government', but in its 'natural course, and in its ordinary haunts . . . . peace sought in the spirit of peace; and laid in principles purely pacific'. Separated economically by the widest diversities of interest and sometimes of practice, there would still remain to these adolescent nations a gentler therapy in the form of common institutions, of many common traditions, of much common history, of a common way of looking at things, of

[1] Walrond, *Letters and Journals of Lord Elgin*, p. 114; *Grey-Elgin Correspondence*, Mar. 23, 1850.

common ideals of world peace and freedom. Elgin was a man of faith; but his historic analogy was based upon worldly wisdom and hard facts, and it may not unfairly be amplified and projected thus into the happier environment of our own day.

Nation and Commonwealth

In many respects Elgin's prophecy has required no less time than this for its fulfilment. The nation which he foresaw in 1850 has matured slowly. There were materials in Canada, as he wrote, 'for the future of Nations'; and Grey added that in the scale of intelligence the province already stood 'very high among the nations of the world'. Elgin's successor, Sir Edmund Head, in the secret *Memorandum* which had been drawn up for Earl Grey in 1854, projected a federation of the British provinces with 'a national destiny', a uniform currency, a mint, and a flag of their own, and with 'the forms and the substance of our constitution come to maturity in this part of America'. Many seers of Confederation also during the next decade had the same vision. Thomas D'Arcy McGee spoke of 'one great nationality bound, like the shield of Achilles by the blue rim of the ocean'; Alexander Tilloch Galt wrote and spoke in terms of 'national prestige', of 'national power and consideration', of building up 'a nation worthy of England from her North American possessions'; Alexander Morris wrote of 'a new nation . . . . with the telegraph and the iron-road connecting the two oceans'. Macdonald, too, at last, was numbered among the prophets: 'We are standing on the very threshold of nations and when admitted we shall occupy no unimportant position among the nations of the world.'

But Confederation was not the idealistic movement it is apt to appear in years of jubilee. Its mainspring in practice was the desperate plight of the old province of Canada, and it was 'extorted', as John Adams said of the Constitution of the United States, 'from the grinding necessities of a reluctant people'. Fifty years were to pass before Macdonald's prophecy could come true. Five great areas, four of them in almost complete isolation, had first to be united into a transcontinental Dominion before the vital forces of nationhood could begin to function. The eastern provinces, with interests almost altogether maritime, looked to the south and across the Atlantic for their commercial future. Cut off from these by an impenetrable wilderness and by all the barriers of race and language was the French population of Canada East.

Beyond, upon the Great Lakes, lay a third vast area already upon an 'inclined plane', as many thought, towards the United States. Separated from Canada West by another impenetrable wilderness was the vast area of Rupert's Land, accessible at that time only by way of Hudson Bay or the United States, and standing, it seemed, directly in the path of American expansion westward and northward, the most rapid and headlong migration of peoples in the range of modern history. Beyond the Rockies lay a fifth area, on the Pacific, to be reached by half-circumnavigating the globe. Nowhere perhaps among modern nations has there been such a contest as this against the barriers of physical geography. In the growth of a national spirit, these magnificent distances were liabilities rather than assets. After the framework of the *B.N.A. Act* of 1867 and the building of transcontinental railways, came the real challenge of nationhood. What if the removal of these physical disabilities were to reveal not mutual sympathies but mutual antipathies? What if varied economic interests, instead of unifying the country, as many of the advocates of Confederation so lightly promised in 1864, were found upon closer analysis to invite conflict and disintegration? The answer to these problems was to be found only in building up, largely in the realm of political traditions and institutions, a consciousness of vital and fundamental interests in common. The Canadian Confederation thus made possible in the end a larger nation, but it postponed for many years the achievement of sentient nationhood as Elgin had conceived it it 1850, and it has resulted in a Dominion which is desperately hard to develop, hard to populate, hard to traverse, hard to govern. For half a century the best energies of Canadian statesmen have gone to the building of giants' causeways across the continent. Only in recent years have the Canadian people recaptured something of the vision which the most discerning of their public men had known long since and lost awhile.

Changes too in international relations have profoundly modified, for the better, some of the conditions under which the 'nation', foreseen by Elgin and Head, now at last begins to function. In the Covenant of the League Canada entered the comity of nations in the spirit of international goodwill. Dedicated to peace and peopled predominantly by two races speaking the two official languages of the League, no country could be more happily situated to avoid those deadlier fumes of nationality which have been seething for a century from the crucible of nineteenth-century

Europe. Even the nations of the old world can claim no longer the unfettered sovereignty of 1914. While the League is not a super-state its members are living in association, and their freedom is no longer the absolute freedom of sovereignty but the contingent freedom of association and law. The rule of law among nations —'the international mind' now abroad in the world—is far from being the force it has been long since within the national state, but every stage in its growth may be relied upon to integrate nations into closer solidarity.

In that sense the British Commonwealth which is so amorphous that observers, unfamiliar with the play of British usage and 'convention', are baffled by its apparent mechanical incoherence, has now for the first time, perhaps, an environment favourable to its own peculiar aptitudes. Even less than the League is the Commonwealth subject to the written bond. The Rt. Hon. Mr. Amery recently remarked that Great Britain and the other nations of the Commonwealth were all Dominions now. It would be equally true perhaps to say that all the Dominions (except the Irish Free State) are now Empires, in control of subordinate territories or mandates which have no immediate contacts whatever with each other. A Canadian 'territory' has no organic contact with an Australian 'territory' or with the British Gold Coast or with Kenya. Thus the British Empire which still exists as an agglomeration of Empires, now associates only as a Commonwealth. In form it is a heptarchy again. Its moral unity, however, belongs to another order. The old ideal of 'romantic loyalty' Elgin found to be passing away seventy-five years ago. In its place it was necessary to prepare the way for a broader conception—a reciprocal loyalty to the political ideals which they hold in common. To give free play to these imponderables—'broad loyalties . . . . common feelings and interests . . . . world ideals of peace and freedom'—is now the genius of the Commonwealth, and it can scarcely fail to respond to the conditions under which it lives. In that sense the growth of self-conscious nationhood in the Dominions, their association as a Commonwealth, and their broader association with each other and with other nations in the League of Nations, are cumulative rather than competitive processes. The three reinforce rather than neutralize each other. For all three, similar motives and aptitudes are brought into play. While this is less obvious in Great Britain where the recent developments in the Commonwealth and in the League may represent a considerable readjustment, it is a very natural tendency in the Dominions where the sense of nationality has burst into activity in all three channels at once. For Canada at least the three are so closely interlocked in origin and method and temper that there would seem to be no valid reason for trying to disentangle the motives which they have in common.

A special interest, however, attaches to the more instinctive associations of the Commonwealth. Their flexibility is such that they may be expected to respond almost automatically to that 'day-to-day opportunism' which Sir Charles Lucas has called the highest genius of the race. Much therefore is likely to be determined by forces that are 'stronger than advocacy'. How far are these likely to carry the 'British Commonwealth of Nations' towards closer integration?

Certain tendencies have been discernible at times in Canada towards separatism and complete independence—not in the literal sense of *in-dependence*, the termination of dependency, but in the narrower sense of formal and complete dissociation from the Commonwealth and from world politics. To many exponents of this view the League of Nations is little more than a myth. The share of Canada in the activities of Assembly, International Labour Organization, and Council, has been but a gesture. The Commonwealth is a verbal abstraction. For a section of Canadian opinion, too, this policy has taken the form not only of isolation but of insulation against all external contacts—a task simplified in many respects by traditions of race, language, and religion.

On the other hand, tendencies, now deep and strong, towards a broader national destiny than this are already gathering momentum, though these are less deliberate in their action, and less dependent therefore upon sheer advocacy. Common to both sets of tendencies perhaps has been the sturdy growth of an indigenous national spirit which is worthy of a tribute wherever it is to be found. Divergencies, however, are beginning to appear with regard both to the past and to the future. A deliberate policy of dissociation or isolation would be a departure from historic traditions at all three of the most critical stages of Canadian national development. Responsible government was the work not of Papineau's Ishmaelitish separatism but of the reasoned goodwill of Howe, Baldwin, and La Fontaine. 'Standing on the very threshold of nations' at Confederation, Macdonald, too, contemplated a broader 'confederacy of free men', destined to 'remain united with the mother country', though 'fast ceasing to be a dependency, and assuming the position of an ally of Great Britain'. Similar in temper were the associations which attended the Dominions into the World War and the League of Nations, and finally launched them upon the high seas of world politics. If there are dangers to be found there for the internal peace of Canada, there are graver dangers to be found in turning back. The hero in Ossian put to sea to ride out the storm. For better or for worse the Dominion is already upon the high seas, and it would seem to be the part of wisdom to make there the best friends it is possible to find. It would be indeed strange, with so many of 'the imponderables' in common, if these were not found to be the nations of the British Commonwealth.

In truth a choice between isolation or insulation on the one hand and more intimate external associations on the other, is perhaps no longer feasible for this country. The cross-roads have long since been passed, and economic as well as political tendencies would seem to confirm the accomplished fact. The export trade of Canada—now fifth in world value—with nine and a half millions of population has reached the figure the United States had with seventy. Canadian wheat is sold and must always be sold in world markets. Economic self-sufficiency, like moral or political self-sufficiency, is a counsel of perfection. Few nations, moreover, have a deeper stake in world peace than Canada, in the interests of peace within her own borders. That this could be safeguarded by withdrawing from all external associations and ignoring the issues of international peace that are now abroad in the world would seem to be the vainest of delusions. Little-Canadianism, as the world is now constituted, would only subserve the dangers which it would be powerless in any case to escape. If world peace, on the other hand, is largely contingent upon the relations between Great Britain, France, and the United States, few nations of the world are more happily associated than Canada with all three; and here again, in the interests of domestic peace if nothing else, it would seem to be the part of wisdom not to blink realities but to throw the modest weight of the Dominion for whatever it may be worth into the scales where alone world peace is to be secured.

Moral integration may be expected to grow out of that kind of experience and association. It is not necessary to emphasize the mechanical integration which has already taken place within the Commonwealth—the 'conventions' of the Imperial Conference of

1926 with regard to consultation before all treaties, to official intercourse through ministers of a common Crown, and to the unanimous reservation of Commonwealth relations from the purview of the League of Nations. These after all are but 'dead instruments', with no more virtue than the old mechanics of governmental subordination without the vitalizing 'spirit of the communion'. In the spontaneous associations of the Commonwealth, however, may be found the widest field for usefulness in world politics, and for a modest measure of world influence, it may be, where Dominion interests are involved. Archimedes in demonstrating the power of the lever asked but a place to stand. Within the circle of the Commonwealth, in the larger associations of the League, the Dominions have a privileged stance which might give to these young nations an influence out of all proportion to their wealth and population.

INDEX

PRINTED IN GREAT BRITAIN AT THE UNIVERSITY PRESS OXFORD
BY JOHN JOHNSON PRINTER TO THE UNIVERSITY